Finding God

Celebrating Church

*As I open this book, I open myself
to God's presence in my life.
When I allow God's grace to help me,
I see with truth, hear with forgiveness,
and act with kindness.
Thank you, God, for your presence in my life.*

Barbara F. Campbell, M.Div., D.Min.

James P. Campbell, M.A., D.Min.

LOYOLA PRESS.
A JESUIT MINISTRY
Chicago

Imprimatur	In Conformity
In accordance with c. 827, permission to publish is granted on August 1, 2012 by Rev. Msgr. John F. Canary, Vicar General of the Archdiocese of Chicago. Permission to publish is an official declaration of ecclesiastical authority that the material is free from doctrinal and moral error. No legal responsibility is assumed by the grant of this permission.	The Subcommittee on the Catechism, United States Conference of Catholic Bishops, has found this catechetical text, copyright 2014, to be in conformity with the *Catechism of the Catholic Church*.

Finding God: Celebrating Church is an expression of the work of Loyola Press, a ministry of the Society of Jesus, the Jesuits.

Senior Consultants
Joe Paprocki, D.Min.
Tom McGrath, M.A.
Robert Fabing, S.J., D.Min.
Richard Hauser, S.J., Ph.D., S.T.L.
Jane Regan, Ph.D.

Advisors
George A. Aschenbrenner, S.J., S.T.L
Most Reverend Gordon D. Bennett, S.J., D.D.
Paul Brian Campbell, S.J., Ph.D.
Paul H. Colloton, O.P., D.Min.
Gerald Darring, M.A.
Eugene LaVerdiere, S.S.S., Ph.D., S.T.L.

Catechetical Staff
Jeanette L. Graham, M.A.
Jean Hopman, O.S.U., M.A.

Grateful acknowledgment is given to authors, publishers, photographers, museums, and agents for permission to reprint the following copyrighted material. Every effort has been made to determine copyright owners. In the case of any omissions, the publisher will be pleased to make suitable acknowledgments in future editions. Acknowledgments continue on page 331.

Cover design: Loyola Press
Cover Illustration: Rafael López
Interior design: Loyola Press

ISBN-13: 978-0-8294-3672-3
ISBN-10: 0-8294-3672-3

LOYOLAPRESS.
A JESUIT MINISTRY

3441 N. Ashland Avenue
Chicago, Illinois 60657
(800) 621-1008

www.loyolapress.com
www.ignatianspirituality.com
www.other6.com

19 20 21 22 23 Web 10 9 8 7 6

Contents

GRADE 8

iv

The Early Church

Saint Peter was one of Jesus' most passionate disciples. He made his living as a fisherman in Galilee, in the northern part of Israel. One day while Peter and his brother Andrew were fishing, Jesus approached them and said, "Come and follow me." The two men left their nets and went with Jesus. Peter was a natural leader who often spoke on behalf of Jesus' disciples. When Jesus asked, "Who do you say I am?" Peter responded for everyone by saying that Jesus is the **Messiah,** a title that means "anointed one."

How the Saint Relates

{

While Peter was both faithful and flawed, Jesus gave him a role of authority in the Church. Peter discovered his purpose by responding to Jesus' call to serve the community. Like Peter, we are called to respond to Jesus' invitation to serve one another.

Past Meets Present

PAST: Jesus gave Peter a position of authority when he gave him the keys to the kingdom and stated that Peter was the rock on whom he would build the Church. According to Catholic Tradition, Peter was the first pope. In listening to the prompting of the Holy Spirit, Peter helped unify a growing faith community.

PRESENT: In 2013 the College of Cardinals elected the 266th pope, Jorge Cardinal Bergoglio, whom we call Pope Francis. Like Peter and every pope that followed him, Pope Francis leads the Church under the direction of the Holy Spirit.

A New Name

When Peter was born, he was named Simon. Jesus gave him the name *Peter*, which means "rock," because of his strong faith. Imagine that Jesus gives you a new name because you are one of his followers. What is this name, and what does it say about your faith?

_____

_____

_____

_____

_____

_____

_____

_____

_____

_____

Peter in Scripture

The Gospels relate many dramatic moments between Peter and Jesus. Once on a mountaintop, Jesus' glory was revealed to Peter, James, and John. Jesus' face glowed, and his clothes shone so brilliantly white that the three disciples who were with him had to look away. During this event, the **Transfiguration,** Peter and the other disciples discovered that Jesus is more than just another good man with a message. He is the Son of God, who reveals God to the world.

Peter clearly was a leader in the early Church. He was the first to preach the Gospel at Pentecost. He led the process by which Matthias was selected to be the replacement for Judas Iscariot, and he performed the first public miracle in Jesus' name when he healed Aeneas. As a leader, Peter made sure that there were no distinctions made among those who joined the Christian community. He welcomed both Jews and **Gentiles,** or non-Jews, into the Church.

A Human Being

In Scripture, Peter appears lovable, impulsive, practical, and sometimes weak under pressure. Peter was also a sinner who turned away from Jesus. The night before Jesus was condemned to death, someone recognized that Peter was one of Jesus' followers. Afraid that he would also be arrested, Peter denied that he knew Jesus. Afterward Peter was ashamed of what he had done. John 21:15–19 describes how Jesus forgave Peter and reaffirmed his ministry of leadership in the Church.

Martyred for His Faith

Peter was sentenced to death by crucifixion for teaching others about Jesus. During the time of Peter's ministry, the leaders of the Roman Empire had condemned Christianity. Peter told his executioners that he was unworthy to die as Jesus died. As a result Peter was crucified upside down. He was buried in an old Roman cemetery where the Basilica of St. Peter is today. Peter was a **martyr,** someone who gave witness to his faith by dying for it.

Jesus' Message

Think about the relationship you have with one of your best friends. How has this relationship changed over time? How has your friend encouraged you to become a better person?

PRAYER

God, thank you for giving us the Church, a community of believers to support us on our journey of faith.

Preaching the Gospel

AFTER Jesus called Peter to follow him, Peter spent the rest of his life following Jesus and preaching the Gospel. Peter gradually realized how important Jesus was, both in Peter's life and for the life of the world. As Peter grew closer to Jesus, he began to more fully understand the meaning of Jesus' name, which in Hebrew means "God saves." Peter understood that by reflecting on Jesus Christ, the "Anointed One" or "the Messiah," and learning from him, we can discover everything God wants us to know about our **Salvation.**

Peter and the disciples learned from the Holy Spirit that God the Father sent his only Son, Jesus, to redeem us. Adam and Eve's decision to turn away from God resulted in the human family being born into Original Sin. A Savior was needed to restore our relationship with God. Jesus is the one who frees all people from the slavery of sin and restores humans to their place as God's children. Peter knew Jesus came to reconcile us to the Father through his life, Death, Resurrection, and Ascension into Heaven.

Saint Peter

READY for Confirmation

We first enter into a relationship with Jesus through the Sacrament of Baptism. As we prepare to celebrate Confirmation, we are invited to reflect on this relationship, and we are encouraged to strengthen it through prayer and the sacraments. When we renew our baptismal promises during the celebration of our Confirmation, we publicly proclaim our belief that Jesus is the true source of our Salvation.

The Our Father

We find the heart of Jesus' teaching—the **Beatitudes**— in the Gospel of Matthew. In this passage, Jesus taught his early followers the Lord's Prayer (Matthew 6:9–13), which we can see as a summary of the Gospel message.

"Our Father" Today, just as he did then, Jesus begins by teaching us that God is our loving Father, who wants to enter into a conversation with us. Since God is our Father, every person on earth is a brother or a sister. There is one human family, whom God loves.

"Who Art in Heaven" Jesus identifies Heaven as our true homeland. Heaven is not some place in space and time. Rather, it is wherever God's love is present. Heaven exists in a hidden way when we are faithful to God and accept his will for us. Following Jesus' footsteps to the Father means that we are headed to a place of peace, eternal rest, and happiness with God when this earthly life is over.

"Hallowed Be Thy Name" We pray that God's name will be "hallowed" so that all people will recognize God's name as holy. This is only possible when the holiness of God is seen in the way we act as his children in the care and concern we have for others.

"Thy Kingdom Come" Jesus came to proclaim the **Kingdom of God** on earth. In his life and teachings, Jesus personifies the kingdom. With the help of the Holy Spirit, we can recognize that we receive the strength to show others that God lives in their midst. For us, living within the Kingdom of God means answering God's call to be a sign of his presence through who we are and how we live.

Saint Matthew

"Thy Will Be Done" We can only be happy as children of God when we follow his will—to live in such a way that others will also want to follow his will. God wants us to love as Jesus loved in every place we find ourselves.

"Give Us This Day" We pray for our daily bread, for our own needs, and for the needs of others. Our loving Father listens to our prayers and wants us to reflect on how we can serve the needs of others.

"And Forgive Us Our Trespasses" What we need most in this world is God's protection and forgiveness. As our loving Father, God forgives our sins, and we show recognition and acceptance of this forgiveness by our willingness to forgive others.

"And Lead Us Not into Temptation" As we come to the end of the Lord's Prayer, we ask God to help us remain faithful to him now and every day of our lives so that we have the strength to reject Satan, who is doing whatever he can to turn us away from God.

Explore

Jesus identifies Heaven as our true homeland.

Study Corner

DEFINE

Salvation, Beatitudes, Kingdom of God

REMEMBER

Like Peter, as we develop our relationship with Jesus, we discover that he is the source of our Salvation. The Lord's Prayer is at the heart of the Gospel message.

The Church Begins

IN the days after Jesus was crucified and rose from the dead, the disciples remained uncertain and afraid. They were fearful that those who had killed Jesus would try to kill them as well. One day when they were huddled together in a locked room, the risen Christ suddenly appeared among them. The disciples, who were amazed, sat down to share a meal with Jesus. During a period of 40 days, the risen Christ appeared to his followers, teaching, encouraging, and sharing meals with them. At the end of these 40 days, Jesus promised he would send the Holy Spirit to his disciples, and then he ascended into Heaven where his humanity is glorified. From there he will come again.

Our Catholic Character

If we think that we alone are responsible for our prayer, we can become discouraged quickly. Our prayer is not just human prayer. It is also divine prayer, because every time we pray, the Holy Spirit leads us and helps us pray with honesty and depth. The Holy Spirit is the living breath of our prayer and the prayer of the whole Church.

Pentecost

After the Ascension, Jesus sent the Holy Spirit to his disciples as he had promised. The descent of the Holy Spirit happened on the Jewish feast of **Pentecost**, when Mary, the Apostles, and some other disciples were gathered together in a house. It was there that the Holy Spirit came down on them. Saint Luke describes this event in the Acts of the Apostles. He tells how a strong wind blew through the house, and tongues of fire came to rest on the disciples.

Everyone was filled with the Holy Spirit. Everyone began to praise God in a loud voice. People from all over the Roman world were outside the house, wondering what was going on. Inside, the disciples now understood their **mission**: to tell everyone about Jesus. All the disciples went out and began speaking to the crowd. The people heard what was being said, and they were amazed that they could understand the disciples in their own languages.

Filled with the Spirit

The Holy Spirit filled the disciples with God's love. He helped them understand the risen **Lord** in ways that they had not grasped before. Because the disciples were filled with the Holy Spirit, Christ, who had risen from the dead and ascended into Heaven, was now present to them in a new way. In sending the Holy Spirit, Jesus made it possible for his disciples to live in friendship with God the Father. The Holy

Spirit who descended on Mary and the disciples is the same Holy Spirit who comes to us in the sacraments. We can always turn to the Holy Spirit for the strength we need to live as Jesus' followers.

The Church

During his life Jesus had gathered a community of followers. Now filled with the Holy Spirit, this community became the **Church.** The Holy Spirit continues to do today what he did for the earliest disciples. He builds up and guides the Church. Catholics believe that the Church is a visible society that is both human and divine. It is made up of people who love one another and work together to build up God's kingdom. The Church is a temple of the Holy Spirit, filled with life so that it can continue the struggle against the forces of evil in the world.

The Holy Spirit fills the lives of each of us and calls us to be part of the Church. We are filled with the Holy Spirit so that we can follow Jesus and live as his disciples. When we love others, care for people in need, and do what Jesus calls us to do, we reveal to others how the Holy Spirit works in us.

Study Corner

DEFINE

Pentecost, mission, Lord, Church

REMEMBER

After his Ascension, Jesus sent the Holy Spirit to the community of his followers. Filled with the Holy Spirit, this community became the Church to which we belong today.

SACRED ART

After Jesus died and ascended into Heaven, his disciples experienced fear and sadness. After receiving the gift of the Holy Spirit, the disciples were filled with the courage of knowing that Jesus was still among them, even if they could not experience his physical presence. Like the early disciples, we experience Jesus' presence through the Holy Spirit, who gives us the strength and courage to share this presence with others.

Pentecost, oil painting, Saint Bavo's Cathedral, Ghent, Belgium.

A Holy Nation

Peter and Paul

proclaimed that Jesus is our Savior. In Baptism, Christians enter into a close relationship with Jesus and with one another.

In the grace we receive through the sacraments, we are better able to resist the temptations that can lead us away from loving God and our neighbors. In Scripture, Peter speaks to his community about the dignity of who they are and who they have become. Through Jesus we are called out of darkness and into God's wonderful light.

A Prayer of Celebration

All: In the name of the Father, and of the Son, and of the Holy Spirit. Amen.

Leader: Peter reminds us of who we are as children of God. Blessed by the grace of the Gospel, we enter into a new relationship with God and with one another.

Reader: A reading from the First Letter of Peter.

> But you are "a chosen race, a royal priesthood, a holy nation, a people of his own, so that you may announce the praises" of him who called you out of darkness into his wonderful light.
>
> Once you were "no people"
> but now you are God's people;
> you "had not received mercy"
> but now you have received
> mercy.
>
> *1 Peter 2:9–10*

The Word of the Lord.

All: Thanks be to God.

Leader: We'll now take a few moments for silent reflection. If you would like, these questions can help you get started.

- **What does it mean to me to recognize that I have been called by God into his wonderful light?**

- **How or when have I experienced God's mercy?**

Let us pray.

All: How good it is to be chosen by God!

Side 1: Shout joyfully to the LORD, all you lands;
serve the LORD with gladness;
come before him with joyful song.

Psalm 100:1–2

All: How good it is when we love one another!

Side 2: Know that the LORD is God,
he made us, we belong to him
we are his people, the flock he shepherds.

Psalm 100:3

All: Amen.

WHERE Do I Fit In?

by Jim Manney

We live in a loud, chaotic world that is filled with many voices, each of which demands our attention. As members of the Church, we are called to listen to the voices that will help us grow in our relationship with Christ. By taking time for prayer, we are able to hear what these voices call us to do. What can you do to take time to hear God's voice? For author Jim Manney, God's voice sounded like nothing he expected.

Reflect

Whose Voice Do I Listen To?

A while ago I was having some very bad days. I had too much work to do. My wife and I had a stack of unpaid bills. Problems kept cropping up, and my solutions weren't working. I felt helpless, and I hated feeling that way. I was angry, then depressed; boastful, then self-pitying. In the middle of all this mental turmoil came a quiet thought: "All will be well. Just do the next thing you have to do. All will be well." I was surprised. My heart settled down. I concentrated on the work at hand and put other worries out of my mind. Things improved.

Another time I had to decide how to deal with someone who had crossed me in a business deal. He hadn't done what he said he would do, but he wouldn't admit that. I felt wronged and said so. We exchanged harsh words. I was furious. Then came a quiet thought: "Maybe you should apologize." Ridiculous, I thought. He should apologize to me. But I thought about it some more and decided that maybe I should apologize. I may have been right about the business deal, but I had acted badly. So I did apologize for my part in the mess. The result was peace in my heart.

Both times the thought was quiet and simple. Both times the thought was virtually the opposite of what I had been thinking. The thought "All will be well" came at a time when nothing was going well and, in fact, seemed to be getting worse. The thought "Maybe you should apologize" came when I was listing all the reasons why the guy should apologize to me.

Upon reflection, I realized that the thoughts were the voice of God. Where else could they have come from? Certainly not from me. And doing what the voice said had good results. Ever since, I pay special attention to quiet thoughts that are contrary to what I'm thinking at the time. That's a sign that they might be from God.

A Clear Voice

On a separate sheet of paper, make a T-chart with the headings *Voice* and *Message*. List some of the voices that are trying to get your attention, such as your friends, your family, and the media. Then write the message that each voice is trying to convey to you. During the next week, spend some time in quiet reflection and determine whether these voices are helping you grow in your relationship with Christ.

JIM MANNEY is the author of *A Simple Life-Changing Prayer.*

What's What?

Write your answers on the lines.

1 Like Peter, what are we called to do? (PAGE 1)

_____

_____

_____

2 What did Peter understand by reflecting on Jesus Christ? (PAGE 4)

_____

_____

_____

_____

3 What do we publicly proclaim when we renew our baptismal promises during the celebration of our Confirmation? (PAGE 4)

_____

_____

_____

4 The heart of Jesus' teaching can be found in the Gospel of Matthew. What is this passage called? (PAGE 5)

_____

_____

5 Because God is our Father, what do we believe about every person on earth? (PAGE 5)

_____

_____

6 What did Jesus make possible for his disciples by sending the Holy Spirit? (PAGE 7)

_____

_____

_____

7 What do Catholics believe is a visible society that is both human and divine? (PAGE 7)

_____

_____

Say What?

Know the definitions of these terms.

Beatitudes	Messiah
Church	mission
Gentiles	Pentecost
Kingdom of God	Salvation
Lord	Transfiguration
martyr	

Now What?

Jesus gave us the Holy Spirit so that we can live in friendship with God the Father. One way we cooperate with the Holy Spirit in developing this friendship is by following Jesus' example. What can you do this week to live as a disciple in the world?

_____

_____

_____

_____

_____

_____

_____

_____

Respond

The Church Grows

Recall a time when you received a message that challenged the way you thought about something. What feelings did the message evoke within you? How did you respond to the message that you received?

PRAYER

God, thank you for those who have preached your message of Salvation. May we share this Good News through our words and actions.

Apostle to the Gentiles

Saint Paul

IT is no accident that the feast for both Saint Peter and Saint Paul is celebrated on the same day, June 29. Peter and Paul are linked as the two great missionaries of the early Church. Jesus chose Peter to lead the Church in its earliest days. Paul was the greatest missionary to the Gentiles.

Paul, who was given the name Saul when he was born, was a Jewish intellectual raised as a **Pharisee,** a sect known for its adherence to the Law. As a Pharisee, Paul knew that the Law had come to the Jews through Moses. Paul was proud of his knowledge and strict following of the Law. His first reaction to Jesus' followers was to lead the persecution against them in Jerusalem. He thought that they were unfaithful to the Law.

One day Paul was on his way to arrest Christians in the city of Damascus. As he traveled, a light flashed around him, and he fell to the ground. He heard Jesus ask him, "Why are you persecuting me?" Paul realized that in persecuting Christians, he was persecuting Jesus as well.

Paul was blinded by the light. His blindness helped him realize that he had been blind to Jesus' true identity. The men traveling with Paul led him to Damascus. There Paul waited three days before a Christian named Ananias laid his hands on Paul in prayer. Paul regained his sight, was filled with the Holy Spirit, and was baptized.

This experience changed Paul's life. He realized that Jesus is alive and present in the Church and that when Christians suffer, Jesus suffers. Paul's experience reflects the Church's belief that physical suffering and moral evils are mysteries that God illuminates through Jesus Christ, the Son of God, who died, was buried, and rose from the dead to overcome evil for the benefit of all people.

Through faith and Baptism, the Christian assumes a new identity in Christ.

Through his experience, Paul discovered that the Holy Spirit was calling him to proclaim Jesus. Paul's essential message was that in Jesus Christ, God has given Salvation to all who believe. This Salvation, the complete realization of which lay in the future, begins in Baptism. Through faith and Baptism, the Christian assumes a new identity in Christ. In the Church the Christian finds the community that proclaims Christ and lives in union with the Holy Spirit.

On the personal level, Christians recognize that when they are united with Christ in Baptism, they are given the help, or **grace,** they need to overcome the temptations that are the result of Original Sin.

Paul teaches that the love of God is being poured into our hearts through the Holy Spirit, who is the source of all love. The Holy Spirit creates a bond between us and God like children bound to a father. Even though we are weak, the Holy Spirit helps us live faithfully within this relationship. It is through the Holy Spirit that we can live in love with all people.

Paul was especially called to bring the message of Christ to the Gentile world. He did so in the Greek cities of Corinth, Philippi, Ephesus, Athens, and finally in Rome. In his preaching Paul emphasized that both Jews and non-Jews were equal members of the Church. He defended his position at the first gathering of early Church leaders during the **Council of Jerusalem,** which was held in A.D. 49. As we will see, Paul's position was also supported by Peter, and the decision was made that non-Jewish people would not have to become Jews first in order to practice the Christian faith.

According to tradition, Paul was arrested and executed during Nero's persecution of Christians around A.D. 67.

Spread the Good News

Paul shared the Good News of Salvation with the Gentiles. With whom can you share the Good News? How might you do so?

_____
_____
_____
_____
_____
_____
_____
_____
_____
_____
_____

Explore

Study Corner

DEFINE

Pharisee, grace, Council of Jerusalem

REMEMBER

Paul became known as the Apostle to the Centiles because he responded to the Holy Spirit's prompting to share the Good News of Salvation with all people, not just the Jews.

Proclaiming Jesus to the World

AFTER Jesus' Death, the disciples preached only to their fellow Jewish believers. They proclaimed that Jesus had come to fulfill the promises of the Old Testament. One day, after the Resurrection, Peter had an experience that would deeply influence the Church's mission. While he was walking to Jerusalem, Peter stopped to pray. During prayer he had a vision in which he saw animals that Jews were forbidden to eat being offered for food.

He saw heaven opened and something resembling a large sheet coming down, lowered to the ground by its four corners. In it were all the earth's four-legged animals and reptiles and the birds of the sky. A voice said to him, "Get up, Peter. Slaughter and eat." But Peter said, "Certainly not, sir. For never have I eaten anything profane and unclean." The voice spoke to him again, a second time, "What God has made clean, you are not to call profane."

Acts of the Apostles 10:11–15

Peter was puzzled by this vision. Its meaning became clear, however, when the servants of a Roman officer named Cornelius came looking for him. They told Peter that Cornelius was told in a vision to seek out Peter. Peter realized the meaning of his vision: While it was unlawful for a Jew to associate or visit with Gentiles, God had shown Peter that it is wrong to call anyone profane or unclean.

The Holy Spirit Descends on Cornelius

Peter went with the servants to Cornelius's home. Upon his arrival, Cornelius told Peter that he was ready to listen to whatever Peter had to say.

While Peter was still speaking these things, the holy Spirit fell upon all who were listening to the word. The circumcised believers who had accompanied Peter were astounded that the gift of the holy Spirit should have been poured out on the Gentiles also, for they could hear them speaking in tongues and glorifying God. Then Peter responded, "Can anyone withhold the water for baptizing these people, who have received the holy Spirit even as we have?" He ordered them to be baptized in the name of Jesus Christ.

Acts of the Apostles 10:44–48

14 *Unit 1 • The Early Church*

Peter told Cornelius how he had come to understand that God shows no partiality—the message of Salvation is for all. Peter proclaimed the basic truths about Jesus and how everyone who believes in Jesus receives forgiveness of sins. Then, to the astonishment of Peter and his associates, Cornelius and his family began to pray in the name of the Holy Spirit. Peter called for water so that they could be baptized.

As we have seen, Paul also preached to the Gentiles. As more Gentiles joined the Church, the disciples needed to discern how these new **converts** were to relate to the Jewish rites of initiation. For example, should the men be circumcised as Jewish men were before they became Christians? Paul objected to this idea. He taught that Gentiles became Christians through their faith in Jesus Christ, rather than through external signs. He thought that to attach Jewish requirements to Gentile converts would hinder his work among the Gentiles.

Council of Jerusalem

Around the year A.D. 49, leaders in the early Church met in council in Jerusalem to discuss the issue. Chapter 15 of the Acts of the Apostles tells the story of how the discussion went. Peter testified to his experience of the Holy Spirit coming down upon the Gentiles. Based on this experience, Peter stated that since God has called them through the Holy Spirit, the Gentiles should not be burdened with the customs of the Jews.

After further discussion and reflection guided by the Holy Spirit, the Church agreed with Peter. The Council of Jerusalem resolved that Jewish laws would not apply to Gentile Christians. Paul and his companion Barnabas were sent to Antioch to announce this teaching.

Study Corner

DEFINE
converts, Eucharist

REMEMBER
During the Council of Jerusalem, the early leaders of the Church decided that Gentile converts to Christianity did not also need to follow Jewish laws and customs.

Past Meets Present

PAST: We learn in Acts of the Apostles 2:42–47 that the early Christians gathered to break bread. They remembered what Jesus did the night before he died. He took bread, said a blessing, broke the bread, and gave it to his disciples. Jesus said that the bread was his Body. Jesus also blessed the wine, distributing it to the disciples, saying that it was his Blood. Jesus then told the disciples to remember him by doing the same thing.

PRESENT: Each day, except Good Friday, the Church gathers to celebrate the **Eucharist,** the source and summit of Christian life. The *Eucharist*, a word which means "thanksgiving," is the Christian prayer of blessing for all that God has done for us in Jesus Christ.

The Eucharist is the celebration of Jesus' sacrifice on the cross. As we celebrate, we remember Christ's Passover, his Death, and his Resurrection from the dead. In remembering Christ's sacrifice, we are reminded that Jesus gives us the grace to live and die as he did—as a person for others. The Eucharist is also our sacrifice, the offering up of ourselves for the good of the world.

During the Eucharist, when the priest prays the words of consecration, the bread and wine become the Body and Blood of the risen Jesus Christ.

When we celebrate the Eucharist, we are directly linked to those early Christians who gathered, broke bread, and celebrated Jesus Christ in their midst. Just as they were, we are also called to receive the Body and Blood of the risen Jesus Christ in the Eucharist.

The Law of Love

The decision

that was made at the Council of Jerusalem was in itself a proclamation of the Good News. Peter, Paul, and the other Church leaders reminded the faithful that God, in his great love, offers the gift of Salvation to all people. At the same time, this gift requires action on our part. Christian believers are called to live lives that are worthy of this gift.

As members of the Church, we share with others the Good News of God's abundant grace through our words and actions. By performing selfless acts of love, we help others open their hearts to God's presence, and we give witness to the unity of the Christian community.

Called to Love

All: In the name of the Father, and of the Son, and of the Holy Spirit. Amen.

Leader: Through his ministry to the Gentiles, Paul reminds us that showing love for one another is at the heart of Christian discipleship.

Reader: A reading from the letter of Paul to the Ephesians.

I, then, a prisoner for the Lord, urge you to live in a manner worthy of the call you have received, with all humility and gentleness, with patience, bearing with one another through love, striving to preserve the unity of the spirit through the bond of peace: one body and one Spirit, as you were also called to the one hope of your call; one Lord, one faith, one baptism; one God and Father of all, who is over all and through all and in all.

Ephesians 4:1–6

The Word of the Lord.

All: Thanks be to God.

Leader: Let us take a moment to reflect silently on how we can live in a manner worthy of the call we have received. These questions can help you get started.

- **How am I being called to practice the virtues of humility, gentleness, and patience with others?**

- **How do my words and actions express to others my belief in God, the Father of all?**

Leader: Let us give thanks to God for his gift of Salvation.

All: The Lord is good to all,
　　compassionate toward all your works.
All your works give you thanks, Lord
　　and your faithful bless you.
They speak of the glory of your reign
　　and tell of your mighty works.

Psalm 145:9–11

All: Amen.

WHERE Do I Fit In?

God has freely chosen to share his love with all people. Families and communities are a reflection of God's love for us and our love for one another. They not only teach us about God's love; they are God's love in action. As members of the Church, we are called to respond to God's gift of love in ways that express our unity with our brothers and sisters in God.

by Maria Mondragon

Reflect

A Place Where I Belong

See, upon the palms of my hands I have engraved you.

Isaiah 49:16

I grew up in New Mexico, the youngest of seven kids. I have six uncles, eight aunts, and 40 cousins. People often assume that in large families it's easy for one child to fall through the cracks. And people often wonder if parents could possibly have enough love for all those kids. I can tell you that in my family, love was (and is) abundant. There were no cracks to fall through because the family was tight-knit.

At family gatherings my uncles would play guitar and sing old favorites. We'd all sing along. It took all our individual voices to make that loud and beautiful sound. And if one voice was a bit off-key (usually mine), it didn't matter because the group as a whole was in tune. When we'd gather for family picnics, we'd all play kickball or baseball. Each of us was cheered on and encouraged. There was room for errors because it was understood that we were all learning to play the game together.

Our church community expanded that circle even more. Members of our extended family and our parish community attended each of our seven First Holy Communion and Confirmation celebrations. My parents also sang in the parish's Spanish choir. For each choir member's birthday, the choir members and their families would gather at sunrise and sing

MARIA MONDRAGON is a managing editor at Loyola Press.

"Las Mañanitas" outside the person's window to celebrate the day on which he or she was born.

It was in these communities that I recognized something—I matter.

My presence among my family members' celebrations was important, just as their presence mattered to me. You might think that if one of the seven of us didn't attend an event, it would go unnoticed. That never happened. People asked for each of us by name. And they still do.

I live in Chicago now, and I miss my family. But here I have helped build a community of families where I know I belong and where people ask for me and for my own children by name.

We Belong

Think of the communities to which you belong. Draw a Venn diagram with three circles and your name in the center where the circles intersect. Label each circle with the name of a community, such as school, church, team, or family. Write the names of the people in each of those communities. Then write a paragraph describing how you feel you belong to each community. How does each community call you by name? How is the Holy Spirit at work in each community?

What's What?

Respond

Complete the crossword by using the clues below.

Across

3 While praying in Jerusalem, Peter had a _____ that deeply influenced the direction of the Church's mission. (PAGE 14)

5 *Eucharist* means "_____." (PAGE 15)

8 Peter and Paul were great _____ of the early Church. (PAGE 12)

10 Paul's physical _____ helped him realize that he had been blind to Jesus' true identity. (PAGE 12)

Down

1 In the Acts of the Apostles, we learn that the early Christians gathered to break _____. (PAGE 15)

2 Peter proclaimed that everyone who believes in Jesus receives _____ of sins. (PAGE 15)

4 Paul teaches us that the love of God is being poured into our hearts through the _____. (PAGE 13)

6 The _____ were known for their strict adherence to the Law. (PAGE 12)

7 During the Council of Jerusalem, the decision was made that non-Jews would not have to first become _____ to practice the Christian faith. (PAGE 13)

9 Paul taught that Gentiles became Christians through their _____ in Jesus Christ. (PAGE 15)

Say What?

Know the definitions of these terms.

converts   grace

Council of Jerusalem   Pharisee

Eucharist

Now What?

In Scripture, Paul reminds us that the Holy Spirit is the source of all love. How can you share this love with others during the next week?

_____

_____

_____

Witnesses to the Faith

> Think about a time when your beliefs were challenged by someone. How did you respond? Were you tempted to go along, or did you find a way to be true to your beliefs in spite of the pressure you faced?

PRAYER

God, thank you for giving us the example of the martyrs. May we always have the strength to remain true to our beliefs.

The Martyrs and the Communion of Saints

BEGINNING with Nero's persecution of the Christian Church in Rome and lasting through the Edict of Milan (issued in A.D. 313), Christians lived under close scrutiny. While the periods of intense persecution were few, Christians were outsiders and considered atheists because they did not celebrate the festivals of the local gods. If crops failed or other natural disasters happened, cities would hear the cry "Christians to the lions!" This discrimination caused the conditions that led to the first Christian heroes, or martyrs. The Greek word for *martyr* means "witness."

Martyrdom was seen as a **charism** in the early Church; however, not all Christians were called to be martyrs. A Christian could not simply confess membership in the Christian faith in the hope of being put to death by the authorities. This act would be considered suicide and would have placed the authorities in the position of being murderers. Commenting on the charism of martyrdom, Saint Augustine said that the intention of the martyrs was to witness to their faith. They were willing to die as a consequence of believing in Jesus. Tertullian (ca. A.D. 160–ca. 225), an early Church father, described martyrdom as Baptism in blood that brought forgiveness of sins. Unbaptized people who died for the sake of their faith were seen as baptized in the giving of their own blood.

Martyrs saw the giving of their lives as a kind of second Baptism. Dying for one's faith was seen as a participation in the Passion of Jesus Christ, who was present with the martyrs, strengthening them.

By confessing their faith to the death, the martyrs showed the Roman state that there were values that transcended the power of the Roman Empire and its gods. Martyrdom was also a witness to unbelievers to the truth of the Gospel. Martyrs are still seen as perfect disciples who immediately realize the blessings promised to all Christians. As such, we believe that they enter Heaven immediately; they do not have to experience Purgatory.

Living with Christ in Heaven, martyrs have direct access to God. Therefore, they can act as **intercessors** and pray for the needs of those left behind. The martyrs are servants of Christ and mediators of grace.

Martyrs are also members of the **Communion of Saints,** which is the community of all those, living and dead, who believe in Jesus and follow his teachings. Since we are also members of the Communion of Saints, we can pray for all those who have died, commending them to God's mercy and offering prayers for them, especially in the Sacrifice of the Mass.

The major periods of persecution were from A.D. 251 to 313. During the most intense persecution, the practice of Christianity was formally outlawed, and everyone in the empire was required to offer sacrifice to the Roman gods. People who did not do so were killed immediately. Some historians believe that nearly 200,000 people were killed during this period. Many other Christians fell away from the faith, and others went into hiding. Therefore, martyrs, as heroes of the Church, were held in high regard.

Honoring the Martyrs

Greeks and Romans celebrated the memories of deceased family members by having meals in their honor. Christian families took up this custom by having special meals on the anniversaries of the martyrs' deaths. In this way Christians ensured that the memories of the martyrs' would not be forgotten.

At first, these commemorations of the martyrs were done locally. As the Church became more aware of its universal mission, Christians realized that the meaning a martyr had for a local church could be celebrated with the whole Church.

Over time the martyrs' grave sites became shrines. The martyrs' **relics,** such as locks of hair or bone fragments, were taken from their original burial sites and housed in churches or basilicas. The names of martyrs were given to Christian children.

The reliquary of Saint Thérèse of Lisieux

Explore

Study Corner

DEFINE

charism, intercessors, Communion of Saints, relics, Gifts of the Holy Spirit

REMEMBER

The early Christians martyrs gave their lives as a witness to their faith in Jesus Christ.

Constantine the Great, woodcut, 1877.

READY for Confirmation

Professing one's faith as a Christian during the period of persecution required faith and courage. In the Sacrament of Confirmation, we receive the gift of courage, one of the seven **Gifts of the Holy Spirit.** *This gift gives us the strength to stand up for our beliefs and to live as Jesus' disciples.*

The Early Martyrs

Saints Perpetua and Felicity

MEMBERS of the early Church followed Jesus' example of love and service by preaching the Gospel and distributing alms—food and money—to widows, orphans, and people who were poor. Before long, so many people were relying on the charity of Christians that the Apostles appointed deacons to oversee the daily distribution of alms. This freed the Apostles to spend time preaching the Gospel. What can you do to preach the Gospel to others?

Saint Stephen (Died 33)

The apostles appointed Stephen to serve as one of the first deacons. He was widely regarded as a man "filled with faith and the holy Spirit." (Acts of the Apostles 6:5) In addition to distributing alms, he also preached the Good News. Some Jewish authorities were so upset with Stephen's message that they found witnesses to testify falsely that he had committed **blasphemy,** which means defying or disrespecting God. Based on this testimony, Stephen was arrested and brought before the **Sanhedrin,**

SACRED ART

The stained-glass windows in our churches serve as sources of light and decorations that fill us with awe. These windows often serve another purpose; they teach us about our faith. Many windows include images of Scripture stories and scenes from the lives of the saints. This window teaches us that Saint Stephen was a leader in the early Church and that he died for his faith. His role as a leader is symbolized by the vestments he is wearing, and the stone he is holding reminds us of how he died.

Saint Stephen, stained glass.

the Jewish court that ruled on matters of faith and practice among the Jews. Stephen spoke passionately in his own defense, drawing on his deep understanding of Scripture to show how everything in Jewish history had been leading up to Jesus. Stephen's adversaries, blinded by rage, dragged him out of town and stoned him to death. His last words were "Lord, do not hold this sin against them." (Acts of the Apostles 7:60) Stephen was the first martyr. We can read more about his ministry and death in the Acts of the Apostles.

Saint Polycarp (69–155)

It was in the middle of the second century, and Polycarp, the bishop of the Greek city of Smyrna, was an old man, well into his 80s. He stood before a Roman judge who liked Polycarp and felt sorry for him. The judge did not want to condemn Polycarp to death because of his faith in Jesus Christ. He tried to save the old man. The judge pleaded with Polycarp to say that the Roman emperor is Lord. All Polycarp had to do was offer a little pinch of incense in front of the statue of the Roman emperor, nothing else. By doing so, Polycarp could save his life.

Polycarp looked to the Roman judge and said, "I have served Christ for 86 years, and he never did me any wrong. How can I turn my back on the king who saved me?" With these words, Polycarp sealed his fate. The Roman judge had Polycarp burned alive. He was executed because he believed in one God and refused to place his faith in any other god.

Saints Perpetua and Felicity (Died 203)

The persecution of Christians affected everyone—men and women, rich and poor. Perpetua, a young noblewoman, was a **catechumen,** an adult who was being formed in the Christian faith through instruction and the example of the community. She sought instruction for herself and for everyone in her household, including Felicity, one of her servants. During the time she was preparing to join the Church, the Roman emperor issued an edict that forbade anyone from being baptized. Perpetua and the members of her household continued to receive instruction until they were arrested. After their arrest they were tried and condemned to death. While

she was in jail, Perpetua's father tried to convince her to change her mind and renounce her faith. She remained steadfast, however. While awaiting their fate, Perpetua, Felicity, and the others were baptized. On the day of their execution, they appeared joyful, as though they were on their way to Heaven.

> # On the day of their execution, they appeared joyful, as though they were on their way to Heaven.

Explore

Study Corner

DEFINE
blasphemy, Sanhedrin, catechumen

REMEMBER
By dying for their faith, Saints Stephen, Polycarp, Perpetua, and Felicity provide examples of how to respond to God's gift of Salvation through Jesus Christ.

Praying to the Saints

There are

times in our lives when we need courage to help us remain faithful to Jesus and his teachings. Maybe we are pressured by our peers to do something that we know is wrong, for example.

During these moments of doubt and uncertainty, we can remember the saints, whose lives exemplify faith and courage. To help us grow in faith, we can pray to the saints and ask them to intercede on our behalf.

A Litany of the Saints

All: In the name of the Father, and of the Son, and of the Holy Spirit. Amen.

Leader: Through their words and actions, the saints have provided examples of Christian living. Let us take a moment to ask them to intercede on our behalf.

Lord, have mercy.

All: Lord, have mercy.

Leader: Christ, have mercy.

All: Christ, have mercy.

Leader: Lord, have mercy.

All: Lord, have mercy.

Leader: Holy Mary, Mother of God,

Response: Pray for us.

Saint Joseph, ℟.
Saint Peter and Saint Paul, ℟.
Saint Stephen, ℟.
Saint Perpetua and Saint Felicity, ℟.
Saint James, ℟.
Saint John, ℟.
Saint Philip, ℟.
Saint Bartholomew, ℟.
Saint Matthew, ℟.

Saint Mary Magdalene, ℟.
Saint Monica and Saint Augustine, ℟.
Saint Benedict and Saint Scholastica, ℟.
Saint Francis and Saint Dominic, ℟.
Saint Ignatius of Loyola, ℟.
Saint Francis Xavier, ℟.
Saint John Vianney, ℟.
Saint Catherine, ℟.
Saint Teresa, ℟.
All the saints and martyrs, ℟.
All holy men and women, ℟.

Leader: Christ, hear us

All: Christ, hear us.

Leader: Christ, graciously hear us.

All: Christ, graciously hear us.

Leader: Let us give thanks to God for giving us the model of the saints.

All: Glory be to the Father,
and to the Son,
and to the Holy Spirit.
As it was in the beginning,
is now, and ever shall be,
world without end.
Amen.

WHERE Do I Fit In?

We often pick up the beliefs of the people around us. Without giving it much thought, we profess to believe the same thing as our parents, friends, and culture. It is often when we are challenged that we take the time to clarify our beliefs. The challenges that the early martyrs faced strengthened their faith so that they could remain true to their convictions.

by Honora Wood

What Do I Stand For?

Growing up, I often took my parents' statements at face value without understanding the facts behind their conclusions. They had done the research already, so why should I? I never even dreamed that my parents could be wrong, so it seemed pointless to ask them why they believed what they did.

When I got older, this passive attitude came back to bite me. I realized that I needed to understand what I truly stand for.

One summer, when I was in high school, I got into a discussion with a guy named Jim, who worked with me in a summer job. We were talking about colleges, and we were on opposite sides of the fence about one particular school. My parents had strong views about this college, and I stated them as my own opinion. Jim had the opposite opinion, with facts and personal experience to back him up. He had visited this college and spoken with many staff members who worked there. I had no such experience. I thought I was right. I knew my parents had reasons for their opinion, but I didn't know what they were. All that I had retained was their opinion, with none of their factual support. Jim asked me, "What proof do you have?" I was completely taken aback; I had no answer to that question. I had to concede to Jim that I simply did not have enough facts to back up my statement. I would have to research it further.

It's easy to listen to parents and other adults because they have so much wisdom and experience. As a young adult transitioning into independence, however, simply parroting the beliefs of my parents will not suffice anymore. God is really pushing me to find out for myself what it means to be Catholic today. I may end up thinking as my parents do, but for my beliefs to shape how I live out God's Word, I have to discern for myself how God is calling me to live out my faith. I am so blessed by the wisdom and the Catholic formation my parents have given me. With their encouragement, I am learning more and more how to make decisions in situations that they never faced.

A Journey of Faith

On a separate sheet of paper, draw a walking path. Include markers along the path that describe events in your life that have challenged and strengthened your faith.

HONORA WOOD is currently studying at the University of Michigan, where she is pursuing a bachelor of fine arts in dance.

What's What?

Circle the letter of the choice that best completes each sentence.

1. Martyrdom was seen as _____ in the early Church. (PAGE 20)

   a. a charism

   b. an atheistic practice

   c. suicide

2. _____ said that the intention of the martyrs was to witness to their faith. (PAGE 20)

   a. Saint Augustine

   b. Tertullian

   c. Nero

3. Dying for one's faith was seen as a _____ the Passion of Jesus Christ. (PAGE 20)

   a. strengthening of

   b. transcending of

   c. participation in

4. The martyrs can act as _____ by praying for the needs of people still on earth. (PAGES 20–21)

   a. perfect disciples

   b. intercessors

   c. forgivers of sin

5. Members of the early Church followed Jesus' example of love and service by distributing _____ to widows, orphans, and people who were poor. (PAGE 22)

   a. food

   b. money

   c. both *a* and *b*

6. Stephen was falsely accused of _____. (PAGE 22)

   a. being a deacon

   b. blasphemy

   c. belonging to the Sanhedrin

7. The stained-glass windows in our churches often teach us about _____. (PAGE 22)

   a. our faith

   b. Saint Stephen's act of blasphemy

   c. the importance of decoration

Say What?

Know the definitions of these terms.

blasphemy	Gifts of the Holy Spirit
catechumen	intercessors
charism	relics
Communion of Saints	Sanhedrin

Now What?

Having faith requires a willingness to stand up for our beliefs, even when it is difficult or unpopular. Who in your life serves as a model of faithfulness and courage? What can you do during the next week to thank that person for his or her example?

_____

_____

_____

_____

_____

_____

_____

_____

_____

The Catechumenate in the Early Church

Think about a time you joined a new group or community, whether it was a sports team, a band, or a school. How were you welcomed into the group? How did others help you feel that you belonged?

PRAYER

God, thank you for all the people who have helped us grow in faith. May we put their examples into practice through our own words and actions.

Joining the Early Church

SINCE the Roman government persecuted the early Christians, choosing to join the Church was a big risk. The process of becoming Christian—the **catechumenate**—took several years, which allowed the catechumens and the community to be sure of the catechumens' desire to become Christian.

During the catechumenate, the catechumens first learned about God the Father. Those who led the catechumenate emphasized that Christians did not consider the emperor to be a god, which was the common belief of the day. By professing loyalty to God rather than the emperor, the catechumens could have been charged with treason and sentenced to death. To determine whether the catechumens were ready to make this commitment, Christian leaders spent time talking and praying with them.

Next, the catechumens were allowed to join the Christian community in **liturgy,** the public worship of God. Listening to Scripture readings and the Homily helped catechumens better understand the Word of God and the Church's teachings. Because the catechumens had not been fully initiated into the Church, they were asked to leave before the Liturgy of the Eucharist, the second part of Mass, began.

In the next step of the catechumenate, the catechumens learned the Lord's Prayer. Leaders from the community again spent time talking with the catechumens to help them discern their readiness to join the Church. The leaders were interested in how the catechumens were living their lives and what they were doing to help people who were poor. The leaders wanted to be sure that the catechumens were freely and consciously choosing to join the Church and that the catechumens understood that the Church would help nurture and support them in their life of faith.

Sacraments of Initiation

Once the Church leaders judged the catechumens to be ready, they were allowed to be initiated fully into the Church. During the Easter Vigil on Holy Saturday, the night before Easter Sunday, the catechumens were baptized, confirmed, and received the Eucharist for the first time. Now that their initiation was complete, the catechumens became known as **neophytes,** beginners in the faith. They were able to remain for the entire celebration of the Mass and to receive Holy Communion.

For the first few centuries of the Church's history, the Sacraments of Initiation were celebrated together at the same time. It was not until five centuries after Jesus died that the Sacraments of Baptism, Confirmation, and the Eucharist were celebrated separately and at different times in one's life. In the Western Church, Christians who were baptized as infants by the local priest waited several years before celebrating the Sacrament of Confirmation.

The Second Vatican Council brought back the process of initiation used in the early Church. Those who join the Church as adults celebrate the Sacraments of Initiation all at once. Those who are baptized as infants generally receive First Holy Communion and Confirmation when they are older. By emphasizing the connection between the Sacraments of Initiation, the Church reminds us that they are the foundation for Christian life.

Through Baptism and Confirmation, we are called to participate in the Church's saving mission. Through participation in the Eucharist, our love of God and all humanity is communicated and nourished. Everyone who is fully initiated into the Church is called to make the Church present in places and circumstances where it can be nourishment for the life of all people.

Through Baptism and Confirmation, we are called to participate in the Church's saving mission.

Past Meets Present

PAST: In the early Church, adults were plunged into water at Baptism, symbolizing their dying to sin and rising to new life in Christ. This practice is called Baptism by immersion. Later, when infant Baptism became more common, so did baptizing by pouring water on the head.

PRESENT: Today, as older churches are renovated and as new churches are built, much thought is being given to the placement and the structure of the baptismal font to allow for Baptism by immersion once again. Immersion is a powerful symbol of the "death to new life" significance of this sacrament.

Study Corner

DEFINE

catechumenate, liturgy, neophytes

REMEMBER

After the catechumenate, the catechumens are welcomed into the Church through the Sacraments of Initiation: Baptism, Confirmation, and the Eucharist.

The Sacraments of Initiation

Baptism

Because of Adam and Eve's choice to turn away from God, we are born into Original Sin and into a world that yearns for the holiness and **justice** that God intended for creation. Catechumens are taught that they are re-created through the waters of Baptism. Just as water cleansed the earth of sin during the great Flood, so too does it cleanse us from the stain of Original Sin. Through Baptism we are born into a new way of life in Christ and can live a life free from sin. Baptism is the first sacrament of the forgiveness of sin. We can only receive this sacrament once in our lives.

Following Jesus' instructions, Christians are baptized "in the name of the Father, and of the Son, and of the holy Spirit." (Matthew 28:19) Whether through immersion or pouring, the water that is used in Baptism symbolizes the new life we receive as disciples. The graces that are bestowed by the Holy Spirit through Baptism confer upon us God's righteousness and leave a **character,** or indelible sign, on our soul. In addition to marking us as Christians, this character consecrates us for worship. Through Baptism the Holy Spirit unites us by faith to the Paschal Mystery so that we can share in Christ's life.

Our Catholic Character

In Scripture, Jesus told Nicodemus that "no one can enter the kingdom of God without being born of water and Spirit." (John 3:5) By saying this, Jesus taught us that Baptism is necessary for Salvation; people who hear the truth and recognize the Gospel must be baptized to be saved. This does not mean that people who are not baptized cannot be saved.

Good people who have no knowledge of the Church or the Gospel it preaches can be saved by searching for the truth and living good lives. People who want to become Christian but die before they are baptized are saved as though they were baptized. The same is true for people who are not baptized but are killed because they believe in Jesus Christ. We call this a baptism of blood, which saves even though it is not a sacrament. We entrust children who die without being baptized to the hands of God, confident that he will care for them.

Because Baptism is necessary for Salvation, the Church teaches that, in imminent danger of death and if no priest or deacon is available, anyone can administer the sacrament, so long as it is done with the Church's intention. To do so, one simply pours water over the head of the person being baptized, while saying "I baptize you in the name of the Father, and of the Son, and of the Holy Spirit." Water is poured three times, once for each time one of the Persons of the Trinity is named.

Confirmation

During the Sacrament of Confirmation, the celebrant, most often the bishop, anoints the forehead of the person being confirmed while he says, "Be sealed with the Gift of the Holy Spirit." The Rite of Confirmation also includes the laying on of hands. Like Baptism, Confirmation leaves a character on a person's soul and can only be received once. This sacrament, which perfects the graces received in Baptism, gives us the Holy Spirit to root us more deeply in our relationship with God the Father and his Son, Jesus Christ. Likewise, this sacrament strengthens our bond with the Church and gives us the strength to build up God's kingdom.

To be confirmed, one must have reached the **age of reason,** usually around seven years of age; be willing to profess freely faith in Christ and his Church; be in a state of grace; have the intention of receiving the sacrament; and be willing to follow Jesus.

The Eucharist

Passover is the most important feast for the Jewish people. During this celebration the Jews remember how God freed them from slavery in Egypt. At his

final Passover meal, the Last Supper, Jesus took bread and said, "This is my body." Then he took a chalice of wine and said, "This is my blood." Jesus asked his followers to remember what he had done. When the early Christians gathered after Christ's Resurrection, they broke bread and remembered the Passover meal that they shared with Jesus the night before he died.

The early Christians had a profound understanding of the meaning of the Eucharist. They realized that their identity as the People of God was based on the presence of the risen Christ in the Eucharist. Today we understand that the Eucharist is the "source and summit" of the Church's life of grace. Through this sacrament we are united with Christ and his act of praise and thanksgiving offered on the cross.

To receive Holy Communion, one must be in a state of grace. The Church recommends that the faithful receive Holy Communion when they participate in the celebration of the Eucharist and obliges the faithful to do so at least once a year.

Explore

READY for Confirmation

When we are confirmed, we participate in God's life of grace through the power of the Holy Spirit. Through Confirmation we are called to be witnesses to the presence of Christ wherever we are, whatever we do. Saint Teresa of Àvila expressed this when she prayed, "Yours are the eyes through which the compassion of Christ must look out on the world. Yours are the feet with which he is to go about doing good. Yours are the hands with which he is to bless his people."

United with God

Our Baptismal Promises

Imagine yourself at a place where you like to go to relax. Take a moment to enjoy being in this place. Then notice that Jesus has come to join you. He knew just where to find you. Greet him and share with him whatever is in your heart.

When you are ready, tell Jesus what you know about your Baptism. If you received the sacrament as an infant, share what you have heard through family stories or through photos or videos that you have seen. Take a few minutes to talk with Jesus.

When we pray, we unite ourselves to the one true God—Father, Son, and Holy Spirit. Sometimes we do this by directing our prayer to God the Father. Other times we pray to his Son, Jesus, and sometimes we pray to the Holy Spirit.

Through the Sacraments of Initiation, we enter into union with Jesus Christ and the entire Church. If you were baptized as an infant, your parents and godparents made promises for you. These baptismal promises express our commitment to our faith. Each year during the Easter season, we have the opportunity to renew our baptismal promises, affirming for ourselves what was promised for us at our baptism.

Then Jesus says that he has a question for you. He wonders if you know what your godparents promised for you when you were baptized. Here are three of the promises that we say during the Sacrament of Baptism. Read them and then spend a moment reflecting on the questions that follow.

Do you believe in God,
the Father almighty,
Creator of heaven and earth?

How have I experienced God's love in my life? How can I show God my love for him?

Do you believe in Jesus Christ, his only Son, our Lord,
who was born of the Virgin Mary,
suffered death and was buried,
rose again from the dead
and is seated at the right hand of the Father?

How can I thank Jesus for the of Salvation that I have received through his Paschal Mystery?

Do you believe in the Holy Spirit,
the holy Catholic Church,
the communion of saints,
the forgiveness of sins,
the resurrection of the body,
and life everlasting?

How can I turn to the Church for the strength to live as a disciple? How can I support others in their life of discipleship?

End by praying the Lord's Prayer.

WHERE Do I Fit In?

by Mary Alice Pratt

As Catholics we are called to share our gifts with all the communities to which we belong. Participating in the life of the community is a way to share our God-given gifts with others. As Mary Alice Pratt reflects here, sometimes we receive as much from the community as we give to them.

Giving and Receiving in Community

When I was around 10 or 11 years old, I read in a Catholic magazine about missionaries working in Africa. This work seemed exciting. I thought I'd like to serve God that way too. I became a nurse, and I joined a society of Catholic women who use their professional skills in developing countries. I went to Amman, Jordan, very near Jerusalem, Bethlehem, and other places of Jesus' life.

Most of the patients at the hospital where I worked were children, including many babies who were dehydrated and undernourished. One of the doctors had developed a formula of bananas, yogurt, water, and a little salt that worked wonders on dehydrated babies. It was wonderful to feed them and watch them recover in a few days.

Many of the children were sicker than that, however. I remember one boy named Sa'id. He was about 13 years old and was sick with typhoid fever, a serious infection caused by contaminated food and water. Most of the children in the hospital were from Muslim families, but Sa'id was a Melkite Christian, one of the Eastern Rites of the Catholic Church. He was very sick. We watched him anxiously, and someone from his family was with him almost all the time.

Sa'id recovered. To thank us, his family brought a lamb to the door of the church, had it blessed and then gave it to the staff of the hospital for a feast.

MARY ALICE PRATT devoted her life to serving others. In addition to serving as a nurse, she also coordinated peace and justice ministries at the University of Kentucky Newman Center.

That was when I realized that being a missionary is about relationships—each one gives and each one receives. We had served Sa'id's family, and they were thanking us.

I learned much from the Arabs, Christians, and Muslims amid whom I lived and worked. I learned to accept customs that were different from my own. My professional skills did not make me superior to the people I helped. That was simply the way I served. The people with whom I lived and worked served me in their own ways. We were equals, giving and receiving from one another, serving Christ together.

Reflect

Gifts to Share

Identify a community into which you have been welcomed. What gifts were you able to share with the community? What gifts did the community share with you? Write your responses on the lines.

_____

_____

_____

_____

_____

_____

What's What?

Write your answers on the lines.

1 Why did the catechumenate often take several years in the early Church? (PAGE 28)

_____

_____

_____

_____

_____

2 What sacraments did the catechumens celebrate when they were initiated into the Church? (PAGE 28)

_____

_____

_____

3 In what do the Sacraments of Baptism and Confirmation call us to participate? (PAGE 29)

_____

_____

4 The water that is used in Baptism is a symbol of what? (PAGE 30)

_____

_____

5 What does Confirmation do to the graces received in Baptism? (PAGE 31)

_____

_____

6 What do the Jews remember during the celebration of the Passover? (PAGE 31)

_____

_____

7 What happens through the Sacrament of the Eucharist? (PAGE 31)

_____

_____

_____

Say What?

Know the definitions of these terms.

age of reason	justice
catechumenate	liturgy
character	neophytes

Now What?

We are welcomed into the Church through the Sacraments of Initiation, which call us to share the Gospel with others through our words and actions. How can you share Jesus' Good News with others this week?

_____

_____

_____

_____

_____

_____

_____

_____

_____

_____

Celebrating Ordinary Time

MANY families use a calendar to keep track of important events, such as school functions, parish celebrations, social events, doctor appointments, birthdays, and holidays. In a similar way, the Church, our family of faith, has a calendar that we use to help us remember and celebrate important events in the lives of Jesus, Mary, and the saints. By celebrating these events, we recall and reflect on the many ways that God has revealed his love to us throughout history. Like many calendars, the liturgical calendar marks entire seasons and individual feasts and celebrations.

During Ordinary Time, one of the seasons of the liturgical year, the Church invites us to think more deeply about the message of the Gospel and how we can respond to Christ's invitation to live as disciples. We hear about this call to discipleship in the Scripture readings that are proclaimed at Mass.

The Church devotes two periods of the liturgical year to Ordinary Time. The first period begins the Monday after the Feast of the Baptism of the Lord and continues until Ash Wednesday. The second period begins the Monday after Pentecost and ends with the beginning of Advent. Together these two periods last for either 33 or 34 weeks.

Green, which symbolizes hope, is the liturgical color for Ordinary Time. This color reminds us of the new life we receive as Jesus' followers. During Ordinary Time the church is filled with green plants, the altar is covered with a green cloth, and priests and deacons wear green liturgical vestments.

The early Christians turned to the saints for direction and strength. Who in your life gives you moral guidance and support? How does the advice you receive help you live as one of Jesus' followers?

PRAYER

Loving God, help us follow the example of the saints so that we may live out our faith in all we do.

35

Saints Show Us the Way

DURING the season of Ordinary Time, we reflect on Jesus' call to discipleship and how we can best use our gifts to respond to that call. We can do this through prayer, celebrating the sacraments, and reading Scripture. To help us learn how others have responded to the call of discipleship, we can study the lives of the saints. The practice of turning to the saints for guidance and inspiration has been part of our Tradition since the earliest days of the Church.

During early periods of persecution, Christians often gathered for safety in the catacombs for prayer and worship. People frequently met in crypts, some of which held bodies of popes and martyrs. Amid the ongoing persecutions, Christians began to **venerate,** or show respect for, these martyrs in special ways. Most frequently this included gathering for prayer on the anniversary of the martyr's death.

In addition to praying to the saints, many people wanted tangible reminders of the saints that they could hold onto. This desire developed into the practice of venerating relics. A first-class relic is a piece of a saint's remains, such as a chip of bone or a lock of hair. As veneration of relics became an important part of early Christian spirituality and as the Church grew in size, the need for additional relics grew. Veneration of two additional types of relics became common. Second-class relics include items that a saint wore, such as an article of clothing, or an item that the person used frequently when he or she was alive. A third-class relic is any object that has been touched to a first- or second-class relic, such as a piece of cloth. The practice of venerating relics continues to be an important part of Catholic spirituality. This practice underscores the sacramental nature of our faith.

Saints and Feast Days

To help keep track of the anniversaries of the martyrs' deaths, the Church began keeping a liturgical calendar. Before long, this calendar included the anniversaries of the deaths of other holy men and women that the Church community considered to be saints. Over the centuries the calendar grew, and multiple local calendars developed. Eventually the number of saints and martyrs whose anniversaries the Church wanted to remember outnumbered the days in the year. In the eighth century, Pope Gregory III named November 1 the Feast of All Saints, the day

Our Catholic Character

Many non-Catholics confuse veneration with worship and think that we worship Mary, the saints, relics, statues, and other physical objects that are an important part of our tradition. In reality, we believe that only God is worthy of our worship. We turn to Mary and the saints in honor, we try to imitate their example of discipleship, and we ask them to intercede on our behalf. The physical objects, often called **sacramentals,** that we use in our sacramental celebrations always point back to God, the true object of our praise and worship.

on which the Church continues to remember all the saints and martyrs who are with God in Heaven. In the 16th century, Pope Gregory XIII approved an official calendar, known as the Roman Martyrology, for the universal Church. This calendar includes all the feast days celebrated by Catholics all over the world. Bishops in each country still have the ability to include important local feast days, such as the feast day of a country's patron saint, in their local liturgical calendars. The Church's calendar of liturgical feast days and celebrations is called the sanctoral calendar.

Originally Christians were recognized as saints without any formal process. In time the Church began to define more clearly **canonization,** the process by which someone is named a saint. The process that is used currently ensures that the person who is a candidate for sainthood lived and died in such an exemplary way that he or she truly can be considered an example of Christian living for the faithful all over the world.

In remembering and celebrating the lives of the saints today, we honor all they did to teach us about God and build up his kingdom. We also commit ourselves to following their example. When we respond to the call to discipleship by following the example of Jesus, Mary, and the saints, we actively profess our membership in the Communion of Saints.

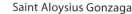

Saint Aloysius Gonzaga

Study Corner

DEFINE

venerate, sacramentals, canonization

REMEMBER

The liturgical calendar includes feast days of the saints and martyrs. By remembering these holy men and women, we recognize their faithfulness and commit ourselves to following their example.

Models of Discipleship

Below is a list of some of the saints whose feast days we celebrate during Ordinary Time. Research how each person followed Jesus' example of love and service. On the lines write how you can follow Jesus' call to discipleship by following the saints' examples.

Saint Francis de Sales (January 24)

_____

_____

_____

_____

Saint Aloysius Gonzaga (June 21)

_____

_____

_____

_____

Saint Teresa Benedicta of the Cross (August 9)

_____

_____

_____

_____

Saint Frances Xavier Cabrini (November 13)

_____

_____

_____

_____

Turn to Mary

DURING **Ordinary Time we grow in discipleship by reflecting on the lives of the saints and committing ourselves to following their example. We can also turn to Mary, who is the perfect model of discipleship.**

Mary's life was a pilgrimage of faith. From her conception she was filled with grace. As she grew older, she also grew in her relationship with God, which enabled her to remain obedient to him. She committed no personal sin in her life. When Mary said yes to God by agreeing to become Jesus' mother, she was a young girl living with her family in a remote part of the Roman Empire. Both she and her fiancé, Joseph, were living simple lives.

Mary was with Jesus from the very beginning of his life, when the Son of God became man for our Salvation. The Church teaches that Mary was ever-virgin, from Jesus' conception through his birth. In becoming Jesus' mother, Mary became the first and the greatest of the disciples. She was also the first to understand the meaning of Jesus' life and ministry. Before Jesus was born, Mary praised God, using words that we now call the *Magnificat.* This song of praise shows how well she understood the purpose of Jesus' life. When Jesus remained behind in Jerusalem as a 12-year-old boy, Mary reflected on the event and learned from it. When Jesus' public ministry began, Mary was there, just as she was there when his public ministry ended with his Crucifixion. After Jesus' Resurrection, Mary remained with the disciples and joined them in their prayer.

READY for Confirmation

Through Confirmation we reaffirm our commitment to our Catholic faith. By following Mary's example and developing an intimate relationship with God through prayer, we can respond "Amen" wholeheartedly when the bishop anoints us and says, "Be sealed with the Gift of the Holy Spirit."

Devotion to Mary

Good things come to the world because of Mary, but they do not come from Mary. They come from Jesus Christ, her Son. Mary shares God's love with us, but it is Jesus who brings us to God the Father. In addition to following Mary's example of discipleship, we respect and revere Mary as someone who intercedes on our behalf. As the mother of our Savior and as a person of great virtue and holiness, Mary has a special place in the life of the Church. Because of this we are encouraged to develop a devotion to her. One way to practice this devotion is to pray the Rosary. We pray with Mary because we believe that she can help us worship the one true God. What can you do in your own life to develop devotion to Mary?

The Church also honors Mary on specific days during the liturgical year. Three of the six U.S. Holy Days of Obligation are devoted to remembering the unique role that Mary has in God's plan of Salvation. On January 1 we celebrate the Solemnity of Mary, Mother of God. On this feast day, we acknowledge that with the human conception of Jesus, Mary became the Mother of God. We celebrate Mary's faith and trust in God alone. We celebrate Mary's **Assumption** into Heaven on August 15. On this feast the Church celebrates when, at the end of her earthly life, Mary was assumed, body and soul, into Heaven. On December 8 we celebrate the Feast of the Immaculate Conception. This feast day celebrates the special grace that Mary received from God when she was conceived without the stain of Original Sin.

In addition to the Holy Days of Obligation, we celebrate other important events in Mary's life. We celebrate her birth on September 8. Mary's parents, Saint Joachim and Saint Anne, loved her and raised her as a child of God. On May 31 we celebrate the Visitation, Mary's visit to her cousin Elizabeth. In the Gospel according to Luke, we read that after the angel Gabriel told Mary that she was going to become Jesus' mother, Mary immediately went to visit Elizabeth. Elizabeth, who was in old age, was also pregnant. As soon as Elizabeth saw Mary, the child that Elizabeth was carrying—John the Baptist—leapt for joy in her womb. We celebrate Mary's role as the Queen of Heaven on August 22. After she was raised body and soul into Heaven, Mary now sits in splendor at the right hand of her Son. From there she intercedes for us on our behalf.

Explore

The Virgin, Joseph Stella, 1926.

SACRED ART

In this image the artist painted Mary as if she were in a garden filled with flowers and fruits that symbolize the meaning of who she is. The lilies and violets symbolize her purity and humility, and the red rose reminds us of the sorrow she felt when witnessing Jesus' Death.

Prayer

Praying with Mary

Mary believed in and responded to God's call in all that she did. Because of this she is an example for all of us. Mary, Jesus' first disciple, shows us what it is like to be a perfect disciple.

Mary found the strength to be a perfect disciple through prayer. While Scripture tells us very little about Mary's life, it does tell us that as the events in Jesus' life unfolded, she pondered these in her heart. Through this pondering, Mary was able to hear what God was revealing to humans through events in the life of his Son, Jesus. We too can reflect on events in Jesus' life so that we can know what God continues to speak to us today.

The *Magnificat*

My soul proclaims the greatness of the Lord,
my spirit rejoices in God my Savior;
for he has looked with favor on his lowly servant.

From this day all generations will call me blessed:
the Almighty has done great things for me,
and holy is his Name.

He has mercy on those who fear him
in every generation.

He has shown the strength of his arm,
he has scattered the proud in their conceit.

He has cast down the mighty from their thrones,
and has lifted up the lowly.

He has filled the hungry with good things,
and the rich he has sent away empty.

He has come to the help of his servant Israel
for he has remembered his promise of mercy,
the promise he made to our fathers,
to Abraham and his children for ever.

WHERE Do I Fit In?

Sacramentality is at the heart of our Catholic experience of God. We believe that music, the arts, people, and physical objects can serve as reminders of God's presence in our lives. The principle of sacramentality teaches us that anything in our life can serve as a visible reminder of God's invisible grace. Relics, one type of sacramental, remind us that we are not alone and that other human beings, both past and present, support us in our journey of faith.

by Michael Cameron

What Good Are Relics?

I confess to an almost incurable habit of saving things. Sometimes the things I haven't thrown out threaten to swallow me up! The saving urge is especially strong when things connect to important people in my life. For instance, for many years I've carried four items in my wallet: a ticket from visiting the Empire State Building with my son, Erik, in 2000; a theater stub from a movie I saw with my son, Matt, in 2002; a receipt from visiting the Mt. St. Helens volcano with my mom and dad in 2005; and an undated love note from my wife, Lorie. Why? Certainly these items flood me with warm thoughts of important people and times. But they give me more than memories of mountaintop moments. Suddenly I'm invaded by the love of the people I love. I vividly recall that I'm not alone in the world—that actual people cherish me as I do them and that we are part of one another no matter what. Strangely, that's somehow even truer since my dad passed away in 2008.

Those four items work like relics. An amazing spiritual power of love at work in the saints leaps to mind as we encounter their lives in things they touched, an item of their clothing, or even a part of their own bodies. But even more than their memory, their love for God surges through us as we open ourselves to their holy memory. The Body of Christ makes us all part of one another—even persons who lived centuries ago!

MICHAEL CAMERON teaches theology at the University of Portland in Oregon. He is married to Lorie Simmons and is the father of two grown sons, Erik and Matthew.

The Church keeps alive their memory and channels God's love to us in special ways by reverence for relics. That's why the Church embeds sacred relics of the saints beneath the altar of every church in the world. While sharing our Lord's Body and Blood there, we also partake of one another's love for God. This spectacular truth of faith shines brightest in our darkest hours: we are never, ever alone without people who love us and love God!

A Living Reminder

Reflect on a person, object, or experience that has served as a reminder of God's presence in your life. In the box below, express how that person, object, or experience helped you grow closer to God. You may wish to write a poem or reflection, compose a song, sketch something, or attach a photograph.

What's What?

Write the letter of the choice that best matches each description.

1 _____ a prayer of devotion to Mary, mother of our Savior and person of virtue and holiness (PAGE 39)

2 _____ Her life was a pilgrimage of faith. (PAGE 38)

3 _____ the feast that celebrates Mary being assumed body and soul into Heaven (PAGE 39)

4 _____ a piece of a saint's remains, such a chip of bone or a lock of hair (PAGE 36)

5 _____ The child she was carrying leapt for joy. (PAGE 39)

6 _____ invites us to think more deeply about the message of the Gospel (PAGE 35)

7 _____ marks entire seasons and individual feasts and celebrations (PAGE 35)

8 _____ a feast that celebrates Mary's visit to her cousin Elizabeth (PAGE 39)

9 _____ a practice that underscores the sacramental nature of our faith (PAGE 36)

a. Mary

b. Ordinary Time

c. Assumption

d. relic

e. Elizabeth

f. The Rosary

g. venerating relics

h. liturgical calendar

i. Visitation

Say What?

Know the definitions of these terms.

Assumption

canonization

Magnificat

sacramentals

venerate

Now What?

During Ordinary Time we can reflect on Jesus' call to discipleship by studying the lives of the saints and committing ourselves to following their example. Which saints appeal to you, and what can you do to follow their example?

_____

_____

_____

_____

_____

_____

_____

_____

_____

_____

_____

_____

_____

_____

Respond

Faith in ACTION

We build up the Church by putting our faith into action. When we freely choose to do this, we respond to Christ's call to discipleship, and we share the Gospel message of peace and love with others. Taking action to create a more just world is not optional behavior. Working for justice is a central component of the Christian faith. Jesus preached not only with words but with how he lived his life. We are called to do the same.

In this unit we explored how Jesus founded the Church by sending the Holy Spirit to his disciples after his Ascension into Heaven. Since then, the presence of the Holy Spirit has filled each of Jesus' followers. In the early Church, this helped the disciples remain true to their faith in the face of persecution. Today, the presence of the Holy Spirit gives us the strength to stand up for people who are marginalized and oppressed.

Defend Life

Purpose

Learn about actions we can take in order to defend the lives of all people, especially those who are marginalized and oppressed by society.

Background

Since its beginning the Church has taught that human life is sacred. We are made in the image and likeness of God. In recent years the bishops have pointed out that respect for human life is not an independent issue. People can only live lives of dignity when they have access to food, clean water, clothing, and shelter. Respect for life is interwoven with the issues of poverty, education, and health care. The bishops in the United States have established the Catholic Campaign for Human Development (CCHD), an organization whose mission is to work for respect for life in relation to these issues.

Steps

1. **Read together the Beatitudes (Matthew 5:3–12). What does Jesus teach us about working for justice? What do the Beatitudes say to us today?**

2. **With an adult, spend some time exploring the CCHD Web site. Learn about the initiatives that are currently under way.**

3. **Develop a plan for how you can advertise CCHD's work within your parish in order to encourage others to get involved in working for justice.**

4. **Make a commitment to complete one action suggested by the CCHD.**

"Blessed are they who hunger and thirst for righteousness, for they will be satisfied."

—Matthew 5:6

Act

Called to Community

Purpose

When Jesus sent the gift of the Holy Spirit at Pentecost, his community of followers became the Church. As the People of God, we are called to participate in the life of the Church and to support one another, regardless of race, gender, or ethnicity. The purpose of this activity is to learn about the importance of immigration reform. Participants will research this issue and then write letters to federal legislators to encourage them to support a more humane immigration policy.

Background

Archbishop José Gomez of Los Angeles is Chairman of the Committee on Migration at USCCB. In a statement released on June 10, 2013, Archbishop Gomez wrote, "Each day in our parishes, social service programs, hospitals, and schools we witness the human consequences of a broken immigration system. … Simply put, the status quo is morally unacceptable." The U.S. bishops continue to encourage national immigration policy reform. They suggest that a just immigration policy should include the following components: anti-poverty efforts, opportunities for family reunification, and provisions for temporary workers.

Steps

1. Research the U.S bishops' position on immigration policy reform by visiting their Web site JusticeforImmigrants.org or by reading the pastoral letter *Strangers No Longer: Together on the Journey of Hope.*

2. Using what you have learned, discuss what your parish community can do to support undocumented immigrants. Choose concrete actions your parish can take and work together to implement a plan.

3. Write letters to your federal legislators, asking them to support immigration policy reform.

4. Raise awareness of this issue by speaking with others about the need for immigration policy reform.

Immigrants marching for reform in Chicago, Illinois.

Act

"**Families are separated, migrant workers are exploited, and our fellow human beings die in the desert. This suffering must end.**"

—Archbishop José Gomez

We Belong

Benedict and Scholastica, whom many believe were twins, were born in Nursia, Italy, during the fifth century. During their lifetime frequent wars and regional conflicts disrupted people's ability to meet their basic needs. People were concerned with remaining safe and finding food and shelter. As a result many people abandoned the practice of daily prayer. Benedict and Scholastica provided an alternative way of life by forming communities for men and women to live together in prayer and meaningful work. Through their example Benedict and Scholastica continue to teach us about the importance of caring for our communities.

How the Saints Relate

By founding religious communities that focused on prayer and work, Benedict and Scholastica began a way of living that provided stability in the midst of chaos. We can also find communities that help us remain true to our faith and allow us to share our gifts in service to others.

Forming a New Community

When he was a child, Benedict's parents sent him to Rome to receive an education. Benedict soon became discouraged by the immoral lives that many people around him were living. He left Rome and settled in a cave on Mount Subiaco, about 50 miles south of the city. There he took time to fast and pray so that he could better discern what God was asking of him. Before long, other men who were interested in a more contemplative way of life joined him. Benedict soon led 12 communities, each of which had 12 monks.

Around A.D. 529, Benedict and a few of the monks moved even farther south. After they arrived at their new location, Benedict built Monte Cassino, a **monastery,** or a place where monks live together in community. The men who lived at Monte Cassino devoted themselves to prayer and manual labor.

Saint Scholastica

While we know little about Scholastica's life, we do know that she eventually settled about five miles south of Monte Cassino. With Benedict's help she founded a community for women, similar to the community that Benedict had founded for men. Scholastica, under Benedict's direction, served as the leader of this new community.

Because Benedict and Scholastica remained busy caring for their respective communities, they were able to visit each other only once a year. Women were not allowed at Monte Cassino, so Scholastica, Benedict, and a few of the monks met at a nearby house. During their last visit together, the group spent time praying and discussing spiritual matters. Benedict and the monks eventually decided to return home. Scholastica, however, begged the men to stay and talk some more. She had a feeling that this would be the last time she and Benedict would see each other alive. Benedict insisted that the monks return to Monte Cassino, because one of their rules was to be in the monastery by nightfall. Disappointed, Scholastica folded her hands, put her head on the table, and began to pray and weep. While Scholastica was praying, a strong storm developed. The weather soon became so bad that Benedict and the other monks could not leave the house. Everyone continued talking and praying well into the night. The men returned home the next day. Scholastica died three days later, and Benedict buried her in a tomb that he had built for himself.

Monte Cassino, Lazio, Italy

We Believe

Think about someone who has helped you grow in faith. What has that person done to help nurture your relationship with Jesus? How can that person's example help you nurture the faith of other people?

PRAYER

Holy Spirit, thank you for helping the Church remain faithful to Jesus and his teachings. Strengthen us so that we may remain people of faith.

The Early Ecumenical Councils

IF someone asked you who Jesus is, how would you respond? In 313, Constantine issued the Edict of Milan, which legalized Christianity. As more people joined the Church, disagreements arose about the Church's answer to this question. The bishops met in **ecumenical councils** to clarify Church teaching.

The Council of Nicaea

Arius, a priest and teacher from Alexandria, believed that Jesus was more than just a human being but less than God. He taught that Jesus had been made by God, just like other creatures. Others, however, believed that because Jesus was fully God, he could not also be fully human.

In 325, Constantine brought the bishops together for a meeting that is known as the Council of Nicaea. He asked the Church's leaders to clarify what the Church believed about Christ's relationship to God the Father. The bishops responded by affirming the Church's belief that Jesus is **consubstantial,** one in being, with his Father, equal in every way. Jesus Christ is God from all eternity, and he was not created.

The Council of Constantinople

The teachings at the Council of Nicaea did not answer all the questions that people had about Jesus. Apollinaris, another priest from Alexandria, accepted that Jesus was God, but he wondered whether Jesus had a human soul. Apollinaris believed that the Word—the Second Person of the **Trinity**—took the place of Jesus' human soul. The bishops met at Constantinople in 381. Acting in their role as the **Magisterium**—teachers of the faith—they stated that Jesus, who was fully human, was just like us in every way except sin. The Church leaders affirmed that, without losing his divinity, Jesus became fully man with a human body and a human soul, and that he lived in complete obedience to his Father. The bishops also declared the Holy Spirit—the Third Person of the Trinity—to be equal to the Father and the Son. These teachings completed those from the Council of Nicaea. The leaders of the Church combined the teachings from these two councils when they wrote the **Nicene Creed.**

The Council of Ephesus

In addition to presenting **heresies,** or false teachings, about the relationship between Jesus and his Father, some people taught heresies about Mary's relationship with the Persons of the Trinity. Nestorius, the bishop of Constantinople, taught that we could call Mary the Mother of Jesus, but that we could not call her the **Mother of God.** Many people within the Church, including the pope, were disturbed by this teaching. If we cannot call Mary, Jesus' mother, the Mother of God, then we cannot call Jesus the Son of God. In 431, the bishops met in Ephesus, where they declared Nestorius's teaching to be incorrect. The council declared that Mary became the Mother of God by the human conception of the Son of God in her womb. The bishops affirmed that she can be called the Mother of Jesus and the Mother of God.

The Council of Chalcedon

Even after the Councils of Nicaea and Constantinople, some people disagreed about Jesus' relationship to God the Father. Eutyches was an influential leader of a monastic community near Constantinople. He taught that Jesus was not really a human being like us because his human nature was completely absorbed by his divine nature as the Son of God. In response the bishops met in Chalcedon in 451. At the Council of Chalcedon, the bishops taught that Jesus Christ is of the same being as his Father in Heaven and that he is also of the same being as all humans.

An Important Question

The early Church leaders knew that it was important to figure out who Jesus Christ is. To be reconciled to God, we need someone who can speak to God for us and speak to us for God. As a human being, Jesus understands our struggles, concerns, and limitations. As God, he understands who God is as our Father and what our Father wants for us. When Jesus talks to us about who the Father is and what he wants for us, Jesus speaks for God in ways that we can understand. Jesus also teaches us how to lift our minds and hearts to God in prayer. The most important prayer he has given us is the Lord's Prayer. Whenever we pray, we grow in our relationship with God, through Jesus, in the power of the Holy Spirit.

SACRED ART

Throughout the history of the Church, stained-glass windows have been used to depict Mary in her role as the Mother of God. Throughout the liturgical year, we honor Mary for the other roles she has played in God's plan of Salvation. On January 1 we celebrate the Solemnity of Mary, Mother of God. We celebrate the Feast of the Assumption on August 15. On March 25, exactly nine months before Christmas, we celebrate the Feast of the Annunciation. On this feast we remember the day that Jesus was conceived in Mary after she said yes to God's will when she was visited by the angel Gabriel.

The Assumption, stained glass.

Explore

Study Corner

DEFINE

ecumenical councils, consubstantial, Trinity, Magisterium, Nicene Creed, heresies, Mother of God

REMEMBER

The bishops clarified the Church's teachings about Jesus, Mary, and the Trinity during the early ecumenical councils.

Professing Our Faith

HOW would you summarize your faith and what it means to you? How would you express to others what motivates you and gives your life meaning? After the ecumenical councils of Nicaea and Constantinople, the bishops wrote the Nicene Creed, a profession of faith that we pray together at Mass. In this Creed we profess the central teachings of the Church.

The Nicene Creed

The Nicene Creed is comprised of three sections, or articles. In the first article, we profess our belief in God the Father, the First Person of the Trinity. We believe that God is the Creator of everything—all that was, all that is, and all that is yet to come. We also believe that God created the universe out of nothing and that the human family is God's greatest creation.

In the second article of the Nicene Creed, we profess our belief in Jesus Christ, the Second Person of the Trinity. The Creed reminds us that Jesus is consubstantial with the Father. This means that Jesus Christ has always existed with God, even before he was born and became man. Jesus was **incarnate,** or became flesh, and Mary was his mother. As a human being, Jesus was like us in all things but sin. His **Paschal Mystery**—Death, Resurrection, and Ascension into Heaven—is the fulfillment of God's plan of Salvation.

In the third article of the Nicene Creed, we profess our belief in the Holy Spirit. We believe that the Holy Spirit was sent by the Father and the Son to give Jesus' followers the strength and courage to fulfill the mission of spreading the Gospel to the ends of the earth. We also acknowledge that in Baptism our sins are forgiven, and we declare our hope and trust in the fullness of God's kingdom that will come at the end of time.

By praying the Nicene Creed, we profess our faith in the one true God; in his Son, Jesus Christ; and in the Holy Spirit. In doing this we declare our willingness to make God the center of our lives. In addition we assent to the Church's Magisterium by proclaiming *Amen,* "I believe," to Church teachings that have been passed on since the time of the Apostles.

I Believe

Read silently the Nicene Creed on page 272. Choose one of the statements of faith presented in the Creed and take a moment to reflect on it. On the lines below, write what the statement means to you.

_____

_____

_____

_____

_____

_____

_____

_____

_____

_____

_____

_____

_____

_____

_____

_____

Our Catholic Character

When the bishops met during the early ecumenical councils, they sought to clarify the relationships among the Persons of the Trinity. By doing so, the bishops emphasized that at the heart of our **faith** is the relationship that we have with God, Jesus, and the Holy Spirit. When we stand to profess our faith by praying the Nicene Creed, we profess that we believe in God the Father, Jesus Christ, and the Holy Spirit. More than that, however, we profess that just as the Persons of the Trinity are in communion with one another, we are in relationship with all three Persons as well. We grow in this relationship when we take the words of the Nicene Creed to heart and allow our relationship with the Persons of the Trinity to guide our lives.

Explore

Study Corner

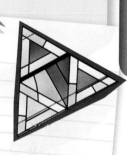

DEFINE

incarnate
Paschal Mystery
faith

REMEMBER

We profess our belief in God, Jesus, and the Holy Spirit through the Nicene Creed; we acknowledge that we are in a relationship with all three Persons of the Trinity.

READY for Confirmation

Before celebrating the Sacrament of Confirmation, we publicly declare our faith by renewing our baptismal promises. While we need the support of the community to help us grow in faith, when we respond "I do" to each promise, we express our personal commitment to the God who has revealed himself to us throughout human history. We acknowledge that we believe and trust in God and that we are willing to work to build up his kingdom by sharing his peace and love with others.

Prayer

What Do I Believe?

The Nicene Creed

is our attempt to put our knowledge and love of God into words. But the Creed is not just a list of what we believe; the Nicene Creed is a prayer.

Like other prayers, the Nicene Creed ends with the word *Amen.* The Hebrew word for *Amen* is a word of faith and trust; when we pray *Amen,* we express our trust that God will hear and answer our prayers. We often pray the Nicene Creed together during Mass, a form of **communal prayer.** We engage in communal prayer any time we worship God together with others.

Reflecting on the Nicene Creed

I believe in one God,
the Father almighty,
maker of heaven and earth,
of all things visible and invisible.

God of all that is, the vastness of your creation extends beyond what we see. With the eyes of faith, we know you to be both the Almighty who is beyond our understanding, and the Father whose tender love sustains us.

I believe in one Lord Jesus Christ,
the Only Begotten Son of God,
born of the Father before all ages,
God from God, Light from Light,
true God from true God.

Lord Jesus Christ, you are truly God, and yet you became man to share life with us. You are Light, and yet chose to dwell in the world that often seems so dark. You brought the life of God close to us so that, in your humanity, we can touch divinity.

I believe in the Holy Spirit, the Lord, the giver of life,
who proceeds from the Father and the Son.

Life-giving Spirit, you come to us as a gift from God the Father and Jesus, his Son. It is through you that we can love others with the love that comes from God.

I believe in one, holy, catholic, and apostolic Church.

Our Church is made up of human beings who strive for unity. May we join those who work to heal divisions among the Church's members.

I look forward to the resurrection of the dead
and the life of the world to come.

Our belief in the risen Jesus gives us hope that we will be united with all our loved ones in the fullness of God's presence.

WHERE Do I Fit In?

by Joe Paprocki

As we grow up, we often have experiences that cause us to question who we are and what we believe. As Jesus' followers, we can turn to the Church to help us navigate this ongoing process of growth and development. By reflecting on the Creed and its meaning, we can remain true to a faith that has been passed down since the time of Jesus.

Who Am I and What Do I Believe?

Reflect

Back in the day, when I was a teenager, I tried really hard to be bad, and I failed miserably. Like many teenagers, I was struggling to find my identity. I didn't want to be the "goody two-shoes" I had been when I was younger. I wanted to be cool. So I grew my hair long. I dressed like a rebel. I hung out with the cool crowd and did cool things. Or so I thought. In reality, I ended up doing a lot of things that were just plain stupid. I did things that were not "me." Why? Because I didn't know who "me" was. Like many teenagers, I went through a difficult period of awkward grasping after some identity or meaning. It wasn't until a few years later, when I began to know what I really believed in and who God was calling me to be, that I began to act accordingly. It's so hard to know how to act when you don't know who you are or what you believe in.

You may be struggling to define yourself too. You may even find yourself doing some things that you're not very proud of. Without a clear sense of identity, it's difficult to act in a consistent manner. All of us need a clear sense of identity, and in order to have that, we need to know what we believe. The Creed is a prayer that expresses our identity. You were baptized into this Creed. At your Baptism, your parents and godparents accepted this identity on your behalf as they responded "I do" to baptismal promises drawn from the Creed.

To symbolize your new identity, you were given a baptismal garment; we are what we wear! The message is clear: If you wish to be Jesus' disciple, place your trust in him. Know who it is you believe in and why. Supported by firm belief, you can find yourself—in Jesus.

Who Am I?

Take a moment to reflect on your personal identity. How has your understanding of who you are changed as you've gotten older? In the box below, draw a symbol that represents your personal identity at this stage in your life. Before you begin, think about what you want your symbol to express to others about who you are.

JOE PAPROCKI is an author, public speaker, and catechist who blogs about his experience at www.catechistsjourney.com.

What's What?

Write the letter of the term that best completes each sentence.

1 The _____ made it legal for people to practice Christianity. (PAGE 48)

2 To say that Jesus is _____ with God is to say that Jesus is one in being with God the Father. (PAGE 48)

3 The _____ is the Third Person of the Trinity. (PAGE 48)

4 The _____ combines the teachings from the Councils of Nicaea and Constantinople. (PAGE 48)

5 Mary became the _____ through the human conception of the Son of God in her womb. (PAGE 49)

6 Jesus' _____ is the fulfillment of God's plan of Salvation. (PAGE 50)

7 At the heart of our _____ is the relationship that we have with God, Jesus, and the Holy Spirit. (PAGE 51)

a. consubstantial

b. Mother of God

c. Edict of Milan

d. Paschal Mystery

e. Nicene Creed

f. faith

g. Holy Spirit

Say What?

Know the definitions of these terms.

communal prayer	Magisterium
consubstantial	monastery
ecumenical councils	Mother of God
faith	Nicene Creed
heresies	Paschal Mystery
incarnate	Trinity

Now What?

By praying the Nicene Creed, we express our common belief in the three Persons of the Trinity: God the Father; Jesus, his Son; and the Holy Spirit. How might your belief in God, Jesus, and the Holy Spirit influence your actions during the next week?

_____

_____

_____

_____

_____

_____

_____

_____

_____

_____

_____

_____

_____

_____

_____

_____

Respond

Praise God in Worship

The people and activities in our day help shape who we are and give us direction. Think about how you organize your day. What are your priorities? Who or what gets most of your time? What is missing from your day that you would like to add? Where does your relationship with God fit into the mix?

PRAYER

Thank you, God, for letting us get to know you by learning about our faith. May all we say and do show our thanks and praise for the gift of Jesus Christ.

Saint Gregory the Great

Saint Gregory the Great, 1799, oil on canvas, Goya y Lucientes.

WE are called to build up God's kingdom. How can you serve others by using the gifts you have received from God? One man used his gifts in many ways. Gregory, who was born around A.D. 540, was concerned with the needs of people who were poor. By the time he was a young man, Gregory had been named the prefect, or governor, of Rome. During his time as prefect, the city was frequently attacked by invaders, and the citizens suffered from poverty, disease, and famine. Gregory used his position of authority to help the people as best he could.

Gregory, who was long drawn to religious life, eventually resigned his position as the prefect of Rome. He sold most of his land and donated the proceeds to people who were poor. Gregory also turned his family's estates into seven different Benedictine monasteries. He lived at one of the monasteries, which he named Saint Andrew.

Eventually, Gregory was ordained a priest. Later the pope asked him to be the papal ambassador to the Court of Constantinople. After serving in this position, Gregory returned to Saint Andrew to live. A few years later, the pope died, and Gregory was chosen to be the next pope. While Gregory wanted to remain a monk at Saint Andrew, he decided to follow God's will for him by serving as the Bishop of Rome.

As pope, Gregory cared for God's people in many ways, including providing for their physical and spiritual needs. For example, he negotiated peace agreements with tribes who tried to invade Rome. He also sent missionaries to Britain to teach people about Jesus. Gregory also developed much of the Church's **doctrine,** the teachings that help us understand and express our experience of the mystery of God.

Gregory, who died in 604, is an example of someone who was filled with the Holy Spirit. In fact, he did so much to serve the Church during his life that he received the title *Great*. He also has been named a **Doctor of the Church.**

Life in the Church

Just as the Holy Spirit helped Gregory the Great live as a faithful disciple, the Holy Spirit helps us live as disciples today. We say that we are animated by the Holy Spirit because the Holy Spirit fills us with God's grace and helps us share his peace and love with others. It is through the ongoing presence of the Holy

Spirit that all of the Church's works, such as teaching, healing, and celebrating the sacraments, are possible.

The Holy Spirit flows from the community we call the Trinity—Three Persons in one God. The Trinity is a community like no other, but it is still a community of Persons. What does that mean for us? It means that the more we are filled with the Holy Spirit, the more we care about our community. For those who follow Jesus, that community is the Church. As members of the Church and as people who are animated with the Holy Spirit, we don't just sit around—we participate. We are involved in the life of the Church, and we celebrate the sacraments, especially the Eucharist. We may also choose to participate in a parish youth group, help with parish service projects, or serve as liturgical ministers.

Gregory's Influence on the Liturgy

The presence of the Holy Spirit in our lives also calls us to participate in the life of the Trinity through our worship of God the Father; Jesus, his Son; and the Holy Spirit. During Gregory's time as pope, he sought to reform the liturgy, or the public worship of the Church. Gregory wrote a book called *Pastoral Care,* which raised the standard for preaching. He asked for simplification of the music assigned to specific liturgical celebrations. This request marked the beginning of a form of liturgical music known as **Gregorian chant,** which is still used today. Gregory was also involved in the development of the Gregorian Sacramentary, a book that contains all the words prayed by the priest during Mass and other liturgical celebrations. This Sacramentary was essential in bringing Catholic worship to new lands, and it guided the celebration of the sacraments for centuries.

Study Corner

DEFINE
doctrine, Doctor of the Church, Gregorian chant

REMEMBER
Gregory the Great, who was animated by the Holy Spirit, did much to serve the Church, including caring for people's physical needs and shaping Church doctrine.

Explore

Our Catholic Character

Today it seems that not a day goes by without someone using the word *great* to describe someone or something, so much so that the word has almost lost its meaning. Yet the word has a powerful definition. *Great* means "remarkable, eminent, noble, or distinguished."

The two popes who have been named *Great* were distinguished men who helped us understand the noble role of the pope as the Bishop of Rome. Pope Leo I the Great was pope around the year 450. He used the special authority of the office of pope to help the Church understand what Scripture teaches about the nature of Jesus Christ as God and man. Gregory used his authority and leadership abilities to serve the good of the people. He made it possible for future popes to make a positive difference in Europe during the Middle Ages.

Because of these two popes, papal leadership became highly respected in Europe. The leadership that both Leo I and Gregory showed enabled them to help people in concrete ways. Both of these remarkable men demonstrated how great Church leaders can build the Church through relationships of understanding and love.

Called to Worship God

GREGORY the Great understood that having the strength to serve the Church was only possible because of his relationship with God. **Adoration,** the act of acknowledging that God is Lord, is one way for us to develop our relationship with God. Through adoration we pray with our entire person—body, mind, and soul. The first three commandments teach us more about how we are called to adore God through our words and actions. God calls us to follow his commandments, and through grace he makes it possible for us to do so.

The First Three Commandments

The First Commandment The First Commandment teaches us that we are called to believe in, hope in, and love God above all else. We do this by making God more important than anyone or anything else in our lives. When something becomes more important to us than God, we commit **idolatry,** which is the act of worshiping a false god. Atheism, which denies or rejects the existence of God, is a sin against the First Commandment.

SACRED ART

One form of adoration that leads back to medieval times is Eucharistic Adoration. Even today, many churches display the Eucharist in a special receptacle called a monstrance and invite the faithful to gaze in reflection and pray before the **Real Presence.** During Eucharistic Adoration many people reflect on the Salvation we receive through Christ's Death and the great gift he gave us in the Eucharist. This prayer, Eucharistic Adoration, is a powerful way to deepen our desire for the Real Presence of Jesus in the Eucharist.

The Second Commandment The Second Commandment teaches us that God's name is holy. We respect God's name by not using it, or the names of Mary and the saints, in ways that dishonor them. This commandment also calls us to honor the promises or oaths that we take in God's name. By not doing so, we show a lack of respect for the Lord.

The Third Commandment The Third Commandment teaches us to take time for God and to give God a central place in our week. We do this by attending Mass on Sunday and making Sunday a day of rest, free from unnecessary work. We also avoid activities that prevent others from worshiping God.

When Moses told the Israelites that the Third Commandment was to keep holy the **Sabbath,** they understood that he meant Saturday, the seventh day of the week. After creating the world, God rested on the seventh day, and God wanted this day, the Sabbath, to be a day of rest for the human family too.

The Lord's Day is to be kept as God's special day.

The early Christians moved the day that they devoted to the worship of God from Saturday, the day of the week when God rested, to Sunday, the day of the week when Jesus rose from the dead. The obligation to keep holy the Sabbath remains the same, however. We can worship God every day of the week, but Sunday is the day set aside for worshiping God together as a community of faith. It also is the day on which we rest from the ordinary routine of our lives. Think of Sunday as a gift that is given to us by God, a day when we can rest in his love by enjoying our family and friends and reaching out to those who need our care.

Our Relationship with Others

The first three commandments teach us about how we are called to live in relationship with God. The remaining commandments teach us about how we are called to live in relationship with others. Jesus underscored the importance of the Ten Commandments when he gave us the Greatest Commandment: "You shall love the Lord your God with all your heart, with all your soul, with all your mind, and with all your strength. . . . You shall love your neighbor as yourself." (Mark 12:31–32)

Keeping the Commandments

Provide a short answer to each question.

The First Commandment: Idols can take the form of seemingly harmless activities that gradually take over our lives and cause us to think that we will find happiness in them instead of in God. What can you do to make sure that God is the true focus of your life?

_____

_____

_____

The Second Commandment: What can you do to honor God's name?

_____

_____

_____

The Third Commandment: Sunday is the Lord's Day, a time to gather as a community at Mass, a time for reflection, and a time to slow down and enjoy God's world. In addition to going to Mass, what is one thing you and your family can to do to keep holy the Sabbath?

_____

_____

_____

Explore

Study Corner

DEFINE
adoration, idolatry, Real Presence, Sabbath

REMEMBER
The first three commandments teach us how we can adore God and grow in our relationship with him.

How Awesome Is Your Name

The words from Psalm 8 echo Genesis 1:28, which says "God blessed them and God said to them: Be fertile and multiply; fill the earth and subdue it. Have dominion over the fish of the sea, the birds of the air, and all the living things that crawl on the earth."

From the beginning God entrusted the earth and its resources to the common use of all humanity. For Pope Gregory the Great, common use meant tending the soil so that it provided food for the community and keeping the water clean for drinking, washing, and bathing.

While the concept of common use hasn't changed much over the centuries, our ability to harm the earth has. As science and technology have advanced, so has our thirst for the earth's resources. We're called to care for these resources, use them in our labor, and enjoy their fruits. The resources of creation are destined for the whole human race. We are not meant to hoard or exploit the natural and living resources of the world. God gives these to be shared equally so that all people may benefit. Showing care for creation is one way to adore God. In being good stewards, we thank God for all that he has given us.

A Psalm as Prayer

Think about the natural beauty in this world. Then pray, using Psalm 8. Adore God for the wonderful glory of creation.

> O LORD, our Lord,
>   how awesome is your name through all the earth!
> When I see your heavens, the work of your fingers,
>   the moon and stars that you set in place—
> What is man that you are mindful of him,
>   and a son of man that you care for him?
> Yet you have made him little less than a god,
>   crowned him with glory and honor.
> You have given him rule over the works of your hands,
>   put all things at his feet:
> All sheep and oxen,
>   even the beasts of the field,
> The birds of the air, the fish of the sea,
>   and whatever swims the paths of the seas.
> O LORD, our Lord,
>   how awesome is your name through all the earth!
>
> Psalm 8:2,4–10

Conclude by praying your own prayer of thanks to God for the gift of creation. You may wish to name something from God's creation for which you are especially thankful or to express to God how you will be a good steward of the gifts he has given us.

WHERE Do I Fit In?

As Catholics we belong to a community with whom we gather to celebrate our joys and sorrows. The teachings, practices, and rituals that are part of our celebrations shape us in ways we don't always realize—at first.

by Catherine O'Connell-Cahill

What Shapes Us?

When my daughter was five, she began singing church songs with great gusto around the house. One of her favorites was a song we sang at our parish all during Lent: "Shepherd me, O God, beyond my wants, beyond my fears, from death into life." It's a version of the well-known 23rd Psalm, which begins, "The Lord is my shepherd." My daughter wanted to know what the words mean, so I tried to explain it to her.

One day, we were driving around town with her cousin, Liam, age four. The two kids had been taking turns, one sitting in the child car seat, and the other riding in the back seat with the seat belt. After each stop they would switch. But then, after the last stop, each of them refused to get into the car seat. After a few mild threats, I said, "Well, let me know who is going to ride where. I can wait." Silence. Then, after a minute or so, my daughter heaved herself into the car seat.

"Liam, I'm doing this for you," she said, "because I know you don't want to sit here, even though it's your turn." Then, realization dawning, she cried, "Mom! It's just like the song, isn't it? 'Shepherd me, O God, beyond my wants!'"

She had found it within herself to be generous and loving even though she didn't have to be. The psalm had done its work in her heart.

This story causes me to think about the things that shape us. Think, for a moment, about all the advertising messages that you hear throughout the day: Buy this phone and you'll be happy. Wear these jeans and you'll be more attractive. If we're not careful, we can let those messages shape us.

We hear a different message at Mass. We are beloved children of a gracious God, and everything we have received in our lives is a gift from God. Jesus, whom we see on the cross at the altar, loved us enough to die for us. With the help of the Holy Spirit, we can be the hands and feet of Christ in the world today.

Reflect

A Message of Faith

Take a moment to reflect on a time you received the message that you're a child of God. Then on a separate sheet of paper write how you can share with others the message that they are also children of God.

CATHERINE O'CONNELL-CAHILL is the author of *At Home with Our Faith*, a monthly family newsletter published by Claretian Publications.

What's What?

Write your answers on the lines.

1 What did Gregory the Great do with his family's estates after resigning as the prefect of Rome? (PAGE 56)

_____

_____

_____

2 When Gregory the Great decided to follow God's will for him, what did he agree to do? (PAGE 56)

_____

_____

3 What makes the Church's works, such as teaching, healing, and celebrating the sacraments, possible? (PAGE 57)

_____

_____

_____

4 What do the first three commandments teach us? (PAGE 58)

_____

_____

_____

5 How can we follow the First Commandment? (PAGE 58)

_____

_____

_____

_____

6 How can we follow the Second Commandment? (PAGE 59)

_____

_____

_____

7 How can we practice the Third Commandment? (PAGE 59)

_____

_____

_____

_____

_____

Say What?

Know the definitions of these terms.

adoration	idolatry
Doctor of the Church	Real Presence
doctrine	Sabbath
Gregorian chant	

Now What?

Jesus' followers, filled with the Holy Spirit, are called to offer praise and adoration to God. How can you offer God your praise and adoration this week?

_____

_____

_____

_____

_____

_____

_____

_____

_____

_____

Respond

Monasteries and Community

Think about a time you had a disagreement with a friend or a family member. How did you respond to the situation? What did the experience teach you about yourself? About the other person? What do you think the Church can teach us about living peacefully with one another?

PRAYER

Thank you, God, for the gift of supportive communities. May we be open to learning from the wisdom of others, and may we be willing to share our wisdom in return.

63

A Response to the Early Middle Ages

Saint Benedict

AFTER Constantine issued the Edict of Milan and declared Christianity to be the official religion of the Roman empire, Rome experienced a period of stability and order. By the fifth century, however, the vast empire had begun to crumble, plunging much of the known world into a period known as the Early Middle Ages, or Dark Ages.

From the fifth century onward, life was difficult for most people. Many of the Roman citizens were peasants, and the few people who were nobles were little more than warriors. Slavery was a common practice, and the empire's infrastructure fell into disrepair. Invaders tried to take control by frequently attacking the empire's borders.

Amid this darkness the Church remained a beacon of light. Church leaders worked to preach the Gospel to invading tribes, heal people who were sick, and reestablish society. Bishops served as civic leaders when government officials were unable to do so.

The bishops also protected the people from tax collectors who wanted to steal whatever they could. By remaining steadfast to the Church's teachings, the bishops preserved and modeled a life of Christian discipleship.

Our Catholic Character

The Rule of Saint Benedict is not the only Rule for monastic communities. Basil wrote a Rule for a community he founded in Cappadocia, in modern-day Turkey, around 356. In this Rule monks were instructed to practice the Christian virtues and avoid vices. Augustine wrote a Rule in the fifth century that focused on a life of common prayer, poverty, obedience, and manual labor. This Rule is still followed by Dominicans and Augustinians. In the 13th century, Albert wrote a Rule for a Carmelite community. His Rule encourages the members of the community to remain faithful to Christ through contemplation and charity.

The Rule of Saint Benedict

During the Early Middle Ages, people lived in fear. But the Church provided a source of hope, and God worked through the community to provide comfort. One alternative offered by the Church was monastic living, in which communities of monks or nuns lived together in monasteries and devoted themselves to prayer and labor. Benedict wanted to be sure that his monks could provide for themselves. He made sure that the monks in the monasteries he founded were able to provide their own food, clothing, and shelter through farming, weaving, and masonry work, respectively. As more and more people were drawn to monastic life, some monasteries grew to cover many acres.

While he was living at Monte Cassino, Benedict wrote a guide for monastic life that today we call the Rule of Saint Benedict. This Rule directs monks to seek God in prayer, silence, work, and service to guests and one another. Chapter 4 of the Rule lists 72 duties of Christian life, which are called "instruments of good works." A short sample from this list includes prescriptions to follow the Ten Commandments, love one's enemies, not to hold grudges, not to swear, not to be lazy, not to grumble, to devote one's self to prayer, and to desire eternal life.

Benedictine monks served the larger Church in many ways. Some of the ministries that the monks provided included offering shelter to travelers and pilgrims; feeding those who were hungry; healing those who were sick; educating boys who wanted to become priests; copying the Bible and other books that otherwise would have been lost; and keeping historical records that are still used now as a means to learn about the Early Middle Ages.

A New Rule

Imagine that you are writing a new Rule for a community of disciples. Rather than being for a group of men or women who live in a monastery, however, your Rule is for a community of people who live among others in the world. What suggestions or practices for community members would your Rule include?

_____

_____

_____

_____

_____

_____

_____

SACRED ART

Benedict's monastery at Monte Cassino has been rebuilt four times since Benedict first built it. Thus, it is surprising that some of the monastery's original artwork still exists. During World War II, the monastery served as a shelter for Italian refugees, and in 1944 the German army—aware that it was a target for attack—began to evacuate the refugees to safety. Before the bombing began, monks, soldiers, and carpenters packed up and transported some of the monastery's artworks. After the war the monastery was rebuilt, and the artworks were returned.

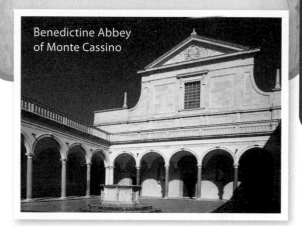

Benedictine Abbey of Monte Cassino

Study Corner

REMEMBER

In the Early Middle Ages, Benedictine monasteries provided stable communities that modeled a life of prayer, work, and care for the wider community.

Neuzelle Abbey, Germany

The Evangelical Counsels

The Cistercians, Gethsemani, Kentucky

"IT is virtuous to live in poverty." Do you agree with this statement? Why or why not? As Catholics we believe that God has called some men and women to live together in religious communities. The members of these communities have consecrated themselves to God by publicly professing the evangelical counsels—poverty, chastity, and obedience—within a stable community that is recognized by the Church. Regardless of our vocation, we are all called to practice these virtues.

Poverty means not to seek or gather material riches. It also means living simply so that we are not distracted by our belongings and, as a result, turn our attention away from God. In Scripture, Jesus challenges us to live simply when he says, "Blessed are the poor in spirit, / for theirs is the kingdom of heaven." (Matthew 5:3) Because we live in a world that often values materialism, it can be difficult to do this. It is important for us, whether we join a religious community or not, to live simply. We can do this by refusing to become attached to our possessions.

For those in religious life, chastity means not having sexual relationships with others. By living chastely, men and women religious are free to devote themselves to serving God and his people wherever they are called to go. We are also called to practice chastity. To do so, we can turn to Christ, who is the model of chaste living. We do this by treating the human body with respect, practicing the virtue of temperance—moderation or self-restraint.

As Jesus' followers, we are called to obedience. We submit to God's authority and follow the Church's teachings. We also practice the virtue of obedience by listening to our parents, teachers, civil authorities, and other adults who have responsibility for our care.

The evangelical counsels help men and women in religious communities focus their minds and hearts on God. The people who respond to God's call to enter religious life choose a way of living that is supported by simplicity, faithfulness, and obedience. These virtues enable religious men and women to dedicate their lives to Christ by serving others.

All baptized Christians are called to live holy lives by practicing the virtues of poverty, chastity, and obedience. When putting these virtues into practice is difficult, we can pray to the Holy Spirit for strength, and we can follow the example of the saints and the other holy men and women in our lives.

Strengthened by the Counsels

The evangelical counsels help free men and women in religious vocations to focus on God and to serve others. Here is an overview of how some communities have been able to serve God and the Church by practicing the evangelical counsels.

Cistercians In 1098 a monk named Robert believed that the Benedictine monastery in Cluny, France, had lost sight of the true spirit of the Rule of Saint Benedict. He, along with 21 other monks, moved into the wilderness, where they followed a stricter version of the Rule. The members of this new community, who became known as Cistercians, engaged in manual labor, prayed many times throughout the day, and lived in near-poverty. One of the best known Cistercian communities is Gethsemani Abbey in Kentucky.

Dominicans Seeing a need for educated preachers, Dominic founded the Order of Preachers in 1215. Members of the community, also known as Dominicans, soon developed a reputation for making intellectual contributions to the Church. Thomas Aquinas, a great **theologian,** was an expert in the study of God and God's Revelation to the world. Today Dominicans still dedicate themselves to education and to preaching the Gospel to people who are hungry for the truth.

Jesuits Ignatius of Loyola began his career as a soldier. While he was recovering from an injury he received in battle, he committed himself to changing his life and to serving God. Ignatius of Loyola's vision for "finding God in all things" soon attracted a group of followers. In 1540 he founded a community of priests and brothers called the Society of Jesus, or the Jesuits. Members of the community continue to help others find God in the world around them. The motto that inspires their work is "for the greater glory of God."

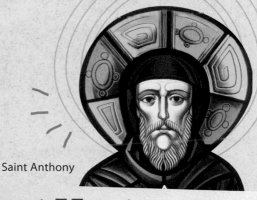

Saint Anthony

Past Meets Present

PAST: Saint Anthony (251–356) is the founder of Christian **monasticism.** He was raised in a wealthy family in Egypt, but he was not comfortable with the surrounding **culture.** When Anthony turned 20, his parents died, and he was put in charge of his young sister. Anthony placed his sister with a community of nuns and went into the Egyptian desert, where he practiced a life of contemplation and self-sacrifice. Anthony spent the rest of his life seeking solitude. He would settle at the edge of civilization, where followers would gather around him so that he could give them spiritual direction. Then he would move farther into the desert to reestablish solitude, and the cycle would start over. He received visitors and gave spiritual advice until his death.

PRESENT: The contemplative tradition in the Church is alive today. Religious orders such as the Camaldolese and the Carthusians live in community, but each monk has a private cell in which he practices the art of contemplative prayer. Women's religious communities devoted to contemplation include the Poor Clares, the Discalced Carmelites, and the Benedictine Sisters of Perpetual Adoration. These communities are called to a ministry of prayer. They also offer a welcoming space for silence, prayer, and spiritual hospitality in an environment of contemplative peace.

Explore

Study Corner

DEFINE

consecrated, evangelical counsels, temperance, theologian, monasticism, culture

REMEMBER

Each of us is called to live out the evangelical counsels according to our state in life, whether we join religious communities, remain single, or get married.

A Faithful Friend

Living as a member of a community can be trying at times. For example, a friend might lie and cause you to doubt him or her. Regardless, it's best not to give up on relationships. You can work at them so that they remain strong.

The love that keeps our relationships alive is a reflection of the love that opens our hearts in prayer. When we have difficulty living in community, we can follow the examples of Jesus, Mary, the saints, and other holy men and women. Jesus is the perfect example of how to live in community with others because he shared God's love through acts of service and by forgiving those who hurt him.

Jesus Leads Us in Community

Leader: We rely on our friends to help soften our struggles and celebrate our achievements.

All: Jesus, teach us to value our friends as you do and to desire to grow in our love for you. We ask this with confidence in your name.

Reader: A reading from the Book of Ben Sira.

Faithful friends are a sturdy shelter;
    whoever finds one finds a treasure.
Faithful friends are beyond price,
    no amount can balance their worth.
Faithful friends are life-saving medicine;
    those who fear God will find them.

Ben Sira 6:14–16

The Word of the Lord.

Leader: Let us bring our prayers before the Lord. We pray in gratitude for our friends. May we show appreciation for them and for all the people in our lives. We pray to the Lord.

All: Lord, hear our prayer.

Leader: We ask forgiveness for the times we have hurt our friends or taken them for granted. Give us the courage to ask for pardon and to spread peace and harmony in our relationships. We pray to the Lord.

All: Lord, hear our prayer.

Leader: We pray for those who find it difficult to make friends. May we reach out to them in kindness. We pray to the Lord.

All: Lord, hear our prayer.

Leader: Let us gather our prayers, those spoken and those in our hearts, and offer them to God in the words that Jesus taught us.

Conclude by praying together the Lord's Prayer.

WHERE Do I Fit In?

We are members of the Church, a community of believers. This is important, because it reminds us that we don't go to God alone. As Sr. Sheryl Chen points out, sometimes living in community can be challenging. It is among the members of our community, however, where we learn what it means to really love others. Love is generated among people.

by Sr. Sheryl Chen, O.C.S.O.

Why Do We Need Community?

Before I entered the monastery, I volunteered at a soup kitchen in Chicago. I was a bit apprehensive about serving the down-and-out, rough characters, mostly men, who came for a free bowl of soup and day-old bread. It turns out that the people who were homeless were fine, but another volunteer almost drove me stark-raving mad with her continuous pious comments. Then it dawned on me that maybe God had inspired me to work here not to learn to serve the unemployed, but to get along with the other staff in the kitchen.

Before I entered the monastery, I had lived alone in an apartment the previous two years. I was pretty faithful to getting up early so that I could pray morning prayer and go to Mass before work, and spending two hours in the evening in prayer. But I suspected that over time I would not be able to keep it up alone, and I would need the support of a community. So I entered a monastery that followed Saint Benedict's Rule for living out Gospel values together in community. Those who live together in monasteries know that they need the support of others to live in the presence of God.

Yet the biggest challenge in monastic life has been my community. Though we each want to live the Gospel according to the Rule, we have very different ideas about what that means in practice. Every day we have to accept one another as different incarnations of Christ, and even, as Saint Benedict says, to prefer what is better for the other to what I myself want. Living in love together calls for a constant yielding of my own will, my preferences, my ideas. It is not easy. It is constant growth in self-knowledge and conversion.

A journalist once asked Blessed Teresa of Calcutta, "What needs to change in the church?" She answered, "You and me."

Called to Community

Identify one or two areas in your life where the support of the community can help you remain faithful to the call of discipleship. On the lines below, write how you can turn to the community for support and how you can support others in their journey of faith.

_____

_____

_____

_____

_____

_____

_____

_____

_____

SR. SHERYL CHEN, O.C.S.O. is a Trappistine sister who lives at Mariakloster Monastery in Tautra, Norway.

What's What?

Circle the letter of the choice that best completes each sentence.

1 By the fifth century, the Roman empire had fallen into a period known as the _____. (PAGE 64)

   a. catechumenate

   b. Early Middle Ages

   c. early Church

2 The Church remained a beacon of light by preaching the Gospel, healing people who were sick, and _____. (PAGE 64)

   a. reestablishing society

   b. selling indulgences

   c. naming new saints

3 Benedict wrote the Rule of Saint Benedict as a guide for how to live _____ life. (PAGE 65)

   a. a sacramental

   b. an educated

   c. a monastic

4 By publicly professing the evangelical counsels, members of religious communities _____ God. (PAGE 66)

   a. slander and betray

   b. consecrate themselves to

   c. ask forgiveness from

5 Obedience means that we are called to _____. (PAGE 66)

   a. live without becoming attached to material goods

   b. respect our bodies and the bodies of others

   c. submit to God's authority

6 Dominic founded a new religious community because he saw a need for _____. (PAGE 67)

   a. educated preachers

   b. social workers

   c. healthcare workers

7 The motto of the Jesuits is _____. (PAGE 67)

   a. "pray and work"

   b. "live in poverty"

   c. "for the greater glory of God"

Say What?

Know the definitions of these terms.

consecrated

culture

evangelical counsels

monasticism

temperance

theologian

Now What?

Practicing the virtues, especially poverty, chastity, and obedience, can help us live together peacefully in our communities. How can you practice these virtues during the next week?

_____

_____

_____

_____

Sent on a Mission

Think about a time you experienced something fresh and exciting that you couldn't wait to share with a friend, such as movie or a book. Why were you so eager to tell your friend? Did you get across your ideas so that he or she understood how great your experience was? How did your friend react to your experience?

PRAYER

God, thank you for experiences that fill us with joy and excitement. May we feel this same enthusiasm about our faith so that we can go out and share it with others.

Saint Columban

The Church's Mission

WHAT mission does Jesus want you to fulfill? Will it always be easy to follow this call? Before his Ascension, Jesus instructed his followers to make disciples of all nations. He did not tell the disciples that this work would be easy or that people would always be happy to hear what the disciples had to say. Jesus knew that sometimes those who set out to preach the Gospel would suffer, just as he had. But he also knew that his message was universal, meant for all to hear.

The early disciples eagerly responded to Jesus' call, and Christianity spread rapidly. Peter and Paul traveled west and brought the Church to Rome, while Thomas traveled as far east as India. Christianity also grew after Constantine declared Christianity the official religion of the Roman empire.

A few centuries later, during the Early Middle Ages, as the Roman empire began to decline, pagan tribes began invading Roman territories, further disrupting Roman rule. By threatening the empire, the invaders threatened Christianity as well. In response Church leaders encouraged **missionaries** to leave their homes and share the Gospel with people who lived beyond the boundaries of the empire. The people who responded to this invitation took on the difficult challenge of preaching to people they had never met, in places they had never seen. It took great effort and a long time, but eventually missionaries spread the Gospel throughout Europe.

Respond to the Call

Church history is filled with examples of people who responded faithfully to the call to preach the Gospel. For many people the response to this call began an adventure that took them to new lands.

READY for Confirmation

Through the Sacrament of Confirmation, we are called to spread the Gospel to others by living as missionaries in our own lives. This does not mean that we have to preach to others or try to convince them to believe as we do. The most persuasive way for us to proclaim the Good News is by living Christian lives and sharing God's peace and love with others through our actions.

Saint Patrick When he was 16 years old, Patrick, who was born in Britain in 385, was captured by pirates and taken to Ireland as a slave. Patrick, who missed his family and friends, turned to God. After six years, Patrick escaped, returned to Britain, and became a priest. Around the time he was ordained, the Church began inviting missionaries to travel to Ireland. At first, Patrick was hesitant to consider this invitation, but he changed his mind after he had a dream in which the Irish people asked him to return. At the age of 42, Patrick returned to Ireland with several companions. Many people in Ireland were pagans who lived in tribes. Eventually an important tribal chief converted to Christianity, and the religion spread. Patrick traveled throughout Ireland, converting thousands of people. He built churches and convents and established monasteries. His feast day is March 17.

Past Meets Present

PAST: Despite the cultural and social constraints they faced, women played an important role in spreading the Gospel in the early Church. Priscilla, for example, is cited by Saint Paul as being a "co-worker in Christ." Phoebe is mentioned as being a Church minister and a benefactor to many. Because Priscilla's and Phoebe's names are recorded in Scripture, we know about their work. Countless others, whose names are lost to history, helped spread the faith in the early days of the Church. The effect of their work continues today.

PRESENT: In the middle of the 20th century, many women responded to the call to serve as missionaries in developing countries. Four women from America, Sisters Maura Clark, Ita Ford, and Dorothy Kazel, and laywoman Jean Donovon responded to this call by traveling to El Salvador. These women paid the ultimate sacrifice for their work on behalf of the Gospel. They were martyred on December 2, 1980. Their lives continue to serve as an inspiration to others.

Saint Columban Born in Ireland, Columban trained in a monastery founded by Saint Patrick. Eventually Columban felt that God was calling him to proclaim the Gospel in what is modern-day France. As he traveled throughout his new homeland, Columban remained firm in his faith. He spoke out against immorality, and he promoted virtues such as chastity. He even went as far as challenging King Theodoric II of Burgundy, who was unfaithful to his wife. As a result of his work, Columban was exiled. He eventually moved to a town outside of Burgundy, where he helped construct a monastery that housed one of Europe's finest libraries during the Middle Ages. We celebrate Columban's feast day on November 23.

Saint Boniface This saint became known as the Saint Paul of his time because of his willingness to travel far and wide to spread the Gospel. He was born in England during the seventh century, and he began his ministry as a Benedictine monk. After he became a missionary, Boniface traveled to Frisia, an area within modern-day Holland. Later the pope sent Boniface to Germany, where he spent more than 30 years teaching and preaching. Eventually Boniface was ordained a bishop. Later in his life, Boniface returned to Frisia. On the eve of Pentecost 754, Boniface and his companions were martyred as they were making preparations for the Confirmation of a group of catechumens. We celebrate his feast day on June 5.

Explore

Study Corner

DEFINE

missionaries

REMEMBER

Through the work of missionaries, millions of people have learned about the Salvation we receive through Jesus' Death and Resurrection. A missionary has the courage to do the right thing, even when it is not popular.

Called to Spread the Good News

HAVE you ever thought that you might be a missionary? All of us are called to spread the Good News of God's love and Salvation to all the world.

The first missionaries had the challenge of proclaiming the Gospel to people who had never heard of Christ and his teachings. Today we face the challenge of reaching out to people who may already know about Jesus and the Gospel message.

The Church recognizes the need for people to serve as missionaries in lands that traditionally have been Christian. This work is called the **New Evangelization**, a term first used by Pope John Paul II. His successors have continued to call us to evangelize anew. During the World Youth Day held in Brazil in 2013, Pope Francis shared his message of the New Evangelization with a crowd of more than three million young people. The pope said, "Jesus is calling you to be a disciple with a mission! … What is the Lord saying to us? Three simple ideas: Go, do not be afraid, and serve…. Where does Jesus send us? There are no borders, no limits: he sends us to everyone. The Gospel is for everyone…. Go, do not be afraid, and serve. If you follow these three ideas, you will experience that the one who evangelizes is evangelized, the one who transmits the joy of faith receives joy."

Live Faith-Filled Lives

One of the best ways for us to share the Good News is to live faith-filled lives and to act with love and kindness in all that we say and do. By giving witness through our example, others may be inspired to seek out a life of faith.

SACRED ART

This painting on steel is a modern American artwork developed by a group of artists known as the American School. Here Jesus is looking over New York City. This artwork reminds us that Jesus Christ watches over all of us and that millions of people can be touched by his Gospel message. In 1992 the bishops of the United States offered three goals for spreading the Gospel: generate enthusiasm in all Catholics for their faith so that they freely share it with others; invite all people to hear the message of Jesus so that they may live his commandment of love; foster Gospel values in our society so that our nation may be transformed by Jesus. The Gifts of the Holy Spirit can help you meet these goals, regardless of your vocation or state in life.

Behold Jesus,
Anonymous.

While we are called to preach the Gospel to others, the Church also calls us to respect the religious freedom of other people. When we work or go to school with people from other religious traditions, it may be helpful to focus on our similarities rather than on our differences. In a 2011 article, Michael Garanzini, S.J., president of Loyola University Chicago, wrote about interacting with people of other faiths: ". . . we need to move past talking about differences and move toward doing things together to improve the lives of all people." We can remain true to our own religious beliefs while also working with those from other religious traditions. Together we can work toward a common cause that will make the world a better place. Through our work, others will see our dedication to our Catholic way of life and will come to know God's loving presence in the world more fully.

Having an active prayer life can also help us serve as missionaries. We can pray to the Holy Spirit for the strength and guidance to share the Good News in ways that people will understand. We can also intercede for others, asking that they be open to developing their relationship with Christ. Through our prayer and good works, we can faithfully spread the Gospel message.

DEFINE

New Evangelization

REMEMBER

We can respond to the call to live as missionaries by living faith-filled lives that give witness to our personal commitment to Jesus and his message.

Explore

A Modern Missionary

Read each situation. Then on the lines below, write how you might choose to act as a modern-day missionary.

1. After a new family moves into your neighborhood, you notice one of the children in your math class. She tells you that she wishes her family would become members of the Catholic Church so that she can join the youth group.

_____

_____

_____

2. One of your aunts is engaged to a man who is not Catholic. Some of your family members are thinking about not going to the wedding because your aunt's fiance is not Catholic.

_____

_____

_____

3. Your best friend, a star athlete, told you that he didn't have time to study for a big test because of a game out of town. Then he said that he found a way to cheat so that he could pass the test.

_____

_____

_____

4. During Mass a missionary who lives in a foreign country shares how she helps others grow in their faith. Then the priest says that the money received during a special collection will be given to the missionary to help support her work.

_____

_____

_____

Witnesses of Love

There are many ways to pray. We often pray with words. Sometimes we pray these words aloud in community. Other times we pray them silently.

Another way to pray is through **meditation.** In this form of prayer, we speak to God and then listen to God's response as we reflect on images, Scripture, events in Jesus' life, or events of our own lives. Meditation, which is a form of **personal prayer,** involves our thoughts, our imagination, and our emotions in conversation with God. The goal of meditation is to grow closer to God and to better recognize his presence in our lives.

Meditation of a Missionary

Our world hungers for God. Signs of his presence are all around us. In fact, we can be signs of God's presence. Each of us is called by God to witness his presence in our own unique way. Read what Pope John Paul II told young people on World Youth Day in 2004.

> Your contemporaries expect you to be witnesses of the One whom you have met and who gives you life. In your daily lives, be intrepid witnesses of a love that is stronger than death. It is up to you to accept this challenge! Put your talents and your youthful enthusiasm at the service of the proclamation of the Good News. Be the enthusiastic friends of Jesus who presents the Lord to all those who wish to see him, especially those who are farthest away from him. . . . God uses human friendship to lead hearts to the source of divine charity. Feel responsible for the evangelization of your friends and all your contemporaries.

Spend some time reflecting on Pope John Paul II's words. Ask yourself these questions:

⇨ What does it mean to be an intrepid witness of a love that is stronger than death?

⇨ How do I show that I am Jesus' friend?

⇨ How can I be a sign of God's love to my friends?

⇨ In what ways am I afraid to let others see my faith?

When you are ready, take a moment to gather your reflections. In your own words, tell God how you will respond to the call to share his love with others.

WHERE Do I Fit In ?

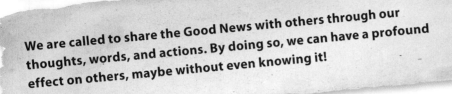

We are called to share the Good News with others through our thoughts, words, and actions. By doing so, we can have a profound effect on others, maybe without even knowing it!

by Fr. Paul Brian Campbell, S.J.

Who Has Carried the Message of Jesus to Me?

Many people have brought Christ to me in my life. The first time it happened was unforgettable. The person who brought Christ to me was Mrs. Brennan, my first grade teacher at a Catholic elementary school in Belfast, Northern Ireland.

We had a religion period every morning. I remember only one of them now, and it has stuck with me through the years. Mrs. Brennan told us the story from Mark's Gospel about the paralyzed man whose four friends brought him to see Jesus. The house was too crowded to enter, so the man's friends opened a hole in the roof and lowered him into the room where Jesus was. Jesus healed the man, who got off his stretcher and walked.

I don't know why it happened, but this story came alive for me. Right then and there, as Mrs. Brennan told it in that Irish classroom, I was transported back to first-century Capernaum. I could see, hear, and experience the whole thing unfolding before me. I was in the crowd. I felt the sun beating down on us, the dust that tickled my throat, the group of people trying to get closer to Jesus. I felt the astonishment as the men climbed on top of the building and started taking off the roof tiles. I listened, spellbound, as Jesus told the paralyzed man to "get up, take your mat and go home." The man, who had been lowered in front of Jesus just a few minutes before, sprang up and marched out of the house with great joy.

Doubtless, it was just another day's work for Mrs. Brennan, but she brought me to meet Jesus for the first time. She almost certainly had no idea that she had opened up the Scriptures for me in a whole new way. My only regret is that I never thought to tell her about it. If people ever do something like that for you, make sure to tell them.

A Model of Faith

Take a moment to think of one or two people who have modeled a life of discipleship for you. Then on the lines below, write what you can do to thank these people for bringing you closer to Jesus.

_____

_____

_____

_____

_____

_____

_____

_____

FR. PAUL BRIAN CAMPBELL, S.J., is the Publisher at Loyola Press.

What's What?

Complete the crossword by using the clues below.

Across

1. Jesus instructed his followers to make _____ of all nations. (PAGE 72)

5. While we are called to serve as missionaries, we also are called to respect other people's religious _____. (PAGE 75)

6. In addition to building churches and convents, Patrick established _____. (PAGE 73)

7. _____ is cited by Paul as being a "co-worker in Christ." (PAGE 73)

8. Each of us is called to spread the Good News of _____ to all the world. (PAGE 74)

Down

2. Columban spoke out against _____. (PAGE 73)

3. We can serve as missionaries through our _____. (PAGE 75)

4. Pope Benedict spoke about the New _____ during the World Youth Day in Madrid. (PAGE 74)

Say What?

Know the definitions of these terms.

meditation

missionaries

New Evangelization

personal prayer

Now What?

God calls each of us to live as a missionary by sharing his love with others. How can you share God's love with the people in your life during the next week?

_____

_____

_____

_____

_____

Celebrating Advent and Christmas

ADVENT, which marks the beginning of the liturgical year, begins four Sundays before Christmas day. The word *Advent* comes from the Latin *adventus*, which means "coming." During Advent, we reflect on the importance of Jesus' coming into the world to fulfill God's plan of Salvation. One way for us to celebrate is to prepare the way of the Lord by proclaiming the Gospel message of peace and love to others. Doing this prepares us to celebrate Christmas with joyful hearts.

During the Christmas season, which lasts through the Feast of the Epiphany in early January, we celebrate the Incarnation—God becoming man in the Person of Jesus. Throughout his life Jesus taught us how to live and offered his own life for us so that we might someday live with him in Heaven. Today Jesus comes to us in prayer, Scripture, and the sacraments. We also experience Christ's presence every time we share love with others. As disciples we know that Jesus will be with us in the future. We wait in joyful hope for his **Second Coming** at the end of time.

Recall a time that you prepared for an important event in your life, such as attending a new school or celebrating a birthday. What did you do to prepare for the celebration? How did your preparations make the celebration more enjoyable?

PRAYER

God, thank you for sending your Son, Jesus. During Advent may we prepare our hearts for his coming so that we can share his love with others during Christmas.

A Time to Prepare

Pope Gregory the Great

ADVENT, which is a time to prepare our minds and hearts for Christmas, has a history that can be traced back to the fourth century. Originally, local communities followed various traditions to help prepare them to celebrate Jesus' birth at Christmas. Around A.D. 600, Pope Gregory the Great issued a liturgical calendar for Catholics all over the world. Since then we have celebrated four Sundays of Advent.

The Advent traditions that have been used by the Church, both then and now, help us reflect on who Jesus is and the impact that the Incarnation has on our lives. These traditions help us answer questions such as the following:

- Who is Jesus to me?

- How does Jesus' coming into the world affect my life and the relationships I have with God, the Church, and other people?

- What does Jesus' coming mean for all humankind?

Often our answers to these questions are shaped by the time in which we live. The early Christians tried to answer these questions amid a time of great persecution. The faithful relied on **apologists**—defenders of the faith—and the Doctors of the Church to help them. These early writers and teachers offered a message of hope, even at a time when many people were killed because of their faith in Jesus. Rather than apologizing, these men and women defended the Christian faith and boldly proclaimed that Jesus is God's Son, who was sent into the world to save humankind.

Our Catholic Character

The title *Doctor of the Church* is bestowed by the pope in recognition of a person's outstanding contribution to the understanding and interpretation of Scripture and the development of Christian doctrine. This title is rarely given. Before someone can be named a Doctor of the Church, he or she must first be declared a saint. Currently there are 33 Doctors of the Church. One of the most recent saints to be named a Doctor of the Church is Saint Thérèse of Lisieux, who was elevated to this position in 1997.

O Antiphons

One Advent tradition that can help us answer the question "Who is Jesus?" is singing the O Antiphons. These **antiphons,** or short verses, are sung between December 17 and December 23 as part of the **Liturgy of the Hours,** the official prayer of the Church. Each antiphon is a name for Jesus that is taken from the Old Testament Book of Isaiah. The authors of this book of the Bible were writing for the Jewish community during a time of hardship and oppression. In response to the people's suffering, God raised up a prophet, who proclaimed a message of faithfulness and hope. Part of that message was a foretelling of the birth of a Savior—Jesus. The names that were used by the prophet to describe the Savior are the names used in the O Antiphons. Each name reveals another dimension of who Jesus is and what his coming means for us.

➡ **O Wisdom** is taken from the passage "The Spirit of the Lord shall rest upon him: / a spirit of wisdom and of understanding, / A spirit of counsel and of strength, / a spirit of knowledge and of fear of the Lord, / and his delight shall be the fear of the Lord." (Isaiah 11:2–3)

➡ **O Adonai,** a name that means "Lord," is taken from the passage "For the Lord is our judge, / the Lord is our lawgiver, / the Lord is our king; / he it is who will save us." (Isaiah 33:22)

➡ **O Root of Jesse** is a title taken from the passage "But a shoot shall sprout from the stump of Jesse, / and from his roots a bud shall blossom." (Isaiah 11:1)

➡ **O Key of David** is taken from the passage "His dominion is vast / and forever peaceful. / Upon David's throne, and over his kingdom, / which he confirms and sustains / By judgment and justice, / both now and forever. / The zeal of the Lord of hosts will do this!" (Isaiah 9:6)

➡ **O Morning Star** is from the passage "The people who walked in darkness / have seen a great light; / Upon those who lived in a land of gloom / a light has shone." (Isaiah 9:1)

➡ **O King of the Nations** is from the passage "For a child is born to us, a son is given to us; / upon his shoulder dominion rests. / They name him Wonder-Counselor, God-Hero, / Father-Forever, Prince of Peace." (Isaiah 9:5)

➡ **O Emmanuel** is from the passage "Therefore the Lord himself will give you a sign; the young women, pregnant and about to bear a son, shall name him Emmanuel." (Isaiah 7:14)

The well-known Advent hymn "O Come, O Come, Emmanuel" is based on the O Antiphons. By reflecting on each antiphon, we prepare our minds and hearts to celebrate the birth of Jesus, **Emmanuel,** a name that means "God is with us."

Study Corner

DEFINE

apologists, antiphons, Liturgy of the Hours, Emmanuel

REMEMBER

During Advent we focus on who Jesus is and how his coming into the world affects our lives. One tradition that can help us reflect on Jesus is singing the O Antiphons.

Explore

READY for Confirmation

As we prepare to celebrate the Sacrament of Confirmation, we reflect on who Jesus is and how our lives are influenced by our relationship with him. The questions we ask ourselves, which are similar to the questions we reflect on during Advent, help us grow in our relationship with him so that we can proudly and confidently profess our faith through our words and actions.

God's Messengers

DURING Advent we prepare for Jesus' birth by reflecting on who Jesus is and how his coming into the world shapes our lives as disciples. During Christmas we celebrate that coming, and we give thanks to God for sending the Savior.

According to Scripture, God sent angels, spiritual creatures who glorify God without ceasing and who serve his saving plans for others, to announce the Good News of Jesus' birth. Throughout history God has sent **heralds,** messengers, to awaken us to Christ's presence among us. This ongoing presence is at the heart of our Christmas celebration.

Biblical Heralds

Isaiah The prophet Isaiah spoke about a child to come who would be named Emmanuel. The Gospel of Matthew makes connections between this prophecy and Jesus' miraculous conception.

Gabriel Before Mary was with child, the angel Gabriel visited her to tell her that she would soon be Jesus' mother. The Bible tells us that Mary was troubled by this visit, but she listened and said yes because her faith was so great.

Angel Gabriel visiting Mary

SACRED ART

This painting reminds us that the Nativity, which took place over 2,000 years ago, is still important to us today. In the painting we see traditional Nativity figures, including angels who are acting as heralds. It appears that the whole town has gathered to witness the miracle of Christ's birth. How does your parish community welcome the Christ Child? In what way might you become involved?

Nativity, Elena Khmeleva, 20th century.

John the Baptist In his role as a herald, John the Baptist preached a message of **repentance** so that people would be ready to welcome Jesus with open hearts. John passionately shared his message with all who would listen. He was determined to tell the world that the Savior promised by God was coming.

Paul After Jesus' Death and Resurrection, Paul brought the message of Jesus' saving grace to the Gentile world. In his Letter to the Romans, Paul shares his joy and concern that all may hear the message of Jesus Christ and be saved.

> For one believes with the heart and so is justified, and one confesses with the mouth and so is saved. For the scripture says, "No one who believes in him will be put to shame." For there is no distinction between Jew and Greek; the same Lord is Lord of all, enriching all who call upon him. For "everyone who calls on the name of the Lord will be saved."
>
> *Romans 10:10–13*

Saintly Heralds

Saint Hildegard of Bingen When Hildegard of Bingen grew up, she became a nun. She was well respected by her community, who chose her to serve as their leader. To help the sisters express their love of God, she composed songs for them to sing. She also composed songs about God's beauty, Mary, the saints, and Heaven. Throughout her life Hildegard had visions of God's beauty. She wrote about her visions to help others come to know God's presence. As more and more people heard about her wisdom, they traveled from all over Germany and France to seek her advice. Even bishops, kings, and popes sought Hildegard's wisdom. She is a Doctor of the Church.

Saint Francis of Assisi On Christmas Eve in Greccio, Italy, in 1223, Saint Francis of Assisi set up the first Nativity scene, or **crèche,** portraying the birth of Christ. He gathered the community and together they set up a manger with hay and used live animals while people reenacted the story of Christ's birth. Blessed Thomas of Celano, the first biographer of Saint Francis, wrote, "Simplicity is honored here, poverty is exalted, humility is commended and a new Bethlehem, as it were, is made from Greccio."

We Are Heralds

Like the saints and people from Scripture, we are called to announce Christ's presence. We do this by living as disciples who share peace and love with others. Practicing the virtues of simplicity, poverty, and humility can help us do this.

➡ **Simplicity:** Live in a kind, loving way. Follow the Ten Commandments, and especially the Great Commandment, the new commandment, and the Golden Rule. Show the world what it means to be Jesus' follower.

➡ **Poverty:** Look beyond your own wants. Help people who are in need. Give of your time and talents to brighten someone's outlook.

➡ **Humility:** Instead of drawing attention to yourself, make a special effort to bring attention to someone else's accomplishments.

Our Catholic Character

A formal Proclamation of the Birth of Christ is traditionally chanted or recited at the beginning of the Mass on Christmas and during the Liturgy of the Hours on Christmas Eve. The proclamation is a prayerful, joyous announcement that heralds Christ's arrival. This Proclamation gives a chronology that begins with the Creation of the world, includes major historical events of the people of Israel, and concludes with Jesus' birth.

Study Corner

DEFINE

heralds, repentance, crèche

REMEMBER

Heralds appear throughout Salvation History to announce the Good News of Jesus' coming and to proclaim his mission here on earth. You can also be a herald of the Gospel message.

God's Greatest Gift

The way the Church prays has developed over time, influenced by history and culture. The words, gestures, melodies, and images that we use in our prayer help us raise our minds and hearts to God the Father through his Son, Jesus.

Because God became man, we can speak the name of God in human form, Jesus, which means "God saves." Because the Holy Spirit, the source of all wisdom, teaches us that Jesus is Lord, we can refer to Jesus as "Lord Jesus Christ, Son of God" in prayer.

Who Do you Say That I Am?

One of the best ways to deepen our relationship with Jesus is to pray with the Gospels.

> When Jesus went into the region of Caesarea Philippi he asked his disciples, "Who do people say that the Son of Man is?" They replied, "Some say John the Baptist, others Elijah, still others Jeremiah or one of the prophets." He said to them, "But who do you say that I am?" Simon Peter said in reply, "You are the Messiah, the Son of the living God."
>
> *Matthew 16:13–16*

Imagine yourself sitting with Jesus now. As you sit together, hear Jesus ask these two questions:

➡ Who do people say that I am?

➡ Who do you say that I am?

Take time to reflect on those questions. Pause to let Jesus speak to you. Share with Jesus anything that is on your mind. Be sure to thank him for your time together.

Pray together:

> Lord Jesus Christ, Son of God, you are our most merciful redeemer, friend, and brother. We pray that we may see you more clearly, love you more dearly, and follow you more nearly, day by day.
>
> *adapted from a prayer by Saint Richard of Chichester, 1253*

WHERE Do I Fit In?

The Feast of the Nativity reminds us that our faith is incarnational—God became man in the Person of Jesus. As members of the Body of Christ, we can also find God's ongoing presence in one another and in the many signs and symbols of our faith.

by Becky Eldredge

Where's God?

One Sunday at Mass during the Christmas season, my two-year old son suddenly asked, "Where's God?" My husband and I, along with several other people around us, were rather surprised by the question. I saw a few smiles and heard a few laughs. One man, however, turned around and looked at my son and answered, "He's not here."

Maybe the man was trying to be funny, but he looked serious. The man's words weighed heavily on me during Mass. They seemed in stark contrast to the signs of our faith that surrounded us and reminded us of God's presence in our past and present—the Nativity scene in front of the altar, the Gospel Reading we heard that day about the Magi coming to visit Jesus, the Eucharist, and the church adorned and radiant with white. Every year we Catholics retell our Christmas story, our story of hope. We celebrate the extent to which God loved us—enough to become man. Our faith refuses to let us forget God's intense interest in each of us that began so long ago.

As I took in the sights of Christmas in the church, I thought about my own personal reminders of God active in my world. I felt God's presence in the way my entire body reacted to the man's answer because I wholeheartedly disagreed with him. I saw God present, not only in the church, but also in each one of us, the gathered Body of Christ. One look at my son reminded me that God dwells in him. God was present in the joy and the curiosity that prompted him to ask his question, "Where is God?"

Toward the end of Mass, I smiled with relief, thankful for the reminders of God's presence, both in the past and in the present. I knew the answer I would give my son, and I knew the answer I wanted to give the man, "God is everywhere! Let me help you see him."

BECKY ELDREDGE works for Charis Ministries, a Jesuit organization that offers retreat and leadership development opportunities to young adults.

God Is Present

Take a moment to reflect on a person, place, or object that has served as a reminder of God's presence in the world. In the box write a poem or reflection, sketch a picture, or attach a photograph of whatever you thought of.

What's What?

Write the letter of the choice that best matches each description.

1 _____ an Advent tradition that includes short verses (PAGE 79)

2 _____ a name that means "Lord" (PAGE 81)

3 _____ God becoming man in the Person of Jesus (PAGE 79)

4 _____ a prophet who spoke about a child to come (PAGE 82)

5 _____ angel who told Mary she would be Jesus' mother (PAGE 82)

6 _____ John the Baptist (PAGE 83)

7 _____ Emmanuel (PAGE 81)

8 _____ marks the beginning of the liturgical year (PAGE 79)

9 _____ composed songs about God's beauty (PAGE 83)

10 _____ set up the first crèche (PAGE 83)

a. Advent

b. Isaiah

c. Saint Francis of Assisi

d. Incarnation

e. preached a message of repentance

f. Adonai

g. Saint Hildegard of Bingen

h. a name that means "God is with us"

i. Gabriel

j. O Antiphons

Say What?

Know the definitions of these terms.

antiphons

apologists

crèche

Emmanuel

heralds

Liturgy of the Hours

repentance

Second Coming

Now What?

Write an Advent prayer that you can pray to help you prepare your heart for Jesus' coming. Pray the prayer each day during the Advent season.

_____

_____

_____

_____

_____

_____

_____

_____

_____

_____

_____

_____

_____

_____

_____

_____

_____

Respond

Faith in ACTION

We strengthen our relationship with our faith community when we live out the call to discipleship. We respond to this call in the attitudes and values we hold and in the ways we relate to the people and world around us. An important part of living as Jesus' disciples is taking action to create a more just world.

In this unit we explored the theme of belonging to the Church, the universal community of Jesus' disciples. Because of his love for each member of the Church, God the Father sent his Son, Jesus, to bring Salvation to the whole human family. We respond to this great gift through our faith and by showing our love for one another.

"The longer I live the more beautiful life becomes."

—Frank Lloyd Wright, architect

Wisdom of the Ages

Act

Purpose

Tap into the wisdom and living history of our elders by talking with them; show our appreciation for all that they have experienced by returning acts of kindness.

Background

When it comes to learning about history, often our first stop is a textbook. But we have a real treasure in our elders, the people who really have "been there and done that."

Steps

1. Read and discuss Wisdom 7:7–31. What are some of the characteristics of wise people? Give examples of people who are wisdom figures for you.

2. Plan a field trip in which you can visit with senior citizens and talk with them about their life experiences. Let them know that you value their experiences and wisdom. One way to structure your time with them is to interview them about their lives. Ask questions that are general yet creative so that you can spark their memories, such as "What is one of your most enjoyable memories?" or "What is one of the greatest life lessons you have learned?"

3. Ask your new friends if you can write what they say. Let them know that you would like to preserve their stories to pass along to others.

4. Come up with a way to show your appreciation for their time and to honor the wisdom of their life experience. For example, you might include the biographies in the parish bulletin or on the parish Web site.

A Quick Response

Purpose

Learn about organizations that serve people by providing emergency-response care after disasters such as wars and hurricanes. Raise awareness of how these organizations have responded to needs in your area and take action to support these organizations.

Background

Catholic Relief Services (CRS) has over 60 years of experience providing direct care to people who have experienced devastating events such as war, famine, and natural disasters. A primary goal of this organization is to ensure that people are able to meet their basic needs so that they can live lives of dignity. CRS provides services such as food and water, health care, and agricultural and infrastructure assistance.

Steps

1. Research local organizations that work to provide emergency care for people in need. Why is this type of care so important? How does providing this type of care help people live lives of dignity?

2. Invite someone from a local organization identified in Step 1 to talk to your group about the needs of his or her organization.

3. As a group, design a project in which you can support local organizations that provide emergency care for people in need. For example, you might organize a food drive to support the organization's disaster-response efforts.

4. Present your project. Discuss with other groups how you might implement it. Establish a time line with achievable goals and complete the project.

Act

> "... nobody needs to wait a single moment before starting to improve the world."
>
> —Anne Frank, young Jewish writer known for her diary

We Worship

Saint Thomas Aquinas was born to a noble Italian family in the early part of the 13th century. When he tried to join the Dominicans against his parents' will, his brothers captured him and had him sent to a family castle where he was detained for two years. His family eventually allowed him to join the Dominicans, after which he spent time studying at the universities in Paris and Cologne. After his education, Aquinas wrote many theological books that drew on the wisdom of the ancient Greek philosophers. Through his writing, Aquinas taught that all truth flows from God.

How the Saint Relates {

Aquinas became the best-known theologian of his time. Part of his writing includes hymns that we still use today to help us grow in our relationship with God and the Church. Like Aquinas, we are called to share our gifts with the world in ways that help others grow closer to God.

Past Meets Present

PAST: The Congregation for the Doctrine of the Faith was founded in 1542 by Pope Paul III. It originally was called the Sacred Congregation of the Universal Inquisition. The scholars who worked in this Vatican office safeguarded the faith, led the Church away from false teachings, and defended the Church against those who denied its truth. Pope Paul VI gave the Congregation its current name in 1965.

PRESENT: Pope John Paul II once wrote this of the Congregation: "the duty proper to the Congregation for the Doctrine of the Faith is to promote and safeguard the doctrine on the faith and morals throughout the Catholic world: for this reason everything which in any way touches such matter falls within its competence." Among other duties, scholars provide works that deepen our understanding of the faith and help us understand how to apply our faith to developments in science and culture. The Congregation for the Doctrine of the Faith also oversees publications that deal with faith and morals, and it investigates writings that seem contrary to the faith.

Pope John Paul II

Writer and Teacher

Aquinas began to write *Summa Theologiae*, his most important work, in 1266. In this five-volume collection of writings, Aquinas systematically presents his thoughts about Christian doctrine. He poses and answers thousands of questions about theology and philosophy, including questions on the sacraments, whether war is ever justified, and whether society should criminalize all vices. The *Summa Theologiae* continues to shape our understanding of theology.

One of the biggest contributions that Aquinas made to the Church was his understanding of the Eucharist. He was the first to use the term **transubstantiation** to teach that during the consecration, the bread and wine truly become the Body and Blood of the risen Christ while retaining their appearance as bread and wine. Aquinas also wrote well-known Eucharistic hymns, including *O Salutaris* and *Pange Lingua*, that many parishes sing today.

Aquinas stopped writing after an experience he had while saying Mass in 1273. When asked about the experience, he responded, "All I have written seems like straw compared to what I have seen and what has been revealed to me." He died a year later while traveling to an ecumenical council in France.

Aquinas, known for his humility, was canonized in 1323. He is regarded as a Doctor of the Church, a teacher known for his or her great scholarship, holiness, and beneficial impact on the Church. He is the patron saint of Catholic universities, colleges, and schools. We celebrate his feast day on January 28.

Have you ever stopped to think about some of the questions raised by Aquinas? Is there such a thing as a just war? Should vices be criminalized? What exactly happens to the bread and wine at the consecration? Taking time to study what the great teachers of the Church tell us can help us grow in our understanding of our faith and direct us toward living moral lives.

The Church and Society

Think about the communities to which you belong. What stories, symbols, or images do these communities use to help their members develop a sense of welcome and belonging?

PRAYER

Holy Spirit, thank you for the guidance you have given the Church. May we continue to listen to your wisdom today.

The Middle Ages

Saint Francis of Assisi

DURING the Middle Ages, the Church continued to face challenges and opportunities. One challenge centered around disagreements between the Eastern and Western Churches. At the same time, the Church used its moral strength to reduce fighting among countries, and it made cultural contributions by supporting the development of cities and universities. The Church also responded to people's needs by approving new religious communities.

Truce of God

From around A.D. 700 to 1300, Europe embraced a warrior culture. The local nobility tried to expand its wealth by raiding neighbors, ransacking villages, and confiscating property. Invading forces of Vikings and other groups from Eastern Europe and northern Africa waged additional battles. The Church realized that ending war completely was impossible, but the bishops decided that they had to do something.

In the 11th century, the Church developed the **Truce of God.** At first the truce declared that fighting could not take place from Sunday evening to Monday morning. This was so successful that the truce was extended to include Thursday and Friday. Battles could only be fought Monday afternoon through Wednesday. Then the truce was expanded so that no fighting could take place during Lent or the season of Easter. Eventually fighting was forbidden for more than half of every year.

The Split Between East and West

After the Roman empire was divided into east and west in A.D. 395, Constantinople became the eastern center of Christianity. Over time, tensions grew between the **patriarch**— the bishop of Constantinople—and the pope in Rome. In 1054, while the patriarch was preparing to celebrate Mass in the cathedral, a western bishop, the ambassador for Pope Leo IX, entered the church and placed on the altar a letter of excommunication from the pope. A few days later, the patriarch sent his own letter of excommunication to the pope in Rome. This split, between the Roman Catholic Church in the west and the **Orthodox Church** in the east, created two separate rites. The communities celebrate liturgy in distinct ways. While the split between the Eastern Church and the Western Church continues, the Church believes that the diversity among authentically recognized rites manifests the catholicity of the Church. The rites communicate the same mystery of Christ.

Cities and Universities

The number of European towns, cities, universities, and cathedrals grew rapidly between 1000 and 1500. Priests, rich merchants, and noble men and women mixed in the cities. Entire communities were involved with building churches and cathedrals. Universities in Italy and France revived the intellectual life of society. Thomas Aquinas lectured at the University of Paris, where he presented the vision of all human life coming from God and being on a journey to God.

Religious Orders

The Church responded to the growth of cities by establishing new religious orders whose rules were more flexible. This allowed the members of the communities to minister directly to people's needs. The monks and sisters at the previously established Benedictine communities seldom left their monasteries and convents. The members of the new orders—Franciscans, Dominicans, Carmelites, Capuchins, and Augustinians—lived in the cities and ministered directly to the people. These new orders were known as **Mendicant Orders** because the members begged for their food. The more mobile way of life for these communities allowed them to be more available to help people in their daily lives.

Francis of Assisi (1182–1226)

Francis of Assisi was raised in a wealthy family. As a young man, he liked spending money on himself. Because he saw himself as a great warrior, Francis joined a campaign against a neighboring city. During the battle he was taken prisoner and had to be ransomed. Being captured and costing his family ransom was a humiliating experience for Francis. This humiliation and the sorrow he felt for his actions during battle caused Francis to examine his life, repent his sins, and pursue a desire to live for God.

After his recovery from the battle, Francis met a person with leprosy. In those days, no one touched people who had leprosy because they thought that the illness was spread by human contact. Still, Francis embraced the person. In that embrace, Francis met Jesus Christ. This marked an important point in Francis's conversion. He began to give away his possessions, and he devoted himself to following Jesus. While he was praying before a crucifix in the abandoned church of San Damiano, Francis heard God speaking to him, "Go and repair my house, which is in ruins." Francis thought that God was talking about the church of San Damiano. So Francis sold some of his father's property to pay for the repairs.

When Francis's father found out, he was furious. He brought Francis before the bishop, who told Francis that it was wrong to sell what was not his. Francis then took off all of his clothes and returned them to his father. The bishop quickly gave Francis a simple robe to wear with a rope to tie around his waist.

Francis began to live a simple life, and soon he had followers who joined him. Together, they started preaching and serving people who were poor. Their followers continue to do this to this day. The simple habit the Franciscans wear today is similar to the robe given to Francis by the bishop. Francis became known for his poverty and for his love of animals. In the later years of his life, he experienced the wounds of the crucified Christ in his hands and feet. Saint Francis of Assisi is still beloved today because of this Christlike love for everyone.

The Cross of Jesus

Saint Francis of Assisi was called by God to minister to the people during difficult times. Francis saw people who were suffering as being like the crucified Christ. In order for human beings to understand the depths of God's love, Francis brought people the image of a human Christ who shares in their suffering.

In this environment of suffering, vivid portrayals of the Crucifixion became popular. Francis wanted people to grasp the meaning of Jesus' Passion and Death. Francis described the humility of Jesus, who never committed a sin but gave up his life for us so that we could be reconciled to God. He also emphasized Jesus' obedience to God the Father. Through his obedience, even dying for our sake, Jesus **atoned** for our sins and opened the gates of Heaven for us. Francis expressed his gratitude to God for Jesus' sacrifice by his care and service to others.

Study Corner

DEFINE

Truce of God, patriarch, Orthodox Church, Mendicant Orders, atoned

REMEMBER

Even though the Church experienced challenges during the Middle Ages, it continued to model discipleship by ministering to people and providing for their needs.

The Marks of the Church

JESUS instructed his followers to continue his work in the world. Sometimes Christians have disagreed about how to do this. To help discern what Jesus wants, we can look to the Marks of the Church. These are four characteristics that Jesus and the Church both share.

The beliefs that are presented in the Marks of the Church have been part of our Tradition since the Church's earliest days. The Marks of the Church were not formally established as part of Church doctrine, however, until the Council of Constantinople in A.D. 381. By declaring that the Church is one, holy, catholic, and apostolic, the bishops sought to help Christians clearly articulate their faith. We profess our beliefs in the Marks of the Church every time we pray the Nicene Creed.

The Church Is One

The Three Persons of the Trinity—the Father, the Son, and the Holy Spirit—call us to be **one** in Christ. Following Christ leads to unity. We display this unity in our prayer and worship of God. We are also one in our celebrations of the sacraments, the seven signs instituted by Christ through which we receive a life of grace. Likewise, we all profess one faith, which is based on central truths. Among these are belief in God's love for us and that we receive Salvation through Christ's life, Death, Resurrection, and Ascension into Heaven.

READY for Confirmation

Each of us is called to be holy. The Gifts of the Holy Spirit—wisdom, understanding, counsel, piety, fortitude, knowledge, and fear of the Lord— help us grow in holiness and live lives of virtue. We receive these seven permanent spiritual gifts at Baptism, and they are strengthened at Confirmation.

As a people of faith, we gather around the bishops, the successors of the Apostles. We especially gather around the Bishop of Rome, the pope, who is the successor of Peter. We see the bishops, united under the pope, as the clearest sign of the Church's unity.

The Church Is Holy

The Church is **holy** because it is one with Jesus Christ. Baptism unites us with the holiness of Christ and calls us to be the holy People of God. Being holy means that we honor God, love Jesus, and share God's love with others. Following Christ and the examples of Mary and the saints can help us grow in holiness.

The Church Is Catholic

Just like Christ's message that God's love is for everyone, the Church is catholic, or universal—for everyone, everywhere. This means that the Church

➤ strives to preach the Gospel to all people.

➤ teaches the total message of Jesus Christ.

➤ offers everything that is necessary for Salvation.

The Church conveys everything that it believes through its teachings and sacramental celebrations. From a small community of disciples in Palestine, the Church has grown to include more than one billion members worldwide.

The Church Is Apostolic

Jesus entrusted the leadership of the Church to Peter. To say that the Church is **apostolic** is to say that Jesus continues to lead the Church through the pope and the bishops, who make up the Magisterium. When the pope and the bishop act in their role as the Magisterium, they exercise the teaching authority of the Church. With the Holy Spirit to guide them, the bishops pass on the faith that has been given to us by the Apostles, and they make sure that the Church teaches the correct understanding of this faith. The Holy Spirit has given the pope and the bishops the gift of **infallibility,** which means that the teachings of the Magisterium are without error when it comes to matters of faith and morals. The bishops lead through their example of service and by calling people to follow Christ.

Explore

Our Catholic Character

Many people's lives demonstrate the meaning of the Marks of the Church. Saint John XXIII is a model of the Church as one. He worked tirelessly to unite Christians in their common beliefs. Saint Thérèse, the Little Flower, is a model of the Church as holy. She spent her entire life trusting God and working to reflect his holiness in daily life. Saint Francis of Assisi is a model of the Church as catholic. His life is admired by Christians and non-Christians alike. He also founded a religious community whose members live all over the world. Saint Paul, who responded to Christ's call to preach the Gospel, is a model of the Church as apostolic.

Through the Marks of the Church, we know who we are as Catholics and how Jesus unites himself with us through the power of the Holy Spirit. The Church holds us together as one, holy, catholic, and apostolic community of believers who are called to love God and one another.

We Are One

Unity comes from God who, as Father, Son, and Holy Spirit, is one. Human beings, made in the divine image of God, are called to establish unity among themselves and to live in solidarity with one another.

The unity of the Church serves as a sign of the unity intended by God for all people. Unity has been a strong sign of the Catholic Church since its beginning. "The community of believers was of one heart and mind." (Acts of the Apostles 4:32) The community was one because Jesus sent the Holy Spirit to unite everyone in his love. Our unity flows from and reflects the unity of the Trinity. The gift of unity that comes from the Spirit helps us live the way Jesus showed us.

A Psalm of Unity

All: How good it is when people live together as one!

adapted from Psalm 133:1

Side 1: Shout joyfully to the LORD, all you lands;
serve the LORD with gladness;
come before him with joyful song.

All: How good it is when people live together as one!

Side 2: Know that the LORD is God,
he made us, we belong to him,
we are his people, the flock he shepherds.

Psalm 100:2–3

All: How good it is when people live together as one!

Leader: Jesus prayed that his followers may be one just as he and his father are one. Let us take a moment to reflect silently on how we can express our unity with Christians all over the world. As you reflect ask yourself the following questions:

How can I express unity through my words and actions?

What parish groups might I join that reach out to other Christians here or abroad?

All: How good it is when people live together as one!

WHERE Do I Fit In?

At the heart of our vocation, whatever it may be, is responding to the needs of others by using the gifts that we have been given. Fr. Kevin O'Brien, S.J., like Saint Francis of Assisi, had an experience that helped him realize his true vocation.

by Fr. Kevin O'Brien, S.J.

How Do We Know What God Wants of Us?

Reflect

Great adventures often have the most unexpected beginnings. For me, the adventure that would lead me to become a Jesuit priest began on a hot day outside a courthouse in southern Florida, in the company of an 80-year-old Jewish woman from Brooklyn.

I was a junior lawyer working on a big case that involved some tragic family history. The stakes were high, and the facts were deeply personal for my client, Miriam. She was immensely kind and gracious. At this stage of her life, the last place she wanted to be was in a courtroom in a long-drawn-out fight over a will. But she knew that in this case it was the right thing to do.

As the junior lawyer, my job was to take care of the client. During the court hearings, recounting some of the painful family history, Miriam sometimes would leave the courtroom, and I would walk with her. She would tell me stories about her family, her dear friends, and about growing up in Brooklyn. She would tell me about her hopes for her future. One day, as we walked outside the courthouse, it hit me: I would rather be outside talking with Miriam than inside the courtroom. There was no blinding light, no thunderbolt from Heaven, just an insight that cut to the heart of the matter.

The thought was not entirely new. I went to law school not intending to practice law but to lay the foundation for a career in politics. From an early age, my family and my faith taught me that, whatever I did in life, I needed to give back to the community. The truth of the Gospel message became part of me: to whom much is given, much is expected. Admittedly, public service fed my ego and my desire for power and prestige, but God works with our mixed motivations, refining over time ambitions that are too self-directed.

That day with Miriam outside the courthouse was a moment when God broke through my cluttered thinking and clearly got my attention. It was a call to figure out what I really wanted to do with my life. I started to pray more regularly, inviting God into the conversation, and the way became clearer from that moment on.

Listen to God

Take a moment to reflect on how you can continue to invite God into your life so that you can hear his call. Then write a prayer that you can pray to help you know the vocation to which God is calling you.

_____

_____

_____

_____

_____

_____

_____

FR. KEVIN O'BRIEN, S.J., is a priest and professor at Georgetown University in Washington, D.C. This essay was excerpted from his book *The Ignatian Adventure*.

What's What?

Write your answers on the lines.

1 What city became the eastern center of Christianity after the Roman empire was divided into east and west? (PAGE 92)

_____

_____

2 What did the bishop of Constantinople do in response to the letter of excommunication that he received from the pope? (PAGE 92)

_____

_____

_____

3 Why were the Franciscans, Dominicans, Carmelites, Capuchins, and Augustinians first known as Mendicant Orders? (PAGE 93)

_____

_____

_____

4 Who calls us to be one in Christ? (PAGE 94)

_____

_____

5 How does the Church convey everything that it believes? (PAGE 95)

_____

_____

_____

6 What do the pope and the bishops do when they act in their role as the Magisterium? (PAGE 95)

_____

_____

_____

7 How was Blessed John XXIII a model of the Church as one? (PAGE 95)

_____

_____

_____

Say What?

Know the definitions of these terms.

apostolic	Orthodox Church
atoned	patriarch
holy	_Summa Theologiae_
infallibility	transubstantiation
Mendicant Orders	Truce of God
one	

Now What?

The Marks of the Church are characteristics that both Jesus and the Church share. To demonstrate to others that you are Jesus' follower, how can you live out the Marks of the Church during the next week?

_____

_____

_____

_____

_____

_____

_____

The Great Cathedrals and Worship

Recall a time when you saw a magnificent structure or walked through an incredible building. What ideas came to mind as you looked at it? What may have inspired the architect to design it that way? Were you inspired by what you saw? If so, how?

PRAYER

God, thank you for all the ways you reveal yourself to us. May we respond to your Revelation with openness and gratitude.

99

The Great Cathedrals

IN the relationship between God and humans, God always acts first by revealing his great love for us. We respond to this Revelation as best we can. One of our most enduring responses has been the building of great **cathedrals,** which are the churches where the bishop of each diocese presides.

The cathedrals of medieval Europe are symbols of people's faith. People sacrificed time and money to build these great cathedrals, which often took generations to complete. Eventually, advances in technology allowed medieval architects to use thin walls; high, arched ceilings; and large stained-glass windows, all of which allowed sunlight to enter into the building. In addition to adding beauty, stained-glass windows served as a source of instruction for the faithful, many of whom were illiterate.

In most cathedrals the entrance is designed so that people walk through a dark narthex, or entryway, into an amazing space of openness and light. This movement echoes the light we experience by modeling our lives on Christ. Through Baptism we are freed from the darkness of sin, and we are born as children of light.

Cathedrals remain a timeless testimony that God is deserving of our focus, devotion, sacrifice, and praise. They serve as beautiful and inspiring reminders that God continuously invites us into his life and love.

Adam and Eve stained-glass detail

1. Adam and Eve in stained-glass windows
2. Symbols of nature in windows
3. Bishop's throne
4. Apse/chancel
5. Crypt
6. Aisle
7. Nave
8. Saints on facade
9. Clerestory
10. Rose window
11. Gargoyles on west front
12. Bell tower
13. Spire

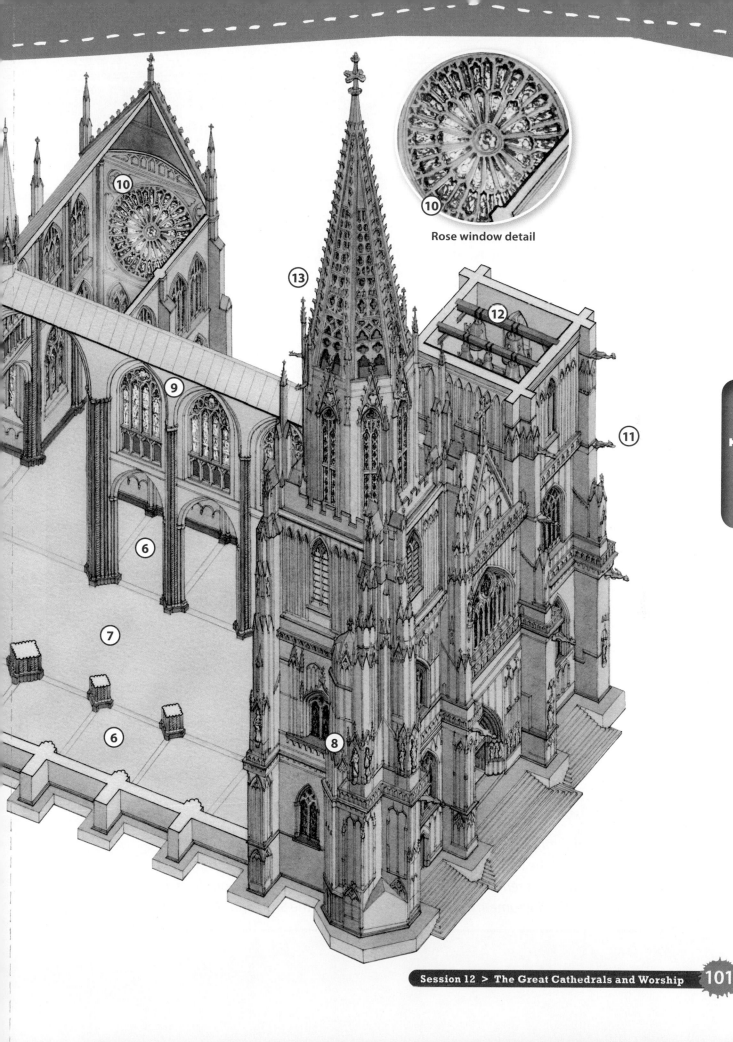

Rose window detail

A Sacramental Church

WHEN we see the word *Church*, many images may come to mind. For some of us, our first thought is the building in which we celebrate the sacraments. For others the word *Church* calls to mind the community, or the People of God who choose to believe in Jesus and follow his teachings. Both of these images are correct.

We can also say that the Church is a sacrament. As Catholics we believe that the Church—which is a sign of the relationship between God and humans—is the source of Salvation for all people. The Church celebrates the communion between God and his greatest creation, human beings, through the seven sacraments, the visible signs of the divine life that God shares with us. The sacraments were instituted by Christ and given to the Church. They are divided into three categories. The Sacraments of Initiation are Baptism, Confirmation, and the Eucharist. The Sacraments of Healing are Reconciliation and the Anointing of the Sick. The Sacraments at the Service of Communion are Matrimony and Holy Orders.

Each sacrament is celebrated by using various **rites.** These ritual words and actions make present the grace of the sacrament that is being celebrated. Participating in these sacramental rites also bears fruit in those who are properly disposed to celebrate

them. An example of a rite is the laying on of hands that is used in the Sacraments of Confirmation and Holy Orders. Receiving Holy Communion is a rite that is part of the Sacrament of the Eucharist.

Rites are meant to help us grow in our relationship with God and the Church. In the Sacrament of Reconciliation, for example, the Holy Spirit helps us move from sorrow for our sins and our broken relationships to forgiveness and reconciliation.

READY for Confirmation

The rites used during Confirmation include the laying on of hands, anointing with Chrism, and the words "Be sealed with the Gift of the Holy Spirit." Chrism is a sacramental that reminds us of the presence of the Holy Spirit in our lives. It is also used in the Sacraments of Baptism, Anointing of the Sick, and Holy Orders.

In the Eucharist, we move from an emptiness and hunger to a state of being nourished by the Body and Blood of Christ.

Rites include sacramentals, which are sacred signs instituted by the Church that prepare those who use them to receive the fruit of the sacraments. Sacramentals **sanctify,** or make holy, the ordinary objects and events of our lives. Blessings, which include praising God and his works, are the Church's primary sacramentals. Other examples of sacramentals include the sacred vessels used during Mass, such as the chalice; holy water; and prayers before and after meals. Sacramentals draw our attention to how God is present among us in the ordinary events of our lives.

A Life of Prayer

Sacraments, rites, and sacramentals foster a life of prayer, which is the raising of our minds and hearts to God. The various types of prayer include blessing, petition, intercession, thanksgiving, and praise. Prayers of blessing ask God to make someone or something holy. When we pray prayers of petition, we ask something of God. We pray on behalf of another person when we pray **prayers of intercession.** Through prayers of thanksgiving, we give thanks to God, and through our prayers of praise, we glorify God.

Prayer may also include acts of **piety,** or devotion. These acts can vary from culture to culture. Some devotional practices are tied to feasts and seasons,

such as getting our throats blessed on the Feast of Saint Blaise, praying the **Rosary** during the month of May, or displaying the palms we receive on Palm Sunday in a place of prominence in our homes.

In addition to the various types of prayer, there are various schools of Christian **spirituality,** or paths to God. Franciscan spirituality, for example, celebrates the wonder of creation. A characteristic of Ignatian spirituality is the awareness of God's presence in the world around us.

The Holy Spirit guides the Church and its members on how to pray so that we can deepen our relationship with the living God. Prayer unfolds throughout the history of Salvation as a mutual call between God and humans. It is through prayer, aided by human reason, that we come to know the one true God who, while he reveals himself to us, remains a total mystery. God calls us to be in relationship with him, but we can never fully know him.

Think about your own prayer life. Which type of prayer do you pray most often? When you notice beauty in nature, do you praise God for the gift of creation? When someone shows you kindness, do you offer a prayer of thanks? Always remember that you can pray in many different ways. You can pray by using your own words, reading Scripture, praying traditional prayers, or even drawing or writing poetry. What is most important is to pray often. As Saint Paul reminds us, we are called to "[P]ray without ceasing." (1 Thessalonians 5:17)

Explore

Our Catholic Character

The sacraments, which unite us with Christ, are one way we participate in the Church's holiness. Through them we grow in faith, and we receive the strength to serve the mission of the Church by sharing God's peace and love with others, especially those who are poor and vulnerable.

Growing Closer to God

JESUS taught us how to pray when he gave us the Lord's Prayer.

The seven petitions in the Lord's Prayer teach us how to place ourselves in God's presence and speak with him in prayer. The first three petitions, which are also statements of praise, unite us with God the Father, and ask that we be able to live as he desires. The fourth and fifth petitions direct us to ask our merciful God for what we need to live and to be healed of sin. In the final two petitions, we ask for God's help in being victorious in our struggle against sin. With these concerns we approach all our prayer, striving to grow closer to God.

Lord's Prayer Reflection

Our Father, who art in heaven,
hallowed be thy name;
thy kingdom come,
thy will be done
on earth as it is in heaven.

Pray the two words *Our Father*. Repeat them slowly as many times as you like, letting them rest deeply in your mind and heart. Ask God to help you know his will for you today. Relax in God's presence. Let him speak to your heart. Listen to what God has to tell you. Then ask for the strength to carry out his will.

Give us this day our daily bread,
and forgive us our trespasses,
as we forgive those who trespass against us;
and lead us not into temptation,
but deliver us from evil.

Jesus tells us to ask God to provide for our needs. Hear Jesus speaking these words to you personally. What is the "daily bread" you need today? Talk it over with Jesus. Do not be afraid to explain what you really need from the people in your life, from the situations in your life, or even from yourself. Let God know how much you want to stay connected with him. Thank Jesus for teaching us how to pray.

WHERE Do I Fit In?

by Margaret Silf

The ability to see God in the world around us is an important part of the Catholic tradition. Here, author Margaret Silf reflects on how an ordinary event—turning on a light switch—can remind others of the truth of God's love.

Let There Be Light!

Can one little light make any difference in the darkness?

On my first visit to New York City, I decided to go to the top of the Empire State Building late one dark night. When the elevator reached the topmost viewing platform, I stepped out and gazed down on a breathtakingly beautiful view. I wasn't the only one to be awed by the sight. A group of youngsters who chattered all the way up immediately fell into a wide-eyed silence as they stepped onto the platform. Everyone was blown away by the sea of beauty sparkling at our feet. New York City was alive with light.

But exactly how did this spectacle come about? It wasn't some lavish Hollywood show put on to draw the crowds. It was simply the result of millions of ordinary people switching on the lights right where they live. None of them thought for a moment that they were contributing to a vision that can take your breath away.

One small light can kindle a fire that changes the world. God's vast visions always begin with the *anawim,* which is Hebrew for "the poor seeking the Lord for deliverance." The Gospel keeps reminding us that we are the poor, the little ones. The light of life is given to us.

When we light a candle, we say to the darkness, "I beg to differ."

MARGARET SILF is the author of *Inner Compass, The Other Side of Chaos,* and *Simple Faith.* She lives in Scotland, United Kingdom.

Reflect

Revealing God's Presence

Reflect on an experience in your life that has served as a source of God's Revelation. On the lines below, write what the event was and what it revealed to you about God's presence in the world today.

_____
_____
_____
_____
_____
_____
_____
_____
_____
_____
_____
_____
_____
_____
_____
_____
_____
_____

What's What?

Respond

Answer each question by filling in the blank.

1 In the relationship between God and humans, _____ always acts first. (PAGE 100)

2 Cathedrals are the churches in which the _____ of each diocese presides. (PAGE 100)

3 Stained-glass windows serve as a source of _____ for the faithful. (PAGE 100)

4 Through _____ we are freed from the darkness of sin, and we are born as children of light. (PAGE 100)

5 The Church is the source of _____ for all people. (PAGE 102)

6 The _____ are all those who choose to believe in Jesus and follow his teachings. (PAGE 102)

7 The three _____ are Baptism, Confirmation, and the Eucharist. (PAGE 102)

8 _____ are the Church's primary sacramentals. (PAGE 103)

9 Examples of _____ include sacred vessels, holy water, and prayers before and after meals. (PAGE 103)

10 Through _____ we lift our minds and hearts to God. (PAGE 103)

Say What?

Know the definitions of these terms.

cathedrals   Rosary

piety   sanctify

prayers of intercession   spirituality

rites

Now What?

We grow in our relationship with God through our participation in the sacramental life of the Church. Choose a sacramental that appeals to you and write how you can use it in your prayer life during the next week.

_____

_____

_____

_____

_____

_____

_____

_____

_____

_____

_____

_____

_____

_____

Nourished by the Eucharist

Think about a time you felt restless because you were unsatisfied. Maybe you were bored, hungry, or tired of waiting for something. Maybe you witnessed some kind of injustice. What was the situation? What did you do to resolve your restlessness? Were you satisfied in the end?

PRAYER

Jesus, thank you for satisfying our hunger for you through the gift of the Eucharist. May we show our thanks for this gift by sharing your presence with others.

Pope Innocent III and the Eucharist

POPE Innocent III, whose birth name was Lotario dé Conti di Segni, was born in approximately 1160 to a noble Italian family. He was first educated in Rome and then attended the University of Paris to study philosophy and theology. Later he studied both civil and canon law in Bologna, Italy. After receiving his education, Lotario returned to Rome and began working for the Church. Because of his knowledge and talent, he was chosen to be an advisor to the pope. When he was only 37 years old, Lotario became pope.

During his papacy, Lotario, who took the name Innocent III, was admired for his brilliant mind and his ability to take action. He restored papal authority within the Church in lands where the nobility had taken governance from the rightful Church officials. Pope Innocent III also launched two Crusades, one to recover Palestine and the Christian lands of the East for Christianity and the other to bring peace to the Christians and Moors of

Pope Innocent III, 1160–1216, fresco, Italy.

READY for Confirmation

By strengthening the Church's concern for people who were poor, Pope Innocent III demonstrated a desire to welcome those in need and offer them food and care. The welcome we receive from the Church in Baptism calls us to welcome others, such as new classmates, new neighbors, or new parishioners. Christ's presence in the Eucharist calls us to give thanks for everything that we have received from God. The Gifts of the Holy Spirit that are strengthened at Confirmation call us to be patient with our brothers and sisters, obedient to our parents, and respectful of ourselves and others.

Spain. In addition, Pope Innocent III recognized that the Church needed to do more to care for people who were poor. So he approved new religious orders, including one founded by Saint Francis of Assisi, to respond to this issue.

The Council of Lateran IV

Pope Innocent III called for the Council of Lateran IV in 1213. Two years later, representatives from the Eastern Church and noblemen from every Catholic kingdom in Europe joined over 400 bishops and 900 abbots at the Lateran Palace, the pope's main residence.

After giving an opening address, the pope presented to the council fathers 70 decrees regarding important points of Church teaching. By approving these decrees, the Church leaders helped define Church **dogma,** or teaching.

In affirming one of the decrees that Pope Innocent III presented, the council accepted transubstantiation as an official Church teaching. Transubstantiation was first defined by Saint Thomas Aquinas as a way to explain how the bread and wine become the Body and Blood of Christ. The dogma of transubstantiation teaches that during the consecration at Mass, the bread, which appears to be bread, and the wine, which appears to be wine, really and truly become the Body and Blood of the risen Christ. Christ makes himself present, Body and Blood, soul and divinity, in the Eucharist.

In addition the council fathers approved a decree requiring the faithful to receive Holy Communion at least once each year. This decree was made because people didn't receive Holy Communion very often during the Middle Ages.

Today, through the **Precepts of the Church,** the Church still calls the faithful to receive Holy Communion at least once per year, during the Easter season. This obligation is a gift that reminds us that the Eucharist strengthens our relationship with Jesus Christ and his Church, forgives venial sin, and gives us the strength to avoid mortal sin. Likewise, through the Eucharist, the relationship of the whole Church as the Body of Christ is strengthened.

Our Catholic Character

Between 1962 and 1965, another ecumenical council, the **Second Vatican Council,** took place. It helped people understand that the Eucharist is the high point of our lives as Catholics. To help us enter more fully into the mystery of the Eucharist, the council suggested changes in the way we celebrate Mass. The council allowed Mass to be prayed in the language of each individual culture rather than in Latin. The priest was allowed to face the people while celebrating Mass, rather than facing the tabernacle. The council made it possible for the people to receive Holy Communion under both forms—the Consecrated Bread and Wine—rather than just one. Lay people were called to participate more fully in the Mass. Lay lectors received permission to proclaim the Scripture readings, and extraordinary ministers of Holy Communion received permission to distribute Holy Communion.

Study Corner

DEFINE
dogma, Precepts of the Church, Second Vatican Council

REMEMBER
At the Council of Lateran IV, Pope Innocent III and the council fathers further defined Church dogma, including the Church's teaching on the Eucharist.

The Sacrament of the Eucharist

THERE are many times in our lives when we stand in lines, waiting to do something. We wait in lines to buy movie tickets. We wait in lines at amusement parks, and we wait in line at the grocery store. We also line up to receive Holy Communion. Unlike most lines, this line is unique. We are not merely lining up. We are processing to the altar to receive the risen Christ in Holy Communion. This procession is a symbol of our lifelong journey to be one with God.

As we process forward to receive Holy Communion, we are called to reflect on what the Eucharist is and what it means for us as Catholics. The word *Eucharist* comes from the Greek, and it means "thanksgiving." Our celebration of the Eucharist is our prayer of praise and thanksgiving to God for everything that he has done for us in Jesus Christ. The Eucharist is our way of thanking God for creating us, redeeming us through Christ's Death and Resurrection, and sanctifying us through the power of the Holy Spirit.

Memorial and Sacrifice

Through the Eucharist we remember Christ's Passion, Death, and Resurrection. The Eucharistic celebration is more than just a remembering, however. Through the celebration of the Mass, Christ's Death is made present to us in the Eucharist. We call this kind of

SACRED ART

On the night before he died, Jesus celebrated the Last Supper—a Jewish celebration of the Passover—with his disciples. During the meal Jesus took bread, blessed it, and said "This is my body." He also took wine and, after giving thanks, gave it to his disciples, saying "This is my blood." By giving his disciples his Body and Blood in the form of bread and wine, Jesus instituted the Sacrament of the Eucharist.

The Last Supper, Florence Martinez, Jacmel, Haiti.

remembering a memorial. We say that the Eucharist is a memorial of Jesus' sacrifice on the cross. In giving thanks for this great gift, we commit to live and die as Jesus did—as a person for others. The Eucharist, therefore, is the celebration of Jesus' sacrifice for our Salvation. But it is also our sacrifice, the offering of ourselves for the good of the world.

Presence

We are always in God's presence, but there are different ways we experience this presence. The most complete way that God reveals himself to us is through the Eucharist, in which Jesus Christ is present in a real way. Christ's presence in the Eucharist is so real that the bread and wine really and truly become his Body and Blood.

To say that Jesus in the Eucharist is the Real Presence is not to downplay or ignore the other ways in which he is present to us. Jesus is among us in the community that gathers together to celebrate the Eucharist. He is present in the Word that is proclaimed at Mass, and he is present in the priest who celebrates the Mass. This is why only a validly ordained priest can celebrate the Eucharist and pray the prayer of consecration through which the bread and wine become Christ's Body and Blood. Jesus' presence in the Eucharist brings all these elements together. In the Eucharist, through the power of the Holy Spirit, Jesus Christ is among us.

During the first part of the Mass, the Liturgy of the Word, we hear God's Word proclaimed to us. During the second part of the Mass, the Liturgy of the Eucharist, the priest calls upon the Holy Spirit to bless our offerings. The priest takes the bread and wine and prays the prayer of consecration over them. Then the community processes forward to receive Holy Communion. In doing so, we follow the instruction Jesus gave to his followers at the Last Supper when he said, "Take and eat. Take and drink."

The Church teaches that to receive the Eucharist, we must be in a state of grace. Anyone who has committed a **mortal sin** is to receive **absolution** through the Sacrament of Reconciliation before receiving Holy Communion.

Christ's work in the liturgy is sacramental. Through the Eucharist the mystery of Salvation is made present. As humans who are born into Original Sin, we are not worthy to receive Holy Communion, but Jesus Christ wants us to take part in this meal so that he can fill us with his life and love.

The Eucharist and Me

Think about this phrase: *The Eucharist satisfies our hunger for Christ's love.* Write a paragraph or draw a picture to describe what this phrase means to you.

_____

_____

_____

_____

_____

_____

_____

_____

_____

Explore

Study Corner

DEFINE

mortal sin, absolution

REMEMBER

The Eucharist is our way of thanking God for creating us, redeeming us through Christ's Death and Resurrection, and making us holy through the action of the Holy Spirit.

Remember Me

IN one of the Eucharistic prayers, we pray, "We offer you in thanksgiving this holy and living sacrifice." Through this prayer we acknowledge that Christ is the source of our Salvation. He is the victim whose Death has reconciled us to God.

Christ, through this sacrifice, has set all creation free from sin and death, created it anew, and returned it to God the Father in thanksgiving. This saving act is made present in every celebration of the Eucharist. In our own lives, every joy we experience, as well as our every need, can also become an offering of thanksgiving. In celebrating the Eucharist, the Church reveals and becomes more fully what it is—a people of thanksgiving.

Jesus in the Eucharist

Over the centuries, Christians have written prayers that inspire images and expand our understanding of the mystery of Jesus present among us in the Eucharist. The Litany of the Blessed Sacrament of the Altar is a prayer that brings to mind images that can help us more fully enter into the Eucharistic mystery.

Slowly and prayerfully read over the images from the Litany below. Spend time with each one.

Living bread that came down from heaven . . .
Bread of life for a hungry world . . .
Precious blood that washes away our sins . . .
Memorial of God's undying love . . .
Food that lasts for eternal life . . .
Mystery of faith . . .
Food of God's chosen . . .

Spend a few moments reflecting on something from your personal experience that you might use to describe the Eucharist. Maybe some other images are beginning to come to you. Your images may be words, drawings, music, or some other artistic form.

All: Thank you, Jesus, for this time together and for giving us yourself in the gift of the Eucharist.

WHERE Do I Fit In?

Jesus has given us a special gift: his Body and Blood in the Eucharist. Sometimes we take Jesus' Real Presence for granted. In this reflection, Tom McGrath reminds us that the Real Presence is both a gift and the primary source of spiritual nourishment in our lives.

by Tom McGrath

Jesus Is There for You

My family moved the day after I graduated from eighth grade. I eventually came to like my new neighborhood, but until high school started, I felt isolated and alone.

Halfway through that long summer, my best friend from the old neighborhood spent the weekend at my house. I was nervous as that weekend approached, wondering how the visit would go. What would we do? Would we still get along?

At first it was awkward, but as we sat on the back porch, Billy asked, "How have you been, Tom? Was it hard moving away from our neighborhood?" Having broken the ice, we were instantly buddies again. We talked and laughed about all the crazy things we did in grammar school. We remembered the good times, and we even shared our fears about what the world of high school would be like.

I felt like I was myself again.

The gift of a person's honest presence is one of the most precious human experiences we can have. When someone is present to us, we, too, become more present. We don't have to hide who we are or what we feel. We begin to learn more about who we most truly are—the person we are down deep, the person God created us to be.

Jesus, who is both human and divine, understood the power of one person being present to another. He knew how being present can transform someone by calling and strengthening him or her to be the person he or she was meant to be. On the night before he died, Jesus gave his disciples the greatest gift, the gift of his own Real Presence. He said, "Take and eat, for this is my body, given up for you."

He said we should do this in memory of him. Jesus gives us that same gift of himself every time we go to Mass and receive him in the Eucharist.

It amazes me that, at Mass, I can go through the motions of receiving Holy Communion without realizing what I'm really doing. At those times, I need to practice noticing and appreciating Jesus' Real Presence and offering my own real presence in return. There are many ways that help me practice the presence of Jesus at Mass.

Here Are Three:

1. **Get to know Jesus in the Gospels.** The more I know about Jesus—how he saw people's needs, healed them, and freed them from their sins—the better able I am to recognize him in the breaking of the bread at Mass.

2. **Practice gratefulness.** Jesus told his disciples that all good gifts around us come from Heaven above. Our job is to recognize those gifts and thank the Lord.

3. **Look for Jesus during the week in the people that I meet.** Jesus said when we are loving to those who are in need, we are also caring for him. Practice recognizing him in those around you who are in need.

At Mass, Jesus promises to always be truly present to us. Let us respond to that great gift by being present to him as well.

TOM MCGRATH is a writer, an editor, and a spiritual director who thinks the Eucharist is the best part of being Catholic.

What's What?

Write the word or words that best complete each sentence.

1 Pope Innocent III called for the Council of

_____. (PAGE 109)

2 During the council called for by Pope Innocent III, Church leaders accepted

the dogma of _____.
(PAGE 109)

3 Christ makes himself present, Body and

Blood, soul and _____, in the Eucharist. (PAGE 109)

4 When we receive Holy Communion,

we walk in a _____ that symbolizes our lifelong journey to become one with God. (PAGE 110)

5 The word *Eucharist* means

"_____." (PAGE 110)

6 The Eucharist is a memorial of Jesus'

_____ on the cross. (PAGE 111)

7 During the first part of the Mass, God's

_____ is proclaimed to us.
(PAGE 111)

8 To receive the Eucharist, we must be in a

state of _____. (PAGE 111)

9 The _____ of the Blessed Sacrament of the Altar contains images that help us describe the experience of Christ's presence among us in the Eucharist. (PAGE 112)

Say What?

Know the definitions of these terms.

absolution   Precepts of the Church

dogma   Second Vatican Council

mortal sin

Now What?

The Eucharist is the Church's primary prayer of thanksgiving to God for all he has done for us. Besides receiving the Eucharist at Mass, what is one way that you can show God your thanks this week?

_____

_____

_____

_____

_____

_____

_____

_____

_____

_____

_____

_____

_____

_____

_____

_____

_____

Respond

Serving Physical and Spiritual Needs

Think about a unique gift that you have. Maybe you're funny, a good listener, or a skilled babysitter. Now think back to a time when you served someone by using this gift. How did others react when you shared your gift? How did the experience affect you? Did you have to sacrifice anything in order to share your gift with others?

PRAYER

God, thank you for the many gifts you have given us. May we always use these gifts to build up your kingdom.

The Church Preserves

Peasants in the Fields,
Camille Pissarro, pastel, 1890.

The Black Death

Life during the Middle Ages was difficult. Most people were poor. The Roman empire had fallen apart as a result of internal decay and attacks by invading tribes from the east. Available food had little protein and few vitamins and minerals, so people suffered from diseases such as scurvy and rickets. The event that had the most impact on people, however, was the Black Death. Also known as the bubonic plague, the Black Death was a deadly disease that seemed to spread without cause, although we now believe it was spread by fleas on rats. This illness was called the Black Death because on the fourth or fifth day of infection, it caused swollen areas on a person's skin to turn black. Some people died within the first day of infection.

Overall, the Black Death killed nearly one-third of Europe's population—approximately 20 million people. In Paris approximately 800 people died each day. Eventually about half the city's population perished. In Venice two-thirds of the population died, at a rate of 600 people per day. Imagine that a mysterious disease began to infect the people of your town, killing half the residents at a rate of 800 people a day. What kind of panic might take hold? Where would people go for help? In the Middle Ages, people turned to the most educated and caring people they knew—the people of the Church.

Priests and religious sisters responded to this crisis by bravely tending to those who were sick. These caretakers helped provide people with food and clothing, and they buried the dead. They also cared for people's spiritual needs by praying with people, providing Christian burials, and celebrating the sacraments. The Black Death eventually put a strain on the Church because many caretakers died while tending to others.

Our Catholic Character

Just as the Church in the Middle Ages answered the call to provide for the needs of people who were suffering, we are also called to extend God's compassion and mercy to others through the Corporal and the Spiritual Works of Mercy. Through the Corporal Works of Mercy, the Church calls us to care for people's material needs—feed the hungry, shelter the homeless, clothe the naked, visit the sick and imprisoned, bury the dead, and give alms to the poor. Through the Spiritual Works of Mercy, the Church calls us to care for people's emotional and spiritual needs. We are to instruct, advise, console, comfort, forgive, and bear wrongs with patience.

The Avignon Papacy

After the papacy of Innocent III, conditions in the Middle Ages, including the Black Death, caused governments, people, and the Church to struggle. In 1305 the French archbishop of Bordeaux was elected pope, and he took the name Clement V. This new pope was strongly influenced by the French king. In 1309 the pope moved to Avignon, France, as a result of unrest in Rome. Between 1305 and 1377, seven popes lived in Avignon. There were many problems with this arrangement. For example, since the pope is the Bishop of Rome, these popes were not present to serve their people. Within Rome the papacy also had military and financial independence from civil governments like France. The papacy was dependent on France during this time, making it difficult for the Church to act freely.

With the help of Catherine of Siena, the papacy finally returned to Rome. Saint Catherine was a Dominican **mystic** and scholar who wrote many letters of spiritual instruction. She is recognized as a saint and a Doctor of the Church. A woman of great knowledge and persuasion, she met with Pope Gregory XI and convinced him to return to Rome. Pope Gregory XI died soon after, and only 16 cardinals went to Rome to elect the next pope. After riots broke out among the people, who wanted an Italian to be elected pope, the cardinals elected an Italian, Urban VI. But the struggles weren't over. Several months later the cardinals from France declared the election invalid and elected another pope, Clement VII. An argument began over who was really the pope.

Christians were confused, and nations took sides. This time was known as the **Great Schism.** *Schism* means "a division or a split between people." Between 1378 and 1417, two, and sometimes three, men claimed that they were the pope at the same time. Finally a Church council met in Constance and restored the authority of the true pope, and the Great Schism ended in the election of Pope Martin V. Despite its struggles the Church found a way to reconcile itself and continue its mission in the world.

Study Corner

DEFINE
mystic, Great Schism

REMEMBER
During the Middle Ages, the Church served the needs of people who were suffering. At the same time, the Church worked to resolve its own internal struggles.

Past Meets Present

PAST: When the Black Death swept through Siena, Italy, Saint Catherine turned her attention to caring for people who became ill. She bravely worked as a nurse at the hospital of Santa Maria della Scala in Siena. She dug graves for those who had died from the plague, and she helped give them Christian burials. Saint Catherine was spared from the disease and went on to play a crucial role in bringing the papacy back to Rome.

PRESENT: Like Saint Catherine of Siena, individuals who work for Catholic Relief Services (CRS) show care for those suffering from disease throughout the world. The other goals of CRS include responding to major emergencies, easing poverty, and nurturing peaceful and just societies. According to their mission statement, Catholic Relief Services is "motivated by the Gospel of Jesus Christ to cherish, preserve and uphold the sacredness and dignity of all human life, foster charity and justice, and embody Catholic social and moral teaching. . . ."

Explore

The Sacraments at the Service of Communion

THROUGHOUT time, God has called people to serve the Church in unique ways, and he has given them the grace to respond to this call faithfully. How has God called you to serve the Church?

Holy Orders

Since Old Testament times, God called members of the community to serve as priests. Among the Israelites, men from the tribe of Levi offered sacrifice to God on behalf of the people. These priests looked to the example of Melchizedek, a holy and blameless priest during the time of Abraham. While these men offered sacrifice to God, they didn't bring Salvation. Jesus Christ, the High Priest, is the one who won Salvation for all people.

We participate in the priesthood of Christ through our Baptism. The Sacraments of Initiation call us to participate in Jesus' ministry as priests, prophets, and kings by offering acts of kindness and love to others.

Some men are called by God to be sacramental priests and to receive **Holy Orders.** These men are called to serve the Church and to represent Christ in the liturgy. After study and preparation, these men are ordained by a bishop. **Ordination** gives priests the authority that Jesus gave his disciples to celebrate the Eucharist and preach the Gospel. Through the ministry of priests, the Holy Spirit makes Christ present in his Church as head shepherd, high priest, and teacher.

Most parish priests are diocesan priests and serve in a particular diocese. They make promises of celibacy and obedience to their bishop. Priests in religious communities are religious-order priests. These men take vows of poverty, chastity, and obedience, and they often live in community. Religious-order priests

READY for Confirmation

When you are confirmed, a bishop will likely preside over the celebration. He will perform a rite called the laying on of hands, in which he will pray for the outpouring of the Holy Spirit upon you. In this way, the bishop follows in the footsteps of the Apostles, who, after receiving the Holy Spirit on Pentecost, went forth to preach and lay hands on others so that they might receive the Holy Spirit.

serve in ministries related to the purpose for which their order was founded. In the Western Church, priests cannot marry. In the Eastern Church, married men can be ordained as priests, but not as bishops.

To become a priest, a man must first be ordained a **deacon.** Some men choose to become and remain ordained deacons. These men, called permanent deacons, serve as deacons their entire lives and dedicate themselves to serving others. Permanent deacons may be married.

The pope selects some priests to serve as bishops. When a man is ordained a bishop, he receives the fullness of the priesthood. The primary ministry of bishops is teaching and preaching. Bishops are assisted in ministry by priests. Most bishops are responsible for leading a diocese.

The Sacrament of Matrimony

Like Holy Orders, marriage, or the Sacrament of Matrimony, is a **Sacrament at the Service of Communion.** Marriage holds an important place in the Bible. In the Book of Genesis, we read that God created Adam and Eve in his likeness and told them to be fruitful and multiply. From this we understand that God created man and woman for each other. In Matrimony they become one flesh that cannot be broken. The covenant that spouses freely enter into entails faithful love. It imposes on them the obligation to observe the bond of marriage for life.

In the New Testament, we read that Jesus was present at the wedding at Cana. By performing his first miracle at this wedding, Jesus helped his disciples understand that marriage between a man and a woman holds a special place in God's eyes. God calls a man and a woman to a commitment of lifelong love for each other. Their union reflects the love of Christ for his Church.

The Sacrament of Matrimony is a vocation that comes from the Holy Spirit, who calls the couple together. While marriage is a couple's personal commitment to each other, it is also a commitment to build the People of God. During the rite of marriage, a man and a woman are ministers of the sacrament for each other. The priest or deacon serves as a witness for the Church. For a valid marriage to take place, the man and the woman have to want to marry, promise to be faithful for life, and be open to having children. The wedding promises must be made freely and publicly before a witness for the Church.

The Domestic Church

The Church teaches that the regulation of birth is an aspect of responsible parenthood. Even if their reasons are legitimate, however, parents must never rely on immoral means to do so. The Church recognizes the role of the family by calling it the "domestic church." Within the family, parents pass on the faith to their children by treating one another with love and respect, by praying together, and by serving others. What the Church does on a large scale, the domestic church does on a smaller scale.

The Church and Divorce

The Church wants Catholics to receive Holy Communion regularly. Catholics who get divorced and remarry while their divorced spouse is still alive are asked not to receive Holy Communion. In such cases Catholics can apply for an **annulment,** which is a finding by a Church tribunal that on their wedding day, at least some essential element for a sacramental marriage was not present. If the Church declares through an annulment that a sacramental marriage did not exist, these Catholics can remarry and receive Holy Communion.

Catholics who have remarried after a divorce without first receiving an annulment still belong to the Church and can still participate in the life of the Church. In fact the Church wants them to be active members and wants the other members of the Church to accept them as participants in the life of the Church.

Explore

Study Corner

DEFINE

Holy Orders, ordination, deacon, Sacrament at the Service of Communion, annulment

REMEMBER

Through ordination men receive the grace to serve the People of God as deacons, priests, and bishops. In the Sacrament of Matrimony, a man and a woman receive the grace to love each other and to care for their children.

Speak, Lord, Your Servant Is Listening

THE domestic church is the first place where we, as children of God, learn to pray as the larger Church prays.

The Church desires that we learn how to pray constantly and that we persevere in prayer. Daily prayer with our families is the first place where we learn to do so, and it is in our families that we learn that prayer and Christian life are inseparable. The love we experience in conversation with God and the love we have for others is the same love. Prayer helps us come closer to Christ Jesus and love others as he loved us.

Vocation Reflection

Leader: Let us take a moment to reflect on how God is calling us to use our gifts to serve the Church.

Reader: A reading from the First Book of Samuel. (Read aloud 1 Samuel 3:1–9.)

The Word of the Lord.

All: Thanks be to God.

Leader: Let us close with a prayer for vocations.

All:

God, in Baptism you called me by name
    and made me a member of your people,
    the Church.

Help all your people to know their vocation in life,
    and to respond by living a life of holiness.

For your greater glory and for the service of
    your people,
    raise up dedicated and generous leaders
    who will serve as sisters, priests, brothers,
    deacons, and lay ministers.

Send your Spirit to guide and strengthen me
    that I may serve your people
    following the example of your Son, Jesus Christ,
    in whose name I offer this prayer. Amen.

WHERE Do I Fit In ?

We are members of the Church, a community of believers who are called to serve the needs of others. We do this by loving people just as they are, not as we wish them to be. We share with all people the love we have received through Jesus so that others can grow in their relationship with him.

by Jim Balmer

I Am Not Alone

I was a smart, creative kid, but I always felt like an outsider. It seemed like other kids were comfortable in their skin, but I was not. As far back as I can remember, I felt that there was something wrong with me and that I would always be alone.

I was unhappy in high school. I got into trouble and did poorly in class. After I graduated, I made some changes. I began to work harder, but I was still alone. I had been raised without any real faith, and frankly, I was embarrassed to be thought of as religious.

Then I met a couple of Catholic priests at a parish who talked with me and shared with me their love of the Church. The priests were completely welcoming to me, which surprised me in light of my background. Despite being clean and sober for a couple of years, I was still pretty rough, and I was very wary of people. These priests didn't seem afraid of me at all.

One of them suggested that I read the four Gospels. Reluctantly, I went to a local bookstore and bought the smallest New Testament I could find. I was worried someone might see me with it.

I sat down to read the Gospels, and I was amazed. This was not a religion of judgment. Here was a Jesus I had never imagined, eating with tax collectors and hanging around with the lowlifes of society. I began to imagine that if he were here, Jesus might want to have lunch with me. With me!

JIM BALMER is the president of Dawn Farm, an organization that helps addicts and alcoholics find recovery.

Could this be real? I went back to the parish and asked for more help finding this Jesus. They helped me come to know him better, and at the Easter Vigil the following year, I joined the Church.

I have never been alone since. Thirty-four years later, my Catholic community and that accessible Jesus still excite me.

The Life of Jesus

On a separate sheet of paper, write a short biography of Jesus that you could give to someone who knows little about him. Be sure to include the stories about Jesus that you find most welcoming.

What's What?

Circle the letter of the choice that best answers each question.

1 Priests and religious sisters showed care for people who were suffering from what? (PAGE 116)
   a. the Roman Empire
   b. the Avignon Papacy
   c. the Great Schism
   d. the Black Death

2 Who was able to convince the pope to return to Rome from France? (PAGE 117)
   a. Pope Gregory XI
   b. Catherine of Siena
   c. Teresa of Ávila
   d. Thérèse of Lisieux

3 In the Old Testament, we read that men from which tribe offered sacrifice to God on behalf of the Israelites? (PAGE 118)
   a. Levi
   b. Melchizedek
   c. Jesus
   d. Abraham

4 We participate in the priesthood of Christ through what? (PAGE 118)
   a. Matrimony
   b. Holy Orders
   c. our Baptism
   d. Ordination

5 What gives priests the authority that Jesus gave his disciples to celebrate the Eucharist and preach the Gospel? (PAGE 118)
   a. diocese
   b. ordination
   c. the priesthood of believers
   d. the Sacrament of Matrimony

6 Most parish priests are what? (PAGE 118)
   a. religious-order priests
   b. married
   c. diocesan priests
   d. Jesuits

7 Who are the minister(s) during a marriage ceremony? (PAGE 119)
   a. the man and the woman
   b. the priest
   c. both *a* and *b*
   d. neither *a* nor *b*

Say What?

Know the definitions of these terms.

annulment
deacon
Great Schism
Holy Orders
mystic
ordination
Sacrament at the Service of Communion

Now What?

Think of a priest or a married couple whom you admire. Take some time this week to let them know why you admire them. Write the name of the priest or couple here.

_____

_____

Celebrating Lent

LENT, which begins on Ash Wednesday, is the 40-day period during which we prepare for Easter, the greatest feast day of the liturgical year. During Lent, a season of repentance, the Church calls us to reflect on how we can more fully turn our lives over to God so that we can celebrate Easter with joyful hearts.

The process of getting back on the right path is known as conversion, which requires action on our part. We turn over our lives to God by asking for forgiveness and by making amends in order to heal the relationships we have damaged through sin. We need to repent as individuals, and sometimes we need to repent as a community.

There are times in its history when the Church has repented for sins it has committed. In 2000, Pope John Paul II issued an apology for past sins committed by the Church. His act of repentance serves as an example for us. In the same way that the pope did for the Church, we can bring our own transgressions into the healing light of Christ's mercy. To repent for our sins is a response to the experience of God's grace and love.

When we know Christ's love, we want to repent for our sins. Think about a time when you "owned up" to doing something wrong. What drove you toward asking for forgiveness and making amends? How did you feel after you repented?

To repent for our sins is a response to the experience of God's grace and love.

PRAYER

God, help us take the path that leads away from temptation and toward forgiveness, gratitude, and faithfulness to you.

Major Struggles in the Middle Ages

Crusade, etching, 1882.

AFTER the decline of the Roman empire during the Middle Ages, the Church sought to protect Christianity and establish a Christian kingdom in the Holy Land. The Church's efforts were not totally successful, and they led to violence and bloodshed.

The Crusades

Between 1095 and 1291, Christian armies from across Europe fought together to establish a Christian kingdom in Jerusalem. Because the Holy Land is sacred to Jews, Muslims, and Christians, the Crusaders faced fierce opposition. While the Crusaders successfully secured the Holy Land for Christians from 1099 to 1187, their long-term efforts failed. During the Crusades many people on both sides of the battle lost their lives. The Crusaders who survived and returned to their homes brought with them memories of terrible violence that occurred near the sacred places where Jesus walked the earth.

Francis of Assisi and the Sultan

In the middle of the Fifth Crusade, in 1219, Francis of Assisi went to Egypt on a mission to bring the Gospel to Muslims. This was his third attempt to reach out to the Muslim community. His first trip was turned back by a violent storm, and his second trip involved an unsuccessful attempt to speak with the sultan in Morocco.

During a period of truce, Francis and his companion crossed battle lines and requested a meeting with Sultan Al-Kamil. Francis told the Muslims that he and his companion had come as messengers on behalf of the Lord God. The sultan was impressed with Francis's faith and holiness. Francis spent several days with the sultan and other teachers of the Muslim faith. The sultan even allowed him to preach to the Muslim soldiers, which was an unthinkable privilege at the time. Francis and his companion left on friendly terms with the Muslims, and he was greatly distressed when the truce ended and bitter fighting continued between Christians and Muslims.

READY for Confirmation

In Scripture we read that if we acknowledge our sins, God, in his mercy, will forgive us and cleanse us of our wrongdoings. As we prepare to celebrate the Sacrament of Confirmation, the Church encourages us to celebrate the Sacrament of Reconciliation. With our sins forgiven, we can celebrate Confirmation with a happy and joy-filled heart.

It was Francis's great hope that Muslims could be converted to Christianity—not through the sword but through the example of Christians who lived out the values of Jesus Christ.

Acknowledging and Asking

On March 12, 2000, Pope John Paul II established a Day of Pardon and asked forgiveness for the sins that the members of the Church had committed throughout history. Pope John Paul II prayed aloud with Cardinal Joseph Ratzinger, who is now Pope Emeritus XVI.

Cardinal Joseph Ratzinger prayed:

> Let us pray that each one of us,
> looking to the Lord Jesus, meek and humble
>   of heart,
> will recognize that even men of the Church,
> in the name of faith and morals,
> have sometimes used methods
>   not in keeping with the Gospel
> in the solemn duty of defending the truth.

Pope John Paul II prayed:

> Lord, God of all men and women,
> in certain periods of history
> Christians have at times given in to intolerance
> and have not been faithful
>   to the great commandment of love,
> sullying in this way the face of the Church,
>   your Spouse.
> Have mercy on your sinful children
> and accept our resolve
> to seek and promote truth
>   in the gentleness of charity,
> in the firm knowledge that truth
> can prevail only in virtue of truth itself.
> We ask this through Christ our Lord.

This humble act of repentance by our Church leaders can teach us a lot. For example, we can see that it is never too late to ask forgiveness for our sins. In asking forgiveness, Pope John Paul II and Cardinal Ratzinger also demonstrated that all people, even the most highly regarded, should never be too proud to ask for forgiveness.

Study Corner

REMEMBER

In response to past sins committed by Church leaders, contemporary leaders of the Church have modeled repentance by asking for forgiveness.

Explore

Past Meets Present

PAST: After Jesus was baptized by John the Baptist, the Holy Spirit led him into the desert, where he spent the next 40 days fasting and praying. While Jesus was in the desert, he was visited by the Devil, who tempted him three times. Jesus responded to the temptations by saying that God's Word was more important than food and should not be tested.

Jesus visited by the Devil

PRESENT: Mirroring Jesus' time in the desert, we observe the practice of fasting and reflective prayer for the 40 days of Lent. We seek God as Jesus did, and we look to the Holy Spirit to be our steadfast guide. We come out of the desert ready to rejoice at Easter, knowing that Christ leads us to Salvation through his sacrifice.

Lent Past and Present

THE origins of Lent are closely connected with those of Easter. In the early Church, until around A.D. 300, most Christians fasted for two or three days before Easter. Then some places began to extend this fast to the entire week before Easter. In Rome the period of fasting lasted up to three weeks. This three-week period also marked an important time of preparation for catechumens, people who are unbaptized and are undergoing instruction in order to join the Church at Easter through the Sacraments of Initiation.

By the fourth century, Lent was observed for a period of 40 days, echoing Jesus' time in the desert after his baptism and before his public ministry. The number 40 symbolizes a long period of time during which one's faith is tested. An example of this is the 40 days of the Great Flood.

During the Second Vatican Council, the Church's leaders identified practices common in the early Church that we could adopt for our modern era. One such practice was the early Church's use of Lent as a time for catechumens to prepare for Baptism. Since we have been baptized already, the Church suggests that we reflect on our baptismal promises to help us identify areas in our lives in which we may need to turn our minds and hearts back to God.

SACRED ART

In this painting, artist Briton Riviere (1840–1920) uses color to draw attention to Jesus, who is sitting in prayer and reflection during his time in the desert. The contrast of the sunset and Jesus' white garments against the dark landscape mirrors Jesus' struggle with the three temptations presented by the Devil. What ideas come to mind as you look at this painting? What do you think Jesus is praying about?

Christ in the Wilderness,
Briton Riviere, 1898.

This year during Lent, consider using the baptismal promises to help you reflect on how God is calling you to conversion. Make an effort to actively renew the promises in the way you think, live, and pray.

➡️ **Do you renounce Satan?**

➡️ **And all his works?**

➡️ **And all his empty show?**

➡️ **Do you believe in God, the Father almighty, Creator of heaven and earth?**

➡️ **Do you believe in Jesus Christ, his only Son, our Lord, who was born of the Virgin Mary, suffered death and was buried, rose again from the dead, and is seated at the right hand of the Father?**

➡️ **Do you believe in the Holy Spirit, the holy Catholic Church, the communion of saints, the forgiveness of sins, the resurrection of the body, and life everlasting?**

Prayer, Fasting, and Almsgiving

The Church also encourages us to engage in the traditional practices of prayer, fasting, and almsgiving during the season of Lent.

Prayer We are called to spend more time in prayer so that we may grow in our relationship with Christ.

Fasting Catholics age 14 and older abstain from meat on Ash Wednesday and the Fridays of Lent, including Good Friday. Catholics between the ages of 18 and 59 also fast on Ash Wednesday and Good Friday by only eating one large meal and two smaller meals. These practices open our hearts and allow us to stand in **solidarity** with people who are

suffering all over the world. Fasting can also help us in our prayer. As we hunger in our bodies, we are reminded that we also hunger for Christ.

Almsgiving When we give to charity, perform the Works of Mercy, or work to promote justice, we express to God our gratitude for all that he has given to us. We also become living examples of the Gospel message.

Each of us has been tempted to sin. When we choose to give in to **temptation,** or sin, we turn our backs on Christ by thinking, saying, or doing something that goes against his teachings. Through the practices of prayer, fasting, and almsgiving, we receive the strength to refrain from giving into temptation. These practices also cleanse our hearts so we may ask for absolution during the Sacrament of Reconciliation, another important Lenten practice.

RCIA

Lent is an important time for the people in the **Rite of Christian Initiation of Adults** (RCIA), the process through which unbaptized adults join the Church. Throughout the RCIA, catechumens receive instruction in preparation for their initiation into the Church. Lent marks the beginning of the catechumens' final period of preparation. During Lent the catechumens participate in the Rite of Election, during which their sponsors stand as witnesses to their faith, moral character, and desire to join the Church. After the Rite of Election, the catechumens are called the Elect. During the Easter Vigil on Holy Saturday, the Elect profess their faith in Christ and his Church, and they promise to live as Jesus' disciples in the world. Then they are welcomed into the Church through the Sacraments of Initiation.

Study Corner

DEFINE

solidarity, temptation, Rite of Christian Initiation of Adults

REMEMBER

Lent is a time to renew our baptismal promises. Prayer, fasting, and almsgiving are three ways that the Church calls us to celebrate Lent.

Our Catholic Character

On Ash Wednesday we receive ashes on our foreheads as a sign of our call to penance and reconciliation. We take this custom from the Jewish tradition of sprinkling ashes on a person's head as a sign of repentance. The ashes that we use on Ash Wednesday come from burning the palms that were used during Masses on Palm Sunday of the previous year.

A Contrite Heart

DURING Lent it is important for us to celebrate the Sacrament of Reconciliation. When we do so, we confess our sins and ask for God's mercy and forgiveness. Many parishes also offer Lenten prayer services as a way to further enrich our Lenten experience. Through prayer and the sacraments, we are reminded of the healing gift of God's mercy and love.

The Act of Contrition is a traditional prayer in which we acknowledge our sins, ask God for forgiveness, and express our desire to repent. We pray this prayer as part of the Sacrament of Reconciliation, but we can also include it in our daily prayers. When we take this prayer to heart, we invite God's grace into our lives so that we can truly know what it means to have a fresh start.

ACT OF CONTRITION

My God,
I am sorry for my sins with all my heart.
In choosing to do wrong
and failing to do good,
I have sinned against you
whom I should love above all things.
I firmly intend, with your help,
to do penance,
to sin no more,
and to avoid whatever leads me to sin.
Our Savior Jesus Christ
suffered and died for us.
In his name, my God, have mercy. Amen.

WHERE Do I Fit In?

Lent provides time for us to reflect on our lives and the choices we have made. In reflection, we realize that our actions not only have an impact on us, but they also affect our relationships with God and with others.

by David Rizzo

How Am I Healed?

In the eighth grade, my friends and I made fun of John, a boy in our class. There was something about him. For starters he had short hair and always wore a sweater vest. This was the 1970s. Long hair, concert T-shirts, and blue jeans were the unofficial uniform of my generation. John stuck out like a sore thumb. He just didn't fit in at all.

As I grew older, I began to regret the way I had treated John. I couldn't shake the feeling that I had done something wrong. I began to realize that when you treat other people badly, you also hurt yourself. Before long I knew I was in need of healing too.

Healing doesn't come easily. Usually it is a long process that takes time. We need time to reflect on our experiences and come to a deeper understanding of our responsibility to God and to others. This is the kind of thing we think about in Lent. It's a time to sit in silence and experience God's healing power.

The season of Lent allows us to step outside our ordinary lives and immerse ourselves in a sacred time and place where we can deepen our understanding of God. Lent begins on Ash Wednesday. When we receive ashes, the priest says, "Remember that you are dust, and to dust you shall return." This always reminds me of the story in the Bible when God fashions the first human being out of clay and breathes his spirit into him. The Church teaches that our inherent dignity and worth as human beings comes from God, who has made each one of us in his image and likeness.

DAVID RIZZO is the author of *Faith, Family and Children with Special Needs*. Along with his wife, Mercedes, he codeveloped the *Adaptive First Eucharist Preparation Kit*.

It took me years to see that all people, including John, share the same divine image and have an inherent dignity and worth. Thinking about things this way helped me understand why what we did to John was so wrong and why I felt so badly about it. I wish I could run into John again so I could tell him I'm sorry. Lenten experiences like these help to heal us. They help us to feel God's love and become more caring persons as a result.

Turn Toward God

Read Joel 2:12–14. Then, on the lines below, write a prayer to pray throughout Lent that can help you turn your mind and heart to God more fully.

_____

_____

_____

_____

_____

_____

_____

_____

_____

What's What?

For each main idea, write at least one supporting detail.

1 Conversion, the process of getting back on the right path, requires action on our part. (PAGE 123)

_____

_____

_____

2 During the Crusades, Christian armies from across Europe fought together to establish a Christian kingdom in Jerusalem. (PAGE 124)

_____

_____

_____

_____

3 It was Francis of Assisi's hope that Muslims could be converted to Christianity. (PAGE 125)

_____

_____

_____

_____

_____

4 During the Second Vatican Council, the Church's leaders identified practices common in the early Church that we could adopt for our modern era. (PAGE 126)

_____

_____

_____

_____

5 When we sin, we turn our backs on Christ by thinking, saying, or doing something that goes against his teachings. (PAGE 127)

_____

_____

_____

_____

_____

_____

Say What?

Know the definitions of these terms.

Rite of Christian Initiation of Adults

solidarity

temptation

Now What?

Think of one thing that you'd like to repent for this Lenten season. Write a brief prayer asking the Holy Spirit to guide you as you seek to repent. Pray the prayer each day this week and throughout Lent.

_____

_____

_____

_____

_____

_____

_____

_____

_____

_____

_____

Respond

Faith in ACTION

As Christians we experience Christ's presence through Scripture, the Church and its sacraments, and in the community of faith. Through our experience of the risen Christ, we are called to share his peace and love with others by putting our faith into action. When we put our faith into action by serving people in need, we build up God's kingdom.

In this unit we explored the theme of celebrating our faith through the sacraments, the seven signs instituted by Christ and given to the Church in order to help us share in a life of grace. Through the grace we receive in the sacraments, we are strengthened in our desire and ability to share the Gospel message of peace and love. We do this whenever we act in ways that help build up the Kingdom of God.

"If you want peace, work for justice."

—Pope Paul VI

A Thousand Paper Cranes

Purpose

Learn about how one young person's simple act became an international symbol of peace; raise awareness about world peace.

Background

Sadako and the Thousand Paper Cranes by Eleanor Coerr is a true story about a young girl named Sadako Sasaki, who developed leukemia from the effects of radiation caused by the bombing of Hiroshima. While Sadako was sick and in the hospital, her best friend, Chizuko, reminded her of an ancient Japanese story about folding a thousand paper cranes in order to become well again. Sadako died before she finished a thousand cranes. Her classmates published Sadako's writings and collected money from young people across Japan to build a monument in memory of Sadako and all the children killed by the atomic bomb. Both Sadako and the paper cranes are symbols of peace today.

Steps

1. Read *Sadako and the Thousand Paper Cranes.* Familiarize yourself with the context of the story by researching World War II and the effects of the atomic bombs on Hiroshima and Nagasaki in 1945.

2. Learn about the traditional art of paper folding called origami. Find a pattern for making a crane.

3. Make a mobile out of folded paper cranes that can be displayed. Or, if you are really ambitious, make a thousand paper cranes that can be sent to Sadako's memorial in the Hiroshima Peace Park in Japan.

The Peacemakers

Nobel Peace Prize winner
Martin Luther King Jr.

Purpose

Study famous peacemakers; organize a group of peacemakers in your community.

Background

In his last will, Swedish industrialist and inventor Alfred Nobel used his wealth to establish the Nobel Peace Prize. The Prize's purpose is to acknowledge people "who shall have done the most or the best work for fraternity between the nations, for the abolition or reduction of standing armies and for the holding and promotion of peace congresses." Though some laureates, or winners of the prize, are considered controversial figures, many are stellar examples of what it means to be a true peacemaker.

Steps

1. Choose a Nobel Peace Prize laureate. Study him or her and report on what this person has done to contribute to world peace. What can you take from his or her example to apply in your own life?

2. Meet with people who are peacemakers in your community. Find out what the issues are in your community. Ask about ways to promote peace.

3. Start a peacemakers group in your parish, school, or community. Decide together what the group's goals will be. What can you all do to make the world or your community a more peaceful place?

Act

"It isn't enough to talk about peace. One must believe in it. And it isn't enough to believe in it. One must work at it."

—Eleanor Roosevelt, U.N. diplomat and former First Lady of the United States

We Are Called

Saint Angela Merici was born in Italy in 1474. Her parents and sister died when she was a teenager, so she lived with her uncle's family. During this time she had a dream in which she understood that God wanted to use her to establish a community of dedicated young women. It would be many years before she understood how to do this. While at her uncle's home, Angela became a member of the Third Order of Saint Francis. This means that she lived as a lay member of a religious community, and she dedicated her life to prayer and good works. Many women were attracted to her spirit and devotion and joined her in her good works.

How the Saint Relates

Saint Angela Merici was chosen to represent Unit 4 because she answered a call from God and recognized a need to help others. In founding the Ursuline Sisters, Angela created a way for women to dedicate their lives in service to God without living behind monastery walls.

Founding a New Religious Community

In 1516 Angela was asked by the Franciscans to go to Brescia and comfort a woman who had just lost her husband and two sons in the war. While there, she met other lay people who were doing works of charity. She joined them and soon became known for her deep love of God and care for girls and widows.

Above: Schoolgirls and nun at an Ursuline convent and orphanage, Guyana, South America.

To help her better understand the will of God, Angela went on a pilgrimage to the Holy Land in 1524. While on that trip, she was temporarily blinded. Angela did not regain her sight until she returned home. She later said that this experience taught her to see with the eyes of her soul. With renewed vigor, Angela continued to serve all those who needed help.

Twenty-eight women joined Angela in her ministry of Christian service. On November 25, 1535, the vision that Angela had as a teenager finally became a reality. On this date, she formally founded the Order of Saint Ursula, named after a saint to whom Angela had a strong devotion. Angela was elected superior of the order by unanimous vote in 1537. She wrote a Rule and Testament for the sisters and leaders to follow. She encouraged them to treat one another as individuals and to use gentleness over force.

Because women in religious communities of the time could only live in monasteries, Angela is recognized for creating a new way for women to serve God in the Church. Saint Angela Merici, whose feast day is January 27, set an example for later communities of women religious who lived and ministered outside the cloister.

Below: Brescia, Italy

The Protestant Reformation

Think about a time you disagreed with someone in a position of authority. How did you express your disagreement? How did the person respond? How was the disagreement resolved?

PRAYER

God, thank you for the gift of free will. May we always choose to use this gift by living faithful lives.

Disagreement in the Church

Martin Luther

IN the 16th century, Christianity was Europe's primary religion. Christianity shaped how people lived both their public and private lives. A confluence of events, however, led to the Protestant Reformation, a movement that sought to reform the beliefs and practices of the Roman Catholic Church. Some of these reforms are still part of our tradition today.

Printing press

Martin Luther

Martin Luther was an Augustinian friar and Scripture scholar who lived in Germany. After he studied theology and was named a professor, Luther began questioning some of the Church's teachings. On October 31, 1517, he posted 95 theses on the door of a church in Wittenberg, Germany. This practice was a common way for theologians to initiate debate on a topic of interest. Luther had planned to present his ideas on Salvation and the nature of the relationship between faith and works in order to develop Catholic thought.

Our Catholic Character

Have you ever had a lingering feeling of shame, even after you made amends for something you did wrong? When we repent from sin, even though we receive forgiveness from God, we can continue to experience the negative effect that sin has on our relationships with others. This suffering, called temporal punishment, can be lessened through prayer and works of charity. The Church uses the word *indulgence* to refer to the lessening of this temporal punishment.

Luther's arguments resulted in controversy. Through the use of the printing press, then a relatively new invention, Luther's ideas spread rapidly. Within a few weeks, the theses were translated from Latin into German, and approximately 250,000 copies were distributed. Luther soon found himself leading a movement that challenged many of the Church's beliefs and practices.

One of Luther's theses challenged the practice of selling **indulgences,** which is a lessening of the temporal punishment due for sins that have been forgiven. Indulgences move us toward our final purification, after which we will live with God forever in Heaven. Luther felt that by marketing indulgences in a carnival-like atmosphere, Church leaders were distorting their spiritual importance. Luther also believed that Scripture alone is the final authority for Christians. In teaching this, Luther rejected the teaching authority of the Magisterium.

Luther rejected the Church's teachings on the sacraments. He believed that Baptism and the Eucharist are the only two sacraments. Luther denied the doctrine of transubstantiation by teaching that when the celebration of the Mass is over, Christ is no longer present in the bread and wine. In addition, while the Church teaches that faith is necessary for Salvation, it also teaches that faith cannot be separated from good works. Luther taught that faith alone is sufficient for Salvation. Through his ultimate denial of Church teaching, Luther helped found a new branch of Christianity known as Protestantism.

Other Voices Call for Reform

Other voices outside Germany joined Luther's call for reform. John Calvin, who lived in Geneva, Switzerland, developed the concepts that came to be known as Calvinism. Calvin's overall view was that as a result of our fallen nature, people are incapable of following God or being saved. Instead, Calvin taught that God has chosen those whom he will save through his mercy, as well as those from whom he will withhold his mercy. This doctrine, which departs from Luther's teaching, is sometimes called "double-predestination," and states that some humans, called the elect, are created for Heaven, while other humans, called reprobates, are created to die unredeemed and will therefore go to Hell.

Calvin also rejected the theology of the Real Presence. He taught, instead, that the words of consecration do not transform the bread and wine into Jesus Christ's Body and Blood. The words simply recall what Jesus said at the Last Supper. Calvin did accept Luther's teaching that Scripture alone is the final source of authority for Christians.

To spread his teachings, Calvin established schools, including the University of Geneva. His followers brought his message to France, the Netherlands, Germany, and Scotland.

The Reformation also spread to England where the Church was challenged by King Henry VIII, who wanted to divorce his wife, Queen Catherine of Aragon. The Church forbade divorce, so Henry VIII rebelled and established the Church of England, making himself its head. As the leader of the Church of England, Henry VIII gave himself permission to divorce Catherine of Aragon.

As groups continued to break away from the Roman Catholic Church, new Protestant denominations formed, including Lutheran, Anabaptist, Presbyterian, Anglican, and Puritan.

Explore

Past Meets Present

PAST: The Protestant Reformation had an impact on the arts in a variety of ways. For example, many medieval artworks were destroyed by Reformers because they were inspired by Roman Catholic teachings. The new art that developed became more secular and focused on daily life rather than religious or scriptural themes. Artists who were interested in Catholic religious themes often had to leave their homelands to find work.

PRESENT: Today's Church understands the importance of preserving artworks so that later generations can view and be inspired by them. Inside Vatican City, the Vatican Museums house an enormous collection of religious art in 54 separate galleries. Rooms I through XIII feature treasured artworks dating from the 12th to the 16th centuries. More than four million visitors see these artworks every year.

Study Corner

DEFINE

indulgences

REMEMBER

The Protestant Reformation was a movement that began as an effort to reform the beliefs and practices of the Roman Catholic Church. Instead it resulted in a split in Christianity. Martin Luther and John Calvin were two prominent Reformers.

God's Gift of Salvation

ONE of Luther's major disagreements with Church teaching centered on Salvation. Our Catholic understanding of this gift is rooted in Scripture.

In the Creation story in the Book of Genesis, Adam and Eve first lived in peace. Eventually, they gave in to temptation and disobeyed God's will. Consequently, the human family is born into Original Sin and suffers the loss of Paradise, the pain of division, and the effects of sin. These divisions, such as murder, slavery, and poverty, are not something that God plans. They are the result of human sinfulness.

When Adam and Eve turned away from God, he did not turn away from them. Instead, God promised that he would send a Savior to forgive sins and restore humans' relationship with him. Jesus is the fulfillment of that promise. Through the Paschal Mystery—his life, Death, Resurrection, and Ascension into Heaven—Jesus Christ offers to all the gift of Salvation.

In reflecting on what human beings need to do in order to earn the gift of Salvation, Luther concluded that faith alone is a sufficient response to this gift. Luther's opinion was in sharp contrast to the Church's teaching that both faith and

Adam and Eve, stained glass.

SACRED ART

The artwork *God Gives* reminds us that God invites everyone to the table and abundantly gives us everything we need. One gift that God shares with us is grace, the gift of God's own self. We believe that grace is the Holy Spirit alive in us. There are two types of grace. **Actual grace** is the freely given gift of God that unites us with the life of the Trinity. This type of grace helps us make choices according to God's will. **Sanctifying grace,** sometimes called habitual grace, is the gift of God that is given to us without our earning it. This type of grace is imparted to us through the sacraments and produces in us a permanent condition in which we are pleasing to God. This kind of grace refers to our God-given inclination and capacity for good.

God Gives, Paula Wiggins.

Study Corner

DEFINE

actual grace, sanctifying grace, free will, particular judgment, Purgatory, Last Judgment

REMEMBER

Jesus Christ is the fulfillment of God's promise of Salvation. We receive the gift of Salvation through faith and good works.

good works are necessary to receive the Salvation offered by God. The basis for the Church's teaching is underscored in the New Testament Letter of Saint James.

> Was not Abraham our father justified by works when he offered his son Isaac upon the altar? You see that faith was active along with his works, and faith was completed by the works. Thus the scripture was fulfilled that says, "Abraham believed God, and it was credited to him as righteousness," and he was called "the friend of God." See how a person is justified by works and not by faith alone. For just as a body without spirit is dead, so also faith without works is dead.
>
> *James 2:21–24,26*

We receive the gift of Salvation through our faith in Jesus and by doing good works that share his peace and love with others. While God desires that all people have faith, he does not force us to believe. God has given us the gift of **free will,** which gives us the ability to choose whether to respond to the gift of Salvation by professing our belief in Christ and his Church and by doing works that bear the fruit of this faith.

Particular Judgment and Purgatory

In the New Testament, Saint Paul rejected the idea that death is the end of everything and that once people die, their lives are over, and no part of them will ever exist again. The Catholic Church accepts Paul's teaching that God has given each of us one body, one soul, and one life to live on earth. This one life is our chance to live as Jesus did. How we live this life determines how we will spend all eternity.

The Church teaches us that at the time of our death, we will be judged based on how willing we were to accept God's grace and how faithful we were to following Jesus. This is called the **particular judgment.** The souls of those who have lived in the grace of Christ will immediately go to Heaven. To us, living in Heaven is "to be with Christ," which is a fulfillment of our deepest longings. At their particular judgement, those who have rejected Christ will live eternally separated from God and his love.

There are many who, although saved in Christ, are not ready to enter into God's presence in Heaven. These souls experience **Purgatory,** a process of purification—a kind of fine-tuning of the soul—before they enter Heaven. Because we are members of the Communion of Saints, our prayers can help the souls in Purgatory on their journey toward God.

Last Judgment

At the end of time, Jesus Christ will come again in glory to bring the Kingdom of God to its fullness. At this **Last Judgment,** everyone will come before Christ to account for all the good he or she has done or failed to do. The just will reign with Christ, glorified in body and soul, and the whole material world will be transformed.

Our Final Goal

After his Crucifixion, Jesus—who is both human and divine—descended into the realm of the dead. Through his Resurrection, Christ opened Heaven's gates for all those who died before him.

Jesus taught us in Scripture that the final goal of human life is to live in Heaven with God the Father; Christ Jesus, his Son; and the Holy Spirit. In Heaven we will know God in an intimate way. Our hopes will be fulfilled, and our happiness will be realized. If, during our lives, we choose to turn away from God and live in mortal sin, we risk not being united with God in Heaven. At the same time, we believe in God's mercy and love. We know that God allows us to ask forgiveness, do penance, and start fresh so that we can live as true followers of Christ and be with him for all eternity.

God's Invitation

ORIGINALLY

written as hymns to be sung, the psalms include songs of lamentation, sorrow, praise, and thanksgiving. The psalms also mirror God's marvelous deeds in the history of his people.

Psalm-based hymns became popular during the Reformation. Many composers, such as William Byrd, wrote hymns for people to use in worship.

Today the psalms are some of the most widely used prayers of the Church, both for communal prayer and for individual reflection. For example, we pray a Responsorial Psalm at every Mass. The psalms are also at the heart of the Liturgy of the Hours, a form of public prayer in which the Church praises God and sanctifies the day.

A Psalm Prayer

I thank you, Lord, with all my heart;
   in the presence of the angels to you I sing.

Sometimes we feel overwhelmed by life. We get absorbed in ourselves and our relationships suffer. Then we remember God's invitation to be still. We realize that we are always in God's presence.

Though I walk in the midst of dangers,
   you guard my life when my enemies rage.
You stretch out your hand;
   your right hand saves me.

Sometimes we have questions that don't seem to have any answers. Why does the world seem to be full of suffering? Is there anything I can do to make a difference? When we accept God's invitation to stillness, we remember that God has the answers.

On the day I cried out, you answered;
   you strengthened my spirit.

Sometimes we define ourselves by what we do rather than who we are. We lose sight of who we are deep down inside—God's cherished one. To keep that knowledge alive, we need to accept God's invitation to sit still with him. When we pay attention, God's voice grows more and more familiar to us.

The LORD is with me to the end.
   LORD, your mercy endures for ever.
   Never forsake the work of your hands!

Psalm 138:1,3,7,8

Share with God whatever is in your heart. Then be silent and allow him to speak to you. Thank God for calling you into existence and for his great love for you.

WHERE Do I Fit In?

While Salvation is a total gift from God that we receive through Jesus' Paschal Mystery, author James Campbell reminds us that through the choices we make, we have the option whether or not to accept this gift and participate in God's plan of Salvation.

by James Campbell

Choose Life

In Deuteronomy 30:15–20, Moses presents the Hebrew people with a choice. This is Moses's last will and testament to the people. It is the time when the people are preparing to enter the Promised Land. Moses will not be crossing with them, so he is giving them a final instruction.

Moses reminds the people of all that God has done for them. He has brought them out of Egypt, through the Red Sea, across the desert of Sinai. It has not been an easy road; there have been times of rebellion. But through Moses's intercession, God has kept the people under his protection.

Now they face the future, and Moses tells them they are at a crossroads in their faith. They can choose not to follow God and be destroyed, or they can follow God and live. Moses tells them, "Choose life, then, that you and your descendants may live." (Deuteronomy 30:19)

Each day we are presented with choices that can lead us either to Salvation or to turn away from God. Each day we are called to reflect on our own history of the grace that we have been given through the sacraments and that lead us to life. Now is the time and the hour to choose life.

It's Your Choice

Think about an important choice you've made during the past week. What options did you have, and what might have been the consequence of choosing each option? Why did you choose the option you did? On the lines below, write a prayer that can help you participate in God's plan of Salvation by making good choices.

_____

_____

_____

_____

_____

_____

_____

_____

_____

_____

_____

_____

JAMES CAMPBELL is the author of *The Stories of the Old Testament: A Catholic's Guide.*

What's What?

Review concepts from this lesson by using the clues to complete the crossword puzzle.

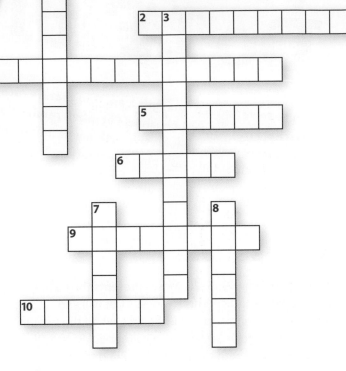

ACROSS

2 Martin Luther believed that _____ alone is the final authority for Christians. (PAGE 136)

4 Luther founded a branch of Christianity known as _____. (PAGE 137)

5 Nailing theses on the door of the local church was a way for theologians to initiate _____ on a topic of interest. (PAGE 136)

6 The Church believes that faith and good _____ are necessary for Salvation. (PAGE 137)

9 As a result of Adam and Eve's choice to turn away from God, humans are born into _____ Sin. (PAGE 138)

10 The _____ mirror God's marvelous deeds in the history of his people. (PAGE 140)

DOWN

1 Martin Luther taught that faith alone is sufficient for _____. (PAGE 137)

3 John Calvin taught that the words of _____ do not transform the bread and wine into Jesus Christ's Body and Blood. (PAGE 137)

7 Angela Merici decided to name the religious community she founded after Saint _____, a saint to whom she had great devotion. (PAGE 134)

8 In response to Adam and Eve's choice to give in to Satan's temptation, God promised that he would send a _____ to save humanity. (PAGE 138)

Say What?

Know the definitions of these terms.

actual grace   particular judgment

free will   Purgatory

indulgences   sanctifying grace

Last Judgment

Now What?

The Church teaches that faith and good works are necessary to receive the gift of Salvation promised by God. What is one work you can do for others this week?

_____

_____

_____

Respond

Renewal in the Church

Think of a time you purposely broke a rule and what the consequences were for making that choice. What role did your conscience play in helping you decide to break the rule? How did your choice affect your relationship with others and with God? How did you make amends for the impact that your choice had on others?

PRAYER

Jesus, thank you for the gift of forgiveness that we receive through the Sacrament of Reconciliation. Help us respond to your gift of Salvation by making good moral choices.

The Bishops Respond

THE Church took seriously the challenges it faced during the Protestant Reformation. From the early 1500s to the mid-1600s, the Church listened to the feedback it was getting and renewed itself by acting upon the call to repent and reform.

This period in history is often called the Counter-Reformation. Think about your own life. How can receiving feedback from other people help us better respond to God's call to serve others?

The Council of Trent

One of the Catholic Church's responses to the challenges of the Protestant Reformation was to convene the Council of Trent, which was held between 1545 and 1563. During this time, Catholic bishops met to offer a collective response to the Protestant Reformation and to determine the steps necessary to renew the Catholic Church.

Saint François de Sales and Saint Jeanne de Chantal, Noël Hallé, oil on canvas.

Teaching the Faith

The *Catechism of the Catholic Church* often helps catechumens in the Rite of Christian Initiation of Adults (RCIA) prepare to enter the Church. Take a moment to reflect on the Church's teachings. Which teachings are essential to pass on to those who want to become Catholic? Write one idea on the lines below and explain why this teaching is important.

_____

_____

_____

_____

_____

... the Council affirmed the Church's teachings on transubstantiation, the Real Presence, and the seven sacraments.

In response to the claims made by Reformers, the Council affirmed the Church's teachings on transubstantiation, the Real Presence, and the seven sacraments. The Council also affirmed that both faith and good works are necessary for Salvation. The bishops clarified the Catholic understanding of Scripture and stated that the Bible must be read within the context of the living teaching of the Church, thereby reaffirming the importance of both Scripture and the Church's Tradition.

In the area of Church practices, the bishops took steps to end abuses, such as the sale of indulgences. Practices around proper devotion to Mary and the saints were also defined and established. The Council affirmed the concept of an ordained priesthood and required that each diocese establish a **seminary,** or school for the proper formation of priests. With this widened focus on forming clergy, there soon were more Catholics preaching and teaching.

Underscoring the importance of the sacraments, the bishops at the Council of Trent encouraged Catholics to receive Holy Communion at least once a week and to receive forgiveness of sins often through the Sacrament of Reconciliation.

The teachings of the Council of Trent inspired the founding of new religious communities, which opened doors for devout Catholics, such as Saint Francis de Sales and Saint Jeanne (Jane) de Chantal, to serve the needs of others. As a result of the Church's response to the Reformers, two-thirds of the Christians in Europe remained Catholic. The work and teachings of the Council of Trent formed and renewed the Church, continuing to guide it into the 20th century.

John Calvin

Past Meets Present

PAST: Martin Luther and John Calvin challenged the Church's teachings and its practices. The Church addressed these challenges at the Council of Trent. The teachings of this council were summarized in the *Catechism of the Council of Trent*. A **catechism** is a collection or summary of the Church's religious teachings. The decisions made at Trent became the foundation for Catholic teaching for the next 400 years.

PRESENT: In 1985 the Church's bishops proposed that a new catechism be written. Their hope was that the new catechism would be a more complete, accurate, and contemporary synthesis of the Catholic faith. Pope John Paul II approved the revised edition of the *Catechism of the Catholic Church* in 1997. When he did so, the pope pointed out that the *Catechism of the Catholic Church* is a collection of the Church's teachings on faith and morals. Through it, the pope noted, people all over the world can know what the Church teaches, celebrates, lives, and prays.

Explore

Study Corner

DEFINE

seminary, catechism

REMEMBER

Through the Council of Trent, the Church responded to the concerns that were raised by the Protestant Reformers by reaffirming the Church's teachings on Scripture, Tradition, and the sacraments.

Sin and Forgiveness

THE Greek word for *sin* means "to miss the mark." When we sin, we hurt others by refusing to follow God's commandments. The choice to sin, or to turn away from God, harms our relationship with God and with others. Thankfully, the Church offers a path to forgiveness through the Sacrament of Reconciliation. The priest to whom we confess our sins in this sacrament can never repeat them to anyone. This is called the "seal of the confessional" or "the sacramental seal." How has the Sacrament of Reconciliation helped you grow in your relationship with God?

When we sin, God calls us to repent and seek forgiveness through the grace of the Holy Spirit. In addition, the Holy Spirit gives us the resolve to make better choices and strengthens us against future temptation.

Types of Sin

Sometimes a person chooses to turn away from God totally and completely by doing something that is seriously wrong. Such an action is a mortal sin. To commit a mortal sin, the action must be a serious offense, the person must know that the action is a serious offense, and the person must freely choose to commit the offense. When someone commits a mortal sin, the Holy Spirit calls the person to contrition. After committing a mortal sin, a person must celebrate the Sacrament of Reconciliation in order to reconcile his or her relationship with God and with others. A person who is in a state of mortal sin is not to receive Holy Communion.

Sometimes people make less serious choices to turn away from God. Such a decision is a **venial sin.** These sins weaken our relationship with God and with others. They can also lead to mortal sins. A person who has committed a venial sin can receive Holy Communion, which forgives venial sins and strengthens us against

Our Catholic Character

The Church has identified certain sins as Capital Sins. These include behaviors that can lead to serious sinful actions. The capital sins are lust (an inordinate craving for bodily pleasure), greed (the desire for material goods or money simply for the sake of having them), envy (a desire for what others have simply because they have it and we don't), gluttony (eating and drinking in excess), sloth (being careless about our spiritual development), pride (having a false image of ourselves that goes beyond what we deserve as God's creation), and anger (uncontrolled feelings of hatred or wrath). The Church teaches that baptized people combat these sins through good will, humility, and trust in God.

the temptation to sin. While the Church does not require us to do so, we are encouraged to receive forgiveness for venial sins through the Sacrament of Reconciliation.

Mortal and venial sins are types of **personal sin.** They are the result of our personal choice to turn away from God. **Social sin,** another type of sin, is an accumulation of personal sins. These sins undermine human dignity, because they perpetuate cultural structures, such as racism and sexism, that allow sinful practices to continue.

The Ten Commandments

The **Ten Commandments** are the ten rules presented by God to Moses at Mount Sinai. They sum up God's law and teach us what is required to love God and our neighbors. The Fourth Commandment instructs us to honor our mother and our father. It is in our families that we first learn how to live moral lives. From our parents and teachers, we learn habits that help us turn toward God and away from evil. These habits include prayer, worship, and the virtues.

The true spirit of the Fourth Commandment teaches us to respect people in positions of authority. We are called to develop relationships with people who will help us in our journey of faith. By developing these relationships, we surround ourselves with people who will help us make good decisions and focus our minds and hearts on God's will for us.

Explore

The Beatitudes

In the Sermon on the Mount, Jesus gave us the Beatitudes, which are instructions for how to live in God's kingdom. In the Beatitudes, Jesus teaches us that disciples are called to live lives of love and humility.

Precepts of the Church

The Precepts of the Church outline the basics of what we are called to do in prayer and in living a moral life. The Church developed the Precepts to help us maintain self-discipline and foster our spiritual development. The Precepts are to attend Mass on Sundays and Holy Days of Obligation, confess serious sins at least once per year, receive Holy Communion at least once a year during the Easter season, observe the days of fast and abstinence, and provide for the needs of the Church.

READY for Confirmation

The Sacrament of Confirmation, which strengthens the grace we receive in the Sacrament of Baptism, is one of the Sacraments of Initiation. As fully initiated members of the community, we have both rights and responsibilities. We have the right to rely on the Church, its teaching, and its members—the People of God—to support us on our journey of faith. We also have the responsibility to support others in their journey. We can do this by modeling a life of discipleship, by choosing to make good moral choices, by praying for others, and by practicing the Works of Mercy.

Restoring Relationships

In the Lord's Prayer, we pray "And forgive us our trespasses, as we forgive those who trespass against us." In this petition we acknowledge that an essential aspect of prayer is to admit that we are sinners.

When we pray the Lord's Prayer, we acknowledge that God's mercy can penetrate our heart only when we are merciful toward others and forgive those who have hurt us. It is not always easy to forgive, but with the help of the Holy Spirit, we can open our hearts to the compassionate love of God.

Forgiveness Reflection

Leader: In the name of the Father, and of the Son, and of the Holy Spirit. Amen.

All: Loving God, we come before you in praise and thanksgiving and ask for your help to see ourselves as you see us. May the Holy Spirit guide our reflection and lead us on the path of reconciliation with you and with one another. We ask this through Christ our Lord. Amen.

Leader: Silently give thanks to God for all the blessings we have received. Ask for God's help to remember the ways we have damaged our relationships with others.

Reader: A reading from the holy Gospel according to Matthew.

Therefore, if you bring your gift to the altar, and there recall that your brother has anything against you, leave your gift there at the altar, go first and be reconciled with your brother, and then come and offer your gift.

Matthew 5:23–24

The Gospel of the Lord.

All: Praise to you, Lord Jesus Christ.

Leader: In light of the Word of God, let's spend a few minutes reflecting on our relationships. Listen to a series of questions that will be read. Silently answer them for yourself.

Leader: The LORD bless you and keep you!
The LORD let his face shine upon you,
and be gracious to you!
The LORD look upon you kindly and
give you peace!

Numbers 6:24–26

All: Amen.

WHERE Do I Fit In?

We often face difficult decisions in our lives. As members of the Church, we are called to develop our conscience so that when we follow our heart, we follow in Jesus' footsteps.

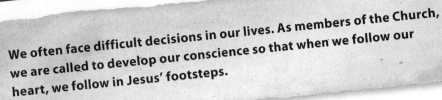

by Chris Lowney

Decisions: Whom Do I Serve?

When I was about your age, my family was not poor, but we did not have lots of money either. And I used to imagine that money could solve every problem in life. If I had lots of money, I could buy whatever toys I wanted, the biggest and best television, and so on.

When I became an adult, I was lucky enough to get a job that paid a good salary, and, over the years, I had a good deal of money. I would not call myself rich, but I had more money than most people, more money than I needed to support myself. And, for sure, money can solve a lot of problems. If I need to pay a doctor or repair a leak in my house, I have the money for those things.

But when you have more money than you need, you also have choices to make. Is it OK for me to buy a brand new cell phone if my old one still works? Is it OK for me to buy the fastest and most expensive car I can find if a child in Africa does not have enough money to pay tuition to go to school? As a Catholic I find that I have to make choices about money all the time. It's natural for a human being to want to have fun and to have whatever things my neighbors have. But my faith teaches me that I'm not supposed to live only for myself and not to make myself the center of the whole world. Instead, I'm also concerned with the needs of the rest of the human family. And the way I interpret that it means that I shouldn't try to have

too many luxurious things for myself if some of my brothers and sisters don't even have the basic things they need in life.

So every time I have extra money, I have a choice to make about how to use it.

Making Decisions

Think about some of the resources you have, such as your time and your talents. On the lines below, write two or three questions you can ask yourself when you are faced with a decision about how to use your resources.

_____
_____
_____
_____
_____
_____
_____
_____
_____

CHRIS LOWNEY is the author of *Heroic Leadership: Best Practices from a 450-Year-Old Company that Changed the World.*

What's What?

Complete each sentence by choosing the correct answer.

1 One of the Church's responses to the challenge of Protestant Reformation was the _____. (PAGE 144–145)

a. Reformation

b. Council of Trent

c. Council of Transubstantiation

d. Real Presence

2 The bishops who met between 1545 and 1563 affirmed the Church's teachings on a variety of issues including _____. (PAGE 145)

a. mortal sin

b. venial sin

c. transubstantiation

d. the catechism

3 When he approved the *Catechism of the Catholic Church*, Pope John Paul II noted that through it, people all over the world can know what the Church _____. (PAGE 145)

a. celebrates

b. forgives

c. repents

d. reflects on

4 The Greek word for *sin* means "_____." (PAGE 146)

a. to refuse to follow God's commandments

b. to harm our relationship with God and with one another

c. to do something we regret

d. to miss the mark

5 When we are slothful, we _____. (PAGE 146)

a. are careless about our spiritual development

b. want what we don't have simply for the sake of having it

c. have a false image of ourselves

d. have uncontrolled feelings of anger

6 In the Sermon on the Mount, Jesus gave us the _____, which are instructions for how to live in God's kingdom. (PAGE 147)

a. Lord's Prayer

b. Ten Commandments

c. Nicene Creed

d. Beatitudes

7 The true spirit of the Fourth Commandment teaches us to _____. (PAGE 147)

a. learn habits that help us turn toward God and away from evil

b. respect people in positions of authority

c. model a life of discipleship, making good moral choices, and praying for others

d. honor only our mother and our father

Say What?

Know the definitions of these terms.

catechism   social sin

personal sin   Ten Commandments

seminary   venial sin

Now What?

We can turn to others for support in living free from sin. To whom can you turn during the next week when you are faced with the temptation to turn away from God?

_____

_____

Respond

The Church Reaches Out

Think about a time you experienced a wonderful surprise. What was good about the experience? What feelings come to mind when you think back on it? Did the experience change your life in any way? If so, how?

PRAYER

God, thank you for the many ways you reveal yourself to us. May we strive to find your presence in the world around us, and may our words and actions reveal your presence to others.

Ignatius of Loyola

Saint Ignatius of Loyola, Peter Paul Rubens.

THE years after the Council of Trent, which the Church called in response to the challenges of the Reformation, brought about renewed theological scholarship, moral betterment, and spiritual growth. Ignatius of Loyola contributed to this renewal in many ways. Like Ignatius, when we follow God's plan for us, we can contribute to the Church in important ways.

A Journey to Faith

Ignatius of Loyola was born in 1491 to a noble family living in Spain. As a young soldier, his life was full of adventure and excitement. He spent time in the palaces of dukes and princes. Ignatius of Loyola believed in God, but he didn't pay too much attention to his faith. He did little more than attend Mass and pray his prayers. In his free time, he used his talents for his own glory and pleasure and not much else. He frequently engaged in activities that were less than admirable.

During one battle, Ignatius was seriously wounded. One of his legs was crushed, and his other leg was badly broken. Ignatius was sent home to recover. While he was at home, Ignatius read whatever he could find, which wasn't much. One book that he read was about Jesus' life, and another book was about the lives of the saints. During his recovery Ignatius began praying very seriously. God's peace filled his heart and assured him that he was on the right path. This experience marked the beginning of Ignatius's conversion.

When Ignatius was well enough to travel, he went to a Benedictine monastery in Montserrat, Spain, where he spent several days in prayer. He then went to Manresa, where he moved into a cave and lived a life of **asceticism,** or self-denial, in order to develop spiritual discipline. During the 10 months Ignatius lived in the cave, he gradually discovered for himself that God totally accepts, loves, and forgives each one of us. After this discovery, Ignatius finally felt ready to reenter society. He wanted to serve others by helping them recognize the presence of God in their lives.

The Jesuits

After his time at Manresa, Ignatius moved to Paris and enrolled in the university there. He wanted to be able to teach in the Church. It was while he was at the University of Paris that Ignatius met the six other men who became his closest friends.

Together, Ignatius and his six friends studied, preached the Gospel, and offered spiritual direction. The men soon decided to form a new religious community, the Society of Jesus. In 1540 they received the blessing of Pope Paul III. The members of the community, commonly known as Jesuits, offered their service to the pope for whatever he wanted of them. In responding to the needs of the day, some of the first Jesuits became teachers in schools and universities, and other Jesuits became missionaries.

Eventually, Ignatius of Loyola and his followers were ordained priests and professed the evangelical counsels of poverty, chastity, and obedience. Unlike the members of most other religious communities of their time, they did not wear a religious habit.

Ignatian Spirituality

All religious communities have their own spirit, or charism, which directs how they preach the Gospel message. While all religious communities have much in common, their individual charisms demonstrate the diversity of the Church in its response to live out Jesus' mission of love and service.

Guided by their charism, the Jesuits strive to help people find God in all things. They do this in many ways, including offering retreats known as the **Spiritual Exercises.** The seeds of the Spiritual Exercises were first sown by Ignatius during his time in Manresa. The Spiritual Exercises include prayers, meditations, reflections, and directions that are led by a spiritual director. Today many people pray by using the Spiritual Exercises.

Part of the Spiritual Exercises is the Daily Examen, in which people are invited to reflect on their day and recognize God's presence in their experiences. The goal of this prayer is to help people develop their relationship with Jesus Christ. The Daily Examen, the Spiritual Exercises, and Ignatian spirituality are gifts to the entire Church.

> **Guided by their charism, the Jesuits strive to help people find God in all things.**

Caring for God's Creation

IGNATIUS of Loyola knew that our awareness of God's presence in the world around us awakens within us an appreciation for the sacredness of all creation. As Jesus' followers, this awareness influences our relationships with others. How might your awareness of God's presence in your life have an impact on your relationships with other people?

The Fifth Commandment

As we grow in our ability to discover God's presence in our lives, we grow in our desire to follow the Fifth Commandment—You shall not kill—which teaches us to respect all life. The Fifth Commandment reminds us that every person has dignity as a human being who is created in God's image and likeness. The Fifth Commandment means more than not taking life; it also means protecting and defending life.

The Fifth Commandment does not prohibit legitimate authorities from safeguarding societies against unjust aggressors. In the *Catechism of the Catholic Church*, however, we read that the use of nonlethal means of protecting people's safety are preferred. Nonlethal means "are more in keeping with the concrete conditions of the common good and more in conformity with the dignity of the human person." (*CCC* 2267)

The Church teaches that some actions are objectively wrong. These actions are moral evils that violate God's **moral law.** We can never choose to engage in moral evils, even if good might result. In addition, the Church has a long history of protecting life, from conception to natural death. The Church has long opposed **abortion, euthanasia,** the practice of child labor, sexual exploitation of human beings, and the use of children as soldiers. The Church also calls for adequate food, health care, and education for all people. Furthermore, the Church instructs us that we must do everything we can to avoid war and safeguard peace.

The Sixth and Ninth Commandments

Our awareness of God's presence in the world also influences our attitudes toward the relationships we have with one another. One way to develop positive relationships is to follow the Sixth and Ninth Commandments, which call us to remain chaste and to respect other people's commitments.

The Sixth Commandment teaches us that we should not commit **adultery,** which is a sin of unfaithfulness. Adultery is an attack on the dignity of marriage, which is a holy union, blessed by God and based on the faithful love between a husband and a wife. We follow the Sixth Commandment by remaining chaste. In its fullest sense, **chastity**

is about having a healthy attitude toward sex and being a sexual person in a responsible way. Chastity also means that sexual relationships can only take place within the context of marriage. For a married couple, chastity means having a joyful sexual life with each other and avoiding anything that might endanger the marriage. Chastity for unmarried people means refraining from sexual activity.

Chastity helps us recognize the boundaries that will help us live in Christian relationships with others. This virtue guides us to connect sexual activity with the lifetime commitment of a husband and a wife in marriage. It teaches us that sex is the total giving of oneself to another. That kind of giving cannot take place outside of marriage. Unmarried people who want to be chaste do not engage in sex with others. They do not dishonor their bodies through masturbation. Their respect for their own bodies and for the bodies of others is total.

The Church recognizes that some people are homosexual (sexually attracted to people of the same gender) and teaches that people with a homosexual orientation should be accepted with respect, compassion, and sensitivity. Homosexuals are invited and encouraged to participate in the life of the Church, and, like all people, they are called to recognize that engaging in sex outside of the Sacrament of Matrimony is wrong.

The Ninth Commandment is "You shall not **covet** your neighbor's wife." The word *covet* is difficult for many people to understand. It means "to wish for enviously or to greedily want something belonging to another." We covet when someone else has something that we want for ourselves. There is nothing wrong with wanting something. What is wrong is to want someone else's possessions so badly that it becomes an obsession. The Ninth Commandment teaches married couples to avoid the road that might lead to adultery. In other words, the Ninth Commandments encourages us to create an environment that helps us practice virtue by selecting books, magazines, movies, music, TV shows, and Web sites that show respect and restraint. It also means dressing so that others can see that we respect ourselves and our body.

Our Catholic Character

Covet is a word that you probably don't often use. Most likely, the word *detachment* does not rank high in the words that you hear every day, either. But the word *detachment* and the idea behind it has always been part of Christian spirituality. When religious men and women take a vow of poverty, they promise to practice detachment. In this context, *detachment* means freedom from the possession of objects—particularly material objects—that might hinder spiritual growth. These religious men and women do so as a reminder that we are all called to live in a spirit of poverty and detachment. By practicing detachment, we overcome the temptation to covet someone else's possessions. Detachment frees us to recognize that only God can bring us true fulfillment. Detachment is the freedom of the poor in spirit, which Jesus spoke of in the first beatitude.

Explore

Study Corner

DEFINE

moral law, abortion, euthanasia, adultery, chastity, covet

REMEMBER

When we are able to see God in the world around us, we have a desire to respect life, relationships, the dignity of others, and the goodness of everything that God has created.

God's Fingerprints

One form of prayer,

the Daily Examen, is an important part of Ignatian spirituality. In the Examen we prayerfully review our day so that we can grow in self-understanding. Being more self-aware frees us to follow God's will for us. Praying the Daily Examen can help us become more aware of God's action in our lives and his presence in the world around us.

Here are the basic steps for praying the Daily Examen. Begin by being aware of all the blessings you have received from God through the events of the day and the people with whom you spent time. Then ask the Holy Spirit to help you know when you might have turned away from God's presence during the day. Review your thoughts, words, and actions since the day began. Think about what brought you closer to God and what led you away from him. Ask God's pardon for any time that you failed to love. Finally, resolve to respond more completely to the generous love of God. End with the Lord's Prayer.

Finding God in All Things

Quiet yourself and remember that you are in God's presence. In your mind, reflect on your day. What good things have come your way? Be specific. Remember the small things, like a smile, a kind word, a blue sky, or your favorite food. Remember the bigger things, too, like passing a test or scoring in a game.

Share with God how grateful you are for all the blessings that you have received.

Before you move deeper into prayer, pause and pray to the Holy Spirit. You may simply want to ask for the help to see whatever God wants you to see.

Now return to your day and look at it with a different focus. Take your time. Ask yourself the following questions or use your own.

➡ Where have I noticed God's presence in my life today?

➡ What brought me closer to God?

➡ What led me away from God?

Tell God that you are sorry for the things that kept you from recognizing his love for you. Ask forgiveness for the times you did not respond to his love.

Remember that God wants to have a close relationship with you. Ask him to help you live your life the way he wants you to. If there is any particular area in which you want God's help, say so. Thank God for his presence in your life.

WHERE Do I Fit In?

Sometimes God's grace comes when we least expect it. Jennifer Courier, a mother, explains how she was able to find God's presence even amid unexpected news.

by Jennifer Courier

Unexpected Blessings

One of the great blessings of my life came in the form of two sparkly, pink pieces of plastic. I was surprised—blessings are supposed to be big things, such as happiness and health, not something that fits in the palm of your hand and most people never see. But it's true.

One day I received a phone call from our daughter Kathryn's teacher. She calmly explained that something seemed to be wrong. "Kathryn just isn't getting it," she said. She appeared to be tuning out during storytime and not following simple verbal instructions. This was unsettling news to us since, at home, Kathryn seemed very well-adjusted. There were no signs of her struggling with simple tasks. My husband and I were extremely worried. Our little girl, the youngest of our four daughters, was struggling. So, now what?

I spent a lot of time praying, asking God for his guidance and grace in this challenging situation. I ended up taking Kathryn to have her hearing checked. My stomach dropped and my heart broke as I watched Kathryn struggle during the battery of tests. She was unable to hear anything at times. She stumbled and struggled to repeat back words and simple sentences at another volume level. All the while, she sat with a smile on her face completely unaware of what was going on. Four weeks later, Kathryn was fitted with a hearing aid. The doctor explained that Kathryn had developed excellent coping mechanisms such as lip reading and picking up on context clues. Now, with the hearing aid, she would begin the exciting journey of being able to hear and process all the

sounds around her. She was thrilled to wear the new hearing aids—beautiful cotton-candy pink with sparkles all over them.

These simple hearing aids have brought overwhelming blessings into my life. I loved seeing the look of awe on Kathryn's face each time she heard a new sound. I was thrilled to see the heartwarming kindness and generous spirit of the boys and girls in Kathryn's class and the dedication of her teachers and doctors who found a solution to help her. I am grateful that the school principal found money in a tight Catholic school budget to purchase equipment for Kathryn's teachers to use to help her. Kathryn now "gets it."

My Catholic faith allows me to see, feel, and accept God's grace and presence each and every day. I've learned that blessings come in all shapes and sizes—even in two little pieces of plastic.

Unexpected News

Recall a time you received news that you did not expect. What was your initial reaction to the news? As you think back, how might God's grace have been present in your experience? Write your ideas on a separate sheet of paper.

JENNIFER COURIER is a writer, editor, wife, and mother of four girls.

What's What?

Review the key concepts in this session by providing a short answer to each question.

1 While Ignatius of Loyola was recovering from wounds he received in battle, he read books about the lives of _____. (PAGE 152)

_____

_____

2 The six men whom Ignatius of Loyola met at the University of Paris joined with him in forming a new religious community known as _____. (PAGE 152)

_____

_____

3 Guided by their charism, the Jesuits strive to _____. (PAGE 153)

_____

_____

4 In the prayer called the _____, people are invited to reflect on their day and recognize God's presence in their experiences. (PAGE 153)

_____

_____

5 The Fifth Commandment teaches us to _____. (PAGE 154)

_____

_____

6 Chastity means that sexual relationships can only take place within the _____. (PAGE 155)

_____

_____

7 The Ninth Commandment encourages us to create an environment that helps us practice _____. (PAGE 155)

_____

_____

Say What?

Know the definitions of these terms.

abortion	covet
adultery	euthanasia
asceticism	moral law
chastity	Spiritual Exercises

Now What?

Praying the Daily Examen helps us recognize God's presence in the world around us. When during your day might you pray the Daily Examen? What can you do to give thanks to God for his ongoing Revelation in your life?

_____

_____

_____

_____

_____

_____

_____

_____

_____

_____

_____

Faith and Reason

Think about a time you heard two conflicting accounts of the same event. What did you do to make sense of the two different stories? How did you determine which source of information was more reliable?

PRAYER

Holy Spirit, thank you for teaching us the truth. May we always turn to you, the source of all wisdom.

The Enlightenment

Galileo

UNTIL the 16th century, people believed that the earth was the center of the universe and that it was God who made everything revolve around our planet. Before long, however, scientists such as Copernicus and Galileo suggested that the earth is not the center of the universe and that the planets in our solar system revolve around the sun. Other scientists took note of the developments in astronomy. Mathematicians such as Descartes and Pascal, for example, developed their own theories about how the universe worked. What is one recent scientific discovery that has altered your understanding of the universe?

These theories of the 16th century began to explain natural phenomena in a different way than religion had done for centuries. These ideas not only changed people's understanding of the world, they also called into question people's beliefs about God and his relationship with creation. For some, God's ongoing role in the creation of the universe seemed diminished. This shift in worldview, which took place during the 1700s, is known as the **Age of Enlightenment.** During this time some people suggested that God was not actively involved in the world. Instead, they suggested that God had created the universe and then sat back as it ran itself. These people believed that God was a distant being. Some even believed that we could solve every human problem through science and mathematics.

The scientific advances made during the Age of Enlightenment also had an impact on people's understanding of morality. Some people began to move away from a belief in **divine law.** Instead, they defined morality as "the greatest good for the greatest number." Philosophers also began looking for ways to encourage people to make their own way in the world and to rely less on the Church and the authority of the government.

Faith and Science Are Complementary

People who believe that we can solve all of humanity's issues by examining them scientifically and mathematically are called **rationalists.**

Faith or Science?

Imagine that a friend asked you to explain the relationship between faith and science. How would you respond? What would you say to him or her about the importance of both?

_____

_____

_____

_____

_____

_____

_____

_____

_____

_____

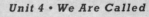

Their philosophy is called rationalism. Some people feel that there is no need for science. They believe that the Bible explains everything. People who take the Bible literally—word for word—are called **fundamentalists.** While Catholics do not read the Bible literally, we do believe that in matters of faith, the Bible is without error. A clue that we should not take the Bible literally can be found in the Book of Genesis, Chapters 1 and 2. Here we find two different stories about how God created the world. Rather than teaching us science or history, these stories teach us about God's relationship with creation.

As Catholics we acknowledge that the achievements of science do not distance God from his creation. Rather, the Church teaches that both faith and science are gifts from God; they complement each other. We look to God and the Church when defining moral behavior, and we accept the ideas of the Church and divine authority as ways to guide us. Science is the study of the way things happen and where things come from. Through faith we explore the meaning of things and how we can find God in them. Science explains the laws of nature. Faith describes the intimate connection between nature and its Creator. Science helps us know why things function. Faith helps us know how all of creation reveals God's presence to us. People of faith do not choose one or the other; we acknowledge the benefits that both have for human beings.

Study Corner

DEFINE

Age of Enlightenment, divine law, rationalists, fundamentalists

REMEMBER

As a result of the scientific discoveries made during the Age of Enlightenment, people began to question God's role in the universe. Unlike the rationalists, the Church teaches that faith and science are complementary.

Past Meets Present

PAST: In 1789 the French Revolution deposed the king, Louis XVI. In place of the king, a government that promoted secularism was established. This new government took land from the Church, and, in a period known as the Reign of Terror, it put priests and nuns to death as enemies of the state. At that time Catholic religious communities were disbanded and forbidden. A group of Carmelite nuns in the city of Compiègne continued to pray together, however. Sixteen Carmelite sisters and one lay person accused of helping them were arrested. They were all condemned to death and beheaded in July 1794. As the women gathered in prayer before their execution, they forgave their enemies. The Martyrs of Compiègne were beatified in 1906.

PRESENT: Even in recent times, priests, religious sisters, and lay ministers have been martyred as enemies of the state. Archbishop Oscar Romero, of El Salvador, was killed on March 24, 1980, while celebrating Mass. He was killed for speaking out against the government's repression of its citizens and its role in violating their basic human rights. Four American women— three religious sisters and one lay woman— were killed in El Salvador on December 2, 1980, because of the ministry that they were providing to people oppressed by the government. On November 16, 1986, six Jesuits, their housekeeper, and her daughter were murdered in El Salvador. They, too, were killed because of their criticism of the government and its abuse of human rights.

Archbishop Oscar Romero of El Salvador

Explore

Choosing to Do Good

THROUGHOUT history many people have believed that the gift of faith and our ability to reason are incompatible. There are saints, however, who have taught that faith is a journey by which we use the gift of reasoning to help us understand the mysteries of faith that have been revealed by God. Both faith and reason are gifts from God that we can use to help us form our conscience. Having a well-formed conscience helps us discern God's will for us so that we can make good moral choices. How else can you discern God's will for you so that you can choose to do the right thing?

Our Catholic Character

According to the *Catechism of the Catholic Church*, a lie is the most direct offense against the truth. It does violence to an individual, destroys trust, and hinders relationships. The Eighth Commandment also forbids **detraction** (revealing another person's faults), rash judgment (assuming without really knowing a moral fault of another), and calumny. Flattery, boasting, and bragging also can be offenses against the Eighth Commandment, when they are not based on truth or are used to make fun of another person.

We rely on our conscience to help us discover the truth. This gift from God leads us to see the morality of our acts and take responsibility for what we do. We are called to form our conscience so that it can properly guide us. We can shape our conscience by following the example set by our family, following Church teaching, and praying for the guidance of the Holy Spirit. We recognize the presence of the Holy Spirit in the Christian ways in which we act. We call these actions the **Fruits of the Holy Spirit.**

The Eighth Commandment

One way we form our conscience is by following the Ten Commandments. The Eighth Commandment—You shall not bear false witness against your neighbor—teaches us that lies are wrong because they can harm our relationships. The lies that we call **calumny** are especially serious. Calumny is slander, which is a lie that hurts someone's reputation. We are also called to refrain from sharing information about a person that might harm his or her reputation, and we are to refrain from breaking confidences that are necessary because of our profession.

Whenever a person tells a lie, he or she should make an effort to repair the damage caused by the lie. The Eighth Commandment challenges us to live in truth so that people can see God reflected in our lives. When people experience us as honest, faithful, and trustworthy, they begin to experience God's presence in our lives.

Making Good Decisions

Every day we are required to make tough choices. Sometimes we have all the information we need to make the right decision, but many times we don't. We might have partial information or even false information. And no matter the situation, we can't always predict the outcome. When faced with difficult situations, it's important for us to do our best to find the truth and to look to our conscience to determine the best course of action. Our conscience is our inner voice that helps us know the law of love that God has placed in our hearts. When we are faced with a difficult choice, we can look to the Holy Spirit for guidance.

The Seventh and Tenth Commandments

Many of the decisions we make in life are connected to the Seventh and Tenth Commandments. The Seventh Commandment states that we shall not steal, but it means so much more. We know that God created the world and filled it with beautiful gifts that he intended to be shared by all. For this reason the Seventh Commandment forbids taking a neighbor's goods. It also teaches us that we should care for the goods of the earth with justice and charity so that these goods can be shared by all.

The Tenth Commandment teaches us that we shall not covet, or desire, our neighbor's goods. Greed can lead people to have feelings of resentment toward others. If we let this resentment grow into anger,

it will sour our lives and ruin our relationships. It is not difficult to see that when we give in to greed, material objects become more important than people and relationships. The Church also forbids greed that arises from a desire for wealth and the power that often comes from having it.

By discovering the truth, forming our conscience, and following the Ten Commandments, we recognize what it means to live in just relationships with others. While God wants us to enjoy the material things that are part of his creation, he also wants us to remember that other people need things and that we are called to respect their needs. When we accept who we are as God created us and thank God for the gifts he has brought into our lives, we can be happy for the gifts that God has given to others.

Explore

SACRED ART

To help us live out the Ten Commandments, we can practice the Corporal Works of Mercy and the Spiritual Works of Mercy. The Corporal Works of Mercy are acts by which we help others with their physical and material needs. The Spiritual Works of Mercy are the kind acts by which we help others with their emotional and spiritual needs. When we choose to practice the Works of Mercy, we build up God's kingdom by following Jesus' example of love and service. By doing so, we acknowledge that everyone has a right to the wonderful gifts we have received from God.

Jesus with Soup, Carolina Arentsen, 21st century.

A Living Work of Art

Through the centuries, Christians have used sacred poetry, music, and images to deepen their experience of prayer. The psalms, for example, includes a number of hymns that were originally written as hymns to be sung during public worship. We can also turn to the beautiful paintings that decorate the Sistine Chapel in Rome or the stained-glass windows in our local churches. In our personal prayer, we can use songs or images, such as well-known paintings of Jesus, as the object of meditation.

The sacred arts express the infinite beauty of God in works made by human hands. All true art gives form to the truth of reality in a language that we not only hear but can also see and touch. Inspired by truth, sacred art makes God's glory more visible, and those of us who experience it are drawn more completely to him.

As God's greatest creation, the members of the human family are God's greatest work of art. We are true revelations of beauty.

Living with Integrity

In your imagination, go to a favorite peaceful place where there are no distractions. Find a comfortable place to sit. Look around. Use your senses to pay attention. What do you see? What do you hear? What do you smell? What can you touch? What do you taste?

Notice that Jesus has come to join you. He sets before you a large, full-length mirror and asks you to look at your reflection. Then he asks you one question: What truth do you see reflected in your life?

At first you think you don't have a clue. But Jesus is patient and gives you lots of encouragement. He asks you questions: Do you have a joyful spirit? Do you have a positive attitude? Are you generous with your talents and possessions? How do you show respect for others and for yourself? How do you resolve conflict?

Spend as much time as you need and feel free to ask Jesus for more clues if you need them. When you decide on your answer, share it with him.

When you are finished, Jesus asks you to take one last look in the mirror. Can you see now that you are God's work of art? You are a person of integrity who lives the truth in a unique and personal way. This may be a new idea for you, and it will take time to understand it fully. Remind yourself to give it some thought whenever you look at yourself in the mirror. Thank Jesus for this time together.

WHERE Do I Fit In?

by John Beilein

We are often tempted to divide our lives into that which is sacred and that which is secular: We go to Mass on Sunday, and we devote the rest of our week to other joys and responsibilities. Coach John Beilein, however, points out that it is important to integrate our spiritual practice into everything that we do.

A Spiritual Practice I Can't Do Without

I coach men's basketball at a Big 10 university. It's a stressful job. The competition is tough; games are close. We perform in public—on television, in big arenas—surrounded by fans who badly want us to win and who are disappointed when we don't. For the players and coaches, the pressure is always on.

One of my biggest responsibilities as coach is to get everyone ready to play. That's what practice is for, and we practice hard almost every day of the week during the season. But practice in the gym is only part of getting ready. Mental preparation is important too. For me, spiritual preparation is also vital.

On the day of every game, I read from a book of daily reflections titled *My Daily Bread* by the Jesuit Anthony Paone. I've had this book for years. These reflections are simple and to the point, and they clear away the obstacles to my peace of mind. This spiritual reading is a big part of my game preparation.

When I'm prepared, I can get my team prepared. Before every game we have a meeting that lasts about 20 minutes. Just before this meeting, I read from my book and settle my spirit. Then I can go in and talk to the players about focusing their minds on what they need to do to play the game well. I read after the game too. The reflections talk about gratitude—something that's easy to feel if we win the game. They also talk about adversity. There's plenty of adversity in college basketball, and you can learn more from losing than you can from winning.

JOHN BEILEIN is the men's basketball coach at the University of Michigan.

I like variety in my spiritual life. At various times, I have prayed the Rosary and practiced other devotions. I pray the Examen of Saint Ignatius Loyola. I go to Mass frequently. I change things up to keep myself fresh. But my reading from *My Daily Bread* is a constant. It's a spiritual practice I can't do without.

Plan Your Week

For each day of the week, write one spiritual practice that you can integrate into your daily activities. Commit to completing each activity.

Monday _____

_____

Tuesday _____

Wednesday _____

_____

Thursday _____

_____

Friday _____

_____

Saturday _____

_____

Sunday _____

_____

What's What?

Write the letter that best matches each description below.

1 _____ people who believe that we can solve humanity's issues by examining them scientifically and mathematically (PAGE 160–161)

2 _____ gifts from God that complement each other (PAGE 161)

3 _____ contain stories that teach us about God's relationship with creation (PAGE 161)

4 _____ a religious truth that we can only know through God's Revelation (PAGE 162)

5 _____ gift from God that leads us to see the morality of our acts (PAGE 162)

6 _____ can harm our relationships (PAGE 162)

7 _____ revealing another person's faults (PAGE 162)

8 _____ can lead people to have feelings of resentment (PAGE 163)

9 _____ acts by which we help others with their physical and material needs (PAGE 163)

a. conscience
b. Genesis, Chapters 1 and 2
c. greed
d. rationalists
e. mystery
f. faith and science
g. lies
h. detraction
i. Corporal Works of Mercy

Say What?

Know the definitions of these terms.

Age of Enlightenment
calumny
detraction
divine law
Fruits of the Holy Spirit
fundamentalists
rationalists

Now What?

We can use the gifts of faith and reason to help us form our conscience. Having a well-formed conscience helps us make good decisions. How can you use the gifts of faith and reason to help you form your conscience this week?

_____

_____

_____

_____

_____

Celebrating Holy Week and Easter

HOLY Week, which is the last week of Lent, is the most important week of the liturgical year. The last three days of this week are known as the **Triduum**—Holy Thursday, Good Friday, and Holy Saturday.

On Holy Thursday we celebrate the Mass of the Lord's Supper, in which we recall the Passover meal that Jesus shared with his followers on the night he was betrayed. During this Mass we give thanks for the Sacrament of the Eucharist, which Jesus instituted when he gave his Body and Blood in the form of bread and wine. We also recall that Jesus washed the disciples' feet as an act of love. In doing this, Jesus gives us an example of how we are called to treat one another.

On Good Friday, during a liturgy that begins and ends in silence, we hear the story of Jesus' Passion, and we venerate the cross by kissing it, bowing before it, or touching it reverently. During the proclamation of the Passion, we pray as we hear about Jesus' suffering during the hours leading up to his **Crucifixion** and Death on the Cross.

Recall one of the most amazing events you have experienced in your life. What impact did this event have on you? What did you to do celebrate this event? What, if anything, do you do to remember or commemorate this event?

On Holy Saturday we celebrate the Easter Vigil to commemorate the night that Jesus rose from the dead. This Mass takes place at nightfall, and it is filled with rich symbolism, including the lighting of the new fire, the lighting of the Paschal Candle, and the sprinkling with holy water. During this Mass we hear Scripture readings that remind us of God's saving deeds, and we welcome new members into the Church.

On Easter Sunday, the highest feast of the year, we celebrate Christ's Resurrection. We recognize that through his Death, Christ saved us from sin and destroyed the hold that death has on us. We see that his Resurrection promises new life, both in this world and in the next. Easter represents the fulfillment of our Christian faith.

PRAYER

Jesus, thank you for the gift of Salvation that we receive through your Resurrection. May we live our lives with the joy of this great gift.

A Message of Hope

THE Triduum ends with the celebration of Jesus' Resurrection on Easter Sunday. This movement from death to new life, from sorrow to joy, is a reflection of our human experience. Throughout history, the Church has cared for all those in sorrow and pain so that all people can experience hope and joy in their lives. How has the Church helped you experience joy?

Saint Vincent de Paul

Vincent de Paul was born in France in the 17th century. Even from a young age, he was concerned with the needs of people who were poor. He knew that by caring for people's needs, he could alleviate their suffering and help them experience the joy of Christ's love.

Vincent's parents made sure that he received an education, and they encouraged him to become a priest. After Vincent was ordained, he moved to Paris and began serving people who were poor or sick. Vincent wanted to serve as many people as possible, so he drew upon his organizational skills and founded the Congregation of the Mission and the Sisters of Charity. With his companion Louise de Marillac, Vincent also organized the Daughters of Charity, a lay organization that enlisted young women to help people in need. Because Vincent and Louise were able to garner support for their ministries, they were able to provide a vast array of social services, including hospital care, soup kitchens, homes for children who had been orphaned, and homes for people who were elderly.

The Society of Saint Vincent de Paul

Blessed Frederic Ozanam, who was born in France in 1813, lived at a time of great political turmoil. As a young adult, Ozanam was inspired by the charitable works performed by Saint Vincent de Paul. He believed that members of society should put the values of mercy and love into action by performing acts of charity. He gathered a small

READY for Confirmation

As we prepare for Confirmation, we examine how the Holy Spirit helps us understand what God is calling us to do, with Christ as our role model. As you reflect on the Gifts of the Holy Spirit, imagine how you might share the hope of the Resurrection with people who are suffering. Try to identify some ways that you can share the message of Easter joy with others throughout the year.

group of university students who shared his beliefs. Originally named the Conference of Charity, Ozanam and his companions tended to the physical and spiritual needs of people who were poor, sick, and unemployed. Ozanam's dedication to justice and social reform led many to join the Conference of Charity. Soon, more than 100 people joined the organization. Ozanam divided the Conference into smaller groups so that it could assist more people.

Frederick Ozanam's legacy, the Society of Saint Vincent de Paul, actively continues the work of Christian charity begun by Saint Vincent de Paul in France in the 17th century. The Saint Vincent de Paul Society came to the United States in 1845, first ministering to people in St. Louis, Missouri. Today over 800,000 people in 130 countries carry out the work of the Society of Saint Vincent de Paul.

Study Corner

REMEMBER

Saint Vincent de Paul and Blessed Frederick Ozanam performed acts of charity for people who were suffering. We, too, are called to share a message of hope with others by following Jesus' example of selfless service.

Jesus Points the Way

Like Saint Vincent de Paul, Saint Louise de Marillac, and Blessed Frederick Ozanam, we are called to act with justice by promoting the dignity of human life and caring for the needs of the most vulnerable among us. Jesus himself gave us this mandate in the Gospels.

"For I was hungry and you gave me food, I was thirsty and you gave me drink, a stranger and you welcomed me, naked and you clothed me, ill and you cared for me, in prison and you visited me." Then the righteous will answer him and say, "Lord, when did we see you hungry and feed you, or thirsty and give you drink? When did we see you a stranger and welcome you, or naked and clothe you? When did we see you ill or in prison, and visit you?" And the king will say to them in reply, "Amen, I say to you, whatever you did for one of these least brothers of mine, you did for me."

Matthew 25:35–40

During the Triduum, as we reflect on Jesus' suffering, we acknowledge the deep suffering that is experienced by people all over the world. At the same time, we are filled with Easter joy, and we proclaim a message of hope. The Easter season offers us the opportunity to celebrate the promise of an end to suffering, fear, and death itself. We celebrate that Christ is risen and that he will come again. We pray that we will open our hearts so that Christ can work through us to help those in need.

SACRED ART

In this painting, we see Saint Vincent de Paul and the Daughters of Charity helping people who are sick with the plague. This painting serves as a reminder that Jesus calls each of us to care unselfishly for the needs of others in whatever ways our gifts allow.

Saint Vincent de Paul, Antoine Ansiaux, oil on canvas, circa 1800.

Choosing Hope Over Despair

The Betrayal of Jesus Christ by Judas, engraving.

THE word *despair* describes the feeling of utter hopelessness. When humans are filled with despair, they might feel as if they can no longer cope with life. Thankfully, despair doesn't have to be a permanent state. It can turn to **hope**, a confident expectation that everything will be OK and a trust in something that we might not be able to see or haven't experienced.

The Scripture readings that we hear proclaimed during Holy Week and Easter are filled with examples of hope and despair. In stories about two of Jesus' Apostles, we learn a lesson about the importance of turning despair into hope and sharing that newfound hope with the world.

Judas

In the Gospel of Matthew, we read that one of Jesus' Apostles, Judas Iscariot, betrayed Jesus by arranging to have him arrested. While Jesus was praying in the garden of Gethsemane after celebrating the Last Supper with his Apostles, Judas arrived with a crowd whose members were carrying swords and clubs. Judas kissed Jesus as a signal that Jesus was the one whom the chief priests sought to arrest. For his betrayal, Judas received 30 pieces of silver.

It is difficult to imagine why Judas—who traveled with Jesus, heard his message, and witnessed his miracles—might betray Jesus and commit such a sin. Judas's actions both before and after his betrayal of Jesus show us that, whatever his motivation, he obviously had lost all hope and was living in despair. In the Gospel of Matthew, we learn that after he saw Jesus being condemned to death, Judas deeply regretted what he had done. Although he felt deep sorrow over his actions, Judas did not do anything to repent of his sins or repair his broken relationship with Jesus. According to tradition, Judas returned the 30 pieces of silver to the priests and elders, admitted that he had betrayed an innocent man, and went off to hang himself. Judas's despair clouded his thoughts and caused him to lose all hope.

Our Catholic Character

Judas, like Jesus and all his early followers, was Jewish. Because of his betrayal and the actions of the Sanhedrin, some Christians have blamed Jews for Jesus' Death. The Church reminds us, however, that **Judaism,** unlike other non-Christian religions, is a response to God's Revelation. We do not believe that Jews were indiscriminately responsible for Jesus' Passion and Death.

Peter

Judas was not the only one of Jesus' Apostles to feel despair over sin. In the Gospels of Matthew and Mark, we read that Peter denied knowing Jesus on three different occasions after Jesus was arrested. It appears that Peter did not want to be associated with a criminal, nor did he want to be arrested as Jesus had been. After his third denial, Peter was so ashamed that he began weeping bitterly. Peter, however, did not remain filled with despair. Despite Jesus' Crucifixion, Peter continued to believe in God's mercy.

The Gospel of John tells us that after the Resurrection, Peter was able to be reconciled with Jesus, who then called Peter to feed and tend Jesus' sheep—all those who were his followers. Three times Jesus asked Peter this question, "Simon, son of John, do you love me?" Three times Peter said that he did. Peter's hope and faith in God's mercy and Christ's love helped him overcome despair and live out his true mission—to be the first leader of the Church.

A Beacon of Hope

Think of a situation in the world today in which people might feel despair. Then on the lines below, write how you can serve as a beacon of hope for the people in the situation.

_____

_____

_____

_____

_____

_____

_____

_____

_____

_____

_____

_____

Past Meets Present

PAST: Saint Peter preached in Rome during the last years of his life. It was there, during the persecutions under Emperor Nero, that he died a martyr's death. Tradition tells us that Peter did not consider himself worthy to be crucified the same way that Jesus was. In response, he was crucified upside down. Origen, an early Christian writer, wrote "Peter was crucified at Rome with his head downward, as he himself had desired to suffer."

PRESENT: Saint Peter's Basilica, considered one of the largest churches in the world, is in Vatican City. The basilica stands on the traditional site where Saint Peter was crucified and buried. The tomb of Saint Peter is under the main altar. Originally founded by Constantine in 324, Saint Peter's Basilica was rebuilt between 1506 and 1615 and includes artistic works by Bramante, Michelangelo, and Bernini. Saint Peter's is one of the holiest Christian sites in the world.

Explore

Saint Peter's Basilica

Study Corner

DEFINE

hope, Judaism

REMEMBER

Peter's hope and faith in God's mercy helped him overcome despair and live out his true mission.

Easter Proclamation

Exsultet Reflection

These, then, are the feasts of Passover,
in which is slain the Lamb, the one true Lamb,
whose Blood anoints the doorposts of believers.

The Easter Proclamation that follows the lighting of the Paschal Candle at the Easter Vigil on Holy Saturday is known as the *Exsultet.* After sunset and in complete darkness, a fire is lit and blessed outside of or at the entrance of the church. Then the Paschal Candle is blessed and lit from this fire. As the candle is carried into the darkened church, we sing, "Christ our light. Thanks be to God!"

The *Exsultet,* traditionally sung by a deacon, proclaims Christ's Resurrection from the dead for our Salvation. Throughout the 50 days of Easter, the Paschal Candle stands in the sanctuary as a sign of the light of the risen Christ, "the one Morning Star who never sets, . . . who, coming back from death's domain, has shed his peaceful light on humanity, and lives and reigns for ever and ever." (The *Exsultet*)

This is the night,
when once you led our forebearers, Israel's children,
from slavery in Egypt
and made them pass dry-shod through the Red Sea.

This is the night
that a pillar of fire
banished the darkness of sin.

This is the night
that even now, throughout the world,
sets Christian believers apart from worldly vices
and from the gloom of sin,
leading them to grace
and joining them to his holy ones.

This is the night,
when Christ broke the prison-bars of death
and rose victorious from the underworld.

WHERE Do I Fit In?

When we experience pain and suffering, it can be difficult to maintain our hope and trust in God. Our tradition, however, reminds us to remain steadfast—for God works in ways that are beyond our human comprehension.

by Fr. Dan Reim, S.J.

Finding Jesus Where I Least Expected

Reflect

Kelly suffered from migraine headaches. They were never bad enough to keep her from her daily activities, but they were a constant, never-ending threat. She saw many specialists and tried many different treatments, but nothing seemed to work.

As time passed, Kelly became more and more depressed. She wondered, "Is this ever going to end?" She asked me, "Why won't God do something? Can't God make this stop?"

I felt helpless. I could have given her all kinds of theological explanations—that God, for example, is a good and loving God. That God doesn't give us pain. Or that God can heal us, but for some mysterious reason, doesn't always do so. But no explanation was going to help her ease the pain. And so we prayed. We prayed that God would heal her, either through her doctors or by some supernatural miracle.

But that prayer wasn't answered. Kelly's migraines continued, and her life became more and more difficult. And yet she continued to pray. She continued to believe that God knew her, loved her, and didn't want her to suffer.

Months passed. I had nearly given up hope that God would help Kelly. (And I'm supposed to be the professional "hoper"!) But there wasn't any reason to have hope.

And then, one day, Kelly called to tell me that it had been two weeks since she had her last migraine. She could see the sunshine in her life again. She felt alive! I was surprised and overjoyed. And I felt humbled that I hadn't trusted

God enough. And I was so impressed with Kelly—that throughout all this time, she had kept praying to God.

Kelly's miracle wasn't just her healing. As she told me, God kept giving her the grace, the strength, and the hope to go on. "Without God," Kelly said, "I could never have made it." Kelly's healing reminded me that Jesus can show up anywhere, at any time.

FR. DAN REIM, S.J., is a campus minister at St. Mary Student Parish in Ann Arbor, which serves the University of Michigan.

Surprise!

Take a moment to reflect on an experience that filled you with hope. Then in the box, make something—a poem, a paragraph, or a drawing—that reflects your experience.

What's What?

Complete each sentence with the correct word or phrase.

1 The *Exsultet* is the Easter Proclamation that follows the lighting of the ———. (PAGE 172)

_____

2 On Holy Saturday, we celebrate the ——— to commemorate the night that Jesus rose from the dead. (PAGE 167)

_____

3 ——— is the founder of the Society of Saint Vincent de Paul. (PAGE 168–169)

_____

_____

4 Despite his feelings of despair, Peter continued to believe in ———. (PAGE 171)

_____

5 Saint Vincent de Paul founded two religious orders, the ——— and the Sisters of Charity. (PAGE 168)

_____

_____

6 We celebrate the Mass of the Lord's Supper on ———. (PAGE 167)

_____

7 In exchange for betraying Jesus, ——— received 30 pieces of silver. (PAGE 170)

_____

8 On ——— we recognize that through his Death, Christ saved us from sin and destroyed the hold that death has on us. (PAGE 167)

_____

Say What?

Know the definitions of these terms.

Crucifixion

Exsultet

hope

Judaism

Triduum

Now What?

Name a time this week when it will be important for you to be a source of hope to yourself or to others. When the time comes, remember to ask the Holy Spirit for guidance.

_____

_____

_____

_____

_____

_____

_____

_____

Faith in ACTION

As Christians we respond to Christ's call to share the Gospel message of hope by treating one another with compassion and by performing acts of charity and service. By performing these works, we put our faith into practice, and we follow Jesus' example in our own words and actions.

In this unit we explored the theme of being called by Christ to share his love with others. Through the sacraments, Scripture, and the Church's teachings, we receive the strength we need to respond to this call. In order to help us respond to this call faithfully, we work with the Holy Spirit to develop our conscience, our inner voice that helps us make good decisions.

Act

> "The Church cannot neglect the service of charity any more than she can neglect the Sacraments and the Word."
>
> —Pope Benedict XVI

Drive for the Basics

Purpose

Understand the importance of the common good; put this teaching into action by identifying needs in your community, organizing a drive to collect goods, and distributing them to people in need.

Background

Housing, food, education, health care, and employment are just some of the basic rights of every human being. In the Acts of the Apostles, Luke tells us that meeting people's basic needs was one of the main responsibilities of the early Church. Luke writes, "There was no needy person among them, for those who owned property or houses would sell them, bring the proceeds of the sale, and put them at the feet of the apostles, and they were distributed to each according to need." (Acts of the Apostles 4:34–35)

Steps

1. Read Acts of the Apostles 6:1–7. In this passage, Luke tells us about two different but related tasks in the early Church: preaching the Good News of Jesus Christ and caring for the needs of the members of the community. How would you retell this story by using your community's circumstances?

2. Talk with local community leaders to find out about some of the pressing needs of the people in your community.

3. Organize a food drive or other drive to collect goods that will help meet the needs of people in your community. Be creative in designing your drive. Find ways to get as many people as possible involved so that people can say about your community, "There was no person in need among them."

Grant a Wish

Asher McGarrah, 5, holding his tree house drawing. The Make-A-Wish Foundation built the tree house in his backyard.

Purpose

Learn how even a small act of kindness can bring hope to a person and mean the world to him or her. Find out what someone's wish is, or the wishes of a group of people, and come up with creative ways to make their wishes come true.

Background

All his life, Christopher Greicius dreamed of becoming a police officer. But after developing a life-threatening illness, realizing his dream seemed far away. In 1980, a group of people worked together with Chris's mom to make his dream come true. With the assistance of the Arizona Department of Public Safety, Chris was able to fly in a police helicopter, wear the motorcycle wings of an Arizona Highway patrol officer, and become the first honorary state trooper in Arizona. Chris died that same year at the age of seven but not before inspiring people around him. The people who worked so hard to make his dream come true decided that they could do the same for others. This was the beginning of the Make-A-Wish Foundation. Since then, more than 144,000 wishes have been granted.

Act

Steps

1. Read the Native American story about Jumping Mouse. A wonderful version of the story is *The Story of Jumping Mouse*, illustrated by John Steptoe. What can we learn from Jumping Mouse about giving?

2. Design your own Grant-A-Wish service project that will give you the opportunity to give to others. Identify a person or group of people who have a wish that seems like an impossibility to them. Work together to grant the wish.

> **"Every person has a . . . duty to work for the advancement of the common good and the well-being of all . . ."**
>
> —United States Conference of Catholic Bishops

We Are Sent

Angelo Giuseppe Roncalli was ordained in 1904. During World War I, he was drafted by the Italian army to serve as a chaplain. After the war, he served the Church in a number of ways. He was the papal ambassador to Turkey and Greece, and he was the bishop of Bulgaria in southeast Europe. On October 28, 1958, Cardinal Roncalli was elected pope and took the name John XXIII. Many of the popes prior to John XXIII had chosen to eat their meals alone so that they could spend more time in prayerful silence. John XXIII, however, hired a cook and started inviting people to join him for dinner. The meals he shared with others helped him remain close to the people he served as pope.

How the Saint Relates { Saint John XXIII was chosen to represent this unit because of his open-hearted willingness to serve God however he was called to do so. His deep prayer life and profound spirituality contributed to his ability to serve God's people throughout his life.

Elected Pope

After the 1958 death of Pope Pius XII, who had served as pope for almost 20 years, Cardinal Roncalli was elected pope, at which time he took the name John XXIII. Because of his age—he was 76—many assumed that he would serve out a short and uneventful papacy. Immediately, however, his actions demonstrated that he would be an active leader who truly cared about his flock. As the Bishop of Rome, John XXIII decided to make pastoral visits to Catholics within the diocese, including to prisoners and children in hospitals.

Pope John XXIII was a spokesperson for social justice, the rights of the working class, people who were poor, and the unity of Christians. He wrote two encyclicals related to Catholic Social Teaching. In *Pacem in Terris (Peace on Earth),* he emphasized the need for universal peace and the right to life for all humans. In addition, he wrote *Mater et Magistra (Mother and Teacher),* an encyclical that explained the need for society to promote human dignity.

Prayer and Reflection

Saint John XXIII lived a life of devout prayer and profound spirituality. As a young man, he began keeping a journal of spiritual reflections, which are included in the book *Journal of a Soul.* In this book, Saint John XXIII shares his thoughts and spiritual development from adolescence until late in life. His loving, trusting relationship with God is apparent through words such as these: "I will not forget that I am never alone, even when I am by myself. . . ."

Calling a Council

Pope John XXIII's most significant contribution to the Church was calling the Second Vatican Council, a gathering of the world's bishops. This council eventually approved significant reforms to the Church and its practices, including allowing priests to celebrate Mass in people's native language rather than in Latin only. Pope John XXIII died before the work of the council was completed, but Pope Paul VI, his successor, resumed the council and brought it to its close. While most feast days are celebrated on the anniversary of a person's death, the feast day of Saint John XXIII is celebrated on October 11, the anniversary of the opening of the Second Vatican Council.

> **Pope John XXIII was a spokesperson for social justice, the rights of the working class, people who were poor, and the unity of Christians.**

Truth Revealed by God

Think about a time someone challenged one of your deeply held beliefs, perhaps by questioning your religious beliefs or family customs. How did you respond to the challenge? Did you talk with the person? Did you ignore him or her? Did you begin to question your own beliefs?

PRAYER

Holy Spirit, thank you for guiding our Church leaders. Help them always remain faithful to the Revelation that we receive from God.

Responding to Modernism

Pope Pius IX

THE modernist movement describes the period during the late 19th and early 20th centuries when many people began to think that human progress was the result of science and reason alone. One aspect of this movement involved the notion that we can use logical, scientific means to understand the world thoroughly and that we can understand and control the world through rational thought. These ideas led some philosophers to suggest that a person could discover truth through scientific inquiry and reasoned thought only, rather than by using faith and reason as equally valid means of discovering the truth as revealed by God.

In response to false claims that had been made by some people who believed in the modernist movement, Pope Pius IX issued the *Syllabus of Errors* on December 8, 1864. This document addressed modernist claims by citing 80 statements made by earlier popes. Each statement included references to Church documents so that readers could look to the *Syllabus* when they wanted to know more about the Church's teachings on various topics.

The final version of the *Syllabus* addressed claims that related to rationalism, **pantheism**—a belief that rejects a personal God and views God and the universe as being identical—socialism, communism, the rights of the Church, the relationship between the Church and civil society, Christian ethics, and marriage.

While Catholics generally accepted the *Syllabus,* many outside the Church viewed the document as the Church's wholehearted rejection of modern culture, which was not the case. Some countries even forbade the *Syllabus of Errors* from being published within their borders.

Study Corner

DEFINE

Syllabus of Errors, pantheism,

REMEMBER

Church teachings tell us that God is a personal God who chose to create the universe out of nothing; faith cannot be fully grasped by reason; the truth revealed by God never contradicts the findings of reason; faith and learning are complementary.

While the *Syllabus of Errors* offered important clarifications about some of the dangers presented in modernist thought, it also reflected some of the Church's own misgivings and fears about advances in science. In other words, over time, Church leaders realized that the teachings presented in the document needed refining.

The First Vatican Council

The Church continued to respond to the modernist movement by clarifying some of its teachings during the First Vatican Council, which Pope Pius IX opened on December 8, 1869. Before this meeting of Church leaders began, Pius IX organized various committees to draft statements to be discussed. Initially, these drafts addressed issues such as Church teaching and practice, the relationship between the Roman Catholic Church and Oriental Churches, and the relationship between Church and state.

In addition to the draft documents, bishops sent additional discussion suggestions, which included requests for revisions of the Liturgy of the Hours and the *Code of Canon Law,* clarification on Church teaching of the bodily Assumption of Mary into Heaven at the end of her earthly life, requests to name Saint Joseph the universal patron of the Church, and clarification on Church teaching regarding papal infallibility.

As the council met, the attendees began an intense debate about the doctrine of papal infallibility. The topic became so important that the council issued several important statements that clearly defined papal infallibility. The definition began with a reminder that the pope—the successor to Saint Peter—has been promised the gift of the Holy Spirit, which gives him the sacred ability to preserve and interpret Revelation as first taught by the Apostles.

In addition, the council produced and received papal approval for the *Constitution on the Catholic Faith*, a document that responded to claims presented by modernist thinkers. This document reminds us that

➡ **God is a personal God who freely has chosen to create the universe *ex nihilo* (out of nothing).**

➡ **faith cannot be fully grasped by reason.**

➡ **the truth revealed by God never contradicts the findings of reason.**

➡ **faith and learning are complementary rather than contradictory.**

The First Vatican Council was the first ecumenical council in over 300 years, and it proved to be a productive way to deal with the issues of the day. The next ecumenical council, the Second Vatican Council, was held less than 100 years later—showing that the Church would continue to respond productively as times changed.

Explore

Our Catholic Character

Questions regarding the teaching around papal infallibility first emerged during the Middle Ages. The First Vatican Council affirmed some of the earlier thinking regarding this doctrine. In regard to faith and morals, for a teaching to be infallible, the teaching must be made by the pope and be held to be true by the universal Church. Since 1870, only one teaching has been designated an official infallible teaching. In 1950, Pope Pius XII's definition of the dogma of the Assumption of Mary was universally held to be infallible. Previously (1854), Pope Pius IX declared the doctrine of the Immaculate Conception of Mary to be infallible.

Witnesses to Truth →

Saint Matthew

THROUGH the *Syllabus of Errors* and the First Vatican Council, the Church began to respond to the major issues of the day while remaining true to its teachings. In doing so, the Church witnessed to a way of life rooted in the truth of the Gospel and courageously countered certain aspects of mainstream culture.

Reach Out to Others

Jesus shows us the importance of reaching out to people through familiar forms of communication and in a way that gets to the heart of people's daily lives. Jesus knew how to tell stories and speak about the Kingdom of God in a way that everyone could understand.

"No one patches an old cloak with a piece of unshrunken cloth, for its fullness pulls away from the cloak and the tear gets worse. People do not put new wine into old wineskins. Otherwise the skins burst, the wine spills out, and the skins are ruined. Rather, they pour new wine into fresh wineskins, and both are preserved."

Matthew 9:16–17

Past Meets Present

Isaac Hecker

PAST: Isaac Hecker (1819–1888), who lived in New York, saw that many people were not adequately receiving the Church's teachings. In response, he became a priest and founded a religious order for men, called the Missionary Society of Saint Paul the Apostle. The members of this community are commonly known as Paulists, and their goal is to spread the truth about the Church and its teachings. After founding the community, Father Hecker began a monthly magazine, the *Catholic World*, to help people learn the truth about the Church's response to the issues of the day.

PRESENT: Like Father Hecker, contemporary Catholic evangelists use various forms of technology. For example, there are over 26 million Catholic Web sites, hundreds of Catholic magazines and newspapers, countless podcasts, and even mobile apps—all of which are used to provide news and information on Church teachings and to foster prayer and faith.

Saint Ignatius of Loyola, the founder of the Jesuits, also believed in the importance of meeting people where they are. A quote attributed to him instructs those in the ministry of **evangelization**—the process of sharing the Good News—to reach out to others by entering through their door. In other words, evangelization is most effective when we work with people where they are and address the questions, concerns, and longings that they carry in their heart. In addition, Saint Ignatius desired to help people find God in all things. Today the Church recognizes that modern technology, when used appropriately, can be used to help people discover God's presence in their lives.

Study Corner

DEFINE
evangelization

REMEMBER
The Church teaches that technology—when used wisely—can be used to spread the Gospel message to others.

Modern Evangelization

Today, the Church continues to provide examples of how to live as disciples while still accepting aspects of modern society. For example, the Church reaches out to people in ways that are familiar to them, such as social media, television, and magazines, to teach others about Christ and his message. Pope Benedict XVI, for example, was the first prelate to use a tablet computer to send a tweet. In his message, Pope Benedict praised Jesus and announced the launch of a Vatican news and information site. Similarly, entire television and radio stations are devoted to presenting Catholic teachings, and many parishes use the Internet to share information about opportunities for faith formation, worship, and service.

Use Technology Wisely

While the Church does not condemn the tools of modern society, it does call us to make good moral choices when using them. The Church points out that media and technology in themselves are not evil or harmful. Rather, the Church condemns the use of media for unwholesome purposes, such as creating and accessing pornography, plagiarizing, or spreading gossip or hurtful remarks about others. Furthermore, the Church warns against overuse of media and technology. Just as gluttony refers to eating too much food, we can also consume too much media. Sometimes we may rely too much on the Internet, television, and movies, or we may use them in unhealthy ways, such as to seek excessive pleasure or to avoid pain. When we are faced with the temptation to make bad choices regarding the use of technology, we can change our habits by limiting the amount of time we spend online or by watching less or better quality TV. We also can choose to access only wholesome Web sites, videos, and music. When we practice good habits, we grow in virtue, and we cooperate with the Holy Spirit in building up God's kingdom.

Explore

READY for Confirmation

As you prepare to celebrate the Sacrament of Confirmation, you will learn about the Gifts of the Holy Spirit. One of these gifts is fortitude, the gift that strengthens us to do the will of God in all things. As you use media and technology, you can pray to the Holy Spirit to strengthen your fortitude so that you can make good choices.

Instruments of Peace

Prayer is the raising of our hearts and minds to God. Traditional prayers give us rich and powerful words to use to talk with God. They are prayers to take to heart over the course of our lives.

When we pray these prayers, we are connected to those who have gone before us in faith. We are part of the community who has prayed the same prayers throughout history. Traditional prayers can be prayed alone, and they also help us pray with others.

The Peace Prayer, usually associated with Saint Francis of Assisi, is one traditional prayer. Saint John Paul II prayed it before representatives of the Christian churches and the world religions when he, as pope, met with them to pray for peace in 1986.

Peace Prayer

Lord, make me an instrument of your peace:
where there is hatred, let me sow love;
where there is injury, pardon;
where there is doubt, faith;
where there is despair, hope;
where there is darkness, light;
where there is sadness, joy.

O divine Master,
*   grant that I may not so much seek*
to be consoled as to console,
to be understood as to understand,
to be loved as to love.
For it is in giving that we receive,
it is in pardoning that we are pardoned,
it is in dying that we are born to eternal life.
Amen.

After praying the Peace Prayer, take a moment to reflect silently on how you can be a peacemaker through your words and actions. You may wish to use these questions to help you.

How can I be a peacemaker within myself?

How can I make peace at home?

How can I make peace at school?

How can I make peace in the world?

Conclude by praying to the Holy Spirit for the strength to share Jesus' peace and love with everyone in your life.

WHERE Do I Fit In?

It's natural to turn to those we trust, such as family members, coaches, and teachers, when we aren't sure what to do. It's also important for us to turn to God. Sometimes he provides guidance even when we don't turn to him in prayer.

by Sr. Dorothy Ederer, O.P.

What Does God Want Me to Do?

My first assignment as a member of the Grand Rapids Dominicans was teaching eighth grade. I loved this work, and I was good at it. I taught for a very happy and rewarding 13 years. Then, I had the premonition that my life was about to turn in a different direction. But I didn't know what this might mean.

The time came when the women in our community come together to reflect on our lives and consider where God may be calling us to serve. One morning I jokingly said to the other sisters, "Well, I will go where God wants me to, but he will have to call me." Seconds later, the phone rang, and laughingly I said, "I might as well answer it. It's probably God." I picked up the phone, and the priest who was head of campus ministry at Western Michigan University was on the line wanting to speak to me. He asked if I would be interested in coming to work with him as a campus minister. I was stunned and made all kinds of objections. All he said was, "I know you will love working with our students here. They need someone like you. You will do just fine." He was right. For 13 years we made Jesus real to the 3,000 students from different faiths on the Western Michigan campus.

I had a dream of someday making Jesus real for people in a travelling ministry, but this wasn't anything more than a dream. Then I read a book, called *Joshua,* and I met the author, Father Joseph Girzone. Soon another phone call came—from Father Girzone, asking me to work with his team in a ministry that went all over the world. For nine wonderful years, we brought Jesus to people throughout the United States and other countries.

God will speak. All we have to do is listen. None of us knows what God has planned for us, but if we keep our hearts and minds open to his call and eagerly follow, it is thrilling what can happen! We will never be disappointed.

Reflect

God Guides

Take a moment to think about the following questions. Then on a separate sheet of paper, write an answer to each. *What is one good decision I've made this school year? When I made the decision, how did I know what God was asking me to do?*

During the next week, focus on your words and actions. Think about how God may be guiding you as you go through your everyday life.

SR. DOROTHY EDERER, O.P., is a Grand Rapids Dominican, campus minister, and author of two books, *Colors of the Spirit* and *The Golfer's Prayer Book.*

What's What?

Review the concepts in this session by providing a short answer to each question.

1 What contributed to Pope John XXIII's ability to serve God's people throughout his life? (PAGE 177)

_____

_____

2 What did Pope John XXIII write about in *Pacem in Terris* and *Mater et Magistra*? (PAGE 178)

_____

_____

_____

_____

3 What was Pope John XXIII's most significant contribution to the Church? (PAGE 178)

_____

4 How did the *Syllabus of Errors* address modernist claims? (PAGE 180)

_____

_____

_____

5 What are four teachings that were included in the *Constitution on the Catholic Faith*? (PAGE 181)

_____

_____

_____

_____

_____

6 What did Saint Ignatius of Loyola believe was an effective way to evangelize others? (PAGE 183)

_____

_____

_____

7 In regard to the tools of modern society, what does the Church call us to do? (PAGE 183)

_____

_____

8 What is one definition of the word *prayer*? (PAGE 184)

_____

_____

Say What?

Know the definitions of these terms.

evangelization

pantheism

Syllabus of Errors

Now What?

The Church calls us to use technology for the good of ourselves and others, without overusing it. What is one change that you can make in your technology use this week?

_____

_____

_____

_____

_____

Respond

Acting on Behalf of Justice

Think about a time you witnessed an injustice. Maybe someone was making fun of an unpopular classmate, or maybe someone was discriminated against because of his or her race. How did you respond? Did you take action or ignore the situation? What was the result of your response?

PRAYER

God, thank you for giving us a body of teachings that helps us make good decisions. May we practice the social teachings of the Church by working to end violence and oppression.

The Industrial Revolution

LEO XIII.
BORN, MARCH 2, 1810. ELECTED POPE, FEBRUARY 20, 1878.

Pope Leo XIII

THROUGH the end of the 18th century, many families made their income by growing and selling crops and livestock. Farmwork was time-consuming and difficult. Advances in technology, however, made farming more efficient and easier. For example, the invention of the cotton gin helped workers clean up to 50 times more cotton than they could by hand. A mechanical replacement for the horse-drawn reaper allowed farmers to cut up to 12 acres of wheat a day rather than just two or three. At the same time, the textile industry developed new machines and work processes that greatly increased production. These rapid changes resulted in new social struggles that the Church tried to address.

To meet the demand for these new technologies, people opened factories to increase production. As a result, the economy began to rely more on manufacturing than on farming. This rapid change in technology regarding how goods were produced is known as the **Industrial Revolution.**

With the Industrial Revolution came the need for a large workforce. The demand for factory-produced products was so high that factory owners hired men, women, and children to work. In the mid-19th century, for example, over 20 percent of the urban workforce was made up of children under the age of 10. Cities soon became overcrowded

SACRED ART

During the Industrial Revolution, people worked long hours and received low wages. Like the people in this painting, they often relied on the charity of others. To address the injustice, Pope Leo XIII called for a **living wage** in his **encyclical,** or letter, *Rerum Novarum* (*On the Condition of Labor*). In this document, he defined a living wage as enough to support a person in reasonable comfort. The Church's insistence on a fair income has been a tenet of its social teaching ever since.

Paupers Having Dinner, Norbert Goeneutte, 1881.

with workers, most of whom worked long hours and earned very little. Entire families needed to work in order to earn enough money to survive. In addition, working conditions were dangerous, both in the factories as well as in the coal mines that produced the fuel that powered the factories.

The Industrial Revolution happened so quickly that most cities were unprepared for the rapid increase in population. Many farmers and their families moved into cities to take factory jobs. Living conditions were poor. Often, entire families lived in one-room apartments that were part of poorly built tenement houses. Clean water and good plumbing were rare, which led to the spread of illness and disease. Soot from burning coal filled the air. Eventually, in response to these conditions, governments passed laws regarding working conditions. These laws, however, were difficult to enforce.

Church Reflection and Action

As the Industrial Revolution progressed, Church leaders recognized the need to improve the deplorable conditions that many people in society were experiencing. Catholics began to reflect on the effects of poverty and the need to work for systematic change rather than relying solely on individual acts of charity. At the same time, people proceeded with optimism and hope for the future. Before long, Pope Leo XIII led the Church to take a stand and work to meet the needs of all people.

Rerum Novarum

To offer the Church's response to the destitution that some people were experiencing as a result of the Industrial Revolution, Pope Leo XIII wrote *Rerum Novarum (On the Condition of Labor)*. In this letter, Pope Leo XIII applied Catholic teaching to the rights of humans to work, make fair wages, own property, and establish professional labor associations. The pope explained the Church's belief that socialism and class struggle were not appropriate ways to develop society. This encyclical also challenged Catholics to work to correct the injustices brought on by the Industrial Revolution and to engage in reform of the new social order. This encyclical is often recognized as the first official document that presents the Church's Catholic Social Teaching.

Explore

Past Meets Present

PAST: *Rerum Novarum (On the Condition of Labor)* was the first encyclical in which a pope discussed economic issues. This encyclical paved the way for future popes to shape Catholic Social Teaching. In 1931 Pope Pius XI issued *Quadragesimo Anno (After Forty Years)* in which he addressed the need for a social order based on justice and **subsidiarity,** the belief that issues are often best handled at the lowest level of authority.

PRESENT: In 2009, Pope Benedict XVI presented *Caritas in Veritate (Charity in Truth)*, in which he discusses Catholic Social Teaching. In this encyclical, the pope tells us, "Charity is love received and given." He explains, "Love is revealed and made present by Christ (John 13:1) and 'poured into our hearts through the Holy Spirit.' (Romans 5:5) As the objects of God's love, men and women become subjects of charity, they are called to make themselves instruments of grace, so as to pour forth God's charity and to weave networks of charity."

Study Corner

DEFINE

Industrial Revolution, living wage, encyclical, subsidiarity

REMEMBER

As a result of the conditions laborers faced during the Industrial Revolution, Pope Leo XII wrote *Rerum Novarum*, which is recognized as the first of many documents that present Catholic Social Teaching.

Catholic Social Teaching

SINCE the time of the Industrial Revolution, the Church has taught that taking action to create a more just world is a central aspect of discipleship. Catholic Social Teaching is a rich treasure of wisdom about how we can build a just society and live holy lives amid the challenges of the modern world.

These teachings identify ways in which the Good News of Jesus can be proclaimed in word and action. In a nutshell, the Catholic Social Teachings instruct us to

- respect everyone, since all life is sacred.
- contribute to family and society by promoting the well-being of all.
- protect the basic human rights of every person.
- help meet the needs of those who are poor and sick.
- work hard and make sure that others have the opportunity to do the same.
- be a peacemaker and recognize that we all depend on one another.
- care for creation and respect plants and animals.

Every pope since Leo XIII has written at least one encyclical about social justice. The issues that the popes have addressed include loving people who are poor, feeding the hungry, sheltering the homeless, abolishing racism, and ending war. Bishops and theologians have also spoken out against injustice and have written about the importance of peace.

Justice, Love, and Peace

Catholic Social Teaching is rooted in the ideas of justice and love. Justice exists when we follow the guidance of the Holy Spirit and treat one another in the same way that God treats us. The Holy Spirit also calls us to love and care for the well-being of each member of the human family, just as Jesus did. We do this by practicing the Beatitudes, in which Jesus taught us the importance of being peacemakers and loving our enemies. In addition, the Church wants us to work for peace in our world.

In his encyclical, *Evangelium Vitae* (*The Gospel of Life*), Pope John Paul II pointed out that human life is sacred because it is a gift from God. We also believe that since Jesus has a unique relationship with every human being, we are able to see the face of Christ in every human face. This respect for human life requires that society respect, defend, and promote the dignity of the human person, beginning at the moment of conception and continuing through every moment and in every condition of each person's life. We demonstrate our belief in the sacredness of human life when we freely choose to respond to the call of justice, peace, and love. Finally, as members of a universal Church, we are called to **participation** in the life of the community. Through participation in the communities to which we belong, we work to build a just and peaceful society.

Solidarity

Jesus identified with all people and even spent time with those whom society considered to be outcasts. As Jesus' followers we are called by the Holy Spirit to live in solidarity with others. This means that we are called to live as one human family—whatever our differences may be. As Pope John Paul II pointed out, to live in solidarity with others is to commit oneself to the common good of every person.

Pope John Paul II wrote about the connection between charity and solidarity in his encyclical, *Sollicitudo Rei Socialis* (*On Social Concern*). This connection, which is fundamental to Catholic Social Teaching, is a distinguishing mark of Christ's disciples. In his encyclical the pope reminds us that through solidarity and charity, we recognize Christ in our neighbor. He points out that our neighbors are not only human beings, who have their own rights as humans, but that they also are the living image of God the Father. Each person is saved through Jesus Christ's Paschal Mystery and placed under the protection of the Holy Spirit.

There are many ways to demonstrate solidarity with others. One way is to take a stand against discrimination. We can do this by standing up for people who are teased, or bullied for being too smart, too dumb, too white, too brown, or too nice. We can also make sure that no one is excluded.

Another way to live in solidarity with others is to care for the earth. By caring for the environment, we show God's love to the people who will come after us.

The resources of creation are destined for the whole human race. When we follow God's commandments, we do not selfishly hoard or exploit the natural resources of the world. God calls us to share the gift of creation equally so that all people benefit. When we recognize our solidarity with others, we become more capable of working with our brothers and sisters to care for and renew the earth.

Our Catholic Character

Death is an important part of the gift and mystery of life. But in modern industrial societies, which tend to measure the value of life by the riches amassed, death can be seen as an unbearable defeat. When we separate death from life, we run the risk of denying death entirely or believing that we can choose death on our own terms to end suffering. Since God is the source of our life, every life is sacred. We must do what we can to lessen suffering, but we are not required to prolong life when death is imminent. We know this because our faith in the Resurrection gives new meaning to our life and death.

Looking Beyond Myself

The world is in need of more love, peace, and justice. Catholic Social Teachings call us to look at our own lives and our behavior as well as to recognize the injustices that exist all around us. These teachings call us to reach out in compassionate love, which is the basis for justice.

For Christians, our inner spiritual life goes hand in hand with our active life in the world. Whenever we nurture our love for God in prayer, we are better able to meet the needs of others and to reach out with love and compassion. In contrast, by acting in solidarity to bring love, make peace, and heal injustice, we can actually enrich our prayer life.

Through action, we encounter God in our present lives. In this way, our prayer can gives us the strength and desire to live in ways that transform the world into a better place for all of God's children.

Litany to Heal Injustice

Reader 1: Think of a person or a group of people who is suffering the effects of an injustice, such as poor living conditions, random acts of violence, false accusations of crime, or discrimination.

Reader 2: In your imagination surround this person or group with care and compassion. Pray a silent prayer for them. *(Pause.)*

Reader 3: Now let us pray together a litany for those who suffer from injustice. If you would like, pray aloud the intention for which you just prayed silently. After each person prays aloud, we will pray together, "Be merciful, O Lord."

CLOSING PRAYER

All: *God of mercy,*
touch with compassion the lives of those
who suffer unjustly.
Help us to be your instruments
of care and healing for others.
We ask this in the name of Jesus,
your Son and our brother. Amen.

WHERE Do I Fit In?

by Palmira Perea Hay

As Catholics we are called to respond to Catholic social and moral teachings. We are guided to assist the poor and vulnerable and to uphold the dignity of human life, each working with the unique gifts that God has given us to serve his kingdom.

How Do I Respond to the Needs Around Me?

Reflect

"For I was hungry and you gave me food, I was thirsty and you gave me drink, a stranger and you welcomed me, naked and you clothed me, ill and you cared for me, in prison and you visited me. . . . Amen, I say to you, whatever you did for one of these least brothers of mine, you did for me."

Matthew 25:35-36,40

I have a distant cousin who is deaf. When I was a child, my mother found out he had no place to live, so she invited him to live with us in our already-crowded house. He lived with us for years. I am now 70, and my mother's example of generosity still moves me and motivates me.

Recently, our parish got a request to visit a family in need. My husband and I are volunteers with the St. Vincent de Paul Society, so we made the visit one cold January day. It was a family in crisis—three children and a single mother. The mother had moved to our town because she had been diagnosed with lymphoma the day before Christmas, and she needed urgent cancer treatment. They also had very little money.

We arranged for the family to receive help. Our parish provided financial assistance with the rent and utilities. The woman needed a course of chemotherapy at the hospital, but she had no way to get there, was very anxious, and spoke only Spanish. I was able to take her to the hospital. I interpreted for her and stayed with her for

every treatment over seven months. The woman calls me her "Angelita." And now she has been declared to be free of lymphoma.

It is a gift and a privilege to participate in the healing of another person. Why did I do it? My mother's example still shows me the way—the way of Jesus.

Needs Chart

On a separate sheet of paper, make a three-column chart with the following headings: *At Home, At School,* and *In My Community.* Under each heading, list at least three areas in which you see a need for care, love, or healing. Then reflect by asking yourself, "How might I bring care, love, or healing in each situation?" Take time in prayer to ask the Holy Spirit to show you how to respond to each need. Notice what happens as you work to meet the needs you listed.

PALMIRA PEREA HAY lives in Albuquerque, New Mexico, with her husband, Steve. Together they engage in ministries such as taking Holy Communion to people in the hospital and visiting people in prison.

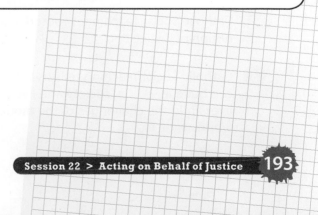

What's What?

Review the concepts from this session by completing the crossword.

ACROSS

5 Our faith in the _____ gives new meaning to our life and death. (PAGE 191)

7 Whenever we nurture our love for God in prayer, we are better able to meet the needs of others and to reach out with _____. (PAGE 192)

8 One way to demonstrate our _____ with others is to take a stand against discrimination. (PAGE 191)

9 As a result of the Industrial Revolution, world economies began to rely more on _____ than on farming. (PAGE 188)

10 In the mid-19th century, over 20 percent of the urban workforce was made up of _____. (PAGE 188)

DOWN

1 Blessed Pope John Paul II pointed out that _____ life is sacred because it is a gift from God. (PAGE 190)

2 Catholic Social Teaching is rooted in the notion of justice and _____. (PAGE 190)

3 Catholic Social Teaching tells us how we can build a _____ society and live holy lives amid the challenges of the modern world. (PAGE 190)

4 In encyclicals on social justice, popes have addressed issues such as loving people who are poor, feeding the hungry, sheltering the homeless, abolishing racism, and ending _____. (PAGE 190)

6 Pope Leo XIII's _____ titled *On the Condition of Labor* was the first to apply Catholic teaching to the rights of humans to work and earn fair wages. (PAGE 189)

Say What

Know the definitions of these terms.

encyclical   participation

Industrial Revolution   subsidiarity

living wage

Now What?

Catholic Social Teaching calls us to stand in solidarity with human beings all over the world. On a separate sheet of paper, write what you can do during the next week to practice solidarity with others.

Respond

Called by God

Think about a time you were invited to serve others without receiving anything in return. What was the situation, and how did you respond? What did you learn from the experience?

PRAYER

God, give us the strength to respond to your invitation to serve others. May we remain faithful to your call to share Christ's love with others.

Pope John XXIII

The Second Vatican Council

IN the mid-20th century, Pope John XXIII called an ecumenical council to address new issues in the Church and society that arose from changes brought about by the Industrial Revolution, war, and the rise of fascism and communism.

The decisions that were made at the Second Vatican Council continue to shape how we practice our faith today. Recall the last time you went to Mass. The fact that the prayers and Scripture readings were in a language other than Latin and that there were lay ministers are just two of the changes that came about as the result of decisions made during the Second Vatican Council.

Providing Direction for the Future

Inspired by the Holy Spirit, Pope John XXIII responded to the challenges of the 20th century by calling the bishops of the world to come together for the Second Vatican Council. Pope John XXIII hinted that he would convene a

Extraordinary Synod, Franklin McMahon, 1985.

SACRED ART

This artwork depicts a meeting convened by Pope John Paul II during which bishops from all over the world met to reaffirm the message of the Second Vatican Council. Meeting such as these, called by the pope to discuss matters of doctrine and pastoral care, are called **synods.** The pope also has the authority to call for an Ecumenical Council, a gathering of all the world's bishops. During a council, Church leaders exercise their role as members of the Magisterium. One of the main differences between a synod and an Ecumenical Council is that with the pope's approval, the decisions of an Ecumenical Council are official teachings of the Church. During a synod, however, the members offer suggestions to the pope, which may or may not become official teachings at a later time.

council in 1959, shortly after he was elected pope. It took more than two years, however, for Church leaders to prepare for this grand event.

Around 2,450 bishops, as well as theologians, members of religious orders, and lay people attended this council, which lasted from 1962–1965. Unlike many previous Ecumenical Councils, the goal of the bishops during the Second Vatican Council was not to respond to people who were teaching heresy. Rather, Church leaders explored how Church teaching could be made clearer. One of the outcomes of the council was the invitation to all Catholics to recognize their call to holiness so that they could be effective evangelizers in the world.

Renewal

During the Second Vatican Council, the bishops approved 16 documents that responded to major issues of the modern day. Some of the Church teachings that were emphasized in the council documents include the role of the **laity** as the People of God and the need for a renewed understanding of the Church and its mission in the modern era. One document, for example, reminds us that each baptized person should recognize his or her call from God to live a life of holiness. The document on the role of the Church in the modern world points out that all members of the Church are called to support goodness and correct evils in the world. The document on the liturgy called for further renewal in the Mass and allowed for priests to celebrate Mass in the language of the people rather than in Latin, as was the custom. In the document on divine Revelation, the council clarified the Church's teaching on Scripture and Tradition and called for Catholics to read the Bible more frequently and with greater devotion. In the document on religious freedom, the Church reaffirmed its commitment to support and work for everyone's right to religious freedom.

The Church continues to renew itself in response to the signs of the times. In 2011, Catholics in the United States began using a new edition of the *Roman Missal*. Previously called the *Sacramentary*, the *Roman Missal* is the book that contains all the prayers that are prayed at Mass. The most current edition of the *Roman Missal* is a closer translation of the Latin original.

Explore

Our Catholic Character

During the Second Vatican Council, Church leaders clearly stated that the Eucharist is the high point of our lives as Catholics. To help us enter more fully into the sacrament, the Council made changes in the way we celebrate the Eucharist. For centuries the Mass was prayed in Latin, with the priest facing an altar built into the wall of the sanctuary, with his back to the assembly. Holy Communion was received only under the form of bread. There were no lay lectors or extraordinary ministers of Holy Communion. Choirs often sang for the people rather than with the people. In many parishes, congregations used English missals while following along with Latin prayers. Think about Mass in your parish today. How is it different from what is described here? The more participatory nature of today's Mass can be attributed to the vision, understanding, and work of the bishops at the Second Vatican Council.

Study Corner

DEFINE

synod, laity

REMEMBER

Pope John XXIII called the bishops together for the Second Vatican Council, during which the Church's leaders responded to major social and religious issues of the day.

Called to Holiness

IN the document titled *Dogmatic Constitution on the Church*, the Second Vatican Council emphasized that all Christians are called to holiness—that we are all called to be saints. The bishops at the council sought to remind us that we are called to live holy lives because we are made in God's image. Through the council's teachings, we learn that each person's unique vocation offers its own way to achieve holiness.

Through the Sacraments of Initiation, we receive the grace we need to respond to this call to holiness. Filled with this grace, we respond to the call to holiness by sharing Christ's love with others through our words and actions—in places and circumstances where it's needed most, whether in our homes, our schools, our communities, or in the world at large.

Scripture clearly tells us that we are to model our lives after Christ as a way to seek holiness. For example, the author of First Peter calls God's people "living stones" who are to model their lives on Jesus Christ, the cornerstone.

> Come to him, a living stone, rejected by human beings but chosen and precious in the sight of God, and, like living stones, let yourselves be built into a spiritual house to be a holy priesthood to offer spiritual sacrifices acceptable to God through Jesus Christ.
>
> *1 Peter 2:4–5*

The *Catechism of the Catholic Church* reinforces the call to holiness by telling us, "All Christians in any state are called to the fullness of Christian life and to the perfection of charity. All are called to holiness." (CCC 2013) The *Catechism* goes on to explain that we should wholeheartedly devote ourselves to the glory of God and to the service of our neighbors.

It's not always easy to choose to build up God's kingdom, to serve others, or to preach the Good News. Through our devotion to the glory of God, we are sometimes called to offer spiritual sacrifices. We know that we are living stones who, united in Christ, can live lives of holiness to help others in many ways, including helping them grow in their relationship with Jesus and his Church.

Many Gifts

In addition to the grace that we receive through the Sacraments of Initiation, each of us has received unique gifts and talents that enable us to respond to God's call of holiness. Paul explained this in his First Letter to the Corinthians.

> There are different kinds of spiritual gifts but the same Spirit; there are different forms of service, but the same Lord; there are different workings but the same God who produces all of them in everyone. To each individual the manifestation of the Spirit is given for some benefit. To one is given through the Spirit the expression of wisdom; to another the expression of knowledge

according to the same Spirit; to another faith by the same Spirit; to another gifts of healing by the one Spirit; to another mighty deeds; to another prophecy; to another discernment of spirits; to another varieties of tongues; to another interpretation of tongues. But one and the same Spirit produces all of these, distributing them individually to each person as he wishes.

1 Corinthians 12:4–11

All Christians, whether married, single, religious, or ordained, cooperate in the building up of the Body of Christ. In the Church there is a diversity of ministries and a unity of mission—to make Christ present in the world today. Regardless of the gifts that we have been given or the ways we have been called to serve, we are all equal before God, who made us in

All Christians, whether married, single, religious, or ordained, cooperate in the building up of the Body of Christ.

his image and likeness. By remembering this, we are reminded that we are all one human family with God as our Father.

Pope John Paul II wrote about the universal call to holiness in his 1988 Apostolic Exhortation *Christifideles Laici (On the Vocation and the Mission of the Lay Faithful in the Church and in the World).*

Everyone in the Church, precisely because they are members, receive and thereby share in the common vocation to holiness. . . . [On] equal par with all other members of the Church, the lay faithful are called to holiness . . . The call to holiness is rooted in Baptism and proposed anew in the other Sacraments, principally in the Eucharist. Since Christians are reclothed in Christ Jesus and refreshed by his Spirit, they are "holy." They therefore have the ability to manifest this holiness and the responsibility to bear witness to it in all that they do.

Explore

Study Corner

REMEMBER

God has called each of us to a life of holiness. We respond to this call by building up God's kingdom. We receive the grace and strength to live holy lives through the sacraments, especially the Eucharist. This grace gives us the strength to practice the gifts we have received from God.

READY for Confirmation

As one who is preparing for Confirmation, it is important to understand the four Marks of the Church, which tell us that the Church is one, holy, catholic, and apostolic. When we say the Church is one, we mean that the Church is unified in the Holy Spirit and that the fullness of Christ's body subsists in the Catholic Church. In the Holy Spirit, her members are united in Christ. When we say the Church is holy, we mean that she is consecrated to the service and worship of God. When we say the Church is catholic, or universal, we mean that she possesses the fullness of Christ's presence and the means of Salvation sent on a mission to the whole human family. When we say the Church is apostolic, we mean that the sole Church of Christ subsists in the Catholic Church and is governed by the successor of Peter and her bishops.

Abundant Harvest

The word *intercession*

means "to ask something on behalf of another." A prayer of intercession is a form of prayer that leads us to pray as Jesus did.

Throughout his life on earth, Jesus interceded with the Father on behalf of all people. The Holy Spirit inspires us to pray in this way so that our hearts are turned outward and focused on the needs of the people around us. When we intercede for others, we are asking for God's mercy on their behalf.

Interceding for Others

All: In the Name of the Father, and of the Son, and of the Holy Spirit. Amen.

Leader: Reflect silently as I read aloud from the holy Gospel according to Matthew. [Read aloud Matthew 9:35–38.]

The Gospel of the Lord.

All: Praise to you, Lord Jesus Christ.

Reader 1: Silently reflect on the passage. Ask yourself: *How might God be calling me to help with the harvest at this time in my life?* Let us ask God to send laborers to spread the Good News.

Reader 2: God of mercy, you sent your Son to teach, preach, and heal. Grant that people everywhere may follow his example and work to serve the Kingdom of God. Let us pray to the Lord.

All: Lord, hear our prayer.

Reader 1: Faithful God, we pray that all people hear your call to serve and respond generously. Let us pray to the Lord.

All: Lord, hear our prayer.

Reader 2: God of love, we pray for ourselves, asking you to reveal to each of us how we can live in service. Grant us the grace to be open to your invitation to join Jesus in his ministry. Let us pray to the Lord.

All: Lord, hear our prayer.

Reader 1: Let's pause to add our own petitions silently. *(Pause.)* Mindful of all our prayers, those spoken and those in our hearts, let us pray.

Reader 2: May Jesus guide our steps and enlighten our hearts. May the Holy Spirit be with us, showing us how to spread the Good News at home, at school, in our communities, and in our world.

All: Amen.

WHERE Do I Fit In?

by Gregory Augustine Pierce

Since before kindergarten, most of us have heard over and over again that it is important to share, take turns, help others, and generally make the world a better place. We know this almost instinctively, and so we might not take time to think about why this concept is important. As Catholics we know that we can look to Jesus Christ for the answer.

Why Am I Being Sent?

At the end of his time on earth, Jesus gathered his disciples together and told them to go out into the entire world to preach, baptize, and build the Kingdom of God. They were sent.

I grew up in New York City. I got sent to Chicago.

My wife and I have three children. I run a small business that produces good products and provides excellent service to our customers. I vote in every election, and I am involved in a variety of community organizations and social justice efforts. This work is how I try to make the world a better place. As a husband, father, businessman, and citizen, I carry out my part of Jesus' mission to proclaim that the reign of God has already begun—that it is within each and every one of us.

Many people think that only priests, nuns, brothers, and deacons have vocations. Actually, every baptized Christian has a calling from God. This call is to build up what Jesus called "the kingdom of God, on earth as it is in heaven." This was Jesus' vision for how the world should be—a very different way for human beings to relate to one another and to our world, because it is based on love, not hatred, power, money, or ambition.

Jesus told a story about two sons. If told today, the story might go something like this. The father said to the first son, "Please go out and mow the lawn." The boy said he would, but his friends showed up and so he went off with them instead. The man then said to his second son, "Please go out and mow the lawn." But the boy complained, "I did it last time. It's my brother's turn. My friends are coming over right now. I won't do it." But when his friends arrived, the boy told them to come back in an hour, and he went out and mowed his father's lawn. Jesus asks us, "Which son did the will of the father?" The correct answer is "the one who mowed the lawn."

So, mow the lawn. Find the work God has for you, and do it.

GREGORY AUGUSTINE PIERCE is a husband, father, publisher, writer, speaker, community organizer, baseball coach, and Cubs and Bulls fan.

Reflect

Witness to Love

Write on the lines two or three sentences to describe a time when you witnessed someone making a decision based on love rather than hatred—even when hatred may have seem justified. Then write a final sentence to describe one positive outcome of this person's decision.

_____

_____

_____

_____

_____

_____

_____

What's What?

Complete each sentence with the correct word or phrase.

1. Church leaders exercise their role as members of the _____ during an ecumenical council. (PAGE 196)

2. Pope John XXIII was inspired by the _____ when he called the bishops of the world to gather for the Second Vatican Council. (PAGE 197)

3. A teaching emphasized in the council documents included the role of the _____ as the People of God. (PAGE 197)

4. The document on _____ allowed priests to celebrate Mass in the language of the people. (PAGE 197)

5. We receive the _____ that we need to live lives of holiness. (PAGE 198)

6. The *Catechism* tells us that we should wholeheartedly devote ourselves to the _____ and to the service of our neighbors. (PAGE 198)

7. There are different kinds of spiritual _____ but the same Spirit. (PAGE 198)

8. One mark of the Church is that the Church is _____ because Jesus, its founder, is holy. (PAGE 199)

9. Throughout his life on earth, Jesus _____ with the Father on behalf of all people. (PAGE 200)

Say What?

Know the definitions of these terms.

laity
synod

Now What?

You have unique gifts and talents that enable you to respond to God's call to holiness. Think about the needs of your family and friends. What is one gift that you will use this week to bring Christ's peace and love to others?

_____
_____
_____
_____
_____
_____
_____
_____
_____
_____
_____
_____
_____
_____
_____
_____

Respond

People for Others

Think about a time you were invited to share a special gift or talent. Perhaps you were asked to show a small child how to play a game or to perform at a family party. What were you invited to do? Why do you think you were asked? How did you respond? In what way did your service help build up the Kingdom of God?

PRAYER

Jesus, thank you for inviting us to spread your message of peace and love with others. May we always be willing to go wherever your Spirit leads us.

203

Hearing the Cry of the Poor

THROUGHOUT Scripture we read about God's concern for people who are poor. In Exodus we learn that God freed the Chosen People from slavery. In Deuteronomy, creditors are called upon to cancel debts after seven years so that no one in the community would be in need. The psalms assure us that the Lord hears the cry of the poor. And in the Gospel of Luke, we read the words that Jesus spoke when he began his public ministry—words first spoken by the prophet Isaiah.

> "The Spirit of the Lord is upon me,
>   because he has anointed me
>   to bring glad tidings to the poor.
> He has sent me to proclaim liberty to captives
>   and recovery of sight to the blind,
>   to let the oppressed go free,
> and to proclaim a year acceptable to the Lord."
>
> *Luke 4:18–19*

Christians have always worked together to care for others in need. For example, in the Acts of the Apostles, we learn that the early Christians collected alms for widows, orphans, and others who were poor. Today, Church leaders call us to do the same—to stand up for and provide for the needs of those who are poor and marginalized.

Blessed Teresa of Calcutta

Blessed Teresa of Calcutta (1910–1997) wholeheartedly responded to the call to care for others. Teresa of Calcutta was born in what is now Macedonia. Her parents, who were of Albanian descent, named her Agnes Gonxha Bojaxhiu. By the time she was 12, Agnes knew that God was calling her to become a religious sister. At the age of 18, she joined the Sisters of Loreto and traveled to a convent in Ireland where she learned English so that she could teach in India. Shorty after beginning her career at Saint Theresa's School in India, Agnes made her first vows and took the name Teresa—the Spanish spelling of the name Thèrésa—in honor of Thèrése of Lisieux, the patron saint of missionaries. Sister Teresa was eventually named headmistress, or principal, of the school.

Our Catholic Character

Saints throughout history have heard God's call to serve people who were poor and sick. In the fourth century, a Roman soldier named Martin of Tours gave his cloak to a man who was shivering in the cold. Later that night Martin dreamed that he saw Jesus dressed in the cloak he had given to the man. This dream had a profound impact on Martin, who converted to Christianity and later was chosen to be a bishop. In addition, Saint Frances of Rome, who lived in the 15th century, founded a community of women who dedicated themselves to caring for people who were poor.

A Call Within a Call

In 1946 Sister Teresa was traveling by train to her annual retreat when she received what she termed "a call within a call." She had an experience which led her to believe that Jesus wanted her to begin caring for people living in the slums of Calcutta, one of India's largest cities. After receiving basic medical training, Sister Teresa began caring for people in need. Other women soon joined her. In 1950 she received permission from the pope to found a new religious community, the Missionaries of Charity. Sister Teresa frequently is called Mother Teresa because she was the longtime **superior,** or leader, of the community.

One of the new religious community's first works was to open a home for the dying, a place for people to receive free medical care and die with dignity. The next major initiatives were to open a home for people with Hansen's disease and a house for children who were homeless or orphaned. As news spread, many others wanted to join the community, including men who wanted to become religious brothers and women who wanted to live a more **contemplative,** or prayerful, life. This growth allowed the Missionaries of Charity to begin working in other parts of the world.

By the time Mother Teresa died in 1997, there were around 4,500 sisters staffing 610 missions in 123 countries all over the world. The work of the community, which continues today, includes caring for people who are sick and dying and who are living with HIV/AIDS. In 1979 Mother Teresa received the Noble Peace Prize, and in 2003 she was **beatified** by Pope John Paul II and given the name Blessed Teresa of Calcutta.

Study Corner

DEFINE

superior, contemplative, beatified

REMEMBER

Throughout history, Christians have worked together to care for people in need. Blessed Teresa of Calcutta is an example of someone who remained faithful to God's call to care for others, even though she experienced moments of doubt.

Explore

Faith and Doubt

During her life, Mother Teresa remained faithful to prayer even though she experienced periods of doubt. Always honest about her faith journey and relationship with God, Mother Teresa provides a good example for us—she chose to remain faithful to what God had called her to do despite times of uncertainty. She followed God's will for her by caring for the poorest of the poor and those who had been rejected by society.

Sister of Charity, Saint Louise de Marillac, ca. 1630.

SACRED ART

Saint Louise de Marillac, who worked with Saint Vincent de Paul in Paris, France, also responded to God's call to help others. In addition to providing charity, Vincent de Paul and Louise worked for long-term change. One way they did this was by founding the Congregation of the Mission and the Daughters of Charity, two religious communities that continue to care for people in need.

Works of Mercy

CHURCH teachings always leads us to Christ. In Scripture, Jesus teaches us that when we care for the needs of others, we serve him as well.

Then the king will say to those on his right, 'Come, you who are blessed by my Father. Inherit the kingdom prepared for you from the foundation of the world. For I was hungry and you gave me food, I was thirsty and you gave me drink, a stranger and you welcomed me, naked and you clothed me, ill and you cared for me, in prison and you visited me.' Then the righteous will answer him and say, 'Lord, when did we see you hungry and feed you, or thirsty and give you drink? When did we see you a stranger and welcome you, or naked and clothe you? When did we see you ill or in prison, and visit you?' And the king will say to them in reply, 'Amen, I say to you, whatever you did for one of these least brothers of mine, you did for me.'

Matthew 25:34–40

Our Catholic Character

Saint Ignatius of Loyola believed that God's loving generosity is revealed through the creation of the world and in Jesus, his Son. He believed that God's generosity challenges us to be generous toward others so that we can mirror God's love to those around us. In this spirit, Ignatius of Loyola gave the Church his Prayer for Generosity, a prayer in which we ask God to help us humbly and generously serve the needs of others.

Corporal Works of Mercy

The Church has given us the Corporal Works of Mercy as a way to help us respond to the call to serve the needs of others. The Corporal Works of Mercy are kind acts by which we can care for our neighbors' physical and material needs.

- **Feed the Hungry** Ways to feed the hungry include donating to a food pantry or volunteering at a soup kitchen.

- **Shelter the Homeless** We can volunteer at a shelter or support organizations that serve people who are homeless.

- **Clothe the Naked** Ways to clothe the naked include donating clothing or baby supplies to organizations that help individuals or families in need.

- **Visit the Sick and Imprisoned** We can reach out to the lonely. We can visit nursing homes, and we can send cards to people who are sick. We can support prison ministries and agencies that fight injustice.

- **Give Alms to the Poor** We can give alms to organizations that serve people who are poor. We can share our time and talents.

- **Bury the Dead** We can attend wakes and funerals, provide food baskets to hospice care centers, and send sympathy cards.

Spiritual Works of Mercy

The Church also guides us to perform Spiritual Works of Mercy, which are ways by which we can care for people's emotional and spiritual needs.

- **Instruct** We can share our faith with others. We can share our knowledge by tutoring or teaching a skill.

- **Advise** We can refuse to participate in gossip, discrimination, or unjust behavior and call others to stop or avoid such behavior.

- **Console** We can assure those in doubt or despair of the loving presence of God.

- **Comfort** We can listen, offer sympathy to those who have experienced a hardship, or be present to those who are struggling or in pain.

- **Forgive** We can receive the grace to forgive others through celebrating the Sacrament of Reconciliation. We can forgive by choosing not to hold grudges. We can be kind even to those who aren't kind to us. We can find ways to make peace with those who have hurt us.

- **Bear Wrongs with Patience** We can turn away from seeking revenge when someone hurts us, by praying for those who have wronged us, and by giving people the benefit of the doubt.

Explore

Study Corner

REMEMBER

The Works of Mercy are ways by which we can care for the needs of others. When we practice these Works, we respond to God's call to care for the most vulnerable among us.

Donations

READY for Confirmation

Confirmation, like all the sacraments, is not about what you are doing but what God is doing through you. Know that the Holy Spirit that descended upon the Apostles at Pentecost is the same Spirit that you receive when you are anointed with Chrism at Confirmation. The Gifts of the Holy Spirit that you receive give you the strength to share in God's work of caring for the needs of others. These gifts also empower you to practice the Works of Mercy and in doing so build up the Kingdom of God.

Make Peace

One way to respond to the needs of others is by being a peacemaker. We make peace in the world by speaking out against violence and by living a virtuous life.

In the Sermon on the Mount in Matthew's Gospel, Jesus teaches that conversion of heart, from anger and hatred to true love of one's neighbor, is essential for Christian living. We are to love our enemies and pray for our persecutors, which the works of Mercy encourage us to do. Another Scripture passage reminds us to reconcile with our brother or sister before bringing our gift to the altar.

Acts of conversion and reconciliation form the basis of fruitful prayer. Through prayerful forgiveness from the depth of a pure heart that seeks the kingdom before all else, we learn to pray as the children of God.

Beatitude Reflection

Family We don't get to choose our families. Our parents, brothers, sisters, and other relatives are all given to us. We journey together through good times and bad, through the ups and downs of life. Nobody's family is perfect, and the peace we desire is not always present. Each of us, however, in our own way, is called to work for peace at home. How can you be a peacemaker in your family?

Blessed are the peacemakers, for they will be called children of God.

Community Peacemakers learn to love their enemies as Jesus taught us. It's easy to pretend you don't have enemies, but there are likely people whom you don't like and try to avoid. Your enemy might be a classmate who, even without saying a word, reminds you that you're not part of the "in" group. Or the enemy might be someone you tease because he or she looks or talks or dresses differently than you do. What gesture of peace can you offer today?

Blessed are the peacemakers, for they will be called children of God.

World Peace doesn't happen by itself. Peace begins with people who are committed to work for justice, not just for themselves but for everyone. When you choose to buy clothing from companies that treat workers fairly, you help create peace. When you volunteer to assist others in need, you help create peace. When you take time to learn about people from another country or religious tradition and reach out in friendship, you are helping create peace. How will you work for justice to create peace?

End by exchanging a sign of peace.

WHERE Do I Fit In?

Do you sometimes get nervous thinking about your future? If so, you are not alone. We all feel some anxiety when we ask ourselves, "What I am supposed to do in my life?" However, here is a truth you can count on: God will show you the way if you learn to pay attention.

by Tom McGrath

Discovering Who You're Meant to Be

How many times have you been asked, "So what are you going to be when you grow up?" I know that I was well into my 20s before I could answer that question, which left me feeling anxious.

Many years later, though, I realized I didn't need to be worried. The truth is that life unfolds. We learn as we go. Some people get a clear sense of what they want to do early on. Most of us take years to understand our purpose and path in life. I know that was true for me.

I have had dozens of jobs in my life—starting with a paper route when I was 11—and I have learned from every single one of them. For example, I thought I'd enjoy the people aspect of being in sales, but I discovered I disliked asking people for their order—a valuable lesson.

I loved working on a landscaping crew because I was outdoors doing physical labor. While that experience didn't lead to a career, it inspired me to weave certain activities—hiking, camping, and gardening—into my life that have brought me much joy.

One summer, hoping to "find myself," I became a camp counselor for troubled kids. Between the archery lessons and ghost stories, I came to recognize the impact that a child's early development has—for good or for ill. That interest shaped my career as a writer and editor leading to a number of books and magazine articles to help parents provide their children a healthy start in life.

So, let me suggest two DOs and one DON'T to you:

1. DO learn to trust that God will show you the way. In fact, God has placed the answer to the question, "Who should I become?" within you. "I will place my law within them, and write it upon their hearts; I will be their God, and they shall be my people." (Jeremiah 31:33)

2. DO start and keep a habit of daily prayer. Pay attention to what God's hopes are for you, and invite God to offer the help he is so eager to provide. A habit of prayer will help you become familiar with God's voice in your life.

3. DON'T compare yourself to others. It's tempting to compare ourselves (usually negatively) to other people. However, realize that you are unique and so is God's path for you. As the saying goes, "Be yourself; everyone else is already taken!"

God wants you to live YOUR life! Try new things. Join clubs and teams. Volunteer to help others. Pursue a new hobby. Find out what stirs joy and enthusiasm in your heart. Ask yourself often what makes you feel more alive and what drains life. Through it all, pray daily, listen for the voice of God, and trust that the path is already unfolding before you.

TOM MCGRATH is a husband, dad, and grandpa as well as the author of *Raising Faith-Filled Kids*.

What's What?

Review the concepts from this session by matching the descriptions on the right with the Works of Mercy listed on the left.

_____ **1** Feed the Hungry (PAGE 207)

_____ **2** Shelter the Homeless (PAGE 207)

_____ **3** Clothe the Naked (PAGE 207)

_____ **4** Visit the Sick and Imprisoned (PAGE 207)

_____ **5** Give Alms to the Poor (PAGE 207)

_____ **6** Bury the Dead (PAGE 207)

_____ **7** Instruct (PAGE 207)

_____ **8** Advise (PAGE 207)

_____ **9** Console (PAGE 207)

_____ **10** Comfort (PAGE 207)

_____ **11** Forgive (PAGE 207)

_____ **12** Bear Wrongs with Patience (PAGE 207)

a. Assure those in doubt or despair of the loving presence of God.

b. Share our faith with others.

c. Volunteer at a shelter.

d. Offer sympathy to those who have experienced a hardship.

e. Visit nursing homes; send cards to people who are sick.

f. Attend wakes and funerals.

g. Donate to a food pantry or volunteer at a soup kitchen.

h. Refuse to participate in unjust behavior and call on others to do the same.

i. Pray for those who have wronged us.

j. Donate baby clothing and supplies.

k. Choose not to hold grudges.

l. Give alms to organizations that serve people who are poor.

Say What?

Know the definitions of these terms.

beatified

contemplative

superior

Now What?

God calls us to respond to the needs of people who are suffering and vulnerable. What can you do this week to respond to this call? Write your ideas on a separate sheet of paper.

Celebrating Pentecost

AS the Church, we are the People of God, a community of believers who share in God's infinite wisdom through Jesus' teachings and the guidance of the Holy Spirit. Each year, on the Feast of Pentecost, 50 days after Easter, we celebrate the birth of the Church.

The Pentecost event, which we remember each year on Pentecost Sunday, occurred nine days after Jesus' Ascension into Heaven. On this day, Mary and the Apostles were gathered together in one room. Here is what Scripture tells us happened next:

> And suddenly there came from the sky a noise like a strong driving wind, and it filled the entire house in which they were. Then there appeared to them tongues as of fire, which parted and came to rest on each one of them. And they were filled with the holy Spirit and began to speak in different tongues, as the Spirit enabled them to proclaim.''

Acts of the Apostles 2:2–4

The Holy Spirit came down upon the Apostles and made it possible for them to share God's Word with people of many different languages. Through the Apostles, with Peter as their leader, the Good News of Salvation quickly spread.

On Pentecost Sunday we celebrate the work of the Holy Spirit in the past and in the present—in the lives of those who came before us, in our own lives, and in the lives of others. We go forth as people filled with grace, guided by the Holy Spirit to serve the Kingdom of God.

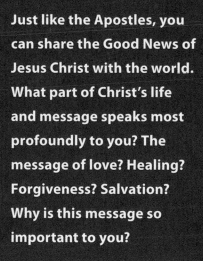

Just like the Apostles, you can share the Good News of Jesus Christ with the world. What part of Christ's life and message speaks most profoundly to you? The message of love? Healing? Forgiveness? Salvation? Why is this message so important to you?

PRAYER

Holy Spirit, help us share the Good News of Jesus Christ in our own unique ways. Empower us to develop our gifts and talents for the service of God's kingdom.

Proclaiming Christ Anew

Saint John Paul II, pope

IN many ways, the circumstances that the members of the Church encounter today are similar to those faced by the Apostles at Pentecost. We are called to proclaim the message of Christ to a world that may not readily accept it.

With Christ's strength, we can go forward with conviction and compassion. We can look for guidance from the Holy Spirit and from other Spirit-led people in our Church whose lives are an example for us.

Saint John Paul II

Karol Wojtyla was born on May 18, 1920, near Krakow, Poland. As a young boy, he enjoyed skiing and swimming. During college he was interested in theater and poetry. When his school was closed by Nazi troops, Wojtyla began studying at a secret seminary run by the archbishop of Krakow. Wojtyla was ordained in 1946. Father Wojtyla was soon recognized as a leading thinker and participated in the Second Vatican Council. Wojtyla was named a bishop, then an archbishop, and, eventually, a cardinal.

For 456 years, from 1522–1978, all the popes had been Italian. In 1978, the cardinals of the Church gathered in Rome and selected Cardinal Wojtyla of Poland to be pope. Wojtyla took the name John Paul II and became the 264th pope.

Pope John Paul II was known as a peacemaker and as someone who lived a life of openness and charity. Pope John Paul II spoke out against war, violence, and capital punishment. He was a defender of the dignity of human life and an advocate for human rights. While pope, he was instrumental in bringing about the fall of communism in Eastern Europe. Often recognized as the pilgrim pope because of his travels to more than 100 countries, Pope John Paul II attracted huge crowds wherever he went.

On April 2, 2005, Pope John Paul II passed away. From the evening of April 2 until his funeral on April 8, more than three million people came to Rome to pay homage to him in Saint Peter's Basilica.

Our Catholic Character

The Church follows a process to beatify and canonize a person who has lived a life of heroic virtue. During the process, two miracles must be proven to be attributed to the intercession of the person—miracles that are instant, able to be proven scientifically, complete, and permanent. Upon canonization, the person is recognized as a saint. As part of the process, experts research the person's life and gather testimonials. In the case of Pope John Paul II, four volumes of information were gathered, and 100 witnesses were interviewed.

World Youth Day

In 1984, Pope John Paul II announced that 1985 would be a **Jubilee Year** for the Catholic Church. The term *jubilee* has been used in the Church since the 1300s to refer to a holy year, a year in which the pope calls people to witness to their faith in specific ways. Aware of the rising number of youth in the Church, Pope John Paul II invited young people from around the world to travel to Rome and gather in Saint Peter's Square for Palm Sunday. More than 300,000 young people responded. After attending this first unofficial World Youth Day, the pope invited the youth to return home to live in virtue and share their renewed faith.

On December 20, 1985, the Holy Father announced the institution of World Youth Day as a regular event. The first official World Youth Day was held in 1986. From that year forward, International World Youth Day has been held every two to three years, in locations such as the Philippines, Spain, Poland, and the United States.

The events at each International World Youth Day take their inspiration from a theme derived from Scripture. For example, in 1993, the theme was "I came that they might have life and have it more abundantly." (John 10:10) During each celebration, it's common to see flags from the world's nations along with singing, dancing, praying, worshiping, and the honoring of both the cultural diversity and the religious unity of the young People of God.

Here is an excerpt from Pope John Paul's message to the participants of the 1993 World Youth Day:

> At this stage of history, the liberating message of the Gospel of life has been put into your hands. And the mission of proclaiming it to the ends of the earth is now passing to your generation. . . . The Church needs your energies, your enthusiasm, your youthful ideals, in order to make the Gospel of life penetrate the fabric of society, transforming people's hearts and the structures of society in order to create a civilization of true justice and love. Now more than ever, in a world that is often without light and without the courage of noble ideals, people need the fresh, vital spirituality of the Gospel.

World Youth Day is one of the many blessings that Saint John Paul II gave to the People of God.

Past Meets Present

PAST: The origins of the designation of a year as a Jubilee Year come from the Old Testament book of Leviticus. According to Jewish law during biblical times, every 50th year, farmland was to remain unplanted, mortgage debts were to be settled, and slaves were to be freed. The Catholic Church adapted this tradition in the 1300s.

PRESENT: In 2009 Pope Benedict XVI officially opened a Jubilee Year for Priests. This Jubilee coincided with the 150th anniversary of the death of Saint John Vianney. The Holy Father called for a year of prayer and renewal that invited Catholics to pray for priests, encourage entry into the vocations, and deepen their love and devotion for the Eucharist and all the sacraments.

Explore

Study Corner

DEFINE

Jubilee Year

REMEMBER

Each year, on the Feast of Pentecost, we celebrate the birth of the Church.

Saint John Paul II was a Church leader who showed us how to share the message of Christ with conviction and compassion.

The New Evangelization

POPE John Paul II realized that one of the greatest problems facing the Church is that some people are indifferent about faith—they don't care to hear about Jesus and his message of Salvation.

The pope taught that Catholics can respond to this indifference by showing how living as a Christian gives meaning to life. Pope John Paul II used the term *New Evangelization* to describe our call to serve as evangelists, both to those who have not yet heard the Gospel, as well as to traditional Christian countries who need to hear the Gospel anew. In his teaching, the pope presented these principles for the New Evangelization.

The New Evangelization is

➡ Christ-centered, founded on Jesus Christ and his Gospel.

➡ the responsibility of all the People of God, not only those in religious vocations.

➡ for all places on earth, not just for foreign missions.

➡ for individuals as well as entire cultures.

➡ the teaching of the Gospel, of catechesis, and of the moral and social teachings of the Church.

➡ a way of spirituality that calls us to know Christ and to make him known to all people.

SACRED ART

The Coming of the Holy Spirit is an oil painting that shows the descent of the Holy Spirit at Pentecost. The waves overhead represent the rush of wind that accompanied the flames. The dove represents the Holy Spirit. It is important to note that the Apostles themselves form a heart—a common symbol that represents the love that Jesus has for all of us and the love that the Apostles had for Jesus. The joined arms of the two Apostles in the center also form a heart shape. The faceless apostles of many shades reminds us that the Holy Spirit has come to and remains with all of us.

The Coming of the Holy Spirit, Soichi Watanabe, 1996.

Pontifical Council for Promoting New Evangelization

Pope Benedict XVI, the successor of Pope John Paul II, reminded Catholics of the need to have a clear understanding of our faith. Only in this way can we prepare ourselves to be a sign of Jesus' love to the world. On September 21, 2010, Pope Benedict XVI wrote an apostolic letter that officially established an office of the Roman Curia called the Pontifical Council for Promoting New Evangelization. This office seeks to turn words into action—to help Catholics around the world be regenerated by the power of the Holy Spirit so that they can give witness to the saving grace and truth that is Jesus Christ. One of the specific responsibilities of this office is to study and promote the use of modern technology in the work of evangelization.

The Gifts and Fruits of the Holy Spirit

Like the Holy Spirit descending upon the Apostles at Pentecost, the Holy Spirit has always inspired people to help serve the Church. This same Holy Spirit is at the center of our lives, ready to help us serve others in the same way. To help us, the Holy Spirit sustains us with gifts that make it possible for us to do what God asks of us. These Gifts of the Holy Spirit are wisdom, understanding, counsel, piety, fortitude, knowledge, and fear of the Lord.

The Fruits of Holy Spirit are signs that show us that the Holy Spirit is active in our life. The more receptive we are to the Holy Spirit in our life, the more we will experience the fruits of God's presence. The **Fruits of the Holy Spirit** are love, joy, peace, patience, kindness, goodness, generosity, gentleness, faithfulness, modesty, self-control, and chastity.

Bearing Fruit

Turn to page 266. Read the section Fruits of the Holy Spirit. Then take a moment to as yourself, "Which Fruit of the Holy Spirit is most present in my life today? What evidence of this fruit do I see?" Write your answers on the lines.

_____

_____

_____

_____

_____

_____

_____

_____

_____

_____

_____

Explore

Study Corner

DEFINE

Fruits of the Holy Spirit

REMEMBER

We are called to be regenerated by the power of the Holy Spirit and to give witness to the saving grace and truth that is Jesus Christ. The Holy Spirit is at the center of our lives, ready to help us.

READY for Confirmation

The introduction to the Rite of Confirmation tells us that through the Sacrament of Confirmation, we are enriched with a special strength of the Holy Spirit and bound even more closely to the Church. As confirmed Catholics, we are called to spread and defend the faith through our words and actions.

Come, Holy Spirit, Come!

At Mass on Easter and Pentecost,

a prayer called a sequence is read or sung before the Gospel Acclamation. A sequence is a piece of liturgical poetry that expands on and explains the meaning of the celebration. Though many sequences were added to the liturgy in the Middle Ages, only four remain today.

When we hear a sequence proclaimed as part of prayer, we are invited to reflect on a specific mystery of faith. The sequence for Pentecost encourages us to meditate on the gift of Salvation we have received through Christ's Resurrection and the outpouring of the Holy Spirit.

Sequence for Pentecost Prayer and Reflection

All: *Come, Holy Spirit, come!*

Leader: Why do you need the Holy Spirit today?

All: *O most blessed Light divine,*
Shine within these hearts of yours,
And our inmost being fill!

Leader: How can you tell when a person is filled with the Holy Spirit? How can others tell when the light of the Holy Spirit is shining within you?

All: *Where you are not, man has naught,*
Nothing good in deed or thought,
Nothing free from taint of ill.

Leader: Do you know someone who seems empty inside or feels as if he or she has nothing? Pray that this person might be guided by the Holy Spirit.

All: *Heal our wounds, our strength renew;*
On our dryness pour your dew;
Wash the stains of guilt away:
Bend the stubborn heart and will;
Melt the frozen, warm the chill;
Guide the steps that go astray.

Leader: What is one good choice you made today? Where have you felt temptation to sin? Pray to the Holy Spirit to guide your steps toward Jesus.

WHERE Do I Fit In?

by James Campbell

Traditionally, we believe that Pentecost marks the birthday of the Church. When we hear the word *church*, we often think of the building where we go to pray or the community with whom we worship. Theologian James Campbell reminds us that our family is a domestic church where we can experience God's love and grace.

What Does It Mean to Be Church?

We live in the presence of God every moment of our lives. I have experienced God with special closeness in my own family.

My younger sister is a member of the Little Sisters of the Poor, whose mission is to care for the elderly. For 25 years she has done this in Colombia, South America. Her particular responsibility is to make sure that there is food on the table every day. For many people, the food my sister provides is all the food they will eat that day. It's difficult work. Every morning my sister receives Jesus in the Eucharist so that she can have the strength to feed his people.

Once, while on a family visit, my brother asked my sister if she wanted to discuss new ideas about Jesus and the Church. My sister wasn't much interested. She told my brother that he should come and live with her community for awhile if he wanted to know what Jesus meant in her life. There he would see that Jesus is present in the Church in all the ways the sisters cared for the needs of people who are poor.

My wife, Barbara, and I experienced the presence of God most joyfully when we were together at the birth of our two daughters. Our second daughter was unexpectedly born at home. When we knew everything would be OK, Barbara and I were so filled with joy that we spontaneously sang a song popular in the Church's liturgy at the time. We sang, "God is love, and he who abides in love, abides in God and God in him."

JAMES CAMPBELL is the author of *Stories of the Old Testament: A Catholic's Guide.*

I think of my family as a small "domestic church." It's where my wife and I have had the honor of watching our daughters grow in wisdom and grace. It's where we see God every day. All of us can celebrate God's presence in the domestic church of our families. We are all fed in the Eucharist so that in one another we can continue to see the face of God.

Reflect

Church

Take a moment to reflect on your experience of the Church. Then, in the box, draw an image that expresses what the Church means to you.

What's What?

Write the word or phrase that best completes each sentence.

1. We are the People of God, a community of believers who share in God's infinite wisdom through Jesus' teachings and the

   guidance of the _____.
   (PAGE 211)

2. Each year, on the Feast of

   _____, we celebrate the birth of the Church. (PAGE 211)

3. Pope John Paul II was a defender of the dignity of human life and an advocate for

   _____. (PAGE 212)

4. Pope John Paul II spoke out against war,

   violence, and _____.
   (PAGE 212)

5. On December 20, 1985, the Holy Father announced the institution of

   _____. (PAGE 213)

6. The _____ describes our call to serve as evangelists to those who have not heard the Gospel as well as those who need to hear the Gospel anew.
   (PAGE 214)

7. The Gifts of the _____ make it possible for us to do what God asks of us. (PAGE 215)

8. The Fruits of the Holy Spirit are

   _____ that show us that the Holy Spirit is active in our life. (PAGE 215)

Say What?

Know the definitions of these terms.

Fruits of the Holy Spirit

Jubilee Year

Now What?

What can you do this week to spread God's message to family, friends, or classmates?

_____

_____

_____

_____

_____

_____

_____

_____

_____

_____

_____

_____

_____

_____

_____

Respond

Faith in ACTION

Our experience of God's grace compels us to go out into the world to share his love with others. We receive the call to participate in this mission through the sacraments, Scripture, and our own personal relationship with Jesus Christ. Through our participation in this mission, we take action to create a more just and peaceful world.

In his own life, Jesus preached not only with words but also with his actions—the way he lived his life. We believe that taking action to create a more just world is an essential component of proclaiming the Gospel.

In this unit we explored the theme of being sent out into the world to share God's love with others. Since its beginnings the Church has called us to participate in its mission to proclaim the Good News by working for justice. We respond to this call by honoring all life and by respecting others.

> "For the Catholic faithful, the commitment to build peace and justice is not secondary but essential."
>
> —Saint John Paul II

Outreach Magazine

Purpose

Learn about the role of communication media in building a just world; create a publication in which young people can voice their opinions about issues of justice and peace and inspire one another to put their beliefs into action.

Background

Truthful communication can be an effective tool in stopping disrespectful, violent, and other unjust behaviors. Open and honest communication has the power to inspire people to act on behalf of justice for the good of all of God's creation.

Steps

1. As a group, start a free magazine or blog that gives young people a voice about justice-and-peace issues such as violence, hunger, sexism, and racism.

2. Enlist the help of your community. Others in your school or parish may be interested in serving as guest writers or in providing graphic or Web design services. If you choose to produce a print publication, volunteers may be willing to donate access to resources such as publishing software, printers, paper, and copiers.

3. Distribute your magazine to local community centers, schools, parishes, restaurants, and coffee shops. Make sure that you ask before you leave the magazines.

Act

Learn a New Language
(Aprende un nuevo idioma)

Purpose

Learn a new language and deepen your appreciation for people of different cultures and backgrounds.

Background

Knowing a second or even a third language can help us increase our awareness and appreciation for people of different cultures and backgrounds. For example, learning sign language may expose us to the culture of people who are deaf. Learning Spanish or Chinese—the first and second most spoken languages after English in the United States—may give us a better sense of the people in our community.

Steps

1. Learn about the different languages of the people in your community. The Modern Language Association (MLA) has an online resource on the most spoken languages in the United States. The United States Census Bureau also has a lot of information arranged according to states and regions. Contact local organizations for people who are deaf to learn how many people in your community use sign language.

2. On the basis of the statistics that you've learned, choose a language that would help you better relate to people in your community.

3. Working together, design a program for yourselves that will accomplish the following goals: learn basic vocabulary of the new language, connect with people who are fluent in the language, study the particular culture(s) associated with the language, and practice, practice, practice!

Act

"A single act of kindness throws out roots in all directions."

—Amelia Earhart
legendary aviator

The Year in Our Church

The Liturgical Calendar

The liturgical calendar shows us the feasts and seasons of the Church year.

Ordinary Time
Lent
Holy Week
Christmas
Easter
Epiphany

Ash Wednesday

Palm Sunday
Holy Thursday
Good Friday
Holy Saturday
Easter Sunday

Christmas

Advent

Winter
Spring
Fall
Summer

First Sunday of Advent

All Souls Day
All Saints Day

Ascension
Pentecost

Ordinary Time

221

The Liturgical Year

The Year in Our Church

Advent marks the beginning of the Church year. It is a time of anticipation that begins four Sundays before Christmas.

The Christmas season includes **Christmas,** the celebration of Jesus' birth, and Epiphany, the day that Jesus was revealed as the Savior to the world.

Lent is a season of conversion that begins on Ash Wednesday. It is a time of turning toward God in preparation for Easter.

During **Holy Week** we recall the events leading to Jesus' Passion and Death. Holy Week begins with Palm Sunday and ends on Holy Saturday.

Easter is the celebration of Jesus Christ's Resurrection from the dead. The Resurrection is the central mystery of the Christian faith. The Ascension celebrates Jesus' return to the Father in Heaven.

The sending of the Holy Spirit from Heaven is celebrated on **Pentecost.** This feast marks the end of the Easter season.

All Saints Day celebrates the victory of all the holy people in Heaven. On **All Souls Day**, we pray for those who have died but are still in Purgatory.

The time set aside for celebrating our call to follow Jesus day by day as his disciples is **Ordinary Time.**

Advent

"And you, child, will be called prophet of the Most High, for you will go before the Lord to prepare his ways."

Luke 1:76

Advent begins on the fourth Sunday before Christmas. This season marks the beginning of the liturgical year. During Advent we remember how the people of Israel awaited the Messiah. We also wait in hope for Christ's return in glory at the end of time.

PRAYER

Thank you, God, for the season of Advent. Help us prepare our hearts to welcome your Son, Jesus.

Prepare the Way

AS the Gospel of Luke tells us, John the Baptist was a prophet who prepared the way for Jesus by preaching a message of repentance. Before reporting John the Baptist's preaching, however, the Gospel of Luke tells the story of John's birth.

Zechariah and Elizabeth were old and had no children. While serving as a priest in the sanctuary, Zechariah was visited by an angel who announced to him that Elizabeth would have a baby. The angel said that this child would grow to be a prophet of God who would prepare the way of the Lord. When Zechariah questioned the angel and asked for a sign that this message was true, the angel said that Zechariah would remain speechless until the promised child was born. It happened as the angel had said. Zechariah wasn't able to speak again until after his son, John, was born.

When an angel visited Mary to announce that she would be Jesus' mother, the angel told Mary that Elizabeth was pregnant. Mary went to visit Elizabeth. John, the child within Elizabeth's womb, was a sign to Mary that the angel's message to her was true. When Mary and Elizabeth met, they rejoiced at the great things God was doing for them.

Beginning with the story of his birth, John, who became known as John the Baptist, pointed the way to Jesus. As an adult, John the Baptist spent time in the desert, preaching a baptism of repentance. Many came to him and were baptized in the Jordan River. John's message of repentance was strong, but he welcomed those who turned to the Lord. Another message

St. John the Baptist, Jacopo Palma, 16th century, oil on panel.

The Annunciation

was clear throughout John's preaching: someone greater than he was coming, someone who would baptize people with the Holy Spirit and fire. John the Baptist was talking about Jesus.

During Advent, we prepare the way of the Lord by praying daily, reading Scripture, and remembering how God kept the promises he made to his people. We also prepare the way of the Lord by seeking opportunities to bring light to darkness by reaching out to people in need.

Jesse Tree

John the Baptist was the last of the prophets who announced the coming of the Messiah whom God had promised to send. Throughout history, God has chosen people to prepare the way of the Lord. One way we can remember the fulfillment of God's promise is through a devotional practice known as the Jesse tree. The Jesse tree helps us remember and celebrate the people and events that prepared the world for Jesus' birth. This devotion is named for Jesse, the father of King David. It's intended to recall Isaiah's prophecy about God's promise to send Emmanuel:

> But a shoot shall sprout from the stump of Jesse,
> and from his roots a bud shall blossom.
>
> *Isaiah 11:1*

The Tree of Jesse, 1499, tempera on panel.

Each week, symbols are added to the Jesse tree. These symbols represent important people and events that prepared the way for the birth of the Messiah. Among the people often symbolized on a Jesse tree are Adam and Eve, Noah, Abraham and Sarah, Moses, Isaiah, King David, Ruth, Mary and Joseph, and John the Baptist. By recalling these people and their stories, we remember that throughout history, God has prepared the way for the Messiah he promised.

In these ancestors of our faith, we find models for our own response to the Lord. God has chosen each of us for an important purpose. We share the mission of John the Baptist and those who came before him by following Christ in our daily lives.

Our Catholic Character

After John the Baptist was born, his father, Zechariah, prayed a prayer that we continue to pray today. This prayer is sometimes called by its Latin name, *Benedictus,* which means "blessed." This prayer is also known as the Canticle of Zechariah, and it is prayed as part of Morning Prayer during the Liturgy of the Hours. The prayer recalls God's mercy and the promise of Salvation he made to the Israelites. It also prophesies the preaching of John the Baptist:

> "And you, child, will be called prophet of the Most High,
> for you will go before the Lord to prepare his ways,
> to give his people knowledge of salvation
> through the forgiveness of their sins."
>
> *Luke 1:76–77*

Our Light and Our Salvation

During Advent we prepare for Jesus' coming. Through our words and actions, we help others open their hearts so that they are ready to accept Christ's light joyfully.

Christ our Light

Leader: The Lord is our light and our Salvation.

All: Praise be to God.

Leader: During Advent we remember God's promise to send the Messiah, a promise that was fulfilled in Jesus' birth. We joyfully recall God's faithfulness to his people. We also look forward to Christ's Second Coming at the end of time. Like John the Baptist, we seek to prepare the way of the Lord. Let us pray that we will be filled with Advent hope as we pray together the Canticle of Zechariah.

All: Blessed be the Lord, the God of Israel; he has come to his people and set them free.

Side 1: He has raised up for us a mighty Savior, born of the house of his servant David.

Side 2: Through his holy prophets, he promised of old that he would save us from our enemies, from the hands of all who hate us.

Side 1: He promised to show mercy to our fathers and to remember his holy Covenant.

Side 2: This was the oath he swore to our father Abraham: to set us free from the hands of our enemies, free to worship him without fear, holy and righteous in his sight all the days of our life.

Side 1: You, my child, shall be called the prophet of the Most High; for you will go before the Lord to prepare his way,

Side 2: to give his people knowledge of Salvation by the forgiveness of their sins.

All: In the tender compassion of our God, the dawn from on high shall break upon us, to shine on those who dwell in darkness and the shadow of death, and to guide our feet into the way of peace. (adapted from Luke 2:68–79)

Leader: Loving God, may you continue to take away our darkness so that we may be revealed as children of light at the coming of your Son, Jesus Christ. We ask this in his name through the Holy Spirit.

All: Amen.

Christmas

> "We saw his star at its rising and have come to do him homage."
> *Matthew 2:2*

The liturgical season of Christmas begins on Christmas Eve. It ends on the Sunday on which we celebrate the Baptism of the Lord. Throughout this holy season, we reflect on and celebrate the mystery of the Incarnation: God sent his Son to share our humanity. On the Feast of the Epiphany, celebrated on the second Sunday after Christmas, we remember that Jesus revealed God to the whole world. Throughout this season, we rejoice in the Salvation given to us through Jesus Christ.

PRAYER

Thank you, God, for loving us so much that you gave us the treasure of your Son. Help us honor this gift by sharing Jesus' love with others.

The Nativity, Laura James, 1996, acrylic on canvas.

Jesus' Birth

THE story of Jesus' birth is recorded in the Gospels of Matthew and Luke. Most of us combine these two accounts of Jesus' birth in our minds. Let's discuss the report of Jesus' birth from Matthew's Gospel. It tells us how the Messiah of the Jewish people is also the Savior of the world.

Matthew's Gospel begins with the genealogy of Jesus. This listing of Jesus' ancestors starts with Abraham. By recalling this ancestry, Matthew connects Jesus' life with the history of God's Chosen People, the Israelites. Matthew then reports Jesus' birth: An angel speaks to Joseph in a dream and tells him to take Mary as his wife, even though Mary was bearing a child before their wedding. The angel tells Joseph that Mary's child was conceived by the Holy Spirit. This child is to be named Jesus, and he will bring the people forgiveness for their sins.

Matthew notes that this story fulfills the prophecy of Isaiah: this child would be Emmanuel, which means "God with us." Throughout his Gospel, Matthew recalls prophecies from the Old Testament to show that Jesus is the Messiah promised to Israel. Joseph obeys the angel's instructions and takes Mary as his wife. Little is said about Jesus' birth, except that Mary "bore a son, and named him Jesus." (Matthew 1:25)

Visitors from the East

It was important to the writer of Matthew's Gospel that we understand Jesus to be the Messiah promised to the Jewish people. But this Gospel writer knew that Jesus' birth is good news for all people. One of the ways he shows this is in the story of the Magi's visit to the infant Jesus. We remember and celebrate the visit of the Magi on the Feast of the Epiphany.

We don't know who the Magi were. We sometimes call them "wise men." Because Matthew's Gospel reports that they noticed the Christmas star, we believe they were astrologers. The Magi sometimes are called kings, based on Old Testament writings thought to prophesy their visit (Psalm 72:10; Isaiah 60:6). Because the Magi arrive from the East, possibly from Persia, it's not likely that they were of Jewish ancestry. We tend to believe that there were three Magi because of the three gifts they presented to Jesus: gold, frankincense, and myrrh.

The Magi arrive in Jerusalem seeking the one they call the "king of the Jews." (Matthew 2:2) The Magi are sent by Herod, the Jewish king appointed by the Romans, to find out about Jesus. Herod is concerned that people will believe Jesus to be the king of the Jews, and Herod believes himself to be this king.

The Magi are told by the chief priests and scribes that the Messiah of the Jews is to be born in Bethlehem. Herod consults with the chief priests and scribes and then secretly asks the Magi to go to Bethlehem. Herod asks them to find this newborn king and to return with the details so that he might give homage. Herod, of course, has no intention of offering homage. Instead, he secretly plans to kill the child.

The Magi follow the star to Bethlehem and find the home of Mary, Joseph, and Jesus. They offer homage to Jesus and present their gifts. Then the Magi are warned in a dream not to return to Herod. So they return home by a different route.

The Magi remind us that God's Salvation is for all people, from every nation. In their journey to find Jesus and in the gifts they bring, the Magi represent all people's search for Jesus. They help us recognize him as the Savior of all people.

Like the Magi, Joseph is also warned in a dream about Herod's desire to kill Jesus. As instructed, Joseph takes Mary and Jesus to Egypt. They remain there until Herod's death. Matthew tells us that Joseph has another dream and reports that Herod orders the massacre of all the infant boys in Bethlehem when he realizes that the Magi are not returning to him. This sad occasion is remembered in our Church's liturgical calendar on December 28, the Feast of the Holy Innocents.

Three Kings,
Karen Cater, 1998.

SACRED ART

Matthew's Gospel tells us that the Magi presented Jesus with gifts of gold, frankincense, and myrrh. Gold is familiar to us, and we would all agree that it would be a tremendous gift to receive. Frankincense and myrrh were also great treasures. Frankincense is a kind of incense that was offered by priests in the Temple. Myrrh is a perfume that was used to prepare bodies for burial and to anoint kings and prophets ritually. The three gifts together symbolize the three aspects of how we understand Jesus to be a Messiah—Jesus is king, priest, and prophet.

All Shall Pay Him Homage

During Christmas we celebrate the Mystery of the Incarnation—God becoming man in the Person of Jesus. We offer our adoration to God for the gift of Salvation that we receive through his Son, Jesus.

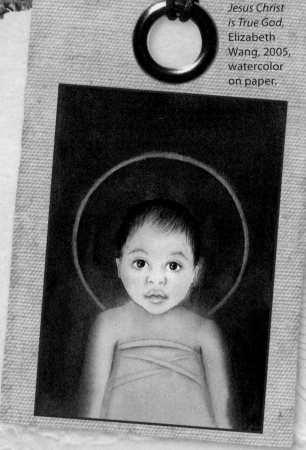

Jesus Christ is True God, Elizabeth Wang, 2005, watercolor on paper.

Gift of God

Leader: God reveals himself to us in the Person of Jesus. This is the great mystery we celebrate during the Christmas season. In the story of the Magi, we learn that all nations shall honor Jesus as Savior.

Reader: A reading from the holy Gospel according to Matthew.
[Matthew 2:1–12]
The Gospel of the Lord.

All: Praise to you, Lord Jesus Christ.

Leader: God has sent Jesus to be the Savior of the world. Let us worship him as the Magi did at his birth.

All: Lord, every nation on earth will adore you.

Side 1: O God, give your judgment to the king;
your justice to the king's son;
That he might govern your people with justice,
your oppressed with right judgment.

All: Lord, every nation on earth will adore you.

Side 2: That abundance may flourish in his days,
great bounty, till the moon be no more.
May he rule from sea to sea,
from the river to the ends of the earth.

All: Lord, every nation on earth will adore you.

Side 1: May the kings of Tarshish and the islands
bring tribute,
the kings of Sheba and Seba offer gifts.
May all kings bow down before him,
all nations serve him.

All: Lord, every nation on earth will adore you.

Side 2: For he rescues the poor when they cry out,
the oppressed who have no one to help.
He shows pity to the needy and the poor
and saves the lives of the poor.

Psalm 72:1–2,7–8,10–11,12–13

All: Lord, every nation on earth will adore you.

Leader: Lord, you brought your Salvation to all in your Son, Jesus. As we adore you, may we experience your justice and peace. We ask this in Jesus' name.

All: Amen.

Lent

Have mercy on me, God, in accord with your merciful love.

Psalm 51:3

During Lent, we reflect on the choices we've made. We ask God to forgive us for the times we have failed to do his will, and we rededicate ourselves to doing good and avoiding sin. We reflect on how Jesus resisted the temptations of the devil in the desert, and we pray that God's grace will help us do the same.

PRAYER

God, help us remain faithful to our Lenten commitments and, by doing so, grow closer to you and to one another.

The Temptation of Jesus

AFTER John the Baptist baptized Jesus in the Jordan River, the Holy Spirit led Jesus into the desert. He fasted and prayed there for 40 days. At the end of the 40 days, Scripture tells us that he was tempted by the Devil.

The temptations that Jesus experienced were real. The Devil tempted Jesus, who was hungry after his long fast. He asked Jesus to prove that he was God's Son by turning stones into bread. Jesus, who was a human being like us in every way but sin, experienced the full effects of hunger. The temptation to have something to eat after fasting for 40 days was real. Yet Jesus refused the Devil's temptation and responded by quoting Scripture, saying that God's Word is more important than food.

Then the Devil took Jesus to the top of the Temple. He quoted Scripture and asked Jesus to test God's promise to protect him. The temptation to seek proof of God's protection was also real. There are times when we all wish to see proof of God's presence and power. Yet Jesus refused this temptation as well. He again responded with Scripture, saying that it's not right to put God to the test.

The Devil tempted Jesus a third time by offering him rule over the whole world if he would worship him instead of God. The temptation to seek power is a great one. Yet Jesus resisted this temptation. Having had enough, Jesus told him, "Get away, Satan!" The Devil then left because Jesus had rebuffed all his temptations. Scripture tells us that the angels then came and ministered to Jesus.

Christ in the Wilderness, Laura James, acrylic on canvas.

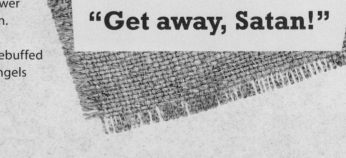

Jesus told him, "Get away, Satan!"

We all experience temptation in our lives. We might be tempted to allow ourselves to forget that remaining faithful to God should be our top priority. We might be tempted to put conditions on our love of God and to test God's care for us. The appeal of showing our power over others might tempt us. For example, we might want to brag about our abilities or to gossip about others' faults. When we give in to temptation, we sin.

Lenten Practices

During Lent, we remember our tendency to sin and try to find ways to resist temptation. Prayer, fasting, and almsgiving are among the habits we practice.

There are many ways to improve our life of prayer during Lent. We renew our commitment to pray daily. We attend Mass more often. We read Scripture with greater frequency and care. We pray the Stations of the Cross, especially the Sorrowful Mysteries. We celebrate the Sacrament of Reconciliation. Through our prayer, we seek to become closer to God.

The Lenten practice of fasting includes several aspects. To fast is to refrain from food for a period of time in order to remember our dependence on God. Another aspect of fasting is called abstinence, which means that we refrain from particular foods, such as meat. Abstinence helps us focus on God and not on the temporary happiness we experience from eating.

The Church designates two days for fasting and abstinence:

Ash Wednesday and Good Friday. On these days, everyone between the ages of 18 and 59 is limited to one full meal and may not eat between meals. People younger and older are encouraged to practice some form of fasting as well.

In addition to Ash Wednesday and Good Friday, all Fridays in Lent are days of abstinence. On these days, we refrain from eating meat. All who have reached their 14th birthday are asked to abstain from meat on these days.

Almsgiving is a third important Lenten practice. During Lent, we strive to remember those who are poor by making financial and material contributions. Some people choose to refrain from certain activities, such as dining out or going to the movies. They give the money they would have spent on these activities to people in need. Almsgiving is another sign of our intention to avoid sin and to be more faithful to God.

During Lent, the Church community focuses on our need for God's forgiveness as individuals and as a community. In the Sacrament of Reconciliation, we confess our sins to God, promise to do penance for our sins, and celebrate God's mercy and forgiveness. During Lent, we may choose to celebrate this sacrament as we prepare ourselves for Easter. We can participate in a parish communal penance service or celebrate the sacrament individually with a priest.

Our Catholic Character

Lent is a season for remembering the grace of our Baptism. For adults who are going to be baptized into the Church at Easter, Lent is a time of intense prayer and preparation for their Baptism. During Lent, the Church community journeys with and prays for these catechumens. At Easter, the catechumens are baptized, and the community renews its baptismal promises. These promises are to reject sin, to reject Satan, and to live the faith that the Church professes.

Have Mercy on Us

During Lent we turn our minds and hearts back to God. We seek forgiveness for the times we have given in to temptation, and we thank God for his mercy.

Forty Days in the Wilderness Tempted by Satan,
William Brassey Hole.

Forgive Me, O God

Leader: Let us praise God. Blessed be God forever.

All: Blessed be God forever.

Leader: Using the words of Psalm 51, let us pray for God's mercy and compassion.

Side 1: Have mercy on me, God, in accord with
　　　your merciful love;
　　　　in your abundant compassion blot out
　　　　my transgressions.
　　　Thoroughly wash away my guilt;
　　　　and from my sins cleanse me.

Side 2: For I know my transgressions;
　　　my sin is always before me.
　　　Against you, you alone have I sinned;
　　　　I have done what is evil in your eyes
　　　So that you are just in your word,
　　　　and without reproach in your judgment.

Side 1: A clean heart create for me, God;
　　　renew within me a steadfast spirit.
　　　Do not drive me from before your face,
　　　　nor take me from your holy spirit.

Side 2: Restore to me the gladness of your salvation;
　　　uphold me with a willing spirit.
　　　Lord, you will open my lips;
　　　　and my mouth will proclaim your praise.

Psalm 51:3–6,12–14,17

Leader: God of mercy, may our Lenten practices during this season of repentance bring us the blessing of your forgiveness and the gift of your light in our lives.

All: Amen.

Holy Week

"[A]s I have done for you, you should also do."

John 13:15

Holy Week begins on Palm Sunday. On this day we remember Jesus' triumphant entry into Jerusalem. Holy Thursday begins the Triduum, three days that comprise one liturgical celebration. On Holy Thursday we remember how Jesus gave us the Eucharist and gave us his example of love as he washed his disciples' feet. On Good Friday we venerate the cross as we recall Christ's Passion and Death. During the Easter Vigil on Holy Saturday, we await Christ's Resurrection. We welcome new members into the Church through the Sacraments of Initiation, and we all renew the promises of our own Baptism.

PRAYER

Jesus, as we remember your Passion and Death, give us the strength to care for those who are suffering among us today.

Jesus Gives Us His Example

Jesus Washing the Disciples' Feet, Laura James, 2000, acrylic on canvas.

THE Gospel of John recounts the events of Holy Week in a slightly different way than the other Gospels. The greatest difference is found in John's description of the Last Supper. The Gospels of Matthew, Mark, and Luke describe the meal and how Jesus broke the bread and shared the chalice of wine. But the Gospel of John describes how Jesus washed his disciples' feet.

John's Gospel tells us that after the meal, Jesus tied a towel around his waist. He then poured water into a basin, washed his disciples' feet, and dried them with the towel. When Jesus came to Simon Peter, Peter protested. He considered Jesus his master and teacher and did not want to be waited on by Jesus.

Jesus' action was a reversal of the social norms of his day. To wash another person's feet was to humble oneself before the other person. But Jesus told Peter that he must permit him to wash his feet, otherwise he couldn't be part of God's plan for Jesus. Peter then said that Jesus should wash Peter's hands and head as well. But Jesus said that this was unnecessary.

After he had washed his disciples' feet, Jesus taught them the importance of what he had just done. He said,

Do you realize what I have done for you? You call me 'teacher' and 'master,' and rightly so, for indeed I am. If I, therefore, the master and teacher, have washed your feet, you ought to wash one another's feet. I have given you a model to follow, so that as I have done for you, you should also do.

John 13:12–15

Jesus continued to teach about the meaning and importance of this action and to prepare his disciples for his Death. This series of teachings is sometimes called the Last Supper discourses. Jesus shared with his disciples many things in these teachings. He told them that he would prepare a place for them in his Father's house and that he is "the way and the truth and the life." (John 14:6) Jesus talked about his relationship with his disciples and told them: "I am the vine, you are the branches." (John 15:5)

In another teaching, Jesus talked about the sacrifice he would make for them through his Death: "This is my commandment: love one another as I love you. No one has greater love than this, to lay down one's life for one's friends." (John 15:12–13) All that Jesus taught is summarized in this new commandment. Jesus also promised to send his disciples the Advocate, the Holy Spirit, who would remain with them forever. The Holy Spirit would help them understand all that Jesus had taught.

The Eucharist

We learn a lot about what Jesus intended for us when he gave us the gift of his presence in the Eucharist. Jesus offers us the greatest gifts of all: his great love poured out for us in his sacrifice on the Cross, the ongoing gift of his presence in the Eucharist, and the gift of peace given to us through the Holy Spirit. In turn, Jesus calls us to follow his example and to do for others what he has done for us. Christ is made known to the world in our love for others.

> **"This is my commandment: love one another as I love you. No one has greater love than this, to lay down one's life for one's friends."**

Our Catholic Character

Traditionally on Holy Thursday, at a Mass called the Chrism Mass, the bishop blesses the oils that will be used throughout the diocese for the Sacraments of the Anointing of the Sick, Baptism, Confirmation, and Holy Orders. Three oils are blessed at this time. The first is the oil of the sick, which is used for the Sacrament of the Anointing of the Sick. The second is the oil of catechumens, which is used during the anointing with oil in the Baptism of both infants and adults. The third oil is called Chrism. It's perfumed oil used at the Baptism of infants and at the Sacraments of Confirmation and Holy Orders. Because this was the kind of oil used to anoint priests and kings, it's a reminder that in our Baptism, we share in Christ's priesthood and kingship. The bishop presides at the Chrism Mass, which is celebrated with priests from throughout the diocese.

Prayer

Love One Another

During Holy Week we reflect on the example that Jesus gave us through his life, suffering, and Death on the Cross. We pray for the strength to follow his example so that all people will experience his love through our words and actions.

Christ Washing the Disciples Feet, 13th century, vellum.

Called to Serve

Leader: The grace of our Lord Jesus Christ be with us all, now and forever.

All: Amen.

Leader: Before his Death on the Cross, Jesus gave us an example of discipleship to follow when he washed his disciples' feet.

Reader: A reading from the holy Gospel according to John.
[John 13:12–17]
The Gospel of the Lord.

All: Praise to you, Lord Jesus Christ.

Leader: Let us pray in thanksgiving for the great gift of love that Jesus gave us through his example of humble, loving service.

All: Where there are charity and love, there is God.

Side 1: Where there are charity and love, there is God.
The love of Christ has gathered us together.
Let us rejoice and be glad in him.
And from our hearts sincerely love each other.

All: Where there are charity and love, there is God.

Side 2: Where there are charity and love, there is God.
Therefore when we gather as one,
Let us be careful not to be divided in mind.
Let there be an end to evil judgments,
an end to quarreling,
And in our midst be Christ our God.

All: Where there are charity and love, there is God.
And when we are united with all the blessed may we see your glorious face,
Christ our God.
With pure and boundless joy
Forever and ever.

Leader: Loving God, your Son, on the night before he died, revealed his great love for us. Help us be his worthy disciples by serving our brothers and sisters, especially those who need us most. Grant this through Jesus Christ, your Son, who reigns with you and the Holy Spirit, one God, forever and ever.

All: Amen.

Easter

"[Y]ou will be my witnesses . . . to the ends of the earth."

Acts of the Apostles 1:8

After Jesus rose from the dead, he appeared to his disciples many times. Scripture tells us that Jesus appeared to his disciples despite locked doors. Jesus showed his disciples the nail marks in his hands and feet and the wound in his side. He walked with them and talked with them. He even shared meals with them. Being with the risen Jesus brought the disciples great joy and peace.

PRAYER

Thank you, God, for the gift of the risen Christ. Help us carry his light and love in our hearts throughout the year.

Jesus Returns to the Father

AFTER Jesus rose from the dead, he continued to appear to his disciples. After spending 40 days with them, Jesus promised to give them the gift of the Holy Spirit.

Jesus told his followers that the Holy Spirit would give them power and enable them to bear witness to Jesus in Jerusalem, throughout Judea and Samaria, and even throughout the world. This may have been an astonishing thought for the disciples. Remember, they were local people with jobs like fisherman and tax collector. Now Jesus was telling them they'd be his witnesses throughout the world!

After making this promise, an amazing thing happened. As the disciples watched, Jesus was lifted up and taken away from them, into the clouds. The disciples stared up at the sky. What else could they do? Their mouths were probably hanging open in disbelief! We call this event, Jesus' ascent to Heaven to sit at God's right hand, the Ascension of the Lord.

As the disciples stood watching, two men in white appeared beside them and asked the obvious question: "[W]hy are you standing there looking at the sky?" (Acts of the Apostles 1:11) Then they

As the disciples watched, Jesus was lifted up and taken away from them, into the clouds.

told Jesus disciples that "This Jesus who has been taken up from you into heaven will return in the same way as you have seen him going into heaven." (Acts of the Apostles 1:11)

Was everything made clear to the disciples as they watched Jesus ascend into Heaven? No. But one thing became apparent: Jesus had left them, but he had given them a job to do. The disciples were to be his witnesses and spread the message of the Gospel to the ends of the earth. The disciples also realized that Jesus would fulfill his promise to send them the Holy Spirit to help with this task. Realizing that they would be guided by this gift, and filled with hope at knowing Jesus would return to them someday, the disciples returned to Jerusalem to wait.

Given a Job to Do

Jesus' Ascension into Heaven confirmed what the disciples had come to believe: Jesus was God who had come to save his people. Now Jesus was returning to God the Father to share in his glory. Jesus had to leave his disciples, but he did not abandon them. His trust in them was apparent, and they had an important job to do. They were to continue the work of Jesus. By doing so, they would bear witness that Jesus was their Lord and God.

As Jesus' disciples today, through our Baptism, we have also received Jesus' promised gift of the Holy Spirit. This gift of the Holy Spirit is strengthened in us through the Sacrament of Confirmation, and it is nourished in the Eucharist. With the Holy Spirit's help, we are sent to be Jesus' witnesses throughout the world.

At the Easter Vigil, and sometimes throughout the Easter season, we renew the promises of our Baptism at the Profession of Faith during Mass. Sometimes a Sprinkling Rite, or a blessing with holy water, is also included as part of the Introductory Rites of Mass. Each of these is a reminder to us of the importance of our Baptism. Easter is the season when we renew our commitment to live faithfully the promises of our Baptism. These promises commit us to be Jesus' witnesses throughout the world.

Our Catholic Character

Since the beginning of the Church, Jesus' Ascension has been a central part of our faith. The statement "He ascended into heaven and is seated at the right hand of the Father" is part of both the Apostles' Creed and the Nicene Creed. On the 40th day after Easter (always a Thursday since Easter is a Sunday), the Church celebrates the Feast of the Ascension of the Lord as a Holy Day of Obligation. In many dioceses in the United States, the Holy Day is moved to the following Sunday, the seventh Sunday of Easter.

Easter

Praise God

During Easter we reflect on the Salvation we have received through Christ's Resurrection. We praise God for this incredible gift, and we go out into the world to fulfill the mission we have been given—to proclaim the Gospel to all people.

Blessed Be God Forever

Leader: Let us praise God, who raised Jesus from the dead. Blessed be God forever.

All: Blessed be God forever.

Leader: Loving God, make us joyful in the Ascension of your Son, Jesus Christ. May we be his witnesses throughout the world as he lives and reigns with you and the Holy Spirit forever and ever.

All: Amen.

Reader: A reading from the Acts of the Apostles [Acts of the Apostles 1:6–12] The Word of the Lord.

All: Thanks be to God.

Leader: During the Easter season, we celebrate the great mystery that Jesus was raised from the dead and appeared to his disciples. We praise God, who has indeed done marvelous deeds!

All: We rejoice in this day that the Lord has made!

Leader: At his Ascension, Jesus returned to the Father so that his disciples might receive his promised gift of the Holy Spirit. We praise God, who has indeed done marvelous deeds!

All: We rejoice in this day that the Lord has made!

Leader: During the Easter season, we recommit ourselves to the promises of our Baptism. We praise God, who continues to do marvelous deeds!

All: We rejoice in this day that the Lord has made!

Leader: As Jesus sent his disciples to be his witnesses throughout the world, so too we have been sent by our Baptism to witness to Jesus in our words and actions. Let us pray that the Holy Spirit will continue to strengthen us and renew within us our baptismal promises.

All: God, through the gift of the Holy Spirit, strengthen us to be witnesses to your love and peace throughout the world. We pray this in Jesus' name. Amen.

Pentecost

For in one Spirit we were all baptized into one body.
1 Corinthians 12:13

On Pentecost we remember and celebrate the outpouring of the Holy Spirit on the first Christian disciples. This Holy Spirit is given to us as well and unites us in the mission of the Church to proclaim the Gospel to all people.

PRAYER

Thank you, God, for the amazing diversity of your Church. Help us celebrate this diversity and always appreciate the many ways you reveal your presence to us.

Building the Church

St. Paul the Apostle, Martino de Bartolomeo, 14th century, tempera on tooled gold ground.

JUST **as a construction project needs a variety of talents, skills, and specialties for a successful building, so too the Church requires a variety of gifts and talents to accomplish the mission Christ gave to us.**

The more difficult and complicated the project, the greater the need for a variety of skills and talents to accomplish the task. It's one thing to build a shed; it's a more difficult task to build a house; it's a far more complicated task to build a skyscraper. Now think about the mission that Jesus gave to his followers: to be his witnesses to the ends of the earth! To accomplish this mission, a great variety of talents, gifts, and specialties would certainly be needed. It would also require the help of the Holy Spirit.

One of the first Christian missionaries, the apostle Paul, knew this to be true. Paul never met Jesus in the flesh. In fact, the Acts of the Apostles tells us that Paul persecuted the first Christians. Paul became a disciple when Jesus appeared to him some time after the Resurrection. This experience was so powerful that Paul instantly became one of Jesus' disciples and set about the task of spreading the Good News. He was so successful in this work that he helped establish many Christian communities. As he continued his missionary journeys, Paul exchanged letters with the communities he founded and answered their questions. He also provided guidance when difficult situations arose. Some of Paul's letters have become part of the New Testament. From these letters we learn about the struggles and questions of these early Christian communities. We also hear Paul's faith and wisdom as he shares the Good News of Jesus with these new Christians.

Paul's Message to the Community in Corinth

The New Testament contains two letters that Paul wrote to the Christian community at Corinth, a major seaport city in Greece. As a center of commercial activity, Corinth was home to a great diversity of people. This diversity was reflected in the Christian community there. Paul thought he had united this diverse community by teaching them the Good News of Jesus. And yet, in the beginning of Paul's first letter to the Corinthians, we learn that Paul has been informed that there are divisions in the Church at Corinth. Throughout the letter we learn how much this disturbs and even angers Paul.

Paul addresses the issues that caused divisions within the community. For example, there are factions claiming allegiance to different disciples. Paul tells them it isn't important who taught each person the Gospel or who baptized a person. Rather, because each person was baptized in Christ's name and lives Christ's teaching, differences within the community are no longer important. The community is Christian, and therefore, one.

As Paul argues that divisions can't exist within a Christian community, he teaches the community at Corinth about the importance of the Holy Spirit in establishing and maintaining Christian unity. Here's what Paul wrote.

> And no one can say, 'Jesus is Lord,' except by the holy Spirit.
>
> There are different kinds of spiritual gifts but the same Spirit; there are different forms of service but the same Lord; there are different workings but the same God who produces all of them in everyone. To each individual the manifestation of the Spirit is given for some benefit.
>
> As a body is one though it has many parts, and all the parts of the body, though many, are one body, so also Christ. For in one Spirit we were all baptized into one body, whether Jews or Greeks, slaves or free persons, and we were all given to drink of one Spirit.
>
> *1 Corinthians 12:3–7,12–13*

Paul recognized and celebrated the diversity of gifts given by the Holy Spirit. Paul taught that different gifts were given to each person for the benefit of all.

He never allowed for this diversity to lead to divisions. He even refused to prioritize or rank based on the gifts received through the Spirit. All are equal in their Baptism; all share in the Gifts of the Holy Spirit; all contribute to the mission of the Church.

On Pentecost we remember and celebrate this message that Paul taught the Corinthians. We pray that the Holy Spirit will continue to unite the members of the Church as we witness to Christ in our world.

Our Catholic Character

The Fruits of the Spirit are signs that show that the Holy Spirit is acting in our lives. Paul's list of the Fruits of the Spirit can be found in Galatians 5:22–23. Church Tradition also includes goodness, modesty, and chastity as Fruits of the Spirit.

The Grace of the Holy Spirit

Holy Spirit Coming, He Qi.

On the Feast of Pentecost, we reflect on the Advocate—the Holy Spirit—that Jesus sent to strengthen his followers. We pray that our hearts may be open to the guidance of the Holy Spirit in our own lives.

Filled with the Spirit

Leader: Blessed be God—Father, Son, and Holy Spirit.

All: Blessed be God.

Leader: At Pentecost, we celebrate the fulfillment of Jesus' promise to his disciples to send them a helper, the Holy Spirit. We offer thanks and praise because this Holy Spirit continues to be with us and guides the Church today.

Reader: A reading from the holy Gospel according to John.
[John 14:15–18]
The Gospel of the Lord.

All: Praise to you, Lord Jesus Christ.

Leader: Lord, send out your Spirit and renew the face of the earth.

All: Lord, send out your Spirit and renew the face of the earth.

Side 1: Bless the LORD, my soul!
LORD, my God, you are great indeed!

Side 2: How varied are your works, LORD!
In wisdom you have made them all;
the earth is full of your creatures.

All: Lord, send out your Spirit and renew the face of the earth.

Side 1: When you hide your face, they panic.
Take away their breath, they perish
and return to the dust.

Side 2: Send forth your spirit, they are created
and you renew the face of the earth.

All: Lord, send out your Spirit and renew the face of the earth.

Psalm 104:1,24,29,30

Leader: We received the Holy Spirit and have been made one in Christ. May the grace of the Holy Spirit we received in our Baptism strengthen us to praise God and unite us in service to others. We pray this in Jesus' name.

All: Amen.

All Souls Day

"I am the resurrection and the life."

John 11:25

The Communion of Saints unites us with all those who have gone before us. On All Saints Day, November 1, and All Souls Day, November 2, we celebrate our unity in Christ, and we pray for those who have died.

PRAYER

Thank you, God, for the gift of our brothers and sisters in Christ—those living, those dead, and those yet to be born. May we support one another on our journey of faith.

Our Hope for Eternal Life

The Raising of Lazarus, Laura James, acrylic on canvas.

AT some point, we all must deal with the death of someone we know or love. Because he shared our humanity, Jesus also faced the reality of death. In the Gospel of John 11:1–44, we learn how Jesus faced the death of his friend, Lazarus. It's an extraordinary story through which Jesus teaches us about the promise of eternal life.

Jesus was close to Lazarus and his two sisters, Mary and Martha. Perhaps Jesus had stayed at their home in Bethany. The Gospel tells us that while Jesus was preaching, he received word from Mary and Martha that Lazarus was ill. Surprisingly, Jesus didn't hurry to Bethany. Instead he waited two days before departing. On the way there, Jesus told his disciples that Lazarus had died and that something would happen that would help the disciples believe in Jesus.

The Gospel describes a very sad scene as Jesus arrived in Bethany. Lazarus was dead and had been buried for four days. Mourners had gathered to comfort Martha and Mary. The sisters greeted Jesus with words that showed both their confidence in his power and their disappointment and sorrow at their brother's death. "Lord, if you had been here, my brother would not have died." (John 11:21) Martha and Mary also expressed their faith in Jesus as the Messiah and their belief that Lazarus would one day share in the resurrection of the dead.

The sadness of everyone who was present touched Jesus' heart, and he wept with the mourners. Then Jesus did an amazing thing. He instructed that the stone be removed from the tomb, prayed aloud to his Father in Heaven, and called Lazarus from the tomb. Incredibly, Lazarus emerged, still wrapped in his burial cloths. In response to Jesus' prayer, God brought Lazarus back from the dead!

What Happens When a Person Dies?

God showed his power over death and the promise of eternal life by raising Lazarus from the dead. Many of those who witnessed this miracle came to believe that Jesus was the Son of God. In John's Gospel the raising of Lazarus marks the turning point in Jesus' ministry, the beginning of Jesus' own journey to death on the Cross. Jesus' Death and Resurrection would bring eternal life to all believers.

Have you ever considered what happens after a person dies? In the prayers of the funeral Mass, we profess our belief that, at death, life is changed but not ended. Our souls continue to exist after our bodies die, while we await the resurrection of the body promised to us by Jesus. Our souls are separated from our body, but one day our body and soul will be rejoined in the resurrection at the end of time.

Those who die with faith in God and in the state of grace—whose sins are forgiven—are said to be with God in Heaven. Only those who are free of sin will experience the vision of God and share in the life of the Trinity. The souls in Heaven enjoy eternal happiness and peace.

God wills that all people share eternal happiness with him in Heaven. Human beings can freely accept God's invitation of love but may also freely and completely reject God's love. Those who reject God's love and forgiveness have chosen to separate themselves from God's presence and choose to be in Hell. The souls in Hell experience sadness and torment because they want what they have rejected: to be in the presence of God.

Purgatory is the third possibility after death. The souls in Purgatory have died united to God. Though their sins have been forgiven, they still need to be purified to be in God's presence. This process of purification happens in Purgatory.

> # The souls in Heaven enjoy eternal happiness and peace.

Our Catholic Character

In Mexico, All Souls Day is known as *Día de los Muertos*, or the Day of the Dead. Altars are constructed in honor of the deceased and are decorated with flowers, candles, photographs, skeleton toys, sugar candy skulls, bread, chocolate, and the favorite food or drink of the deceased. Families then go to cemeteries to clean and decorate the tombstones of their loved ones. Today many urban Mexican families commemorate the Day of the Dead with a family supper that includes the "Bread of the Dead" (*pan de muerto*).

Pray with Confidence

On the Feast of All Souls, we reflect on the example of discipleship that we have received from the members of the Communion of Saints. We pray that our lives will provide an example of Christian living for all the people we encounter.

The Raising of Lazarus,
Sadao Watanabe, 1970, serigraph.

Let Us Pray

Leader: Praise be to God, who fills our lives with joy.

All: Praise be to God.

Leader: Let us pray for the strength to remain steadfast in our belief that we will be raised from the dead at the end of time.

Reader: A reading from the First Letter of Paul to the Corinthians.
[1 Corinthians 15:20–26]
The Word of the Lord.

All: Thanks be to God.

Leader: Let us pray for those who have died with hope in God's mercy and forgiveness.

Leader: God, hear the prayers we offer this day for those who have died. May our prayers and the faith of our deceased brothers and sisters lead them into the joy of your presence. We pray also for ourselves. God, help us live with hope in your promise of resurrection. We ask this through Christ, our Lord.

All: Amen.

Prayers and Practices of Our Faith

Luke

John

251

The Story of God's Promise

GOD speaks to us in many different ways. One way that he has revealed himself to us is through Scripture. These collected writings make up the Bible. Together, the Scriptures tell the story of God's promise to care for us, especially through his Son, Jesus. At Mass, readings from the Bible are proclaimed during the Liturgy of the Word. Christians all over the world pray with Scripture when they pray the Liturgy of the Hours. We can also pray with Scripture by reading the Bible on our own.

The Bible is a collection of books that is made up of two parts, the Old Testament and the New Testament. Many of the stories that are included in the Bible were first developed in oral cultures. The stories were passed down by word of mouth from one generation to the next. Eventually the stories were written down. The writings that make up the Bible were inspired by the Holy Spirit and were written by different authors who used various literary styles, such as history, poetry, narratives, and parables.

God speaks to us in many different ways.

The Old Testament

The Old Testament contains 46 books that tell stories about the Jewish people and their faith in God before Jesus was born. The sections of the Old Testament are the Torah, the historical books, the wisdom books, and

Torah

the prophetic books. The Old Testament as we know it today did not begin to take shape until a period of **exile** known as the Babylonian Exile (587–537 B.C.). It was in Babylon that members of the priestly class took many of the oral and written accounts of God's saving work and put them together in what we now know as the Torah.

The Torah The first five books of the Old Testament—Genesis, Exodus, Leviticus, Numbers, and Deuteronomy—are referred to as the Torah, meaning "instruction" or "law." The stories from the prehistory of Israel that are in the Book of Genesis were probably the first part of the Old Testament to be written. The author is probably King David's court historian, who wrote the stories around 1000 B.C. The author referred to God as Yahweh and spoke of God in human terms. It was this author who wrote the story of God walking in the Garden with Adam and Eve and the story of God's orderly creation of the world in six days and his rest on the seventh.

Moses

The central story in the Torah is the Exodus. After the Hebrews had been enslaved by the Egyptians, God called Moses to lead them out of Egypt to the **Promised Land.** During the journey, God gave Moses and the people the Ten Commandments.

The Historical Books The historical books were put together from the court accounts of various kings of Israel and Judah, such as Saul, David, and Solomon. This section of the Old Testament records the story of the Israelites who fought to establish and maintain control of the Promised Land, to which God had delivered them during the Exodus.

The Wisdom Books These books are a collection of the wisdom teachings of the Israelites that accumulated over thousands of years. These writings

Ruth and Naomi

The Book of Ruth, one of the historical books, begins in crisis. An Israelite couple, Elimelech and Naomi, live in the country of Moab with their two sons and their sons' Gentile wives. All three husbands die, leaving three widows—Naomi and her daughters-in-law Ruth and Orpah—without support. Naomi is an Israelite, and the other two women are not.

Naomi decides to return to Israel. She tells Ruth and Orpah to stay in Moab and find new husbands. Orpah agrees, but Ruth has formed a deep relationship with her mother-in-law. Ruth says to Naomi, "I'm your daughter-in-law, and I will never leave you. I will go to your country with you, and I will worship your God."

The rest of the story tells how Ruth is rewarded for her faithfulness to her mother-in-law. She eventually marries Boaz, a prominent member of Naomi's family, and she becomes the great-grandmother of King David. Ruth followed her heart, faithfully supporting her mother-in-law, Naomi.

Ruth, Laura James, 1999, acrylic on canvas.

Prayers and Practices of Our Faith

include wisdom about when the people wandered the desert during the Exodus, their time living in the Promised Land, and their struggle during the Babylonian Exile.

One of the best-known wisdom books is the Book of Psalms. A psalm is a prayer in the form of a poem. Each psalm expresses an aspect, or feature, of the depth of human emotion. Over several centuries, 150 psalms were gathered to form the Book of Psalms. They were once sung at the **Temple,** the house of worship first built by King Solomon in Jerusalem. The psalms have been used in the public worship of the Church since its beginning. We often pray the psalms as part of our private prayer and reflection.

The Prophetic Books A large part of the Old Testament, 18 books, presents the messages and actions of the prophets. These were people called by God to speak for him to urge the Jewish people to be faithful to the **Covenant.**

The New Testament

The second part of the Bible, the New Testament, contains 27 books that tell the story of Jesus' life, Death, and Resurrection and the experience of the early Christians. For Christians the most important books of the New Testament are the four Gospels— Matthew, Mark, Luke, and John. While the first three Gospels write about Jesus in different ways, they tell stories that are similar enough to be read side-by-side. Because of this, we call them the Synoptic Gospels.

Many of the 27 books of the New Testament are letters written by early Christian leaders such as Paul. In reading about Jesus' public ministry, his Paschal Mystery, and the life of the early Church, we discover our own call to discipleship.

Mark

Mark writes his Gospel to reassure his community that the persecutions they are enduring are not a sign that God has abandoned them.

The Gospel of Mark This was the first Gospel written. In fact, the author was the first to develop the type of literature we call Gospel. This Gospel was written for Jewish and Gentile Christians living through Nero's persecutions in Rome during the second half of the A.D. 60s. The central message of this Gospel is that the only way to be a true follower of Jesus is to take up the cross and follow him. Almost immediately after Peter's profession of faith—"You are the Messiah"—the disciples begin to misunderstand Jesus' true identity. Finally, at the Crucifixion, Jesus is all alone. None of the disciples could follow him to the end. The Roman centurion at the foot of the cross says, "Truly this man was the son of God." (Mark 15:39) This echoes the beginning of the Gospel, "The gospel of Jesus Christ [the Son of God]." (Mark 1:1) Mark writes his Gospel to reassure his community that the persecutions they are enduring are not a sign that God has abandoned them. Rather it is only through suffering that they can really know Jesus as the Son of God.

The Gospel of Matthew The author of the Gospel of Matthew used the Gospel of Mark as a starting point. The Gospel of Matthew was written in the A.D. 80s for a mainly Jewish Christian community, probably in the city of Antioch. It was a community that wanted to continue to assert its Jewish identity while at the same time profess that Jesus was the awaited Messiah. Because of their belief in Jesus as the Messiah, the members of the community were in conflict with Jews, who did not accept Jesus. To support his community's belief, Matthew often quotes the Jewish scriptures to show how Jesus was the long-awaited Messiah. He begins his Gospel with two chapters about the birth of Jesus that emphasize that Jesus was predicted in the Old Testament. This created a comparison between Jesus and Moses. Herod, like Pharaoh, kills the male children. Jesus escapes to Egypt so that like Moses he can one day leave Egypt. Matthew divides his Gospel into five sections, like the five books of Moses. As Moses received the Ten Commandments on a mountain, Jesus delivers the new law in the Sermon on the Mount. In Matthew, Jesus is the new Moses.

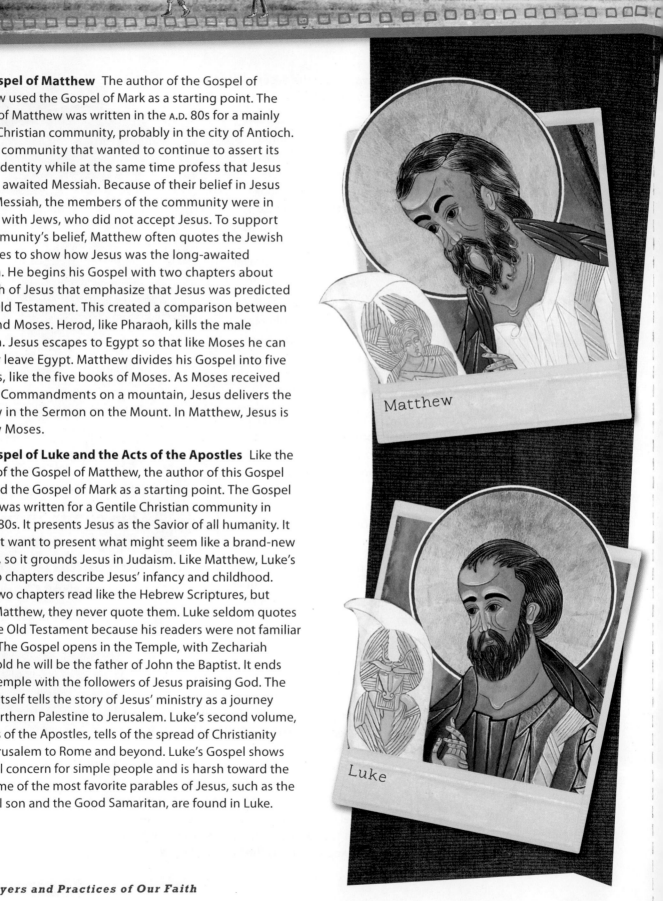

Matthew

Luke

The Gospel of Luke and the Acts of the Apostles Like the author of the Gospel of Matthew, the author of this Gospel also used the Gospel of Mark as a starting point. The Gospel of Luke was written for a Gentile Christian community in the A.D. 80s. It presents Jesus as the Savior of all humanity. It does not want to present what might seem like a brand-new religion, so it grounds Jesus in Judaism. Like Matthew, Luke's first two chapters describe Jesus' infancy and childhood. These two chapters read like the Hebrew Scriptures, but unlike Matthew, they never quote them. Luke seldom quotes from the Old Testament because his readers were not familiar with it. The Gospel opens in the Temple, with Zechariah being told he will be the father of John the Baptist. It ends in the Temple with the followers of Jesus praising God. The Gospel itself tells the story of Jesus' ministry as a journey from northern Palestine to Jerusalem. Luke's second volume, the Acts of the Apostles, tells of the spread of Christianity from Jerusalem to Rome and beyond. Luke's Gospel shows a special concern for simple people and is harsh toward the rich. Some of the most favorite parables of Jesus, such as the prodigal son and the Good Samaritan, are found in Luke.

Prayers and Practices of Our Faith

Finding a Passage in the Bible

Bible passages are identified by book, chapter, and verse, for example, Genesis 1:28. The name of the book comes first. Sometimes it is in abbreviated form. Your Bible's table of contents will help you determine what the abbreviation means. In our example, the name of the book of the Bible is Genesis. After the name of the book, there are two numbers. The first one identifies the chapter, which in our example is chapter one. This number is followed by a colon. The second number identifies the verse or verses, which in the example below is verse 28.

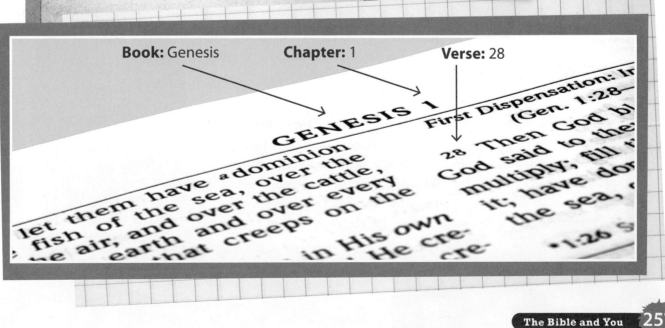

Book: Genesis   **Chapter:** 1   **Verse:** 28

GENESIS 1

let them have dominion
fish of the sea, over the
air, and over the cattle,
earth and over every
that creeps on the
in His own
He cre-

First Dispensation: In
(Gen. 1:28–

28 Then God bl
God said to the
multiply; fill
it; have dor
the sea,
cre-

•1:26 s

The Gospel of John The Gospel of John, written in the mid-to-late A.D. 90s, is very different from the three Synoptic Gospels. Most of the miracles and sayings of those Gospels are not found in John. In addition, the Gospel of John is different in tone and theology. In John, Jesus speaks in long, symbolic speeches. Instead of the story of Jesus' infancy, John's Gospel begins, "In the beginning was the Word, / and the Word was with God, / and the Word was God." (John 1:1) In John, Jesus only performs seven miracles, which are called signs. Their purpose is to strengthen the disciples' faith in Jesus. Jesus goes to great length to explain the significance of these signs. His ministry takes place over the period of three years. Every year a trip to Jerusalem at Passover plays a central role. The Gospel of John was written for a Jewish Christian community who resented being rejected by the main Jewish community. The last chapter is a later addition. It shows the attempt of the community of John to be reconciled with the more mainstream Church centered around Peter.

"My Lord and My God"

Many of us would like to have seen and heard Jesus while he lived on earth. Perhaps we think that it would be easier to believe in him if we met him face-to-face. The apostle Thomas had that opportunity as he followed Jesus during his ministry. He also witnessed Jesus' arrest, and he hid in fear when Jesus was crucified.

After the Resurrection, the other Apostles told Thomas that Jesus has risen from the dead. Unable to believe such wonderful news, Thomas demanded proof. The Gospel of John tells the story of Thomas's encounter with Jesus and Jesus' generosity in meeting Thomas's demands so that he might believe. Thomas responded with his great affirmation of faith, "My Lord and my God!"

The Doubting Thomas, Andrea del Verrocchio, bronze, 1466–83.

Paul and His Letters About the year 50, Paul wrote his first letter to the first Christian community he founded, in the city of Thessalonica. A year later he wrote a second letter to the Thessalonians to correct some misunderstandings that had arisen. These letters were written more than 20 years after the Death and Resurrection of Jesus. Over the next 10 years or so, Paul wrote letters to the other Christian communities he had founded in response to their questions or improper behavior. He also wrote a letter to the Christians of Rome, a city he hoped to visit. He wrote this letter because he wanted to convince the Christians in Rome that he was an orthodox Christian with a true teaching of the message of Jesus. Paul's letter to Philemon is a personal letter on behalf of a Christian slave being returned to his master. Paul's writings also include the letters to Timothy and Titus.

Other Epistles and the Book of Revelation The remaining letters include the letters of Peter, which reflected the concerns of the Church in Rome; the letter to the Hebrews, a homily on early Christian themes; the letter of Jude; the letters of John; and the Revelation of John. Revelation is an example of a type of writing popular in Judaism at the time. It presents a vision of the end of the world in which the good and the just triumph. These visions actually address a crisis facing the writer and the community. In the case of John, the crisis is the persecution of Christians by the Roman Emperor Domitian. Revelation is John's way of offering words of encouragement to the people. †

> The remaining letters include the letters of Peter, which reflected the concerns of the Church in Rome.

> About the year 50, Paul wrote his first letter to the first Christian community he founded, in the city of Thessalonica.

Saint Paul

Church and World Time Line

Church History

Birth of Jesus. Rome takes over governance of Jerusalem. Sadducees and Pharisees are active.

Jesus is proclaimed. Paul travels to Athens. Council of Jerusalem occurs (50). Romans conquer Jerusalem and destroy the Temple. New Testament written.

Church spreads throughout Roman empire. Church affirms that the God of the Old Testament is the Father of Jesus.

Councils of Nicaea (325), Ephesus (431), Chalcedon (451) take place. Monasticism spreads. Basilica of St. Peter erected in Rome and replaced by present church in the 1500s. Saint Patrick begins his mission to Ireland (432).

Ministry of Jesus takes place, culminating with his Crucifixion, Death, and Resurrection.

World History

Rome occupies the Holy Land.

Romans control Palestine. Herod's kingdom is divided among his sons and Roman procurators.

Sporadic persecution of Christians (250–303). Constantine becomes Roman emperor (306). Edict of Milan grants tolerance to all religions (313).

Persecution of Christians in 65 and 90. Jewish leaders redefine Judaism as religion of the Scriptures.

Roman government fails in the West (476). Eastern Empire flourishes. Clovis, king of the Franks, coverts to Christianity with his tribe (496).

260 *Prayers and Practices of Our Faith*

| 500 – 1000 | 1000 – 1300 | 1300 – 1500 | 1500 – 1700 | 1700 – 2000 |

Schism with the Eastern Church occurs (1054). Church becomes predominant spiritual force in West. Truce of God established (c. 1000–1300). Cistercians founded (1098). Dominicans founded. (1215). Augustinians founded (1243). Franciscans founded and the Crusades occur (1095–1291).

Avignon Papacy (1309–1377)
Western Schism (1378–1417)

Reformation begins. Jesuits founded (1540). Angela Merici founds Order of St. Ursula, first women's teaching order in the Church (1535). Council of Trent meets (1545–1564). Missionary activity expands to Asia and the Americas.

Saint Benedict founds Western monasticism on Monte Cassino (529) and writes his Rule. Pope Gregory the Great becomes pope (590). Pope Gregory II sends Boniface on mission to German tribes. Cyril and Methodius sent as missionaries to Slavs (862).

Church spreads to United States. Declaration of the Immaculate Conception occurs (1854). Pope Leo XIII issues encyclical *On Capital and Labor* (1891). Vatican Council I (1869–1870) and Vatican Council II (1963–1965) meet. Catholics martyred in Central America (1970–1980). Pope John Paul II meets with representatives of major world religions at Assisi (1986, 2002).

| 500 – 1000 | 1000 – 1300 | 1300 – 1500 | 1500 – 1700 | 1700 – 2000 |

Muhammad and his followers leave Mecca for Medina: Islam begins (622). Europe experiences the Dark Ages. Pope Leo III crowns Charlemagne as Holy Roman Emperor (800).

The Black Death: one-third of Europe dies of bubonic plague (1348–1353). Johann Gutenberg prints first Bible (1455–1458).

The following events and movements occur: The Enlightenment; Rationalism; French Revolution (1789–1804); Nationalism; Colonialism; World War I (1914–1918); and World War II (1939–1945).

Rise of cities and commerce. Rise of universities. Gothic cathedrals built. National monarchies rise in England and France.

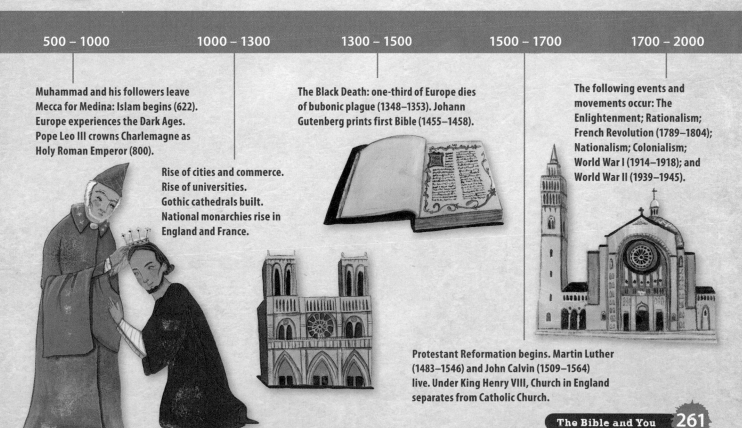

Protestant Reformation begins. Martin Luther (1483–1546) and John Calvin (1509–1564) live. Under King Henry VIII, Church in England separates from Catholic Church.

What Every Catholic Should Know

The Great Commandment

The Ten Commandments are fulfilled in Jesus' Great Commandment.

"You shall love the Lord your God with all your heart, with all your soul, with all your mind, and with all your strength. . . . You shall love your neighbor as yourself."

Mark 12:30–31

The New Commandment

Before his death on the cross, Jesus gave his disciples a new commandment.

"[L]ove one another. As I have loved you, so you also should love one another."

John 13:34

The Golden Rule

"Do to others whatever you would have them do to you."

Matthew 7:12

The Beatitudes

The Beatitudes are the teachings of Jesus in the Sermon on the Mount. They can be found in Matthew 5:1–10. Jesus teaches us that if we live according to the Beatitudes, we will live a happy life. The Beatitudes fulfill God's promises made to Abraham and his descendants and describe the rewards that will be ours as loyal followers of Christ.

"Blessed are the poor in spirit,
    for theirs is the kingdom of heaven.
Blessed are they who mourn,
    for they will be comforted.
Blessed are the meek,
    for they will inherit the land.
Blessed are they who hunger and thirst
      for righteousness,
    for they will be satisfied.
Blessed are the merciful,
    for they will be shown mercy.
Blessed are the clean in heart,
    for they will see God.
Blessed are the peacemakers,
    for they will be called children of God.
Blessed are they who are persecuted
      for the sake of righteousness,
    for theirs is the kingdom of heaven."

Matthew 5:1–10

Sermon on the Mount,
Laura James.

The Ten Commandments

As believers in Jesus Christ, we are called to make moral choices that keep us united with God and help us follow Jesus' example. With the help and grace of the Holy Spirit, we can choose ways to act to keep us close to God, to help other people, and to be witnesses to Jesus.

The Ten Commandments guide us in making choices that help us live as God wants us to live. The first three commandments tell us how to love God; the other seven tell us how to love our neighbor.

1. I am the Lord your God: you shall not have strange gods before me.

2. You shall not take the name of the Lord your God in vain.

3. Remember to keep holy the Lord's Day.

4. Honor your father and your mother.

5. You shall not kill.

6. You shall not commit adultery.

7. You shall not steal.

8. You shall not bear false witness against your neighbor.

9. You shall not covet your neighbor's wife.

10. You shall not covet your neighbor's goods.

Precepts of the Church

The Precepts of the Church describe the minimum effort we are called to make in prayer and in living a moral life. All Catholics are called to move beyond the minimum by growing in love of God and love of neighbor. The Precepts are as follows:

✝ attendance at Mass on Sundays and Holy Days of Obligation

✝ confession of sins at least once a year

✝ reception of Holy Communion at least once a year during the Easter season

✝ observance of the days of fast and abstinence

✝ providing for the needs of the Church

The Four Last Things

There are four things that describe the end of all human life.

death   judgment   Heaven   Hell

First is the death of the individual. Then immediately after death is the judgment by Christ. The result of this judgment is either Heaven, perhaps with a stay in Purgatory, or Hell.

Justification

Paul thought that God's justice was saving justice at its best. God, who is faithful, fulfilled the promises he made in the Covenant with his Chosen People. God has taken the initiative to call the human family back to him through Jesus Christ. This process of reuniting the human family with God is called justification. (Romans 3:21–31) We cannot justify ourselves. We can only be justified by being united in faith with Jesus Christ and by accepting the grace won by Christ. (Romans 5:1–2) People can only be made right with God and set free from a life of immorality by accepting God's reconciling grace.

Because of Adam and Eve's choice to turn away from God, we are born into Original Sin. As a result, we cannot make things right with God by ourselves. The good news is that God has reached out to us to repair the relationship and reconcile us to himself. Paul calls this saving action of God justification.

Justification is the action of the Holy Spirit that cleanses us from sin in Baptism and that continually gives us the grace to walk in right relationship with God. Through justification we are healed, and our relationship with God is made right.

Since justification is an action of God, there is nothing we can do to merit Salvation on our own. In the process of cooperating with the grace of God, however, we can merit for ourselves and others the continuing graces that we need to be saved. ✝

We cannot justify ourselves. We can only be justified by being united in faith with Jesus Christ and by accepting the grace won by Christ.

Christ on the Cross,
Barthelemy d'Eyck,
circa 1445–1450.

Virtues

Virtues are gifts from God that lead us to live in a close relationship with him. Virtues are like habits. They need to be practiced; they can be lost if they are neglected.

Theological Virtues

The three most important virtues are called Theological Virtues because they come from God and lead to God.

faith   hope   charity

Cardinal Virtues

The Cardinal Virtues are human virtues, acquired by education and good actions. *Cardinal* comes from *cardo*, the Latin word for "hinge," meaning "that on which other things depend."

prudence   justice   fortitude   temperance

Gifts of the Holy Spirit

The Holy Spirit makes it possible for us to do what God asks of us by giving us these many gifts.

wisdom	understanding	counsel	piety
fortitude	knowledge	fear of the Lord	

Fruits of the Holy Spirit

The Fruits of the Holy Spirit are signs of the Holy Spirit's action in our lives.

love	kindness	faithfulness
joy	goodness	modesty
peace	generosity	self-control
patience	gentleness	chastity

Virtues are like habits. They need to be practiced; they can be lost if they are neglected.

Works of Mercy

The Corporal and Spiritual Works of Mercy are actions we can perform that extend God's compassion and mercy to those in need.

Corporal Works of Mercy

The Corporal Works of Mercy are kind acts by which we help our neighbors with their material and physical needs:

✝ feed the hungry

✝ give drink to the thirsty

✝ clothe the naked

✝ shelter the homeless

✝ visit the sick

✝ visit the imprisoned

✝ bury the dead

Spiritual Works of Mercy

The Spiritual Works of Mercy are acts of compassion by which we help our neighbors with their emotional and spiritual needs:

✝ counsel the doubtful

✝ instruct the ignorant

✝ admonish sinners

✝ comfort the afflicted

✝ forgive offenses

✝ bear wrongs patiently

✝ pray for the living and the dead

Prayer and Forms of Prayer

GOD, who is always with us, wants us to talk to him and listen to him. We do this in prayer, which is the lifting of our minds and hearts to God.

What Is Prayer?

Being a Christian requires that we believe all that God has revealed to us, that we celebrate it in the liturgy and the sacraments, and that we live what we believe. All of this depends on a vital and personal relationship with the living and true God. This relationship is found in prayer. Prayer is, first of all, a gift from God. We can pray because God first seeks us out and calls us to meet him. We become aware of our thirst for God because God thirsts for us. Prayer arises from our heart, beyond the grasp of reason. Only the Spirit of God can understand the human heart and know it fully. Prayer is the habit of being with God—Father, Son, and Holy Spirit. This communion with God is always possible because through our Baptism we are united with Christ. By being united with Christ, we are united with others. Christian prayer is communion with Christ that branches out to all the members of his body, the Church.

We Meditate and Contemplate

One way to pray is to meditate. To meditate is to think about God. We try to keep our attention and focus on God. In meditation we may use Scripture, prayer books, or icons, which are religious images, to help us concentrate and to spark our imagination.

Another way to pray is to contemplate. This means that we rest quietly in God's presence.

We Get Ready to Pray

We live in a busy, noisy, and fast-paced world. Sometimes, because of this, we have difficulty concentrating. In order to meditate or reflect, we need to prepare ourselves.

We can get ready for meditation by resting our bodies in a comfortable position. Sitting with our backs straight and both feet on the floor is one comfortable position. We can close our eyes, fold our hands in front of us, silently take a deep breath in, and then let it out slowly. We can establish a rhythm by slowly counting to three while breathing in and slowly counting to three while breathing out. Concentrating on our breathing helps us quiet our thoughts.

We Avoid Distractions

If we become distracted by thinking about something, such as the day at school or a sports event, we can just go back to thinking about our breathing.

After a little practice, we will be able to avoid distractions, pray with our imagination, and spend time with God or Jesus in our hearts.

The Five Basic Forms of Christian Prayer

The Holy Spirit, who teaches us to pray, leads us to pray in a number of ways. This conversation with God can take the form of blessing, petition, intercession, thanksgiving, or praise.

Blessing

To bless someone is to acknowledge his or her goodness. A prayer of blessing or adoration is our response to God's goodness because of all the gifts he has given us. When we pray a prayer of blessing, God's gifts and our acceptance of them come together. We bless God, the source of every blessing, because he has blessed us.

Petition

A prayer of petition is much more than asking God for things we want or need. When we pray a prayer of petition, we express our relationship with God as our Creator. Sometimes we sin and turn away from God.

So the first step in a prayer of petition is turning back to him and asking for his forgiveness. We can then ask God for what we need, confident that he knows what we need before we ask.

Intercession

In prayers of intercession, we ask something on behalf of another. As a prayer form, intercession is a prayer of petition that leads us to pray as Jesus did. Throughout his life on earth, Jesus interceded with the Father on behalf of all people. To pray in this way means that our hearts are turned outward, focused on the needs of others.

Thanksgiving

Thanksgiving is a characteristic of Christian prayer, especially the celebration of the Eucharist. When we celebrate the Eucharist, we give thanks for the sacrifice that Jesus made on the Cross. Through his Death, Resurrection, and Ascension, Christ has reconciled us to God. In celebrating the Eucharist, we more fully become a people of thanksgiving.

Praise

Praise is the form of prayer that recognizes that God is God and gives him glory. Praise goes beyond thanking God for what he has done for us and gives him glory simply because he is. Praise embraces the other forms of prayer and carries them to God, who is the source of all that is. ✝

Prayers to Take to Heart

WE can pray with any words that come to mind. Sometimes, when we find that choosing our own words is difficult, we can use traditional prayers. Likewise, when we pray aloud with others, we rely on traditional prayers to unite our minds, hearts, and voices. Taking traditional prayers to heart can be helpful. Taking prayers to heart means that we not only learn the words but also try to understand and live them.

Pope Benedict XVI has identified four prayers that are shared by the universal Church. If they are learned in Latin they could be prayed as a sign of the universal nature of the Church. All Catholics throughout the world would be praying in the same language. The Latin for these four prayers is included across from each of them.

The Lord's Prayer

Our Father, who art in heaven,
hallowed be thy name;
thy kingdom come,
thy will be done
on earth as it is in heaven.
Give us this day our daily bread,
and forgive us our trespasses,
as we forgive those who trespass against us;
and lead us not into temptation,
but deliver us from evil.
Amen.

Pater Noster

Pater noster, qui es in caelis,
sanctificetur nomen tuum.
Adveniat regnum tuum.
Fiat voluntas tua,
sicut in caelo et in terra.
Panem nostrum quotidianum da nobis hodie,
et dimitte nobis debita nostra
sicut et nos dimittimus debitoribus nostris.
Et ne nos inducas in tentationem,
sed libera nos a malo.
Amen.

Hail Mary

Hail Mary, full of grace,
the Lord is with you.
Blessed are you among women,
and blessed is the fruit of your womb, Jesus.
Holy Mary, Mother of God,
pray for us sinners,
now and at the hour of our death.
Amen.

Ave Maria

Ave Maria, gratia plena,
Dominus tecum.
Benedicta tu in mulieribus,
et benedictus fructus ventris tui, Iesus.
Sancta Maria, Mater Dei,
ora pro nobis peccatoribus,
nunc, et in hora mortis nostrae.
Amen.

The Sign of the Cross

In the name of the Father, and of the Son, and of the Holy Spirit.
Amen.

Glory Be to the Father (Doxology)

Glory be to the Father, and to the Son, and to the Holy Spirit. As it was in the beginning, is now, and ever shall be, world without end.
Amen.

Morning Offering

My God, I offer you my prayers, works, joys and sufferings of this day in union with the holy sacrifice of the Mass throughout the world. I offer them for all the intentions of your Son's Sacred Heart, for the salvation of souls, reparation for sin, and the reunion of Christians.
Amen.

Prayer Before Meals

Bless us, O Lord, and these your gifts which we are about to receive from your goodness. Through Christ our Lord.
Amen.

Prayer After Meals

We give you thanks
for all your gifts,
almighty God,
living and reigning
now and for ever.
Amen.

Signum Crucis

*In nomine Patris, et Filii,
et Spiritus Sancti.
Amen.*

Gloria Patri

*Gloria Patri, et Filio, et Spiritui Sancto.
Sicut erat in principio, et nunc, et semper,
et in saecula saeculorum.
Amen.*

Act of Contrition

My God,
I am sorry for my sins with all my heart.
In choosing to do wrong
and failing to do good,
I have sinned against you
whom I should love above all things.
I firmly intend, with your help,
to do penance,
to sin no more,
and to avoid whatever leads me to sin.
Our Savior Jesus Christ
suffered and died for us.
In his name, my God, have mercy.

Prayer to the Holy Spirit

Come, Holy Spirit, fill the hearts of your faithful.
And kindle in them the fire of your love.
Send forth your Spirit and they shall be created.
And you will renew the face of the earth.

Lord,
by the light of the Holy Spirit
you have taught the hearts of your faithful.
In the same Spirit
help us to relish what is right
and always rejoice in your consolation.
We ask this through Christ our Lord.
Amen.

Apostles' Creed

I believe in God,
the Father almighty,
Creator of heaven and earth,
and in Jesus Christ, his only Son, our Lord,
who was conceived by the Holy Spirit,
born of the Virgin Mary,
suffered under Pontius Pilate,
was crucified, died and was buried;
he descended into hell;
on the third day he rose again from the dead;
he ascended into heaven,
and is seated at the right hand of God
   the Father almighty;
from there he will come to judge the living
   and the dead.

I believe in the Holy Spirit,
the holy catholic Church,
the communion of saints,
the forgiveness of sins,
the resurrection of the body,
and life everlasting. Amen.

Nicene Creed

I believe in one God,
the Father almighty,
maker of heaven and earth,
of all things visible and invisible.

I believe in one Lord Jesus Christ,
the Only Begotten Son of God,
born of the Father before all ages.
God from God, Light from Light,
true God from true God,
begotten, not made, consubstantial
   with the Father;
through him all things were made.
For us men and for our salvation
he came down from heaven,
and by the Holy Spirit was incarnate of the
   Virgin Mary,
and became man.

For our sake he was crucified under
   Pontius Pilate,
he suffered death and was buried,
and rose again on the third day
in accordance with the Scriptures.
He ascended into heaven
and is seated at the right hand of the Father.
He will come again in glory
to judge the living and the dead
and his kingdom will have no end.

I believe in the Holy Spirit, the Lord,
   the giver of life,
who proceeds from the Father and the Son,
who with the Father and the Son is adored
   and glorified,
who has spoken through the prophets.

I believe in one, holy, catholic and
   apostolic Church.
I confess one Baptism for the forgiveness of sins
and I look forward to the resurrection of the dead
and the life of the world to come. Amen.

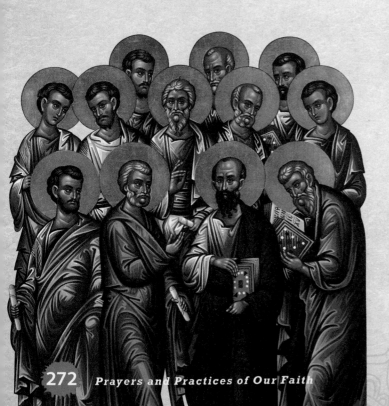

Act of Faith

O my God, I firmly believe that you are one God in three divine Persons, Father, Son, and Holy Spirit. I believe that your divine Son became man and died for our sins, and that he will come to judge the living and the dead. I believe these and all the truths which the holy Catholic Church teaches, because you have revealed them, who can neither deceive nor be deceived.
Amen.

Act of Hope

O my God, relying on your infinite mercy and promises, I hope to obtain pardon of my sins, the help of your grace, and life everlasting, through the merits of Jesus Christ, my Lord and Redeemer.
Amen.

Act of Love

O my God, I love you above all things with my whole heart and soul, because you are all good and worthy of all my love. I love my neighbor as myself for the love of you. I forgive all who have injured me and I ask pardon of those whom I have injured.
Amen.

Prayer for Vocations

God, in Baptism you called me by name
and made me a member of your people, the Church.
Help all your people to know their vocation in life,
and to respond by living a life of holiness.
For your greater glory and for the service
    of your people,
raise up dedicated and generous leaders
who will serve as sisters, priests,
brothers, deacons, and lay ministers.

Send your Spirit to guide and strengthen me
that I may serve your people
following the example of your Son, Jesus Christ,
in whose name I offer this prayer.
Amen.

Jesus Prayer

Lord Jesus Christ, Son of God,
 have mercy on us sinners.

Prayer for Generosity

Eternal Word, only begotten Son of God,
Teach me true generosity.
Teach me to serve you as you deserve,
To give without counting the cost,
To fight heedless of wounds,
To labor without seeking rest,
To sacrifice myself without thought of any
reward
Save the knowledge that I have done your will.
Amen.

Suscipe

Take, Lord, and receive all my liberty,
my memory, my understanding,
and my entire will.
All I have and call my own.

You have given all to me.
To you, Lord, I return it.

Everything is yours; do with it what you will.
Give me only your love and your grace.
That is enough for me.

Magnificat

My soul proclaims the greatness of the Lord,
my spirit rejoices in God my Savior,
for he has looked with favor on his lowly
     servant.
From this day all generations will call me
     blessed:
the Almighty has done great things for me,
and holy is his Name.
He has mercy on those who fear him in every
     generation.
He has shown the strength of his arm,
he has scattered the proud in their conceit.
He has cast down the mighty from their thrones,
and has lifted up the lowly.
He has filled the hungry with good things,
and the rich he has sent away empty.
He has come to the help of his servant Israel
for he has remembered his promise of mercy,
the promise he made to our fathers,
to Abraham and his children forever.

Memorare

Remember, O most gracious Virgin Mary,
that never was it known
that anyone who fled to thy protection,
implored thy help,
or sought thy intercession,
was left unaided.
Inspired by this confidence
I fly unto thee,
O Virgin of virgins, my Mother.
To thee do I come,
before thee I stand,
sinful and sorrowful.
O Mother of the Word Incarnate,
despise not my petitions,
but in thy mercy hear and answer me.

Angelus

Verse: The Angel of the Lord declared unto Mary.

Response: And she conceived of the Holy Spirit.

Hail Mary, . . .

Verse: Behold the handmaid of the Lord.

Response: Be it done unto me according to thy
word. Hail Mary.

Verse: And the Word was made flesh.

Response: And dwelt among us. Hail Mary.

Verse: Pray for us, O holy Mother of God.

Response: That we may be made worthy of the
promises of Christ.

Let us pray;
Pour forth, we beseech thee, O Lord,
thy grace into our hearts, that we, to whom the
Incarnation of Christ, thy Son, was made known by
the message of an angel, may by his Passion and
Cross be brought to the glory of his Resurrection.
Through the same Christ, our Lord. Amen.

The Madonna of the Magnificat,
Alberto Giacometti.

Art © Alberto Giacometti
Estate/Licensed by VAGA and
ARS, New York, NY.

Regina Caeli

Queen of heaven, rejoice, alleluia.
The Son whom you merited to bear, alleluia,
has risen as he said, alleluia.
Rejoice and be glad, O Virgin Mary, alleluia!
For the Lord has truly risen, alleluia.

Let us pray:
O God, who through the resurrection of your
Son, our Lord Jesus Christ, did vouchsafe to
give joy to the world; grant, we beseech you,
that through his Mother, the Virgin Mary, we
may obtain the joys of everlasting life. Through
the same Christ our Lord. Amen.

Act of Consecration to Mary

O my Queen, O my Mother, I love you and give
myself to you. I give to you this day my eyes,
my ears, my mouth, my heart, my whole self.
Since I am yours, keep me and guard me as
your child forever. Amen.

Prayer to St. Joseph, the Protector of the Church (adapted)

Blessed Joseph, we ask you to pray for us.

Through the love you had for Mary and by the
love you expressed to Jesus, we humbly ask
you to help us in all our needs.

Watchful guardian of the holy family,
defend us from sin, shield us from harm,
    and protect us from evil.

Through your prayers and examples, guide us
to live a holy life and obtain eternal happiness
in heaven. Amen.

Saint
Joseph

Crowning Mary

The Daily Examen

SAINT Ignatius of Loyola gave the Church a great gift—the Spiritual Exercises. Praying with the Spiritual Exercises helps us discover God's plan for us.

The Daily Examen is an important part of the Spiritual Exercises. When we pray the Daily Examen, we reflect on the events of the day so that we can discover God's presence and discern his will for us. The Daily Examen helps us recognize God's presence in our everyday lives.

The following steps are a version of the Daily Examen that we can use in our personal prayer.

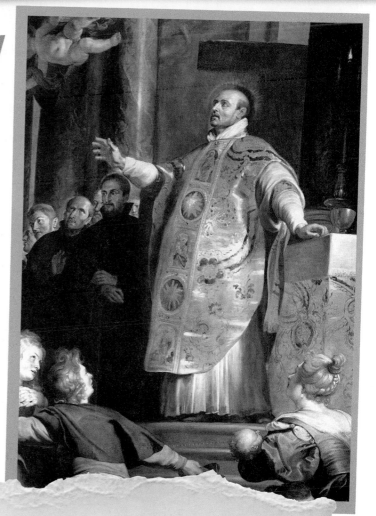

The Vision of St. Ignatius of Loyola,
Peter Paul Rubens, oil on canvas.

1. **Become aware of God's presence.** Take a moment to reflect on all the blessings you have received from God throughout the day. Ask yourself, "How did God reveal himself to me in the events I experienced and the people I met?

2. **Review the day with gratitude.** Take a moment to thank God for the joys and delights you have experienced throughout the day. Ask yourself, "What joys have I experienced in my interactions with others? What sights, sounds, and smells have filled me with delight?"

3. **Pay attention to your emotions.** Reflect on the feelings you have experienced throughout the day. Ask yourself, "Have any of my emotions drawn me closer to God or led me away from him? What might God be telling me through my emotions?"

4. **Choose one feature of the day and pray with it.** Ask the Holy Spirit to help you identify something from your day that seems especially important. It may be a feeling, an encounter, or a recurring thought you've had. Spend a moment reflecting on the experience and pray a prayer from your heart.

5. **Look toward tomorrow.** Ask God for the grace to help you remain faithful to the call of discipleship. Then ask him to open your mind and heart so that you can continue to discover his presence in your everyday experience.

By praying this version of the Daily Examen, you can become more aware of God's action in your life so that you can find God in all things.

The Rosary

THE Rosary helps us pray to Jesus through Mary. When we pray the Rosary, we think about the special events, or mysteries, in the lives of Jesus and Mary.

In his apostolic letter *Rosary of the Virgin Mary,* Pope John Paul II wrote that the Rosary could take on a variety of legitimate forms adapted to different spiritual traditions and different Christian communities. "What is really important," he said, "is that the Rosary should always be seen and experienced as a path of contemplation." When we pray the Rosary, we contemplate the gift of Salvation that we have received through Jesus, who was born of Mary.

Hail, Holy Queen (Salve Regina)

Hail, holy Queen, Mother of mercy,
hail, our life, our sweetness, and our hope.
To you we cry, the children of Eve;
to you we send up our sighs,
mourning and weeping in this land of exile.
Turn, then, most gracious advocate,
your eyes of mercy toward us;
lead us home at last
and show us the blessed fruit of your womb, Jesus:
O clement, O loving, O sweet Virgin Mary.

The Rosary is made up of a string of beads and a crucifix. We hold the crucifix in our hands as we pray the Sign of the Cross. Then we pray the Apostles' Creed.

Next to the crucifix, there is a single bead, followed by a set of three beads and another single bead. We pray the Lord's Prayer as we hold the first single bead and a Hail Mary at each bead in the set of three that follows. Then we pray the Glory Be to the Father. On the next single bead, we think about the first mystery and pray the Lord's Prayer.

There are five sets of 10 beads; each set is called a decade. We pray a Hail Mary on each bead of a decade as we reflect on a particular mystery in the lives of Jesus and Mary. The Glory Be to the Father is prayed at the end of each set. Between sets is a single bead on which we think about one of the mysteries and pray the Lord's Prayer. In some places it is traditional to pray the Hail, Holy Queen after the last decade. We end the prayer by holding the crucifix in our hands as we pray the Sign of the Cross.

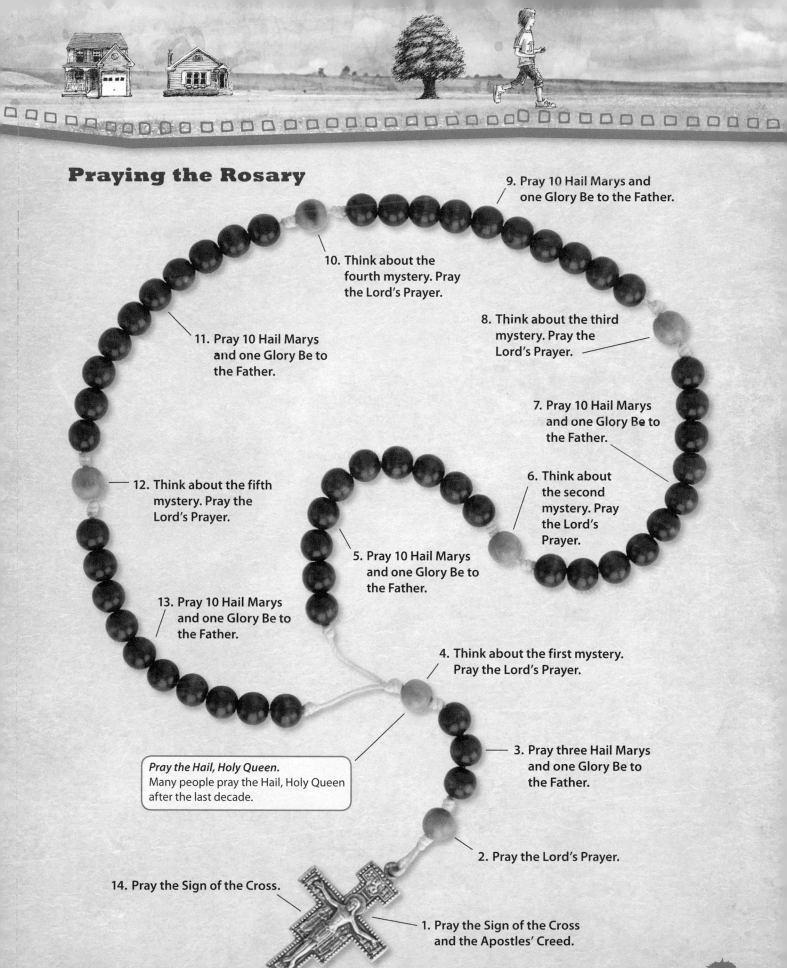

Praying the Rosary

9. Pray 10 Hail Marys and one Glory Be to the Father.

10. Think about the fourth mystery. Pray the Lord's Prayer.

11. Pray 10 Hail Marys and one Glory Be to the Father.

8. Think about the third mystery. Pray the Lord's Prayer.

7. Pray 10 Hail Marys and one Glory Be to the Father.

12. Think about the fifth mystery. Pray the Lord's Prayer.

6. Think about the second mystery. Pray the Lord's Prayer.

5. Pray 10 Hail Marys and one Glory Be to the Father.

13. Pray 10 Hail Marys and one Glory Be to the Father.

4. Think about the first mystery. Pray the Lord's Prayer.

Pray the Hail, Holy Queen.
Many people pray the Hail, Holy Queen after the last decade.

3. Pray three Hail Marys and one Glory Be to the Father.

2. Pray the Lord's Prayer.

14. Pray the Sign of the Cross.

1. Pray the Sign of the Cross and the Apostles' Creed.

Mysteries of the Rosary

THE Church has used three sets of mysteries for many centuries. In 2002, Pope John Paul II proposed a fourth set of mysteries—the Luminous Mysteries, or the Mysteries of Light. According to his suggestion, the four sets of mysteries might be prayed on the following days: the Joyful Mysteries on Monday and Saturday, the Sorrowful Mysteries on Tuesday and Friday, the Glorious Mysteries on Wednesday and Sunday, and the Luminous Mysteries on Thursday.

The Annunciation

The Joyful Mysteries

1. **The Annunciation** Mary learns that she has been chosen to be the mother of Jesus.

2. **The Visitation** Mary visits Elizabeth, who tells her that she will always be remembered.

3. **The Nativity** Jesus is born in a stable in Bethlehem.

4. **The Presentation** Mary and Joseph take the infant Jesus to the Temple to present him to God.

5. **The Finding of Jesus in the Temple** Jesus is found in the Temple discussing his faith with the teachers.

The Luminous Mysteries

Wedding Feast at Cana

1. **The Baptism of Jesus in the River Jordan** God proclaims that Jesus is his beloved Son.

2. **The Wedding Feast at Cana** At Mary's request, Jesus performs his first miracle.

3. **The Proclamation of the Kingdom of God** Jesus calls all to conversion and service to the Kingdom.

4. **The Transfiguration of Jesus** Jesus is revealed in glory to Peter, James, and John.

5. **The Institution of the Eucharist** Jesus offers his Body and Blood at the Last Supper.

The Agony in the Garden

The Sorrowful Mysteries

1. **The Agony in the Garden** Jesus prays in the Garden of Gethsemane on the night before he dies.

2. **The Scourging at the Pillar** Jesus is lashed with whips.

3. **The Crowning with Thorns** Jesus is mocked and crowned with thorns.

4. **The Carrying of the Cross** Jesus carries the cross that will be used to crucify him.

5. **The Crucifixion** Jesus is nailed to the cross and dies.

The Glorious Mysteries

1. **The Resurrection** God the Father raises Jesus from the dead.

2. **The Ascension** Jesus returns to his Father in Heaven.

3. **The Coming of the Holy Spirit** The Holy Spirit comes to bring new life to the disciples.

4. **The Assumption of Mary** At the end of her life on earth, Mary is taken body and soul into Heaven.

5. **The Coronation of Mary** Mary is crowned as Queen of Heaven and Earth.

The Ascension

Stations of the Cross

THE 14 Stations of the Cross represent events from Jesus' Passion and Death. Even before the Gospels were written, Jesus' followers told the story of the Paschal Mystery. When people went on pilgrimages to Jerusalem, they were anxious to see the sites where Jesus lived and died. Eventually, following in the footsteps of the Lord on the way to his Death became an important part of the pilgrimage.

The stations, as we know them today, came about when it was no longer easy or even possible to visit the holy sites in Palestine. In the 1500s, villages all over Europe started creating replicas of the Way of the Cross, with small shrines commemorating the places along the route in Jerusalem. Eventually, these shrines became the set of 14 stations we now know.

The first thing to remember about the stations is that they are a prayer. They are not an exercise in remembering events from the past. They are an invitation to make present the final hours of Jesus' life. The Stations of the Cross become a prayer when we open our hearts to be touched by Jesus' final journey to the Cross. Jesus wants to use any means available to move our hearts to know his love for us.

At each station we use our senses and our imagination to reflect prayerfully on Jesus' suffering, Death, and Resurrection. The stations can allow us to visualize the meaning of his Passion and Death and lead us to gratitude. They can also lead us into a sense of solidarity with all our brothers and sisters, especially those who suffer, who are unjustly accused or victimized, who sit on death row, who carry difficult burdens, or who face terminal illnesses.

1

Jesus Is Condemned to Death.
Pontius Pilate condemns Jesus to death.

2

Jesus Takes Up the Cross.
Jesus willingly accepts and patiently bears the Cross.

3

Jesus Falls the First Time.
Weakened by torments and by loss of blood, Jesus falls beneath the Cross.

4

Jesus Meets His Sorrowful Mother.
Jesus meets his mother, Mary, who is filled with grief.

 Prayers and Practices of Our Faith

5

Simon of Cyrene Helps Jesus Carry the Cross.
Soldiers force Simon of Cyrene to carry the Cross.

6

Veronica Wipes the Face of Jesus.
Veronica steps through the crowd to wipe the face of Jesus.

7

Jesus Falls the Second Time.
Jesus falls beneath the weight of the Cross a second time.

8

Jesus Meets the Women of Jerusalem.
Jesus tells the women not to weep for him but for themselves and for their children.

9

Jesus Falls the Third Time.
Weakened almost to the point of death, Jesus falls a third time.

10

Jesus Is Stripped of His Garments.
The soldiers strip Jesus of his garments, treating him as a common criminal.

11

Jesus Is Nailed to the Cross.
Jesus' hands and feet are nailed to the Cross.

12

Jesus Dies on the Cross.
After suffering greatly on the Cross, Jesus bows his head and dies.

13

Jesus Is Taken Down from the Cross.
The lifeless body of Jesus is tenderly placed in the arms of Mary, his mother.

14

Jesus Is Laid in the Tomb.
Jesus' disciples place his body in the tomb.

The closing prayer—sometimes included as the 15th station—reflects on the Resurrection of Jesus.

The Mystery of Faith Made Present

THE Church was revealed to the world with the coming of the Spirit on Pentecost. This gift of the Spirit ushered in a new era in the history of Salvation. This era is the age in which Christ makes present and communicates his work of Salvation through the liturgy of the Church. The Church, as Christ's Body, is the first sacrament, the sign and instrument through which the Holy Spirit dispenses the mystery of Salvation. Christ lives and acts through the sacraments.

The Seven Sacraments

Jesus touches our lives through the sacraments. The sacramentals—water, bread, wine, and oil—that are part of our rites are signs of Jesus' presence.

Sacraments of Initiation

These sacraments lay the foundation of Christian life.

Baptism In Baptism we are born into new life in Christ. Baptism takes away Original Sin and makes us members of the Church. Its sign is the pouring of water.

Confirmation This sacrament seals our life of faith in Jesus. Its signs are the laying on of hands on a person's head, most often by a bishop, and the anointing with oil. Like Baptism, it is received only once.

Eucharist The Eucharist nourishes our life of faith. We receive the Body and Blood of Christ. Its signs are bread and wine.

Sacraments of Healing

These sacraments celebrate the healing power of Jesus.

Penance and Reconciliation In the Sacrament of Penance and Reconciliation, we receive God's forgiveness through the absolution we receive from the priest. To receive the gift of forgiveness, we must have contrition for our sins. The signs of this sacrament are our confession of sins, our repentance and satisfaction, and the words of absolution.

Anointing of the Sick This sacrament unites a sick person's sufferings with the suffering of Jesus. Oil, a symbol of strength, is the sign of this sacrament. A person is anointed with oil and receives the laying on of hands from a priest.

Sacraments at the Service of Communion

These sacraments help members serve the community.

Matrimony In Matrimony, a baptized man and woman are united with each other as a sign of the unity between Jesus and his Church. Matrimony requires the consent of the couple, as expressed in the marriage promises. The couple is the sign of this sacrament.

Holy Orders In Holy Orders, men are ordained as priests and bishops to be leaders of the community. Deacons, who are ordained, serve as a reminder of our baptismal call to serve others. The signs of this sacrament are the laying on of hands and the prayer by the bishop, who asks God for the outpouring of the Holy Spirit.

Celebrating the Lord's Day

THE Sabbath, the day on which God rested after creating the world, represents the completion of creation. Saturday has been replaced by Sunday for Christians because it recalls the beginning of the new creation through the Resurrection of Jesus Christ. The Sunday celebration of the Lord's Day is at the heart of the Church's life. That is why on Sundays and other Holy Days of Obligation, we are required to participate in the Mass. We also rest from work, take time to enjoy our families and enrich our cultural and social lives, and perform Works of Mercy. On Sunday people from all over the world gather at God's Eucharistic table.

The Order of Mass

The Mass is the high point of Catholic life, and it always follows a set order.

Introductory Rites—preparing to celebrate the Eucharist

Entrance Chant
We gather as a community and praise God in song.

Greeting
We pray the Sign of the Cross. The priest welcomes us.

Penitential Act
We remember our sins and ask God for mercy.

Gloria
We praise God in song.

Collect
We ask God to hear our prayers.

Liturgy of the Word—hearing God's plan of Salvation

First Reading
We listen to God's Word, usually from the Old Testament.

Responsorial Psalm
We respond to God's Word in song.

Second Reading
We listen to God's Word from the New Testament.

Gospel Acclamation
We sing "Alleluia!" to praise God for the Good News. During Lent we use a different acclamation.

Gospel Reading
We stand and listen to the Gospel of the Lord.

Homily
The priest or the deacon explains God's Word.

Profession of Faith
We proclaim our faith through the Nicene Creed.

Prayer of the Faithful
We pray for our needs and the needs of others.

Liturgy of the Eucharist—celebrating Christ's presence in the Eucharist

Presentation and Preparation of the Gifts
We bring gifts of bread and wine to the altar.

Prayer over the Offerings
The priest prays that God will accept our sacrifice.

Eucharistic Prayer
This prayer of thanksgiving is the center and high point of the entire celebration.

✝ **Preface**—We give thanks and praise to God.

✝ **Holy, Holy, Holy**—We sing an acclamation of praise.

✝ **Institution Narrative**—The bread and wine become the Body and Blood of Jesus Christ.

✝ **The Mystery of Faith**—We proclaim the mystery of our faith.

✝ **Amen**—We affirm the words and actions of the Eucharistic Prayer.

Communion Rite—preparing to receive the Body and Blood of Jesus Christ

The Lord's Prayer
We pray the Lord's Prayer.

Sign of Peace
We offer one another Christ's peace.

Lamb of God
We pray for forgiveness, mercy, and peace.

Communion
We receive the Body and Blood of Jesus Christ.

Prayer after Communion
We pray that the Eucharist will strengthen us to live as Jesus did.

Concluding Rites—going forth to glorify the Lord by our lives

Final Blessing
We receive God's blessing.

Dismissal
We go in peace, glorifying the Lord by our lives.

Holy Days of Obligation

The Holy Days of Obligation are the days other than Sundays on which we celebrate the great things God has done for us through Jesus and the saints. On Holy Days of Obligation, Catholics attend Mass.

Six Holy Days of Obligation are celebrated in the United States.

January 1—Mary, Mother of God

40 days after Easter—Ascension

August 15—Assumption of the Blessed Virgin Mary

November 1—All Saints Day

December 8—Immaculate Conception

December 25—Nativity of Our Lord Jesus Christ

Making Good Choices

OUR conscience is the inner voice that helps us know the law God has placed in our hearts. Our conscience helps us judge the moral qualities of our own actions. It guides us to do good and avoid evil.

The Holy Spirit can help us form a good conscience. We form a good conscience by studying the teachings of the Church and following the guidance of our parents and pastoral leaders.

God has given every human being free will. This does not mean that we have the right to do whatever we please. We live in true freedom when we cooperate with the Holy Spirit, who gives us the virtue of prudence. This virtue helps us recognize what is good in every situation and make correct choices. The Holy Spirit gives us the gifts of wisdom and understanding to help us make the right choices in life in relationship to God and others. The gift of counsel helps us reflect on making correct choices in life.

The Ten Commandments help us make moral choices that are pleasing to God. We have the grace of the sacraments, the teachings of the Church, and the example of the saints and fellow Christians to help us make good choices.

Making moral choices involves the following steps:

1. Ask the Holy Spirit for help.

2. Think about God's law and the teachings of the Church.

3. Think about what will happen as a result of your choice. Ask yourself, "Will the consequences be pleasing to God? Will my choice hurt someone else?"

4. Seek advice from someone you respect and remember that Jesus is with you.

5. Ask yourself how your choice will affect your relationships with God and others.

Making moral choices means taking into consideration the object of the choice, our intention in making the choice, and the circumstances in which the choice is made. It is never right to make an evil choice in the hope of gaining something good.

Human Sinfulness

Original Sin

When Adam and Eve gave in to the temptation of the Devil, they let their trust in God, the Creator, die in their hearts. By giving in to temptation, they abused the gift of freedom they received from God. They believed the Devil. As a result, they chose to do what they wanted rather than doing what God wanted for them. All subsequent sins would be further acts of disobedience toward God and would demonstrate a lack of trust in his goodness. Adam and Eve committed a personal sin, but this sin affected the human nature that they would then transmit to humanity. Human nature would now be deprived of the original holiness and justice that God had intended. Original Sin is not a sin we commit but a state into which we are born. Baptism, by giving us the life of Christ's grace, erases Original Sin and turns us back toward God. But the consequences of our nature, weakened and inclined to evil, remain in us.

Mortal Sin

Mortal sin destroys the love of God in our heart. A conversion of heart, through the Sacrament of Penance and Reconciliation, is necessary to experience God's mercy again. For a sin to be mortal, three conditions must be met. First, the matter of the sin must be serious. Second, mortal sin requires full knowledge of the seriousness of the act. Third, there must be complete consent. In other words, the sin is really a personal choice.

Venial Sin

Venial sin allows the love of God to remain in our heart, but it offends and wounds that love. One commits a venial sin when the offense is of a less serious matter or, if the matter is serious, it is chosen without full knowledge or complete consent. Venial sin interferes with our practice of the virtues, makes it harder to do good, and can lead us to mortal sin. Venial sin is forgiven through the Sacrament of Penance and Reconciliation, the practice of good works, and reception of the Eucharist.

Capital Sins

Saint John Cassian and Saint Gregory the Great distinguished seven sins they called Capital Sins. These sins produce other sins and vices.

pride	covetousness	envy	anger
lust	gluttony	sloth	

God's Forgiveness

When we seek forgiveness, we return to God, the only one who can forgive sin. Throughout his public ministry, Jesus talked a lot about forgiveness. He called the Church to be a forgiving community, and he gave the Church the authority to forgive sins, In fact, we can say that the Church is a sign of God's forgiveness because it is through the Church that God forgives our sins.

In the early days of the Church, someone who sinned and wanted to be forgiven would enter the **Order of Penitents** for a period of time. During this time, a person could not attend liturgy, and he or she would ask for the prayers of the community. During Holy Week, the bishop would call the person up before the whole community to be reconciled publicly. Later on, the Irish monks made it more popular to celebrate the Sacrament of Penance and Reconciliation one-on-one with a priest. This sacrament has been celebrated in different ways over the centuries, but gradually the rite has developed into the way it is celebrated today.

The Morality of Human Acts

Human beings are able to act morally only because we are free. If we were not free to decide what to do, our acts could not be good or evil. Human acts that are freely chosen after a judgment of conscience can be morally evaluated. They are either good or evil.

The morality of human acts depends on

✝ the object chosen;

✝ the end in view or the intention; and

✝ the circumstances of the action.

For an act to be good, what you choose to do must be good in itself. If the choice is not good, the intention or the circumstances cannot make it good. You cannot, for example, steal a digital camera because it is your father's birthday and it would make him happy to have one. But a good act done with a bad intention is not necessarily good either. Participating in a hunger walk not out of concern for people who are poor but to impress a teacher from whom you want a good grade is not necessarily a good act. Circumstances can affect the morality of an act. They can increase or lessen the goodness of an act. Acting out of fear of harm lessens a person's responsibility for an act.

Conscience

Do we know what a good choice is? How do we know our intentions are good? God has established rules for living, called the moral law, which direct us to know what is right and what is wrong. Deep within us there is a voice through which we come to know some of that moral law. But it is often difficult to decide what the right thing to do is. When we take time to put aside distractions and look inside ourselves, we get in touch with our conscience, which directs us to do good.

Our conscience leads us to see the morality of our acts and to take responsibility for what we do. But we aren't born with a fully working conscience. The education of our conscience is a lifelong task and an extremely important one. The formation of our conscience begins in our family and continues through the friendships we make and the situations in which we choose to live our lives. We learn what is right from examples set by our parents and teachers, from the advice of others, by listening to the teaching of the Church, by praying for guidance from the Holy Spirit, and by learning from our mistakes. These experiences all help form our conscience.

It is, however, our responsibility to see that our conscience is formed through all these influences. We can make mistakes through ignorance, but if we do not take the opportunities given to us to learn the correct choice, we are still culpable to some degree. In the end, if we are to be moral people, we don't make good choices only because others tell us what is right. We make good choices because, with the help of others, we come to know what is right as best we can. Then we can say, "I know this is the right thing to do, so I must do it."

Our conscience is a wonderful guide for making moral decisions. But forming our conscience doesn't happen on its own. Unlike the image of conscience that is depicted in popular culture, our conscience is not a little voice in our head or an angel sitting on our shoulder whispering in our ear. Our conscience is a gift that needs to be developed. Forming our conscience is a lifelong endeavor.

Here are some suggestions on how to develop an informed conscience.

✝ Study Scripture.

✝ Get to know Church teaching.

✝ Seek advice from someone knowledgeable.

✝ Form the habit of choosing and doing good.

✝ Pray and receive the sacraments.

When we are faced with a difficult decision, we can ask ourselves the following questions to help us know what our conscience is telling us to do.

✝ What are the choices I am faced with, and what are the positives and negatives of each one?

✝ What is my motivation for making each choice?

✝ What have I learned about God's law and the teachings of the Church that will help me know which is the right choice?

✝ Who can help me with my decision?

✝ How will my final decision affect me? How will it affect others?

✝ What will my final decision say about my relationship with God and with others?

Our conscience is a gift that needs to be developed.

An Examination of Conscience

An examination of conscience is the act of looking prayerfully into our hearts to ask how we have hurt our relationships with God and other people through our thoughts, words, and actions. We reflect on the Ten Commandments and the teachings of the Church.

The questions below help us in our examination of conscience.

My Relationship with God

☐ What steps am I taking to grow closer to God and to others? Do I turn to God often during the day, especially when I am tempted?

☐ Do I participate at Mass with attention and devotion on Sundays and Holy Days of Obligation?

☐ Do I pray often and read the Bible?

☐ Do I use God's name and the names of Jesus, Mary, and the saints with love and reverence?

My Relationships with Family, Friends, and Neighbors

☐ Have I set a bad example through my words or actions? Do I treat others fairly? Do I spread stories that hurt other people?

☐ Am I loving towards those in my family? Am I respectful of my neighbors, my friends, and those in authority?

☐ Do I value human life? Do I do what I can to promote peace and end violence? Do I avoid talking about others in ways that could harm them?

☐ Do I show respect for my body and for the bodies of others? Do I keep away from forms of entertainment that do not respect God's gift of sexuality?

☐ Have I taken or damaged anything that did not belong to me? Have I cheated or copied homework?

☐ Have I told the truth even when it was difficult?

☐ Do I show concern for the poor and offer assistance to them in the ways I am able? Do I show concern for the environment and care for it as God has asked?

☐ Do I quarrel with others so I can get my own way? Do I insult others to try to make them think they are less than I am? Do I hold grudges and try to hurt people who I think have hurt me?

How to Make a Good Confession

An examination of conscience is an important part of preparing for the Sacrament of Penance and Reconciliation. The sacrament includes the following steps:

1. The priest greets us, and we pray the Sign of the Cross. He invites us to trust in God. He may read God's Word with us.

2. We confess our sins. The priest may help and counsel us.

3. The priest gives us a penance to perform. Penance is an act of kindness or prayers to pray, or both.

4. The priest asks us to express our sorrow, usually by reciting the Act of Contrition.

5. We receive absolution. The priest says, "I absolve you from your sins in the name of the Father, and of the Son, and of the Holy Spirit." We respond, "Amen."

6. The priest dismisses us by saying, "Go in peace." We go forth to perform the act of penance he has given us.

Respecting Religious Traditions of Others

CHRISTIANITY is divided into hundreds of faith traditions. The Holy Spirit calls members of the Church to work for unity among the Christian traditions. This effort is known as **ecumenism.** One way we can engage in the work of ecumenism is by praying for Christian unity.

The Church teaches that Jesus is the source of Salvation for all people. At the same time, we are called to respect the religious freedom of all people. One way to demonstrate respect is to work toward building relationships among people of different religions. This work is referred to as **interreligious dialogue.** The following are some of the world's most widely practiced non-Christian religions.

Judaism

The faith of Judaism is rooted in the Old Testament stories of Abraham and the Patriarchs, Moses and the Exodus, and the teachings of the prophets. The most important celebration is the Passover, usually celebrated in a family meal, in which Jewish people remember the night in which God prepared for their liberation from slavery in Egypt. In retelling the story of the Exodus, the people recognize that the God who saved the people in ancient Egypt is the same God who calls them to freedom and obedience today.

Star of David

Islam

Islam celebrates the Muslim's submission to God following the teachings of the prophet Muhammad. Five times a day, a Muslim stops and kneels, facing Mecca in Saudi Arabia, and prays. The Five Pillars of Islam that the Muslim follows are to say and believe that there is no God but God, and Muhammad is his Prophet; to pray five times a day; to give to people who are poor; to fast during the month of Ramadan; and, if possible, to make a pilgrimage to Mecca at least once in a lifetime.

Star and Crescent

Buddhism

Buddhism follows the teachings of Siddhartha Gautama—the Buddha (ca. 563–483 B.C.). The Buddha provided a prescription for leading a peaceful life. He taught the people to follow the Noble Eightfold Path: right seeing, right thought, right speech, right action, right livelihood, right effort, right mindfulness, and right contemplation. This path leads a person to the Six Perfections: giving to others and serving and helping them; living a good moral life; overcoming anger, ill will, and hatred; being energetic rather than lazy; and developing awareness, concentration, and insight. In this way people can see the true nature of things.

The Buddha

Hinduism

Hinduism celebrates the belief in 330 million gods. Hindus worship the divine in the form of gods and goddesses that resemble humans, animals, or natural forces such as wind, water, fire, sun, and moon. They celebrate their gods in temples dedicated to particular gods and at home in personal and family shrines.

Ganesha

Issue of Salvation

Can people be saved if they do not specifically believe in Jesus Christ? The Catholic Church says they can. In the *Pastoral Constitution on the Church in the Modern World*, the Church teaches that the grace of Salvation through Jesus Christ is offered to every person in ways known only to God. ✝

Catholic Social Teaching

THE Catholic Church has developed a large body of teaching on social justice issues because action on behalf of justice and working to create a more just world are essential parts of preaching the Gospel. In the story of the Good Samaritan (Luke 10:29–37), Jesus makes clear our responsibility to care for those in need.

The major development of the social doctrine of the Church began in the 19th century when the Gospel encountered modern industrial society. There were new structures for the production of consumer goods, new concepts of society, new types of states and authorities, and new forms of labor and ownership.

Since that time the Church has been making judgments about economic and social matters that relate to the basic rights of individuals and communities. The Church's social teaching is a rich treasure of wisdom about how to build a just society and live holy lives amid the challenges of the modern world. The Catholic Church teaches this responsibility in the following themes of Catholic Social Teaching.

Life and Dignity of the Human Person

All human life is sacred, and all people must be respected and valued over material goods. We are called to ask whether our actions as a society respect or threaten the life and dignity of the human person.

Call to Family, Community, and Participation

Participation in family and community is central to our faith and to a healthy society. Families must be supported so that people can participate in society, build a community spirit, and promote the well-being of all, especially the poor and vulnerable.

Rights and Responsibilities

Every person has a right to life as well as a right to those things required for human decency. As Catholics, we have a responsibility to protect these basic human rights in order to achieve a healthy society.

Participation in family and community is central to our faith and to a healthy society.

Option for the Poor and Vulnerable

In our world many people are very rich, while at the same time, many are extremely poor. As Catholics, we are called to pay special attention to the needs of the poor by defending and promoting their dignity and by meeting their immediate material needs.

The Dignity of Work and the Rights of Workers

The basic rights of workers must be respected: the right to productive work, fair wages, and private property; and the right to organize, join unions, and pursue economic opportunity. Catholics believe that the economy is meant to serve people and that work is not merely a way to make a living but an important way in which we participate in God's creation.

Solidarity

Because God is our Father, we are all brothers and sisters with the responsibility to care for one another. Solidarity is the attitude that leads Christians to share spiritual and material goods. Solidarity unites rich and poor, weak and strong, and helps create a society that recognizes that we all depend on one another.

Care for God's Creation

God is the creator of all people and all things, and he wants us to enjoy his creation. The responsibility to care for all God has made is a requirement of our faith. ✝

Glossary

A

Abba the Aramaic word for "father" but more like the informal "papa" or "daddy." When Jesus spoke to God the Father, he called him "Abba." [Abba]

abortion the deliberate ending of a pregnancy that results in the death of the unborn child. The Church teaches that since life begins at conception, abortion is a serious crime against life and is gravely against the moral law. [aborto]

Abraham the model of faith and trust in God in the Old Testament. God made a covenant with Abraham, promising him land and many descendants. He became the father of the Chosen People. [Abrahán]

absolution the forgiveness we receive from God through the priest in the Sacrament of Penance and Reconciliation. Absolution places us in a state of grace and prepares us to receive other sacraments. [absolución]

abstain the choice to avoid certain foods or activities. Abstaining is a form of fasting that helps remind us that God comes first in our lives and that we are dependent on God for everything. [abstenerse]

Acts of the Apostles the second volume of Luke's two-volume work. Written for a Greek Christian audience, it continues the story of Jesus' Resurrection and Ascension and reports the beginnings of the Church at Pentecost. It then tells stories of the Apostles, including Paul, and how their evangelism spread the Church from Jerusalem to the ends of the earth. [Hechos de los Apóstoles]

actual grace the gift of God, freely given, that unites us with the life of the Trinity. Actual grace helps us make the choices that conform our lives to God's will. (See *grace, habitual grace,* and *sanctifying grace.*) [gracia actual]

adoration the act of giving reverence to God by recognizing and worshiping the Real Presence of Jesus Christ in the Blessed Sacrament, displayed in a monstrance. [adoración]

adultery a sin of unfaithfulness to one's marriage vows that injures the bond of the marriage covenant. It occurs when two people have sexual relations while at least one of them is married to another person. The Sixth Commandment forbids adultery because it undermines the institution of marriage and is harmful to children, who need the stability of their parents' marriage commitment. [adulterio]

Advent the four weeks before Christmas. It is a time of joyful preparation for the celebration of the Incarnation, Jesus' birth as our Savior, and a time for anticipating the coming of Jesus Christ at the end of time, which is known as the Second Coming. [Adviento]

Advocate Jesus' name for the Holy Spirit. The Holy Spirit comforts us and makes Jesus present to us. [Defensor]

Age of Enlightenment the shift in worldview that took place during the 1700s. The Age of Enlightenment included great advances in science and scientific understanding but also led to questions about religion, morality, and the existence of God. [Ilustración, la]

age of reason the age one must reach in order to receive Confirmation, usually around seven years old. The Church also requires that one reach the age of reason before celebrating the Sacraments of Reconciliation and the Eucharist. [edad de la razón]

Agony in the Garden the time Jesus spent in fervent prayer in the Garden of Gethsemane the night before his Crucifixion. Jesus' Agony in the Garden reminds us to remain true to our identity as sons and daughters of God, especially when we are tempted to run away from God. [Oración de Jesús en el Huerto, la]

All Saints Day November 1, the day on which the Church honors all who have died and now live with God as saints in Heaven. This group includes those who are officially recognized as saints as well as people who have not been officially declared saints but now live in God's presence in Heaven. The feast celebrates our union with those who have gone before us and points to our ultimate goal of union with God. [Día de Todos los Santos]

All Souls Day November 2, the day on which the Church prays that all who have died in friendship with God may rest in peace. Those who have died may need purification in Purgatory before living fully in God's presence. Our prayers and good works can help them in this process. Along with All Saints Day, this feast reminds us that all who love God, living and dead, are united with Jesus Christ and one another in the Communion of Saints. [Día de los Fieles Difuntos]

Alleluia a prayer of praise to God. It is usually sung as the Gospel Acclamation before the proclamation of the Gospel Reading at Mass except during Lent. [Aleluya]

almsgiving the offering of money, possessions, time, or talent to those in need. Along with fasting and prayer, almsgiving is an important spiritual practice during Lent. [limosna, dar]

altar the table in the church on which the priest celebrates Mass, where the sacrifice of Christ on the Cross is made present in the Sacrament of the Eucharist. The altar represents two aspects of the mystery of the Eucharist. It is the place where Jesus Christ offers himself for our sins and where he gives us himself in the Eucharist as food for eternal life. [altar]

ambo a raised stand from which a person proclaims the Word of God during Mass [ambón]

Amen the Hebrew word used to conclude Jewish and Christian prayers. It means "This is true," "So be it," or "Let it be so." We end prayers with *Amen* to show that we mean what we have just said. [amén]

angel a spiritual creature who worships God in Heaven. Angels serve God as messengers. They tell us God's plans for our Salvation. [ángel]

Angelus a Catholic devotion recited three times a day—morning, noon, and evening. The devotion reflects on the mystery of the Incarnation—the coming of the angel to Mary, her acceptance of the invitation to be the mother of Jesus, and the Word made flesh. [Ángelus]

anger an emotion that is not in itself wrong, but when not controlled can harden into resentment and hate, becoming one of the seven capital sins (See *Capital Sins*.) [ira]

annulment a finding by a Church tribunal that at least one essential element for a marriage was not present on the day of the wedding. The Church can declare that the Sacrament of Matrimony did not take place if one of the parties did not freely choose to marry, had been married before and that marriage was not annulled, or was not open to having children. An annulment cannot be considered until after a person is divorced. Catholics who receive an annulment are free to marry in the Church. [anulación]

Annunciation the announcement to Mary by the angel Gabriel that God had chosen her to be the mother of the Messiah. She would conceive a child through the Holy Spirit and name him Jesus. The Feast of the Annunciation is celebrated on March 25, nine months before Christmas. [Anunciación]

Anointing of the Sick one of the seven sacraments. In this sacrament a seriously ill person is anointed with holy oil and receives the strength, peace, and courage to overcome the difficulties associated with illness. Through this sacrament, Jesus brings the sick person spiritual healing and forgiveness of sins. If it is God's will, healing of the body is given as well. [Unción de los Enfermos]

antiphon one or more psalm verses sung in response during the liturgy. Although the Mass also uses antiphons, they are used in the Liturgy of the Hours to pray about the central events of the Christian faith. [antífona]

apocalyptic literature a form of writing that uses symbolic language and imagery to describe the eternal struggle between good and evil. The Book of Revelation is an example of apocalyptic literature. [literatura apocalíptica]

apologist a defender of the faith. Apologists defend Christianity against critics and proclaim the truths of the faith. [apologista]

Apostle one of the twelve chosen men who accompanied Jesus in his ministry and were witnesses to the Resurrection. *Apostle* means "one sent." These were the men sent to preach the Gospel to the whole world. [Apóstol]

Apostles' Creed a statement of Christian belief that developed out of a creed used in Baptism in Rome. The Apostles' Creed lists simple statements of belief in God the Father, Jesus Christ the Son, and the Holy Spirit. The profession of faith used in Baptism today is based on it. [Credo de los Apóstoles]

apostolic the Mark of the Church that indicates that Jesus continues to lead the Church through the pope and the bishops. The pope and the bishops are the successors of the Apostles. (See *Marks of the Church*.) [apostólico]

Ark of the Covenant the sacred box that God commanded Moses to build out of acacia wood to hold the restored tablets of the Law (Exodus 25:10–16) [Arca de la Alianza]

Ascension the entry of Jesus into God's presence in Heaven. In the Acts of the Apostles, it is written that Jesus, after his Resurrection, spent 40 days on earth, instructing his followers. He then returned to his Father in Heaven. [Ascensión]

asceticism the practice of self-denial and spiritual discipline as a way of training and forming oneself for the service of God and others. Asceticism can take many forms such as abstinence, fasting, celibacy, and prayer. [ascetismo]

Ash Wednesday the first day of Lent, on which we receive ashes on our foreheads. The ashes remind us to prepare for Easter by repenting and showing sorrow for offending God and hurting our relationships with others. [Miércoles de Ceniza]

assembly the People of God when they are gathered together to worship him [asamblea]

Assumption when Mary was taken into Heaven, body and soul. Mary had a special relationship with her Son, Jesus, from the very beginning when she conceived him. Because of this relationship, she enjoys a special participation in Jesus' Resurrection and has been taken into Heaven where she now lives with him. We celebrate this event in the Feast of the Assumption on August 15. [Asunción]

atone to make amends for sin. Jesus' obedience to God the Father by dying on the Cross atoned for the sins of the whole world. [expiar]

B

Baptism the first of the seven sacraments. Baptism frees us from Original Sin and is necessary for Salvation. Baptism gives us new life in Jesus Christ through the Holy Spirit. The celebration of Baptism consists of immersing a person in water while declaring that the person is baptized in the name of the Father, the Son, and the Holy Spirit. [Bautismo]

baptismal font the water vessel where the Sacrament of Baptism is celebrated. The baptismal font may be located in a separate baptistry, near the entrance of the church, or in the midst of the community. [pila bautismal]

basic rights the human rights a government should protect, such as religious liberty, personal freedom, access to necessary information, right to life, and protection from terror and torture [derechos básicos]

basilica the term used to designate a certain church of historical significance in a local area. Major basilicas are in Rome and are designated churches of ancient origin that serve as places of pilgrimage. Minor basilicas are designated churches that have historical or devotional importance in local areas throughout the world. [basílica]

beatified recognized by the Church as having lived a life of great Christian virtue and declared to be in Heaven. Beatified persons are referred to as *Blessed* and can be publicly venerated by the Church. [beatificado]

Beatitudes the teachings of Jesus in the Sermon on the Mount in Matthew's Gospel. The Beatitudes are eight guidelines for Christlike living that lead to happiness in this life and eternal joy in the next. They are the fulfillment of the Ten Commandments given to Moses. [Bienaventuranzas]

Bible the collection of books that contains the truths of God's Revelation. These writings, inspired by the Holy Spirit and written by different authors using different styles, are the Word of God. The Bible is made up of 46 books in the Old Testament and 27 books in the New Testament. [Biblia]

bishop a man who has received the fullness of Holy Orders. As a successor to the original Apostles, he cares for the Church and is a principal teacher in it. [obispo]

blasphemy any word, thought, or action done in hatred or defiance against God. It extends to using language that disrespects the Church, the saints, or holy things. It is also blasphemy to use God's name as an excuse to enslave people, to torture them, or to put them to death. Using God's name to do these things can cause others to reject religion. [blasfemia]

Blessed Sacrament the Eucharist that has been consecrated by the priest at Mass. It is kept in the tabernacle to adore and to be taken to those who are sick. [Santísimo Sacramento]

blessing a prayer that calls for God's power and care upon some person, place, thing, or special activity [bendición]

Body and Blood of Christ the Bread and Wine that has been consecrated by the priest at Mass. In the Sacrament of the Eucharist, all the risen Lord Jesus Christ—body, blood, soul, and divinity—is present in the consecrated Bread and Wine. [Cuerpo y Sangre de Cristo]

Bread of Life a title that Jesus gives himself in John 6:33–35. Jesus is food for the faithful. [Pan de Vida]

Buddhism a religion based on the teaching of Siddhartha Gautama, who was known as the Buddha, which means "Enlightened One." The Buddha was born to a royal family in northern India about five and a half centuries before Jesus. At age 29 he became disillusioned with life and left his comfortable home to find an answer to the question of why humans suffer. [Budismo]

Glossary

C

calumny (slander) a false statement about someone's reputation that makes others think bad of that person. Calumny is a sin against the Eighth Commandment. [calumnia]

Canaan the name of the land between Syria and Egypt in which the Israelites settled [Caná]

canon the official list of the 73 books that make up the Old and New Testaments of the Bible [canon]

canonization the process by which someone is declared a saint. The process ensures that the person who is a candidate for canonization lived an exemplary Christian life and can serve as a model for Christians around the world. [canonización]

canonize to declare that a Christian who has died is already a saint in Heaven and may be looked to as a model of Christian life who may intercede for us [canonizar]

Capital Sins those sins that can lead to more serious sin. They are pride, covetousness, envy, anger, gluttony, lust, and sloth. [pecados capitales]

Cardinal Virtues the four virtues that lead a person to live in relationship with God and with others. Prudence, justice, fortitude, and temperance can be acquired by education and good actions. (See *fortitude, justice, prudence,* and *temperance.*) [virtudes cardinales]

cast lots to throw down small stones or pebbles called lots to help determine a decision needing divine guidance. Lots were cast to choose the disciple to replace Judas in the Acts of the Apostles 1:23–26. Roman soldiers also cast lots to divide Jesus' clothing among them as in John 19:24. [echar a suertes]

catechism a collection or summary of Church teachings for the education of the faithful. The current *Catechism of the Catholic Church* provides a contemporary summary and explanation of the Catholic faith. [catecismo]

catechumen a person being formed in the Christian life through instruction and by the example of the faith community. Through conversion and maturity of faith, a catechumen is preparing to be welcomed into the Church at Easter through the Sacraments of Baptism, Confirmation, and the Eucharist. [catecúmeno]

catechumenate the process of becoming a Christian. In the early Church, the process took several years. [catecumenado]

cathedral the main church in a diocese where a bishop presides and where the bishop's *cathedra*, or chair, is located. The *cathedra* represents the bishop's authority as the main teacher of the faith in the diocese. [catedral]

catholic one of the four Marks of the Church. The Church is catholic because Jesus is fully present in it, because it proclaims the fullness of faith, and because Jesus has given the Church to the whole world. The Church is universal. (See *Marks of the Church.*) [católica]

Catholic Social Teaching the body of teaching on social justice issues, action on behalf of justice, and work toward a more just world. The Church makes judgments about economic and social matters that relate to the basic rights of individuals and communities. The Church's social teaching is a rich treasure of wisdom about how to build a just society. [enseñanza social católica]

celebrant a bishop or priest who leads the people in praying the Mass. A deacon who baptizes or witnesses a marriage is also a celebrant. [celebrante]

celebrate to worship, praise, and thank God for what he has done for us with prayers and songs, especially in the celebration of the Eucharist [celebrar]

census a systematic counting of the citizens of a particular place. In addition to the census taking place when Jesus was born, the Bible records several censuses, including two in the Book of Numbers and one by King David. [censo]

character a permanent spiritual mark. Character shows that a person has a new relationship with Jesus and a special standing in the Church. Baptism, Confirmation, and Holy Orders each have a specific permanent character and therefore may be received only once. [carácter]

charism a special gift of the Holy Spirit given for the service of others, the good of the world, and particularly for the building up of the Church [carisma]

charity a virtue given to us by God that helps us love God above all things and our neighbor as ourselves. (See *Theological Virtues.*) [caridad]

chastity the integration of our physical sexuality with our spiritual nature. Chastity helps us be completely human, able to give to others our whole life and love. All people, married and single, are called to practice chastity. [castidad]

chasuble the visible liturgical vestment worn by the bishop or priest at Mass. A newly ordained priest receives a chasuble as part of the ordination ritual. [casulla]

Chosen People the people set apart by God to have a special relationship with him. God first formed a Chosen People when he made a covenant, or solemn agreement, with Abraham. He reaffirmed the Covenant through Moses at Mount Sinai. The Covenant is fulfilled in Jesus and his Church. [Pueblo Elegido]

Chrism a perfumed oil, consecrated by a bishop, that is used in the Sacraments of Baptism, Confirmation, and Holy Orders. Anointing with Chrism signifies the call of the baptized to the threefold ministry of priest, prophet, and king. [crisma]

Christ a Greek version of the Hebrew word *Messiah*, or "anointed one." It is another name for Jesus as priest, prophet, and king. [Cristo]

Christian the name given to all those who have been anointed through the gift of the Holy Spirit in Baptism and have become followers of Jesus Christ [cristiano]

Christmas the feast of the birth of Jesus (December 25) [Navidad]

Church the people of God throughout the whole world, or diocese (the local Church), or the assembly of those called together to worship God. The Church is one, holy, catholic, and apostolic. [Iglesia]

clergy those men who are set apart as sacred ministers to serve the Church through the Sacrament of Holy Orders [clero]

commandment a standard, or rule, for living as God wants us to live. Jesus summarized all the commandments into two: love God and love your neighbor. [mandamiento]

common good the sum total of the social conditions that allow people, individually and as a group, to reach their full potential. The common good requires peace, security, respecting everyone's rights, and meeting everyone's spiritual and worldly needs. People have a responsibility to contribute to the good of the entire society. It is one of the basic principles at the center of Catholic Social Teaching. [bien común]

communal prayer the worship of God together with others. The Liturgy of the Hours and the Mass are the main forms of communal prayer. [oración comunitaria]

Communion of Saints the unity of all, dead or living, who have been saved in Jesus Christ. The Communion of Saints is based on our one faith, and it is nourished by our participation in the Eucharist. [Comunión de los Santos]

community Christians who are gathered in the name of Jesus Christ to receive his grace and live according to his values [comunidad]

compassion God's fundamental attitude toward his people. This is best seen in Jesus' reaching out to heal those in need. Acting with compassion and mercy toward those in need identifies a person as belonging to God. [compasión]

confession the act of telling our sins to a priest in the Sacrament of Penance and Reconciliation. The sacrament itself is sometimes referred to as confession. [confesión]

Confirmation the sacrament that completes the grace we receive in Baptism. It seals, or confirms, this grace through the seven Gifts of the Holy Spirit that we receive as part of Confirmation. This sacrament also makes us better able to participate in worship and the apostolic life of the Church. [Confirmación]

conscience the inner voice that helps each of us judge the morality of our own actions. It guides us to follow God's Law by doing good and avoiding evil. [conciencia]

consecrate to make a thing or a person to be special to God through a prayer or blessing. At Mass the priest's words at the consecration transform the bread and wine into the Body and Blood of Jesus Christ. People or objects set apart for God in a special way can also be consecrated. For example, men or women living in religious communities consecrate themselves to God through the evangelical counsels. [consagrar]

consubstantial the doctrine affirming that Jesus, the Son of God, assumed human nature while maintaining the same divine nature as God the Father. The Nicene Creed was written in part to make clear that Jesus is consubstantial with the Father. [consustancial]

consumerism giving undue value to the acquisition of material goods, acting in a way that puts things at the center of one's life where God alone should be [consumismo]

contemplate to focus on God while quieting and emptying our minds of all other distractions [contemplar]

contemplation the act of prayerfully and continuously focusing on God. Many religious communities and spiritualities in the Church are devoted to contemplation. [contemplación]

contemplative the character of an activity or a way of life that is prayerful and continuously focused on God. Many religious communities in the Church are devoted to contemplative life. [conemplativo]

Glossary

contrition the sorrow we feel when we know that we have sinned, followed by the decision not to sin again. Contrition is the most important act of the penitent preparing to celebrate the Sacrament of Penance and Reconciliation. (See *imperfect contrition* and *perfect contrition*.) [contrición]

conversion a radical or serious change of the whole life, a turning away from sin and toward God. The call to change of heart is a key part of the preaching of Jesus. Throughout our entire lives, Jesus calls us to change in this way. [conversión]

convert one who embraces a new faith or religion. At the beginning of the Church, whether Gentile converts needed to observe Jewish law was a major controversy resolved at the Council of Jerusalem. [converso]

convocation a gathering of people called together. We are called together in the Church as a convocation to work for the Salvation of all people. [asamblea]

Corporal Works of Mercy kind acts by which we help our neighbors with their everyday material needs. Corporal Works of Mercy include feeding the hungry, giving drink to the thirsty, clothing the naked, sheltering the homeless, visiting the sick and the imprisoned, and burying the dead.
[obras de misericordia corporales]

Council of Jerusalem the name of the meeting around A.D. 50 that is described in Acts of the Apostles. The meeting was the result of a disagreement between Paul and his followers and the Jewish Christian followers of James, the leader of the Jerusalem Church. James felt that those who became Christians should also observe Jewish customs. Paul said that there should be no such necessity. [Concilio de Jerusalén]

counsel one of the seven Gifts of the Holy Spirit. Counsel helps us make correct choices in life through reflection, discernment, consultation, and advisement. (See *Gifts of the Holy Spirit*.) [consejo]

Covenant, the in the Old Testament, the solemn agreement between God and the Chosen People, Israel, that involved mutual commitments. God made covenants with Noah, Abraham, and Moses and prepared his people for Salvation. In the New Testament, God's new and final Covenant was established through Jesus' life, Death, Resurrection, and Ascension. *Testament* is another word for *covenant*. [Alianza]

covet to desire something belonging to someone else out of envy or jealousy. Coveting something is a desire that becomes an obsession. We are forbidden by the Ninth and Tenth Commandments from coveting others' spouses or possessions. [codiciar]

covetousness having a craving for wealth or for another's possessions (See *Capital Sins*.) [avaricia]

creation God's act of making everything that exists outside himself. Creation also refers to everything that exists. God said that all of creation is good. [creación]

Creator God, who made everything that is and whom we can come to know through everything he created [Creador]

crèche a Nativity scene depicting the birth of Christ. Crèches are popular ways to observe Advent and Christmas, and they can be found in homes, churches, and public places. [belén]

creed a brief statement of faith. The word *creed* comes from the Latin *credo*, meaning "I believe." The Nicene Creed and the Apostles' Creed are the most important summaries of Christian beliefs. [credo]

crosier the staff carried by a bishop that shows he cares for us in the same way that a shepherd cares for his sheep. It also reminds us that a bishop represents Jesus, the Good Shepherd. [báculo]

crucified the way in which Jesus was put to death, nailed to a cross. As the crucified one, Jesus died for the sake of the world. [crucificado]

Crucifixion refers to Jesus' Death on the Cross. In the ancient method of crucifixion used by the Romans, the victim was tied or nailed to a wooden cross and left to hang until dead, usually from suffocation. The cross with an image of the crucified Jesus on it is called a crucifix. [Crucifixión]

culture the activity of a group of people that includes their music, art, language, and celebrations. Culture is one of the ways people experience God in their lives. [cultura]

D

Daily Examen a prayer from the Spiritual Exercises that helps us become aware of God's presence, give thanks for the day we are given, pay attention to how we feel about our actions, and resolve to act more intentionally in the future. [examen diario de conciencia]

deacon a man ordained through the Sacrament of Holy Orders to the ministry of service in the Church. Deacons help the bishops and priests by serving the various charitable ministries of the Church. They help by proclaiming the Gospel, preaching, and assisting at the Liturgy of the Eucharist. Deacons can also celebrate Baptisms, witness marriages, and preside at funerals. [diácono]

detraction the act of talking about the faults and sins of another person to someone who has no reason to hear this and who cannot help the person. Detraction damages the reputation of another person without any intent to help that person. [detracción]

dignity of the human person a basic principle at the center of Catholic Social Teaching. It is the starting point of a moral vision for society because human life is sacred and should be treated with great respect. The human person is the clearest reflection of God among us. (See *Catholic Social Teaching*.) [dignidad de la persona humana]

dignity of work a basic principle at the center of Catholic Social Teaching. Since work is done by people created in the image of God, it is not only a way to make a living but also an important way we participate in God's creation. In work, people fulfill part of their potential given to them by God. All workers have a right to productive work, decent and fair wages, and safe working conditions. (See *Catholic Social Teaching*.) [dignidad del trabajo]

diocese the members of the Church in a particular area, united in faith and the sacraments, and gathered under the leadership of a bishop [diócesis]

disciple a person who has accepted Jesus' message and tries to live as he did, sharing his mission, suffering, and joys [discípulo]

discipleship for Christians, the willingness to answer the call to follow Jesus. The call is received in Baptism, nourished in the Eucharist, strengthened in Confirmation, and practiced in service to the world. [discipulado]

discrimination the act of mistreating other people because of how they look or act or because they are different [discriminación]

Dismissal the part of the Concluding Rites of the Mass in which the people are sent forth by the priest or deacon to do good works and praise and bless God (See *The Order of Mass*.) [despedida]

divine law the moral law as revealed by God in the Bible [ley divina]

Divine Praises a series of praises beginning with "Blessed be God," traditionally prayed at the end of the worship of the Blessed Sacrament in Benediction [alabanzas de desagravio]

Divine Providence the guidance of God over all he has created. Divine Providence exercises care for all creation and guides it toward its final perfection. [divina providencia]

Doctor of the Church a man or a woman recognized as a model teacher of the Christian faith [doctor(a) de la Iglesia]

doctrine the teachings that help us understand and accept the truths of our faith as revealed by Jesus and taught by the Church [doctrina]

dogma a teaching that the Church assures Catholics is true and that Catholics are obliged to believe. Papal infallibility, the Assumption, and the Immaculate Conception are all dogmas of the Church. [dogma]

domestic church the Christian home, which is a community of grace and prayer and a school of human virtues and Christian charity [iglesia doméstica]

doxology a Christian prayer praising and giving glory to God, often referencing the three divine Persons of the Trinity. The Glory Be to the Father and the *Gloria* at Mass are two common doxologies. [doxología]

E

Easter the celebration of the bodily raising of Jesus Christ from the dead. Easter is the festival of our redemption and the central Christian feast, the one from which other feasts arise. [Pascua]

Easter Vigil the celebration of the first and greatest Christian feast, the Resurrection of Jesus. It occurs on the first Saturday evening after the first full moon of spring. During this night watch before Easter morning, catechumens are baptized, confirmed, and receive the Eucharist for the first time. [Vigilia Pascual]

Eastern Catholic Churches a group of Churches that developed in the Near East in countries such as Lebanon and are in union with the Roman Catholic Church. These Churches have their own liturgical, theological, and administrative traditions. They show the truly catholic nature of the Church, which takes root in many cultures. [iglesias católicas orientales]

ecumenical council a gathering of Catholic bishops from the entire world, meeting under the leadership of the pope or his delegates. Ecumenical councils discuss pastoral, legal, and doctrinal issues. There have been 21 ecumenical councils recognized by the Catholic Church. The first was the First Council of Nicaea in 325. The most recent was the Second Vatican Council, which took place between 1962 and 1965. [concilio ecuménico]

Glossary

ecumenism the movement to bring unity among Christians. Christ gave the Church the gift of unity from the beginning, but over the centuries, that unity has been broken. All Christians are called by their common Baptism to pray and to work to maintain, reinforce, and perfect the unity Christ wants for the Church. [ecumenismo]

Emmanuel a Hebrew name from the Old Testament that means "God with us." In Matthew's Gospel, Jesus is called Emmanuel. [Emanuel]

encyclical a letter written by the pope and sent to the whole Church and sometimes to the whole world. It expresses Church teaching on some specific and important issue. [encíclica]

envy a feeling of resentment or sadness because someone has a quality, a talent, or a possession that we want. Envy is one of the seven capital sins, and it is contrary to the Eighth Commandment. (See *Capital Sins*.) [envidia]

epiphany an event in the life of Christ when Jesus' divinity revealed itself. The Church recognizes four epiphanies: the Nativity, the adoration of the Magi, Jesus' baptism, and Jesus' sign at the wedding feast at Cana. [epifanía]

Epistle a letter written by Saint Paul to a group of Christians in the early Church. Twenty-one books of the New Testament are letters written by Paul or other leaders. The second reading at Mass on Sundays and holy days is usually from one of these books. [epístola]

eternal life living happily with God in Heaven when we die in grace and friendship with him. Jesus calls all people to eternal life. [vida eterna]

Eucharist, the the sacrament in which we give thanks to God for the Body and Blood of Christ. The Eucharist nourishes our life of faith. We receive the Body and Blood of Christ in the consecrated Bread and Wine. [Eucaristía, la]

Eucharistic liturgy the public worship, held by the Church, in which the bread and wine are consecrated and become the Body and Blood of Jesus Christ. The Sunday celebration of the Eucharistic liturgy is at the heart of Catholic life. [Liturgia Eucarística]

Eucharistic Prayer during the Mass the liturgical expression of praise and thanksgiving for all that God has done in creation and in the Paschal Mystery (Christ's dying and rising from the dead) and through the Holy Spirit (See *The Order of Mass*.) [Plegaria Eucarística]

euthanasia an act with the intent to cause the death of a person who is handicapped, sick, or dying. Euthanasia is considered murder and is gravely contrary to the dignity of the human person and to the respect due to the living God, our Creator. [eutanasia]

evangelical counsels the virtues of poverty, chastity, and obedience that help men and women live holy lives in accordance with the Gospel. All Christians are called to live the evangelical counsels, although members of religious communities consecrate themselves by making vows to live according to the evangelical counsels. [consejos evangélicos]

Evangelist one of the writers of the four Gospels: Matthew, Mark, Luke, and John. The term is also used to describe anyone engaged in spreading the Gospel. Letters in the New Testament and in the Acts of the Apostles list Evangelists, along with Apostles and prophets, as ministers of the Church. [evangelista]

evangelization the declaration by word and example of the Good News of Salvation we have received in Jesus Christ. It is directed both to those who do not know Jesus and to those who have become indifferent about him. Those who have become indifferent are the focus of what is called the New Evangelization. [evangelización]

examination of conscience the act of prayerfully thinking about what we have said or done in light of what the Gospel asks of us. We also think about how our actions may have hurt our relationship with God and with others. An examination of conscience is an important part of our preparing to celebrate the Sacrament of Penance and Reconciliation. [examen de conciencia]

Exile the period in the history of Israel between the destruction of Jerusalem in 587 B.C. and the return to Jerusalem in 537 B.C. During this time many of the Jewish people were forced to live in Babylon, far from home. [Exilio]

Exodus God's liberation of the Hebrew people from slavery in Egypt and his leading them to the Promised Land. It is also one of the first five books in the Bible. [Éxodo]

Exsultet an Easter hymn of praise sung during the Service of Light that begins the Easter Vigil [Exsultet]

F

faith a gift of God that helps us believe in him. We profess our faith in the Creed, celebrate it in the sacraments, live by it through our good conduct of loving God and our neighbor, and express it in prayer. It is a personal adherence of the whole person to God, who has revealed himself to us through words and actions throughout history. (See *Theological Virtues.*) [fe]

fasting a spiritual practice of limiting the amount we eat for a period of time to express sorrow for sin and to make ourselves more aware of God's action in our lives. Adults ages 18–59 fast on Ash Wednesday and Good Friday. The practice is also encouraged as a private devotion at other times of penitence. [ayuno]

fear of the Lord one of the seven Gifts of the Holy Spirit. This gift leads us to a sense of wonder and awe in the presence of God because we recognize his greatness. (See *Gifts of the Holy Spirit.*) [temor de Dios]

feast day important liturgical celebrations in the life of the Church that mark an event in the life of Jesus or the life of a particular saint [día de fiesta]

Feast of Our Lady of Guadalupe feast day during the Advent season that celebrates Mary's appearance to Juan Diego. Widely celebrated on December 12, this feast is an important religious day for Catholics, especially those from Mexico and other parts of Latin America. [Solemnidad de Nuestra Señora de Guadalupe]

Feast of the Holy Family celebrated on the Sunday that falls within the octave of Christmas or, if no Sunday falls within the octave, on December 30. The feast celebrates the family of Jesus, Mary, and Joseph as a model for all Catholic families. [Fiesta de la Sagrada Familia]

forgiveness the willingness to pardon those who have hurt us but have then shown that they are sorry. In the Lord's Prayer, we pray that since God will forgive us our sins, we are able to forgive those who have hurt us. [perdón]

fortitude the strength to choose to do the right thing even when that is difficult. Fortitude is one of the seven Gifts of the Holy Spirit and one of the four central human virtues, called the Cardinal Virtues, by which we guide our conduct through faith and the use of reason. (See *Cardinal Virtues* and *Gifts of the Holy Spirit.*) [fortaleza]

four last things our belief in the four realities of death, judgment, Heaven, and Hell. The Church invites us to think about how the choices we make each day have consequences now and in the future. [los novísimos]

free will the ability to choose to do good because God has made us like him. Our free will is what makes us truly human. Our exercise of free will to do good increases our freedom. Freely choosing to sin makes us slaves to sin. [libre voluntad]

Fruits of the Holy Spirit the demonstration through our actions that God is alive in us. The Fruits of the Holy Spirit are love, joy, peace, patience, kindness, goodness, generosity, gentleness, faithfulness, modesty, self-control, and chastity. [frutos del Espíritu Santo]

fundamentalist a person who believes the Bible is literally true, word for word. Fundamentalists fail to recognize that the inspired Word of God has been expressed in human language, under divine inspiration, in different literary forms, by human authors possessed of limited capacities and resources. [fundamentalista]

G

Garden of Eden a garden created by God, filled with trees and lush vegetation, where God first placed Adam and Eve and from which they were later expelled [Jardín del Edén]

genealogy a listing of a person's ancestors through generations. Jesus' genealogy is listed in Matthew 1:1–17. [genealogía]

Gentile the name given by the Jews after the Exile to a foreign person. Gentiles were considered to be nonbelievers who worshiped false gods. They stand in contrast to the Jewish people who received God's Law. [gentil]

genuflect to show respect in church by touching a knee to the ground, especially before the Blessed Sacrament in the tabernacle [genuflexión]

gesture the movements we make, such as the Sign of the Cross or bowing, to show our reverence during prayer [gestos]

gift of peace the peace that Jesus gives to us that flows from his relationship with his Father. This is the peace that the world cannot give, for it is the gift of Salvation that only Jesus can give. [don de la paz]

Gifts of the Holy Spirit the permanent willingness, given to us through the Holy Spirit, that makes it possible for us to do what God asks of us. The Gifts of the Holy Spirit are wisdom, understanding, counsel, fortitude, knowledge, piety, and fear of the Lord. [dones del Espíritu Santo]

gluttony excessive indulgence in food or drink (See *Capital Sins.*) [gula]

God the Father, Son, and Holy Spirit, one God in three distinct Persons. God created all that exists. He is the source of Salvation, and he is Truth and Love. [Dios]

godparent a witness to Baptism who assumes the responsibility for helping the baptized person along the road of Christian life [padrino/madrina]

Good News the meaning of the word *Gospel* in Greek. The spreading of the Good News began on Pentecost and continues today in the ministry of the Church. [Buena Nueva]

Gospel the Good News of God's mercy and love that we experience by hearing the story of Jesus' life, Death, Resurrection, and Ascension. The story is passed on in the teaching ministry of the Church as the source of all truth and right living. It is presented to us in four books in the New Testament: the Gospels according to Matthew, Mark, Luke, and John. [Evangelio]

grace the gift of God, given to us without our meriting it. Grace is the Holy Spirit alive in us, helping us live our Christian vocation. Grace helps us live as God wants us to live. (See *actual grace, habitual grace,* and *sanctifying grace.*) [gracia]

Great Commandment Jesus' commandment that we are to love both God and our neighbor as we love ourselves. Jesus tells us that this commandment sums up everything taught in the Old Testament. [mandamiento mayor]

Great Commission Jesus' command to the Apostles to spread the Good News to all people. Jesus commissioned the disciples before his Ascension. [misión de los discípulos]

Great Schism a split in the Church during the Middle Ages when two and then three men all claimed to be pope. The split began because the papal court had moved between Rome and Avignon, France. The schism was resolved at the Council of Constance (1414–1418) with the election of Martin V. [Gran Cisma]

Gregorian chant a form of liturgical music that began its development during the time of Pope Gregory the Great [canto gregoriano]

guardian angel the angel who has been appointed to protect, pray for, and help a person live a holy life [ángel de la guarda]

H

habit the distinctive clothing worn by members of religious orders. It is a sign of the religious life and a witness to poverty. [hábito]

habitual grace another name for sanctifying grace, as it refers to our God-given inclination and capacity for good. Habitual grace is a participation in God's own spirituality. (See *actual grace, grace,* and *sanctifying grace.*) [gracia habitual]

Heaven union with God the Father, Son, and Holy Spirit in life and love that never ends. Heaven is a state of happiness and the goal of the deepest wishes of the human heart. [cielo]

Hebrew a descendant of Abraham, Isaac, and Jacob, who was enslaved in Egypt. God helped Moses lead the Hebrews out of slavery. [Hebreo]

Hell a life of total separation from God forever. In his infinite love for us, God can only desire our Salvation. Hell is the result of the free choice of a person to reject God's love and forgiveness once and for all. [infierno]

herald a messenger who announces important news. Angels served as the heralds of the birth of Christ. [heraldo]

heresy a false teaching that distorts a truth of the Catholic faith. Many of the Church councils have taught against heresies about the Trinity, Jesus, or the faith of the Church. [herejía]

holiness the fullness of Christian life and love. All people are called to holiness, which is made possible by cooperating with God's grace to do his will. As we do God's will, we are transformed more and more into the image of the Son, Jesus Christ. [santidad]

holy the Mark of the Church that indicates that the Church is one with Jesus Christ. Holiness is closeness to God, and therefore the Church is holy because God is present in it. (See *Marks of the Church.*) [santo]

Holy Communion the consecrated Bread and Wine that we receive at Mass, which is the Body and Blood of Jesus Christ. It brings us into union with Jesus and his saving Death and Resurrection. [Comunión]

Holy Day of Obligation a principal feast day, other than Sundays, of the Church. On Holy Days of Obligation, we celebrate the great things that God has done for us through Jesus and the saints. Catholics are obliged to participate in the Eucharist on these days, just as we are on Sundays. [día de precepto]

Holy Family the family of Jesus as he grew up in Nazareth. It included Jesus; his mother, Mary; and his foster father, Joseph. [Sagrada Familia]

Holy of Holies the holiest part of the Temple in Jerusalem. The High Priest entered this part of the Temple once a year to address God and ask his forgiveness for the sins of the people. [Sanctasanctórum]

Holy Orders the sacrament through which the mission given by Jesus to his Apostles continues in the Church. The sacrament has three degrees: deacon, priest, and bishop. Through the laying on of hands in the Sacrament of Holy Orders, men receive a permanent sacramental mark that calls them to minister to the Church. [sacramento del Orden]

Holy Spirit the third Person of the Trinity, who is sent to us as our helper and, through Baptism and Confirmation, fills us with God's life. Together with the Father and the Son, the Holy Spirit brings the divine plan of Salvation to completion. [Espíritu Santo]

Holy Thursday the Thursday of Holy Week on which the Mass of the Lord's Supper is celebrated, commemorating the institution of the Eucharist. The season of Lent ends with the celebration of this Mass. [Jueves Santo]

holy water water that has been blessed and is used as a sacramental to remind us of our Baptism [agua bendita]

Holy Week the celebration of the events surrounding Jesus' establishment of the Eucharist and his suffering, Death, and Resurrection. Holy Week commemorates Jesus' triumphal entry into Jerusalem on Palm Sunday, the gift of himself in the Eucharist on Holy Thursday, his Death on Good Friday, and his Resurrection at the Easter Vigil on Holy Saturday. [Semana Santa]

Homily the explanation by a bishop, a priest, or a deacon of the Word of God in the liturgy. The Homily relates the Word of God to our lives as Christians today. (See *The Order of Mass*.) [homilía]

honor giving God or a person the respect that they are owed. God is given this respect as our Creator and Redeemer. All people are worthy of respect as children of God. [honrar]

hope the confidence that God will always be with us, make us happy now and forever, and help us live so that we will be with him forever (See *Theological Virtues*.) [esperanza]

human condition the general state of humankind. While the human family is created in the image and likeness of God, it is also wounded by sin and often rejects the grace won by Jesus Christ. So while called by God to the highest good, too often human behavior leads to personal and social destruction. [condición humana]

I

idolatry the act of worshiping something other than God. Originally idolatry meant the worship of statues or other images of gods, but the pursuit of money, fame, or possessions can become forms of idolatry. (See *consumerism*.) [idolatría]

Immaculate Conception the Church teaching that Mary was free from Original Sin from the first moment of her conception. She was preserved through the merits of her Son, Jesus, the Savior of the human race. Declared a dogma of the Catholic Church by Pope Pius IX in 1854, the Feast of the Immaculate Conception is celebrated on December 8. [Inmaculada Concepción]

imperfect contrition Sorrow for sin that is motivated by reasons other than loving God above all else. Imperfect contrition comes from fear of punishment or other consequences of our sin. Contrition is the most important act of the penitent preparing to celebrate the Sacrament of Penance and Reconciliation. (See *contrition* and *perfect contrition*.) [contrición imperfecta]

incarnate to take human form. The word *incarnate* comes from a Latin term meaning "to become flesh" and describes what happened in the mystery of the Incarnation when the Son of God, Jesus, became man, conceived and born of Mary. [encarnar]

Incarnation Jesus Christ, the Son of God, is God made flesh. The Son of God, the Second Person of the Trinity, is both true God and true man. [Encarnación]

indulgence a lessening of temporal punishment gained through participation in prayer and works of charity. Indulgences move us toward our final purification, after which we will live with God forever. [indulgencia]

Industrial Revolution the rapid economic change beginning at the end of the 18th century and continuing into the 19th century that resulted in a shift away from homemade and agricultural production and toward industry and manufacturing. [Revolución industrial]

inerrancy the absence of error in the Bible when it tells us a religious truth about God and his relationship with us. The Church teaches the inerrancy of Scripture on moral and faith matters. [inerrancia]

Glossary

infallibility the inability to be in error or to teach something that is false. On matters of belief and morality, the Church is infallible because of the presence and guidance of the Holy Spirit. [infalibilidad]

infallible the quality of Church teachings in areas of faith and morals that have been proclaimed by the pope and the bishops, in their role as the Magisterium and guided by the Holy Spirit, to be without error [infalible]

Infancy Narrative an account of the infancy and childhood of Jesus that appears in the first two chapters of Matthew's and Luke's Gospels. Matthew's Infancy Narrative reveals Jesus as the fulfillment of prophecies. Luke's Infancy Narrative reveals Jesus as a Savior who came for everyone, not the privileged few. The intention of these stories is to proclaim Jesus as Messiah and Savior. [narración de la infancia]

inspiration the quality that explains God as the author who, through the Holy Spirit, enlightened the minds of human authors while they were writing the books of the Bible. God blessed the writers of Scripture with inspiration that enabled them to record religious truths for our Salvation. [inspiración]

inspired influenced by the Holy Spirit. The human authors of Scripture were influenced by the Holy Spirit. The creative inspiration of the Holy Spirit made sure that the Scripture was written according to the truth God wants us to know for our Salvation. [inspirado]

Institution Narrative the words prayed by the priest at the Eucharist that recall Jesus' words and actions at the Last Supper. During the Institution Narrative, the bread and wine become the Body and Blood of the risen Christ. [narración de la institución]

intercession a form of prayer on behalf of others. We ask for the intercession of those in Heaven, such as Mary and the saints, or those still with us here on earth. [intercesión]

intercessor a person who prays for the needs of others. An intercessor can be someone still alive on earth or a saint in Heaven. [intercesor]

interpretation coming to an understanding of the words of Scripture, combining human knowledge with the wisdom and guidance of the teaching office of the Church [interpretación]

interreligious dialogue the ongoing discussions between Christians and those of other faiths [diálogo interreligioso]

Islam the third great religion, along with Judaism and Christianity, that professes belief in one God. *Islam* means "submission" to that one God. [islamismo]

Israelite a descendant of Abraham, Isaac, and Jacob. God changed Jacob's name to "Israel," and Jacob's twelve sons and their children became the leaders of the twelve tribes of Israel. (See *Hebrew*.) [israelita]

J

Jerusalem the city conquered by David in 1000 B.C. to serve as his capital. David also made it the center of worship by bringing in the Ark of the Covenant, which held the tablets of the Law. [Jerusalén]

Jesse Tree an Advent activity that helps us prepare to celebrate Jesus' birth. A small or an artificial tree is decorated with images of Jesus' ancestors. The image is based on Isaiah 11:1, "But a shoot shall sprout from the stump of Jesse, / and from his roots a bud shall blossom." [tronco de Jesé]

Jesus the Son of God, who was born of the Virgin Mary and who died and was raised from the dead for our Salvation. He returned to God and will come again to judge the living and the dead. *Jesus* means "God saves." [Jesús]

Jews the name given to the Hebrew people, from the time of the Exile to the present. The name means "the people who live in the territory of Judah," the area of Palestine surrounding Jerusalem. [judíos]

Joseph the foster father of Jesus who was engaged to Mary when the angel announced that Mary would have a child through the power of the Holy Spirit. In the Old Testament, Joseph was the son of Jacob, who was sold into slavery in Egypt by his brothers and then saved them from starvation when famine came. [José]

Jubilee Year a holy year in which the pope calls people to witness to their faith in specific ways. Pope John Paul II announced that 1985 was a Jubilee Year. [Año jubilar]

Judaism the name of the religion of Jesus and all the people of Israel after they returned from exile in Babylon and built the second Temple [judaísmo]

justice the virtue that guides us to give to God and others what is due them. Justice is one of the four Cardinal Virtues by which we guide our Christian life. (See *Cardinal Virtues*.) [justicia]

justification the action of the Holy Spirit that cleanses us from sin in Baptism and that continually gives us the grace to walk in right relationship with God. Justification is the saving action of God that restores the right relationship between God and an individual. [justificación]

K

Kingdom of God God's rule over us, announced in the Gospel and present in the Eucharist. The beginning of the kingdom here on earth is mysteriously present in the Church, and it will come in completeness at the end of time. [Reino de Dios]

Kingdom of Heaven the term for the Kingdom of God in Matthew's Gospel. The Beatitudes help us enter into the Kingdom of Heaven by guiding us in ways to live according to the values of Jesus. [Reino de los cielos]

knowledge one of the seven Gifts of the Holy Spirit. This gift helps us perceive what God asks of us and how we should respond. (See *Gifts of the Holy Spirit*.) [ciencia]

L

laity those who have been made members of Christ in Baptism and who participate in the priestly, prophetic, and kingly functions of Christ in his mission to the whole world. The laity is distinct from the clergy, whose members are set apart as ordained ministers to serve the Church. [laicado]

Lamb of God the title for Jesus that emphasizes his willingness to give up his life for the Salvation of the world. Jesus is the Lamb without blemish or sin who delivers us through his sacrificial Death. [Cordero de Dios]

Last Judgment the final judgment of all human beings that will occur when Christ returns in glory and all appear in their own bodies before him to give an account of all their deeds in life. In the presence of Christ, the truth of each person's relationship with God will be laid bare, as will the good each person has done or failed to do during his or her earthly life. At that time, God's kingdom will come into its fullness. [Juicio Final]

Last Supper the meal Jesus ate with his disciples on the night before he died. At the Last Supper, Jesus instituted the Sacrament of the Eucharist. [Última Cena]

lectio divina a reflective way of praying with Scripture. *Lectio divina* is Latin for "sacred reading" and is an ancient form of Christian prayer. It involves four steps: sacred reading of a Scripture passage, meditation on the passage, speaking to God, and contemplation or resting in God's presence. [*lectio divina*]

Lectionary for Mass the official book that contains all the Scripture readings used in the Liturgy of the Word [*Leccionario*]

Lent the 40 days before Easter (not counting Sundays) during which we prepare through prayer, fasting, and almsgiving to change our lives and live the Gospel more completely [Cuaresma]

Light of the World a name that helps us see that Jesus is the light that leads us to the Father. Jesus lights up our minds and hearts, replacing sin and darkness with the knowledge of God. [luz del mundo]

litany a prayer that consists of a series of petitions, often including requests for the intercession of particular saints [letanía]

literary forms the different styles of writing found in the Bible. Some forms are history, proverbs, letters, parables, Wisdom sayings, and poetry. They all have as their purpose the communication of the truth found in God's Word. [géneros literarios]

liturgical year the celebration throughout the year of the mysteries of the Lord's birth, life, Death, Resurrection, and Ascension. The cycle of the liturgical year constitutes the basic rhythm of the Christian's life of prayer. [año litúrgico]

liturgy the public prayer of the Church that celebrates the wonderful things God has done for us in Jesus Christ, our High Priest, and the way in which he continues the work of our Salvation. The original meaning of *liturgy* was "a public work or service done for the people." [liturgia]

Liturgy of the Eucharist the part of the Mass in which the bread and wine are consecrated and become the Body and Blood of Jesus Christ. We then receive Christ in Holy Communion. [Liturgia de la Eucaristía]

Liturgy of the Hours the public prayer of the Church to praise God and sanctify the day. It includes an office of readings before sunrise, morning prayer at dawn, evening prayer at sunset, and prayer before going to bed. The chanting of psalms makes up a major portion of this prayer. [Liturgia de las Horas]

Liturgy of the Word the part of the Mass in which we listen to God's Word from the Bible and consider what it means for us today. The Liturgy of the Word can also be a public prayer that is not followed by the Liturgy of the Eucharist. [Liturgia de la Palabra]

Glossary

living wage the amount of income that is enough to support a person and a family in reasonable comfort. Pope Leo XIII defined what a living wage was in his encyclical *On the Condition of Labor*. [salario digno]

Lord a title that indicates the divinity of God. *Lord* replaced *Yahweh*, the name God revealed to Moses and was considered too sacred to pronounce. The New Testament uses the title *Lord* for both the Father and for Jesus, recognizing him as God himself. (See *Yahweh*.) [Señor]

lust the excessive craving for or indulgence of bodily pleasure that makes the other a victim of our desires (See *Capital Sins*.) [lujuria]

M

Magi, the the men who came from the East to Bethlehem by following a star. They were the first Gentiles to believe that Jesus was the Messiah. [Reyes Magos]

Magisterium the living, teaching office of the Church. This office, through the bishops and with the pope, provides an authentic interpretation of God's Revelation. It ensures faithfulness to the teaching of the Apostles in matters of faith and morals. [Magisterio de la Iglesia]

Magnificat Mary's song of praise recorded in the Gospel of Luke. Sung before Jesus' birth, the *Magnificat* shows Mary's understanding of Jesus' mission and her role as a disciple. [*magníficat*]

manna the food provided by God when the Israelites were in the desert [maná]

marginalized those who are viewed as unimportant or powerless in society. We find Jesus among the marginalized, such as people who are poor, mistreated, discriminated against, and the victims of war. [marginados]

Marks of the Church the four most important aspects of the Church found in the Nicene Creed. According to the Nicene Creed, the Church is one, holy, catholic, and apostolic. (See *apostolic, catholic, holy*, and *one*.) [atributos de la Iglesia]

martyr one who has given his or her life for the faith. *Martyr* comes from the Greek word for "witness." A martyr is the supreme witness to the truth of the faith and to Christ to whom he or she is united. In chapter 7 of Acts of the Apostles, the death of the first martyr, the deacon Stephen, is recounted. [mártir]

Mary the mother of Jesus. She is called blessed and "full of grace" because God chose her to be the mother of the Son of God, the Second Person of the Trinity. [Virgen María]

Mass the most important sacramental celebration of the Church, established by Jesus at the Last Supper as a remembrance of his Death and Resurrection. At Mass we listen to God's Word from the Bible and receive Jesus Christ in the consecrated Bread and Wine that are his Body and Blood. [Misa]

Matrimony a solemn agreement between a woman and a man to be partners for life, for their own good and for bringing up children. Marriage is a sacrament when the agreement is properly made between baptized Christians. [Matrimonio]

meditate to focus the mind prayerfully on an image or a word in order to experience God and understand God's will [meditar]

meditation a form of prayer using silence and listening. Through imagination, emotion, and desire, it is a way to understand how to adhere and respond to what God is asking. By concentrating on a word or an image, we move beyond thoughts, empty the mind of contents that get in the way of our experience of God, and rest in simple awareness of God. [meditación]

memorial a remembrance of events that have taken place in the past. We recall these events because they continue to affect us since they are part of God's saving plan for us. Every time we remember these events, we make God's saving action present. [memoria]

Mendicant Order a unique variety of religious order that developed in the 13th century. Unlike monks who remain inside a monastery, members of Mendicant Orders have ministries of preaching, teaching, and witnessing among people. They are called mendicant from the Latin word for "begging," which is their major means of supporting themselves. The two main Mendicant Orders are the Dominicans, founded by Saint Dominic de Guzman, and the Franciscans, founded by Saint Francis of Assisi. [orden mendicante]

mercy the gift to be able to respond with care and compassion to those in need. The gift of mercy is a grace given to us by Jesus Christ. [misericordia]

Messiah a title that means "anointed one." It is from a Hebrew word that means the same thing as the Hebrew word *Christ*. Messiah is the title given to Jesus as priest, prophet, and king. [Mesías]

ministry service or work done for others. All those baptized are called to a variety of ministries in the liturgy and in service to the needs of others. [ministerio]

miracle a sign or an act of wonder that cannot be explained by natural causes and that is the work of God. In the Gospels, Jesus works miracles as a sign that the Kingdom of God is present in his ministry. [milagro]

mission the work of Jesus Christ that is continued in the Church through the Holy Spirit. The mission of the Church is to proclaim Salvation through Jesus' life, Death, Resurrection, and Ascension. [misión]

missionary a person sent by Church authority to spread the Gospel through evangelization and catechesis. Missionaries may serve in areas where few people have heard about Jesus or in small, underserved communities of isolated believers. [misionero]

monastery a place where men or women live out their solemn vows of poverty, chastity, and obedience in a stable community. People who live in monasteries spend their days in public prayer, work, and meditation. [monasterio]

monasticism a form of religious life in which men and women live out their vows of poverty, chastity, and obedience in a stable community. The goal of monasticism is to pursue a life of public prayer, work, and meditation under the guidance of a rule for the glory of God. Saint Benedict of Nursia, who died about 550, is considered the father of Western monasticism. [monacato]

monstrance a vessel that holds the Blessed Sacrament for adoration and Benediction [custodia]

moral choice a choice to do what is right or not to do what is wrong. We make moral choices because they help us grow closer to God and because we have the freedom to choose what is right and avoid what is wrong. [decisión moral]

moral law a rule for living that has been established by God and people in authority who are concerned about the good of all. Moral laws are based on God's direction to us to do what is right and avoid what is wrong. Some moral laws are "written" in the human heart and can be known through our own reasoning. Other moral laws have been revealed to us by God in the Old Testament and in the new law given by Jesus. [ley moral]

mortal sin a serious decision to turn away from God by doing something that we know is wrong. For a sin to be mortal, it must be a very serious offense, the person must know how serious it is, and the person must freely choose to do it anyway. [pecado mortal]

Mother of God the title for Mary proclaimed at the Council of Ephesus in 431. The council declared that Mary was not just the mother of Jesus, the man. She became the Mother of God by the conception of the Son of God in her womb. Because Jesus' humanity is one with his divinity, Mary is the mother of the eternal Son of God made man, who is God himself. [Madre de Dios]

Muslim a follower of the religion of Islam. *Muslim* means "one who submits to God." [musulmán]

mystery a religious truth that we can know only through God's Revelation and that we cannot fully understand. Our faith is a mystery that we profess in the Creed and celebrate in the liturgy and the sacraments. [misterio]

mystic a person who has a special understanding of God from intense, private experiences [místico]

Mystical Body of Christ the members of the Church formed into a spiritual body and bound together by the life communicated by Jesus Christ through the sacraments. Christ is the center and source of the life of this body. In it, we are all united. Each member of the body receives from Christ gifts fitting for him or her. [Cuerpo Místico de Cristo]

N

Nativity the mystery of Jesus' birth as told in the Gospels of Matthew and Luke. Although the two Nativity stories focus on different details, they relate the same truth that Jesus is the promised Savior. [Natividad]

natural law the moral law that is "written" in the human heart. We can know natural law through our own reason because the Creator has placed the knowledge of it in our hearts. It can provide the solid foundation on which we can make rules to guide our choices in life. Natural law forms the basis of our fundamental rights and duties and is the foundation for the work of the Holy Spirit in guiding our moral choices. [ley natural]

neighbor according to Jesus, this includes everyone, as each person is made in God's image. We are all meant to develop mutually supportive relationships. [prójimo]

neophyte a person who has recently been initiated into the Church through the Sacraments of Initiation [neófito]

New Evangelization the work of missionaries in traditionally Christian areas with people who may already know about Jesus and the Gospel [nueva evangelización]

Glossary

New Testament the 27 books of the Bible that tell of the teaching, ministry, and saving events of the life of Jesus. The four Gospels present Jesus' life, Death, and Resurrection. Acts of the Apostles tells the story of Jesus' Ascension into Heaven. It also shows how Jesus' message of Salvation spread through the growth of the Church. Various letters instruct us in how to live as followers of Jesus Christ. The Book of Revelation offers encouragement to Christians living through persecution. [Nuevo Testamento]

Nicene Creed the summary of Christian beliefs developed by the bishops at the first two councils of the Church held in A.D. 325 and 381. It is the Creed shared by most Christians in the East and the West. [Credo Niceno]

novena a Catholic tradition repeated over a set number of days, usually nine, in devotion to a particular mystery or saint [novena]

novice a monk or nun who has not yet taken vows. Novices deepen their faith and learn about the customs, practices, and obligations of the religious life. [novicio]

O

obedience the act of willingly following what God asks us to do for our Salvation. The Fourth Commandment requires children to obey their parents, and all people are required to obey civil authority when it acts for the good of all. To imitate the obedience of Jesus, members of religious communities make a special vow of obedience. [obediencia]

obey to follow the teachings or directions given by God or by someone who has authority over us [obedecer]

oil of catechumens the oil blessed by the bishop during Holy Week and used to anoint catechumens. This anointing strengthens them on their path to initiation into the Church. Infants are anointed with this oil right before they are baptized. [óleo de los catecúmenos]

oil of the sick the oil blessed by the bishop during Holy Week and used in the Sacrament of the Anointing of the Sick, which brings spiritual and, if it is God's will, physical healing [óleo de los enfermos]

Old Testament the first 46 books of the Bible, which tell of God's Covenant with the people of Israel and his plan for the Salvation of all people. The first five books are known as the Torah or Pentateuch. The Old Testament is fulfilled in the New Testament, but God's Covenant presented in the Old Testament has permanent value and has never been revoked. [Antiguo Testamento]

one the Mark of the Church that indicates the unity of the Church as a community of Christian believers as well as the unity of all the members with Christ (See *Marks of the Church.*) [una]

option for the poor the principle of Catholic Social Teaching that holds that Christians must promote social justice and serve those who are poor (See *Catholic Social Teaching.*) [opción por los pobres]

ordained men who have received the Sacrament of Holy Orders so that they may preside at the celebration of the Eucharist and serve as leaders and teachers of the Church [ordenado]

Order of Mass, The the sequence of the prayers, gestures, readings and Eucharistic rites of the Mass [Ordinario de la Misa, el]

Order of Penitents a group of people within the Church, practicing intense repentance. The Order of Penitents first began in the early centuries of the Church, and many of the practices of Lent, including the use of ashes, come from the Penitents. [orden de penitentes]

Ordinary Time the longest liturgical season of the Church. It is divided into two periods—the first after the Christmas season and the second after Pentecost. The first period focuses on Jesus' childhood and public ministry. The second period focuses on Christ's reign as King of Kings. [Tiempo Ordinario]

ordination the rite of the Sacrament of Holy Orders by which a bishop gives to men, through the laying on of hands, the ability to minister to the Church as bishops, priests, and deacons [ordenación]

Original Sin the consequence of the disobedience of the first human beings. Adam and Eve disobeyed God and chose to follow their own will rather than God's will. As a result, human beings lost the original blessing God had intended and became subject to sin and death. In Baptism we are restored to life with God through Jesus Christ, although we still experience the effects of Original Sin. [pecado original]

Orthodox Church the Eastern Churches that split with the Roman Catholic Church in 1054. These Churches are distinct from the Roman Catholic Church in their liturgy and some of their traditions. [Iglesia Ortodoxa]

P

Palm Sunday the celebration of Jesus' triumphant entry into Jerusalem on the Sunday before Easter. Today it begins a week-long commemoration of the saving events of Holy Week. [Domingo de Ramos]

pantheism the belief that rejects a personal God and instead considers that God and the universe are identical. Pantheism was condemned in the *Syllabus of Errors*. [panteísmo]

parable one of the stories that Jesus told to show us what the Kingdom of God is like. Parables present images drawn from everyday life. These images show us the radical choice we make when we respond to the invitation to enter the Kingdom of God. [parábola]

Paraclete another name for the Holy Spirit. Jesus promised to send a Consoler and Advocate who would help the Apostles continue his mission. [Paráclito]

parish a stable community of believers in Jesus Christ who meet regularly in a specific area to worship God under the leadership of a pastor [parroquia]

participation one of the seven principles of Catholic Social Teaching. All people have a right to participate in the economic, political, and cultural life of society. It is a requirement for human dignity and a demand of justice that all people have a minimum level of participation in the community. (See *Catholic Social Teaching*.) [participación]

particular judgment Christ's judgment made of every person at the moment of death that offers either entrance into Heaven (after a period of purification in Purgatory if needed) or immediate and eternal separation from God in Hell. At the moment of death, each person is rewarded by Christ in accordance with his or her works and faith. [juicio individual]

Paschal Mystery the work of Salvation accomplished by Jesus Christ through his Passion, Death, Resurrection, and Ascension. The Paschal Mystery is celebrated in the liturgy of the Church, and we experience its saving effects in the sacraments. In every liturgy of the Church, God the Father is blessed and adored as the source of all blessings we have received through his Son in order to make us his children through the Holy Spirit. [Misterio Pascual]

Passion the suffering and Death of Jesus. The Passion is part of the Paschal Mystery that accomplished Jesus Christ's saving work and that we celebrate and remember in the Eucharist. [Pasión]

Passover the Jewish festival that commemorates the delivery of the Hebrew people from slavery in Egypt. In the Eucharist, we celebrate our passover from death to life through Jesus' Death and Resurrection. [pascua]

pastor a priest who is responsible for the spiritual care of the members of the parish community. It is the job of the pastor to see that the Word of God is preached, the faith is taught, and the sacraments are celebrated. [párroco]

patriarch, Catholic the title used by leaders of certain Eastern Catholic Churches [patriarca, católico]

patriarch, Old Testament a leader of a family or clan within ancient Israel. More specifically, in biblical studies, the patriarchs are the founders of the Hebrew people described in Genesis chapters 12–50. Prominent among the patriarchs are Abraham, Isaac, Jacob, and Jacob's twelve sons. [patriarca, Antiguo Testamento]

patriarch, Orthodox the title used by leaders of Orthodox Churches. The bishop of Constantinople is known as the Ecumenical Patriarch. [patriarca, ortodoxo]

peacemaker a person who teaches us to be respectful in our words and actions toward one another [paz, los que trabajan por la]

penance the turning away from sin with a desire to change our life and live more closely the way God wants us to live. We express our penance externally by praying, fasting, and helping those who are poor. Penance is also the name of the action that the priest asks us to take or the prayers that he asks us to pray after he absolves us in the Sacrament of Penance and Reconciliation. (See *Sacrament of Penance and Reconciliation*.) [penitencia]

Penance and Reconciliation, Sacrament of the sacrament in which we celebrate God's forgiveness of sin and our reconciliation with God and the Church. This sacrament includes sorrow for the sins we have committed, confession of sins, absolution by the priest, and doing the penance that shows our willingness to amend our ways. [sacramento de la Penitencia y de la Reconciliación]

Penitential Act a formula of general confession asking for God's mercy at Mass. The priest may lead the assembly in praying the *Confiteor* ("I confess to almighty God . . .") or a threefold invocation echoed by "Lord have mercy . . . Christ have mercy . . . Lord have mercy" in English or in Greek. (See *The Order of Mass*.) [acto penitencial]

Pentecost the 50th day after Jesus was raised from the dead. On this day the Holy Spirit was sent from Heaven, and the Church was born. It is also the Jewish feast, called *Shavuot* in Hebrew, that celebrated the giving of the Ten Commandments on Mount Sinai 50 days after the Exodus. [Pentecostés]

People of God another name for the Church. In the same way that the people of Israel were God's people through the Covenant he made with them, the Church is a priestly, prophetic, and royal people through the new and eternal Covenant with Jesus Christ. [Pueblo de Dios]

Glossary

perfect contrition the sorrow for sin that arises from a love of God above all else. Perfect contrition is the ideal act of the penitent preparing to celebrate the Sacrament of Penance and Reconciliation. (See *contrition* and *imperfect contrition*.) [contrición perfecta]

personal prayer the kind of prayer that rises up in us in everyday life. We pray with others in the liturgy, but also we can listen and respond to God through personal prayer every moment of our lives. [oración personal]

personal sin a sin we choose to commit, whether serious (mortal) or less serious (venial). Although the consequences of Original Sin leave us with a tendency to sin, God's grace, especially through the sacraments, helps us choose good over sin. [pecado personal]

petition a request to God, asking him to fulfill a need. When we share in God's saving love, we understand that every need is one that we can ask God to help us with through petition. [petición]

Pharaoh the Egyptian word for "Great House," referring to the royal palace of the king of Egypt. The reference to Pharaoh became known for the king himself, just as "White House" might refer to the president. Pharaoh was both the political and religious leader of Egypt. [faraón]

Pharisee a member of a party or sect in Judaism that began more than 100 years before Jesus. Pharisees saw Judaism as a religion centered on the observance of the Law. The Gospels depict tension between Jesus and the Pharisees. Pharisees were later found in the Christian community in Jerusalem. (Acts of the Apostles 15:5) Before his conversion, Paul was proud to call himself a Pharisee. [fariseo]

piety one of the seven Gifts of the Holy Spirit. It calls us to be faithful in our relationships both with God and with others. Piety helps us to love God and to behave responsibly and with generosity and affection toward others. (See *Gifts of the Holy Spirit*.) [piedad]

plague a natural calamity or disease that is seen as being inflicted by God as a remedial event to make people more conscious of their duties toward God and one another. In the Book of Exodus, the plagues inflicted on the Egyptians are seen as the means by which God convinced the Egyptians to free the Hebrew people from slavery. [plaga]

pope the Bishop of Rome, successor of Saint Peter, and leader of the Roman Catholic Church. Because he has the authority to act in the name of Christ, the pope is called the Vicar of Christ. The pope and all the bishops together make up the living, teaching office of the Church, the Magisterium. [papa]

poverty the quality of living without attachment to material goods. All baptized persons, not only those called to religious life, are called to live a holy life by practicing the virtues of chastity, obedience, and poverty. [pobreza]

praise the expression of our response to God, not only for what he does, but also simply because he is. In the Eucharist, the whole Church joins with Jesus Christ in expressing praise and thanksgiving to the Father. [alabanza]

prayer the raising of our hearts and minds to God. We are able to speak to and listen to God in prayer because he teaches us how to pray. [oración]

prayer of intercession a prayer of petition in which we pray as Jesus did to the Father on behalf of people. Asking on behalf of others is a characteristic of a heart attuned to God's mercy. Christian intercession recognizes no boundaries. Following Jesus' example, we pray for all people—for those who are rich, for political leaders, for those in need, and even for persecutors. [oracione de intercesión]

Precepts of the Church those positive requirements that the pastoral authority of the Church has determined are necessary to a moral life. The Precepts of the Church ensure that all Catholics move beyond the minimum by growing in the love of God and neighbor. [mandamientos de la Iglesia]

precursor a title for John the Baptist as the immediate forerunner of Jesus, the Messiah. John the Baptist is considered the last of the prophets. [precursor]

presbyter a word that originally meant "an elder or a trusted advisor to the bishop." From this word comes the English word *priest*, one of the three degrees of the Sacrament of Holy Orders. All the priests of a diocese under the bishop form the presbyterate. [presbítero]

pride a false image of ourselves that goes beyond what we deserve as God's creation. Pride puts us in competition with God. It is one of the seven capital sins. (See *Capital Sins*.) [soberbia]

priest a man who has accepted God's call to serve the Church by guiding it and building it up through the ministry of the Word and the celebration of the sacraments [sacerdote]

priesthood all the people of God who have been given a share of the one mission of Christ through the Sacraments of Baptism and Confirmation. The ministerial priesthood, which is made up of those men who have been ordained bishops and priests in Holy Orders, is essentially different from the priesthood of all the faithful because its work is to build up and guide the Church in the name of Christ. [sacerdocio]

Promised Land the land first promised by God to Abraham. It was to this land that God told Moses to lead the Chosen People after they were freed from slavery in Egypt and received the Ten Commandments at Mount Sinai. [Tierra Prometida]

prophecy a divine communication that comes through a human person. Prophecy in the Old Testament often tells of the coming of Jesus or conveys an important message to God's people. [profecía]

prophet one called to speak for God and to call the people to be faithful to the Covenant. Eighteen books of the Old Testament present the messages and actions of the prophets. [profeta]

prudence the virtue that directs us toward the good and helps us choose the correct means to achieve that good. When we act with prudence, we carefully and thoughtfully consider our actions. Prudence is one of the Cardinal Virtues that guide our conscience and influence us to live according to the Law of Christ. (See *Cardinal Virtues*.) [prudencia]

psalm a prayer in the form of a poem, written to be sung in public worship. Each psalm expresses an aspect of the depth of human prayer. Over several centuries, 150 psalms were assembled into the Book of Psalms in the Old Testament. Psalms were used in worship in the Temple in Jerusalem, and they have been used in the public worship of the Church since its beginning. [salmo]

Purgatory a possible outcome of particular judgment following death. Purgatory is a state of final cleansing after death of all our human imperfections to prepare us to enter into the joy of God's presence in Heaven. [purgatorio]

R

racism the opinion that race determines human traits and capacities and that a particular race has an inherent, or inborn, superiority. Discrimination based on a person's race is a violation of human dignity and a sin against justice. [racismo]

rationalist a person who regards human reason as the principal source of all knowledge. Rationalism was developed by René Descartes and dominated European thought in the 17th and 18th centuries. Rationalists recognize as true only those religious beliefs that can be explained rationally and stress confidence in the orderly character of the world and in the mind's ability to make sense of this order. [racionalista]

Real Presence the way in which the risen Jesus Christ is present in the Eucharist in the consecrated Bread and Wine. Jesus Christ's presence is called real because in the Eucharist his Body and Blood, soul and divinity, are wholly and entirely present. [Presencia Real de Cristo]

reconciliation the renewal of friendship after that friendship has been broken by some action or lack of action. In the Sacrament of Penance and Reconciliation, through God's mercy and forgiveness, we are reconciled with God, the Church, and others. [reconciliación]

Redeemer Jesus Christ, whose life, sacrificial Death on the cross, and Resurrection from the dead set us free from the slavery of sin and bring us redemption [Redentor]

redemption our being set free from the slavery of sin through the life, sacrificial Death on the cross, and Resurrection of Jesus Christ. [redención]

reform to put an end to a wrong by introducing a better or changed course of action. The prophets called people to reform their lives and return to being faithful to their Covenant with God. [reforma]

refugee a person who flees his or her home country because of a natural or a manmade disaster. Jesus was a refugee when Joseph and Mary escaped to Egypt to keep Jesus safe from King Herod. [refugiado]

relic a piece of the body of a saint, something that belonged to a saint. The first relics were from the bodies of martyrs and were enshrined in Christian basilicas and churches. [reliquia]

religious life a state of life recognized by the Church. In religious life, men and women freely respond to a call to follow Jesus by living the vows of poverty, chastity, and obedience in community with others. [vida religiosa]

repentance our turning away from sin, with a desire to change our lives and live more closely as God wants us to live. We express our penance by prayer, fasting, and helping those who are poor. [arrepentimiento]

Resurrection the bodily raising of Jesus Christ from the dead on the third day after his Death on the cross. The Resurrection is the crowning truth of our faith. [Resurrección de Cristo]

Glossary

Revelation God's communication of himself to us through the words and deeds he has used throughout history to show us the mystery of his plan for our Salvation. This Revelation reaches its completion in his sending of his Son, Jesus Christ. [Revelación]

righteousness an attribute of God used to describe his justice, his faithfulness to the Covenant, and his holiness in the Old Testament. As an attribute of humans, righteousness means being in a right relationship with God through moral conduct and observance of the Law. We have merit in God's sight and are able to do this because of the work of God's grace in us. Paul speaks of righteousness in a new way that is no longer dependent on observance of the Law. It comes through the faith in Jesus and his saving Death and Resurrection. To be made righteous in Jesus is to be saved, vindicated, and put right with God through his grace. [rectitud]

rights and responsibilities an important idea within Catholic Social Teaching. All people have the right to the necessities for a full and decent life, such as dignified work, health care, and education. All people also have responsibilities to promote the common good and to help others. (See *Catholic Social Teaching*.) [derechos y responsabilidades]

rite one of the many forms followed in celebrating liturgy in the Church. A rite may differ according to the culture or country where it is celebrated. A rite is also the special form for celebrating each sacrament. [rito]

Rite of Christian Initiation of Adults (RCIA) the process through which unbaptized adults join the Church. Catechumens receive instruction in preparation for their initiation into the Church. Lent marks the beginning of the catechumens' final period of preparation. During Lent they participate in the Rite of Election, during which their sponsors stand as witnesses to their faith, moral character, and desire to join the Church. During the Easter Vigil on Holy Saturday, the Elect profess their faith in Christ and the Church, and they promise to live as Jesus' disciples in the world. They are welcomed into the Church through the Sacraments of Initiation. [Ritual de la Iniciación Cristiana de Adultos]

Rosary a prayer in honor of the Blessed Virgin Mary. When we pray the Rosary, we meditate on the mysteries of Jesus Christ's life while praying the Hail Mary on five sets of ten beads and the Lord's Prayer on the beads in between. In the Latin Church, praying the Rosary became a way for ordinary people to reflect on the mysteries of Christ's life. [Rosario]

S

Sabbath the seventh day, when God rested after finishing the work of creation. The Third Commandment requires us to keep the Sabbath holy. For Christians the Sabbath became Sunday, the Lord's Day, because it was the day that Jesus rose from the dead and the new creation in Jesus Christ began. [sabbat]

sacrament holy, visible signs that signify a divine reality. Through the sacraments, Christ acts in us to save us. Grace received through the Holy Spirit enables us to carry out our mission as disciples. [sacramento]

sacramental an object, a prayer, or a blessing given by the Church to help us grow in our spiritual life [sacramental]

sacramental seal the obligation of priests to keep absolutely secret the sins confessed during the Sacrament of Penance and Reconciliation [sello sacramental]

Sacraments at the Service of Communion the Sacraments of Holy Orders and Matrimony. These two sacraments contribute to the personal Salvation of individuals by giving them a special way to serve others. [sacramentos al Servicio de la Comunidad]

Sacraments of Healing the Sacraments of Penance and Reconciliation and Anointing of the Sick, by which the Church continues Jesus' healing ministry of body and soul [sacramentos de la Curación]

Sacraments of Initiation the sacraments that are the foundation of our Christian life. We are born anew in Baptism, strengthened by Confirmation, and receive in the Eucharist the food of eternal life. By means of these sacraments, we receive an increasing measure of the divine life and advance toward the perfection of charity. [sacramentos de la Iniciación]

sacrifice a ritual offering of animals or produce made to God by the priest in the Temple in Jerusalem. Sacrifice was a sign of the people's adoration of God, giving thanks to God, or asking for forgiveness. Sacrifice also showed union with God. The great High Priest, Christ, accomplished our redemption through the perfect sacrifice of his Death on the Cross. [sacrificio]

Sacrifice of the Mass the sacrifice of Jesus on the Cross, which is remembered and made present in the Eucharist. It is offered in reparation for the sins of the living and the dead and to obtain spiritual or temporal blessings from God. [sacrificio de la Misa]

saint a holy person who has died united with God. The Church has said that this person is now with God forever in Heaven. [santo]

Salvation the gift, which God alone can give, of forgiveness of sin and the restoration of friendship with him [Salvación]

sanctify to make holy. Sacramentals and other Church practices make holy the everyday events and objects in our lives. [santificar]

sanctifying grace the gift from God, given to us without our earning it, that introduces us to the intimacy of the Trinity, unites us with its life, and heals our human nature, wounded by sin. Sanctifying grace helps us respond to our vocation as God's adopted children, and it continues the work of making us holy that began at our Baptism. (See *actual grace, grace,* and *habitual grace.*) [gracia santificante]

sanctuary a holy place to worship God. A sanctuary in church is the place where a religious rite is celebrated. [santuario]

Sanhedrin the Jewish court that ruled on matters of faith and practice among Jews. The Sanhedrin was the only Jewish court allowed to inflict the death penalty. [Sanedrín]

Satan a fallen angel and the enemy of anyone attempting to follow God's will. Satan tempts Jesus in the Gospels and opposes his ministry. In Jewish, Christian, and Muslim thought, Satan is associated with those angels who refused to bow down before human beings and serve them as God commanded. They refused to serve God and were thrown out of Heaven as a punishment. Satan and the other demons tempt human beings to join them in their revolt against God. [Satanás]

Savior Jesus, the Son of God, who became man to forgive our sins and restore our friendship with God. *Jesus* means "God saves." [Salvador]

scriptorium the room in a monastery in which books were copied by hand. Often beautiful art was added to the page to illustrate a story. [scriptorium]

Scriptures the holy writings of Jews and Christians, collected in the Old and New Testaments of the Bible [Sagradas Escrituras]

seal of confession also called the sacramental seal. It declares that the priest is absolutely forbidden to reveal under any circumstances any sin confessed to him in the Sacrament of Penance and Reconciliation. (See *sacramental seal.*) [sigilo sacramental]

Second Coming the return in glory of Jesus Christ to the world. The Church looks forward to the Second Coming with joy. [Segunda Venida]

Second Vatican Council the 21st and most recent ecumenical council of the Catholic Church. It met from October 11, 1962, to December 8, 1965. Its purpose, according to Pope John XXIII, was to renew the Church and to help it promote peace and unity among Christians and all humanity. [Concilio Vaticano Segundo]

seminary a school for the training and spiritual formation of priests. Seminaries first became widespread in the Church during the renewals of the 1500s. [seminario]

seraphim the heavenly beings who worship before the throne of God. One of them purified the lips of Isaiah with a burning coal so that he could speak for God. (Isaiah 6:6–7) [serafín]

Sermon on the Mount the words of Jesus, written in Chapters 5–7 of the Gospel of Matthew, in which Jesus reveals how he has fulfilled God's law given to Moses. The Sermon on the Mount begins with the eight Beatitudes and includes the Lord's Prayer. [Sermón de la Montaña]

sexism a prejudice or discrimination based on sex, especially discrimination against women. Sexism leads to behaviors and attitudes that foster a view of social roles based only on sex. [sexismo]

Sign of Peace the part of the Mass in which we offer a gesture of peace to one another as we prepare to receive Holy Communion. This signifies our willingness to be united in peace before we receive the Lord. (See *The Order of Mass.*) [Rito de la Paz]

Sign of the Cross the gesture we make that signifies our belief in God the Father, the Son, and the Holy Spirit. It is a sign of blessing, a confession of faith, and a way that identifies us as followers of Jesus Christ. [Señal de la Cruz]

signs events in the world that point to a deeper reality. The first half of the Gospel of John presents seven signs that reveal the glory of God and give us a glimpse of what the Kingdom of God is like. [signos]

sin a deliberate thought, word, deed, or failure to act that offends God and hurts our relationships with other people. Some sin is mortal and needs to be confessed in the Sacrament of Penance and Reconciliation. Other sin is venial, or less serious. [pecado]

Glossary

sloth a carelessness of heart that leads a person to ignore his or her development as a person, especially spiritual development and a relationship with God. Sloth is one of the seven capital sins, and it is contrary to the First Commandment. (See *Capital Sins.*) [pereza]

social justice the fair and equal treatment of every member of society. It is required by the dignity and freedom of every person. The Catholic Church has developed a body of social principles and moral teachings described in papal and other official documents issued since the late 19th century. This teaching deals with the economic, political, and social order of the world. It is rooted in the Bible as well as in the traditional theological teachings of the Church. [justicia social]

social sin social situations and institutions that are against the will of God. Because of the personal sins of individuals, entire societies can develop structures that are sinful in and of themselves. Social sins include racism, sexism, structures that deny people access to adequate health care, and the destruction of the environment for the benefit of a few. [pecado social]

solidarity the attitude of strength and unity that leads to the sharing of spiritual and material goods. Solidarity unites rich and poor, weak and strong, to foster a society in which all give what they can and receive what they need. The idea of solidarity is based on the common origin of all humanity. (See *Catholic Social Teaching.*) [solidaridad]

Son of God the title revealed by Jesus that indicates his unique relationship to God the Father. The revelation of Jesus' divine sonship is the main dramatic development of the story of Jesus of Nazareth as it unfolds in the Gospels. [Hijo de Dios]

soul the part of us that makes us human and an image of God. Body and soul together form one unique human nature. The soul is responsible for our consciousness and our freedom. The soul does not die and will be reunited with the body in the final resurrection. [alma]

Spiritual Exercises a spiritual retreat written by Ignatius of Loyola, designed to help people become aware of the presence of God in all things. The Spiritual Exercises are a major part of Ignatian spirituality. [Ejercicios Espirituales]

spirituality our growing, loving relationship with God. Spirituality is our way of expressing our experience of God in both the way we pray and the way we love our neighbor. There are many different schools of spirituality. Examples of these schools are Franciscan and Jesuit.

These are guides for the spiritual life and have enriched the traditions of prayer, worship, and living in Christianity. [espiritualidad]

Spiritual Works of Mercy the kind acts through which we help our neighbors meet the needs that are more than material. The Spiritual Works of Mercy include counseling the doubtful, instructing the ignorant, admonishing sinners, comforting the afflicted, forgiving offenses, bearing wrongs patiently, and praying for the living and the dead. [obras de misericordia espirituales]

Stations of the Cross a prayer for meditating on the final hours of Jesus' life, from his condemnation by Pontius Pilate to his Death and burial. We pray the Stations by moving to each representation of 14 incidents, based on events from Jesus' Passion and Death. [Vía Crucis]

stewardship the careful and responsible management of something entrusted to one's care, especially the goods of creation, which are intended for the whole human race. The sixth Precept of the Church makes clear our part in stewardship by requiring us to provide for the material needs of the Church, according to our abilities. [corresponsabilidad]

subsidiarity the principle that the best institutions for responding to a particular social task are those closest to it. The responsibility of the closest political or private institution is to assist those in need. Only when issues cannot be resolved at the local level should they be resolved at a higher level. [subsidiaridad]

Summa Theologiae a work of Christian theology in five volumes written by Saint Thomas Aquinas. In the *Summa Theologiae*, Aquinas asks questions about thousands of theological topics that continue to influence Christian theology today. [*Summa Theologiae*]

superior the leader of a community of consecrated religious men or women [superior]

swaddling wrapping an infant in strips of cloth for warmth and comfort. Jesus' swaddling clothes symbolized the humility and poverty of his birth and foreshadowed the shroud he would be wrapped in after his Crucifixion. [envolver en pañales]

Syllabus of Errors a document issued by Pope Pius IX condemning false claims and ideas about the nature of God and the world. The condemned views included claims related to pantheism, socialism, communism, the rights of the Church, and many other topics. [Syllabus Errorum]

synagogue the Jewish place of assembly for prayer, instruction, and study of the Torah. After the destruction of the Temple in 587 B.C., synagogues were organized as places to maintain Jewish faith and worship. Jesus attended the synagogue regularly for prayer and to teach. When visiting a city, Paul would first visit the synagogue. The synagogue played an important role in the development of Christian worship and in the structure of Christian communities. [sinagoga]

synod a meeting of bishops from all over the world to discuss doctrinal or pastoral matters. Synods offer suggestions to the pope, which may or may not become official teachings at a later time. [sínodo]

synoptic the way in which three of the four Gospels—Matthew, Mark, and Luke—tell similar stories in similar ways about the life and Death of Jesus. The Gospel of John's structure and stories are often different from the other three. Although none of the Gospels agree on every detail, each one conveys unique truths from their own perspectives about Jesus' life and mission. [sinóptico]

T

tabernacle the container in which the Blessed Sacrament is kept so that Holy Communion can be taken to those who are sick and dying. It is also the name of the tent sanctuary in which the Israelites kept the Ark of the Covenant from the time of the Exodus to the construction of Solomon's Temple. [sagrario]

temperance the Cardinal Virtue that helps us control our attraction to pleasure so that our natural desires are kept within proper limits. This moral virtue helps us choose to use goods in moderation. (See *Cardinal Virtues.*) [templanza]

Temple the house of worship of God, first built by Solomon. The Temple provided a place for the priests to offer sacrifice, to adore and give thanks to God, and to ask for forgiveness. It was destroyed and rebuilt. The second Temple was also destroyed and was never rebuilt. Part of the outer wall of the Temple mount remains to this day in Jerusalem. [Templo]

temptation an attraction, from outside us or inside us, that can lead us to disobey God's commands. Everyone is tempted, but the Holy Spirit helps us resist temptation and choose to do good. [tentación]

Ten Commandments the 10 rules given by God to Moses on Mount Sinai that sum up God's law and show us what is required to love God and our neighbor. By following the Ten Commandments, the Hebrews accepted their Covenant with God. [Diez Mandamientos]

theologian an expert in the study of God and his Revelation to the world [teólogo]

Theological Virtues the three virtues of faith, hope, and charity that are gifts from God and not acquired by human effort. The virtue of faith helps us believe in God, the virtue of hope helps us desire eternal life and the Kingdom of God, and the virtue of charity helps us love God and our neighbor as we should. [virtudes teologales]

Torah the Hebrew word for "instruction" or "law." It is also the name of the first five books of the Old Testament: Genesis, Exodus, Leviticus, Numbers, and Deuteronomy. [Torá]

Tradition the beliefs and practices of the Church that are passed down from one generation to the next under the guidance of the Holy Spirit. What Christ entrusted to the Apostles was handed on to others both orally and in writing. Tradition and Scripture together make up the single deposit of faith, which remains present and active in the Church. [Tradición católica]

Transfiguration an event witnessed by the apostles Peter, James, and John that revealed Jesus' divine glory. Jesus' face shone like the sun, his clothes became dazzlingly white, and he spoke with Elijah and Moses on the mountain. [Transfiguración]

transubstantiation the unique change of the bread and wine in the Eucharist into the Body and Blood of the risen Jesus Christ, while retaining their physical appearance as bread and wine [transubstanciación]

trespasses unlawful acts committed against the property or rights of another person or acts that physically harm a person [ofensas]

Triduum a Latin word meaning "three days" that refers to Holy Thursday, Good Friday, and Holy Saturday. The liturgies of the Triduum are among the most solemn celebrations of the Catholic faith. [Triduo Pascual]

Trinity the mystery of the existence of God in three Persons—the Father, the Son, and the Holy Spirit. Each Person of the Trinity is God, whole and entire. Each Person is distinct only in the relationship of each to the others. [Trinidad, Santísima]

Truce of God an act of the Church in the 11th century that banned fighting on Sundays and that was eventually extended to more than half the year [tregua de Dios]

Glossary

U

understanding one of the seven Gifts of the Holy Spirit. This gift helps us make the right choices in life and in our relationships with God and with others. (See *Gifts of the Holy Spirit*.) [consejo]

universal Church the entire Church as it exists throughout the world. The people of every diocese, along with their bishops and the pope, make up the universal Church. (See *catholic*.) [Iglesia universal]

V

venerate to show respect for someone or something. Although only God should be worshiped, Christians venerate the saints and objects associated with them to show respect for God's work in their lives. [venerar]

venial sin a choice we make that weakens our relationship with God or with other people. Venial sin wounds and lessens the divine life in us. If we make no effort to do better, venial sin can lead to more serious sin. Through our participation in the Eucharist, venial sin is forgiven when we are repentant, strengthening our relationship with God and with others. [pecado venial]

viaticum the Eucharist that a dying person receives. It is spiritual food for the last journey we make as Christians, the journey through death to eternal life. [viático]

Vicar of Christ the title given to the pope who, as the successor of Saint Peter, has the authority to act in Christ's place. A vicar is someone who stands in for and acts for another. (See *pope*.) [Vicario de Cristo]

virtue an attitude or a way of acting that enables us to do good [virtud]

Visitation one of the Joyful Mysteries of the Rosary, a reference to Mary's visit to Elizabeth to share the good news that Mary is to be the mother of Jesus. Elizabeth's greeting of Mary forms part of the Hail Mary. During this visit, Mary sings the *Magnificat,* her praise of God. [Visitación]

vocation the call each of us has in life to be the person God wants us to be and the way we each serve the Church and the Kingdom of God. Each of us can live out his or her vocation as a layperson, as a member of a religious community, or as a member of the clergy. [vocación]

vow a deliberate and free promise made to God by people who want especially to dedicate their lives to God. Their vows give witness now to the kingdom that is to come. [voto]

Vulgate the Latin translation of the Bible by Saint Jerome from the Hebrew and Greek in which it was originally written. Most Christians of Saint Jerome's day no longer spoke Hebrew or Greek. The common language, or vulgate, was Latin. [Vulgata]

W

Way, the what Saint Paul called the early faith and those who follow Jesus. Like the disciples on the road to Emmaus, our life is a journey of faith on "the Way" for which Jesus gives strength in the Eucharist. [Camino, el]

wisdom one of the seven Gifts of the Holy Spirit. Wisdom helps us understand the purpose and plan of God and live in a way that helps bring about this plan. It begins in wonder and awe at God's greatness. (See *Gifts of the Holy Spirit*.) [sabiduría]

Wisdom Literature the Old Testament books of Job, Proverbs, Ecclesiastes, Song of Songs, Wisdom, and Ben Sira. The purpose of these books is to give instruction on ways to live and how to understand and cope with the problems of life. [literatura sapiencial]

witness the passing on to others, by our words and our actions, the faith that we have been given. Every Christian has the duty to give witness to the good news about Jesus Christ that he or she has come to know. [testimonio]

worship the adoration and honor given to God in public prayer [culto]

Y

Yahweh the name of God in Hebrew, which God told Moses from the burning bush. *Yahweh* means "I am who am" or "I cause to be all that is." [Yavé]

Index

A

Abba, 301
abortion, 154, 301
Abraham, 301
absolution, 111, 295, 301
abstain, 301
abstinence, in Lent, 233
Act of Consecration to Mary, 276
Act of Contrition, 128, 271
Act of Faith, 273
Act of Hope, 273
Act of Love, 273
Acts of the Apostles, 6, 14, 23, 96, 175, 204, 211, 239, 242, 244, 256, 301
actual grace, 138, 301
Adam, 30, 138, 254, 291
adoration, 58, 301
adultery, 154, 301
Advent, 79, 80–83, 222, 223–26, 301
Aeneas, 2
Age of Enlightenment, 160, 261, 301
age of reason, 301
Agony in the Garden, 281, 301
Albert, Rule of, 64
All Saints Day, 222, 247, 289, 301
All Souls Day, 222, 247–49, 301
Alleluia, 302
almsgiving, 127, 233, 302
altar, 302
ambo, 302
Amen, 38, 50, 52, 287, 302
Ananias, 12
Andrew, 1
angel, 224, 228, 302.
    See also guardian angel
Angelus, 275, 302
anger, 146, 291, 302
Anglicans, 137
Anne, Saint, 39
annulment, 119, 302
Annunciation, 224, 280, 302
anointing, for Confirmation, 102
Anointing of the Sick, Sacrament of the, 102, 237, 285, 302
Anthony, Saint, 67
antiphons, 81, 302
apocalyptic literature, 302
Apollinaris, 48
apologist, 80, 302
Apostles, 22, 258, 302. *See also* Acts of the Apostles; disciple
    bishops as successors to, 95
Apostles' Creed, 241, 272, 278, 279, 302
apostolic, 95, 302
Apostolic Exhortation (John Paul II), 199
Aquinas, Thomas, Saint, 67, 89–90, 109
    Church in Middle Ages and, 92–93
Arius, 48
Ark of the Covenant, 302
art, Protestant Reformation and, 137
    in Vatican Museum, 137

B

Ascension, 4, 72, 94, 222, 240–41, 281, 289, 302
asceticism, 152, 302
Ash Wednesday, 123, 127, 129, 233, 303
assembly, 303
Assumption, 39, 49, 181, 281, 289, 303
atone, 93, 303
Augustine, Saint, Rule of, 20, 64
Augustinians, 64, 93, 261
Ave Maria, 270
Avignon papacy, 116–17, 261

Babylonian exile, 254, 255
Baptism, Sacrament of, 4, 12, 13, 20, 29, 30–31, 94, 102, 118, 136, 284, 303
    of Jesus, 232, 280
baptismal font, 29, 303
basic rights, 303
basilica, 303
    of St. Peter, 2, 171, 260
beatified, 205, 212, 303
Beatitudes, 5, 190, 208, 263, 303
Benedict, Saint, 45, 64
    community of, 46, 64–65
Benedict XVI, Pope Emeritus, 2, 74, 125, 175, 183, 189, 213, 215, 270
Benedictine Sisters of Perpetual Adoration, 67
Benedictus, 225
Ben Sira, Book of, 68
Bethlehem, 229
Bible, 82, 145, 161, 253–59, 303. *See also* New Testament; Old Testament
birth of Jesus, 82, 228–29
bishop, 44, 95, 118, 119, 144–45, 237, 303
Black Death, 116, 261
blasphemy, 22, 303
Blessed Sacrament, 303
blessing, 157, 303
    prayers of, 103, 269
Boaz, 254
Body and Blood of Christ, 15, 31, 103, 109, 110, 111, 303
Boniface, Saint, 73
book(s), of Old Testament, 254
bread and wine, 111
Bread of Life, 303
Buddhism, 297, 303

C

calling, 74–75, 118–19, 175–76, 195, 209.
    See also vocation
calumny (slander), 162, 304
Calvin, John, 137, 145, 261
Calvinism, 137
Camaldolese, 67
Campion, Edmund, Saint, 153
Canaan, 304
canon, 304
canonization, 37, 212, 304
canonize, 304
Canticle of Zechariah, 225
Capital Sins, 146, 291, 304. *See also* sin
Cappadocia, 64

Capuchins, 93
Cardinal Virtues, 266, 304
Caritas in Veritate (Benedict XVI), 189
Carmelites, 67, 93, 161
Carrying of the Cross, 281
Carthusians, 67
Cassian, John, Saint, 291
cast lots, 304
catechism, 145, 304
Catechism of the Catholic Church, 144, 145, 154, 162, 198
Catechism of the Council of Trent, 145
catechumen, 23, 126, 144, 233, 304
catechumenate, 27, 28–29, 304
cathedral, 99, 100–101, 261, 304
Catherine of Aragon, Queen of England, 137
Catherine of Siena, Saint, 117
catholic, 95, 304
Catholic Church. *See* Church, the
Catholic Relief Services (CRS), 88, 117
Catholic Social Teaching, 189, 190–91, 192, 298–300, 304
celebrant, 304
celebrate, 304
celibacy, of priests, 118
census, 304
Chalcedon, Council of, 49, 260
chalice, 103
character, 30, 304
charism, 20, 304
    of Jesuits, 153
charity, 163, 189, 304
Charlemagne, 261
chastity, 66, 154–55, 245, 304
chasuble, 304
child labor, 154
child soldiers, 154
choice, 149, 162–63, 290–95
Chosen People, 204, 305
Chrism, 102, 237, 305
Chrism Mass, 237
Christ, 305. *See also* Jesus
Christian, 305
Christianity, 64, 72, 136–37
Christian kingdom, in Jerusalem, 124
Christians, persecution of, 20, 21, 36, 260
Christmas, 79, 80, 85, 222, 227–30, 305
Church, the, 1, 6–7, 11, 28–29, 43, 72–73, 91–96, 102–3, 116–17, 121, 123, 143–145, 189, 211, 217, 305.
    See also domestic church
    Marks of, 94–95
    Precepts of, 109, 147, 264
church and state, 181
Church of England, 137
Cistercians, 66, 67, 261
Clark, Maura, Sister, 73
Claver, Peter, Saint, 153
Clement V, Pope, 116–17
Clement VII, Pope, 117
clergy, 305
Code of Canon Law, 181
Collect, 286
College of Cardinals, 2
Columban, Saint, 73

commandment, 305.
    See also Ten Commandments
    Great Commandment, 59, 262, 310
    New Commandment, 262
common good, 305
common use, 60
communal prayer, 52, 305
communication, Catholic, 182
Communion. *See* Holy Communion; Service of Communion, Sacraments at the
Communion of Saints, 21, 37, 139, 247, 250, 305
Communion Rite, 288
community, 7, 16, 17, 28, 45, 68, 69, 121, 190, 193, 299, 305
    Church and society, 91–96
    monastic, 46, 63, 64–67, 69
    of women religious, 134
compassion, 305
Concluding Rites, 288
confession, 295, 305. *See also* examination of conscience; Penance and Reconciliation, Sacrament of
    seal of, 146, 321
Confirmation, Sacrament of, 4, 21, 29, 31, 38, 51, 72, 81, 94, 102, 118, 147, 168, 183, 199, 207, 215, 237, 284, 305
Congregation for the Doctrine of the Faith, 90
Congregation of the Mission, 168, 205
conscience, 163, 290, 292–93, 305
    examination of, 294, 308
consecrate, 66, 305
Constantine, Roman Emperor, 48, 260
    Edict of Milan and, 64
Constantinople, 92
Constantinople, Council of, 48, 94
Constitution on the Catholic Faith, 181
consubstantial, 48, 305
consumerism, 305
contemplate, 305
contemplation, 67, 268, 305
contemplative, 205, 305
contrition, 306
    imperfect, 311
    perfect, 317
conversion, 306
    acts of, 208
convert, 15, 306
convocation, 306
Copernicus, 160
Corinthians, Paul's Letters to, 198–99, 243, 245
Cornelius, 14
Coronation of Mary, 276, 281
Corporal Works of Mercy, 116, 163, 207, 267, 306
council. *See* ecumenical council; specific councils
counsel, 306
    evangelical, 66
Counter Reformation, 144–45
Covenant, 255, 306
covet, 155, 306
covetousness, 291, 306
creation, 60, 161, 191, 254, 306

Index

Index

Acknowledgments

Excerpts from the *New American Bible, revised edition* © 2010, 1991, 1986, 1970 Confraternity of Christian Doctrine, Washington, D.C., and are used by permission of the copyright owner. All rights reserved. No part of the *New American Bible* may be reproduced in any form without permission in writing from the copyright owner.

The English translation of the Act of Contrition from *Rite of Penance* © 1974 International Commission on English in the Liturgy Corporation (ICEL); excerpt from the English translation of *Rite of Confirmation* © 1975, ICEL; the English translation of *Memorare, Regina Caeli,* Prayer to the Holy Spirit and Hail, Holy Queen *(Salve Regina)* from *A Book of Prayers* © 1982, ICEL; the English translation of Prayer Before Meals and Prayer After Meals from *Book of Blessings* © 1988, ICEL; the English translation of Nicene Creed and Apostles' Creed from *The Roman Missal* © 2010, ICEL. All rights reserved.

The English translation of the *Magnificat* by the International Consultation on English Texts.

Excerpts from the English translation of the *Catechism of the Catholic Church, Second Edition* for the United States of America © 2000 United States Catholic Conference, Inc.—Libreria Editrice Vaticana.

Excerpt from *Faithful Citizenship: A Catholic Call to Political Responsibility* © 2003 United States Conference of Catholic Bishops, Washington, D.C. All rights reserved. Used by permission.

Excerpt from *Strangers No Longer: Together on the Journey of Hope* © 2003 United States Conference of Catholic Bishops, Washington, D.C. All rights reserved. Used by permission.

Excerpts from papal encyclicals and other Vatican documents are © Libreria Editrice Vaticana. All rights reserved.

The Prayer for Generosity and the *Suscipe* are from *Hearts on Fire: Praying with Jesuits* by Michael Harter, S.J. © 2005 Loyola Press.

Loyola Press has made every effort to locate the copyright holders for the cited works used in this publication and to make full acknowledgment for their use. In the case of any omissions, the publisher will be pleased to make suitable acknowledgments in future editions.

Art and Photography

When there is more than one picture on a page, positions are abbreviated as follows: **(t)** top, **(c)** center, **(b)** bottom, **(l)** left, **(r)** right, **(bg)** background, **(bd)** border.

Photos and illustrations not acknowledged are either owned by Loyola Press or from royalty-free sources including but not limited to Art Resource, Alamy, Bridgeman, Corbis/Veer, Getty Images, iStockphoto, Jupiterimages, Media Bakery, PunchStock, Shutterstock, Thinkstock, and Wikipedia Commons. Loyola Press has made every effort to locate the copyright holders for the cited works used in this publication and to make full acknowledgment for their use. In the case of any omissions, the publisher will be pleased to make suitable acknowledgments in future editions.

Frontmatter: i Rafael Lopez. **iii** (t) © iStockphoto.com/samgrandy. **iii** (c) © iStockphoto.com/reddydesign. **iii** (b) © iStockphoto.com/aldomurillo. **iv** (t) The Crosiers/Gene Plaisted, OSC. **iv** (c) Loyola Press Photography. **iv** (bl) Peter Reali/Media Bakery. **iv** (br) Darren Greenwood/Media Bakery.

© **iStockphoto.com: 5** (t) rusm; (b) Teacept. **6** (t) aldomurillo. **7** (tl, cr) blue67. **12–13** (cl, b) Beastfromeast. **13** (tl) Teacept; (cr) diane555. **14** (t) rusm. **16** (t) sefaoncul. **20** (t) duncan1890. (c) Luso. **21** (t) ZU_09. **22** (br) DRW-Artworks. **24** (t) Blend_Images. **27** (t) pixdeluxe. **28** (t) duncan1890. **30–31** stdemi. **32** (t) wweagle. **36** (b) bubaone. **38** (t) javarman3. **48–49** Beastfromeast. **49** (br) Floortje. **50** (tl, b) Beastfromeast. **58** (t) CEFutcher. **58–59** blue67. **64** rusm **65** (br) typo-graphics. **68** (t) digitalskillet. **74** (cl) blue67. **75** (t) blue67; (c) jcarillet. **79** (t) Juanmonino. **80–81** (b, t) Beastfromeast. **81** (cr) adaszku. **83** Hogie. **87** (t) reddydesign. **88** (b) cnicbc. **91** (t) CEFutcher. **92** (t) makkayak. **95** (t) rusm; (b) terminator1. **99** (t) Ron_Thomas. **108–109** (t, br) blue67. **109** (c) kryczka. **111** (c) jjshaw14. **119** (t) Fos4o. **120** (t) nojustice. **124** stocksnapper. **126** (t) kulicki. **131** (t) iamagoo; (c) akiyoko; (b) PacoRomero. **132** (c) traffic_analyzer. **136** (t) ZU_09; (c) duncan1890. **137** (r) beastfromeast. **143** (t) goldenKB. **145** (t) Grafissimo. **152** (bd) makkayak. **154** RapidEye. **156** (t) 1001nights. **160** (t) wynnter. **164** (t) rivers_photography. **167** (c) MentalArt. **170** (t) wynnter. **171** (cl) majaiva; (cr) xenotar. **178** (t) rusm; (tr) Kalistratova. **180** (cr, b) jammydesign. **183** (tr) hanibaram. **184** (t) LindaYolanda. **189** (br) duncan1890. **191** (t, b) Beastfromeast. **195** (t) Bryngelzon. **196** (t) largeformat4x5. **197** princessdlaf. **199** (cr) SilviaJansen. **205** (t) T-Immagini. **206–207** Maydaymayday. **207** (cr) WendellandCarolyn. **211** (cr) aldomurillo. **216** JLBarranco. **219** (t) kali9. **220** (t) powerofforever; (b) oneclearvision. **221** (tr) 7io; (bg) Jasmina007; (bl) beastfromeast. **224** (tl, b) blue67; (bd)ithinksky; (c) blue67. **229** (t) Alexan2008; **230** (tr) smartstock; (cr) beastfromeast. **233** (c) ma-k; (r) Smileyjoanne. **237** (tr) 7io; (c) McIninch; **248** (t) bopshops; **251** (t, bd) Jasmina007; (tr) WPChambers. **257** (bg) javarman3. **259** (c) Ekely. **265** (bd) makkayak. **267** (b) redmal. **268** (b) Trifonov_Evgeniy. **269** (br) grandriver. **270** livjam. **274** (t) ankh-fire; (b) Slonov. **281** (t) ajt. **288** (b) duckycards. **294** (c) AndrisTkachenko. **296** (cr) risamay. **297** (tr) wesvandinter; (cr) vladj55. **298** (l) LeggNet. **300** (b) eurobanks. (br) ChepeNicoli.

Thinkstock: 87 (b) iStockphoto. **138–139** (b, r) iStockphoto. **221** (t) iStockphoto. **298** (r) Jupiterimages/Brand X Pictures.

Unit 1: 1(t) **1** Andrew R. Wright. **2** (br) Andrew R. Wright. **3** (t) Image Source Photography/Veer. **4** The Crosiers/Gene Plaisted, OSC. **5** (t) The Crosiers/Gene Plaisted, OSC. **7** (tr) The Crosiers/Gene Plaisted, OSC; (br) The Crosiers/Gene Plaisted, OSC. **8** (t) Ocean Photography/Veer. **11** Patrick Lane/Veer. **12** (cr) The Crosiers/Gene Plaisted, OSC. **14** (b) The Crosiers/Gene Plaisted, OSC. **15** (br) Loyola Press Photography. **19** (t) Ocean Photography/Veer. **21** (t) James Boardman/Alamy. **22** (t) Saints Perpetua and Felicity. Bancel La Farge (1927), Chapel of Saints Perpetua and Felicity. Photo courtesy of the Basilica of the National Shrine of the Immaculate Conception, Washington, D.C.; (bc) The Crosiers/Gene Plaisted, OSC. **28** (tr, bl, br) Alessandra Cimatoribus. **29** (bc) Phil Martin Photography. **29** (br) "Leon Vanella/Alamy. " **30** (tr) David Grossman/Alamy. **31** (bl) The Crosiers/Gene Plaisted, OSC. **35** (cr) Collage Photography/Veer. **36** (t) W.P. Wittman Limited. **37** The Crosiers/Gene Plaisted, OSC. **38** (tr) The Crosiers/Gene Plaisted, OSC. **39** (tr) The Crosiers/Gene Plaisted, OSC; (bl) Gift of Adolf Lewisohn/The Bridgeman Art Library International/The Brooklyn Museum. **40** (t) The Crosiers/Gene Plaisted, OSC. **43** (t) Greenshoots Communications/Alamy; (b) Marjorie Kamys Cotera/Bob Daemmrich Photography/Alamy. **44** (t) David McNew/AP/Corbis; (b) Scott Olson/Staff/Getty Images News/Getty Images.

Unit 2: 45 (t) Andrew R. Wright. **46** (tl) Andrew R. Wright; (c) imagebroker/Alamy. **47** (t) Image Source Photography/Veer. **48** (t) The Crosiers/Gene Plaisted, OSC. **49** (cl) The Crosiers/Gene Plaisted, OSC. **50** (tr) The Crosiers/Gene Plaisted, OSC. **51** (cr) The Crosiers/Gene Plaisted, OSC. **52** (t) W.P. Wittman Limited. **55** (t) Media Bakery. **56** Museo Romantico, Madrid, Spain/The Bridgeman Art Library International. **57** (tr) Loyola Press Photography. **58** (br) Media Bakery. **60** (t) Thomas Odulate/Media Bakery. **63** (t) cultura Photography/Veer. **64** (t) The Crosiers/Gene Plaisted, OSC. **65** (c) Wojtek Buss/Media Bakery. **66** (t) Courtesy of Br. Paul Quenon. The Cistercians, Gethsemani, Kentucky. **67** (t) The Crosiers/Gene Plaisted, OSC. **71** (t) OJO Images Photography/Veer. **72** (t) The Crosiers/Gene Plaisted, OSC. **73** (t) Godong/Robert Harding/Media Bakery. **74** (t) rickbl/Veer; (b) Photo © Boltin Picture Library/The Bridgeman Art Library International. **76** (t) REB Images/Media Bakery. **77** Loyola Press Photography. **79** (cr) Warling Studios. **80** (t) The Crosiers/Gene Plaisted, OSC. **82** (tl) SeDml/Veer; (tr) The Crosiers/Gene Plaisted, OSC; (br) Private Collection/The Bridgeman Art Library International. **84** (t) Tim Pannell/Media Bakery. **88** (t) Photo Mere Spazz/Alamy.

Unit 3: 89 (t) Andrew R. Wright. **90** (c) N.N./dpa/Corbis; (br) Andrew R. Wright. **92** (t) The Crosiers/Gene Plaisted, OSC. **94** The Crosiers/Gene Plaisted, OSC. **96** SW Productions/Media Bakery. **100–101** Stephen Conlin. **102** (t) imagebroker/Alamy. **103** (br) Zulhazmi Zabri/Shutterstock.com. **104** (t) Lea Roth/Media Bakery. **107** (t) Alloy Photography/Veer. **108** (t) SeDmi/Veer; (c) Roger-Viollet, Paris/The Bridgeman Art Library International. **110** (t) W.P. Wittman Limited; (br) Florence Martinez. **112** (t) Media Bakery. **113** Warling Studios. **115** (t) Terry Vine /Media Bakery. **116** (t) Giraudon/The Bridgeman Art Library International. **117** (c) Loyola Press Phototgraphy/www.saintsforsinners.com. **118** (t) Godong/Media Bakery. **123** (cl) Warling Studios; (cr) W.P. Wittman Limited. **125** The Crosiers/Gene Plaisted, OSC. **126** (b) © Guildhall Art Gallery, City of London/The Bridgeman Art Library International. **127** (t) Phil Martin Photography; (br) Pascal Deloche/Media Bakery. **128** Mike Booth/Alamy. **132** (t) UK History/Alamy; (b) VisionsofAmerica/Joe Sohm/Media Bakery.

Unit 4: 133 Andrew R. Wright. **134** (t) imagebroker/Alamy; (bl) Image licensed by Depositphotos.com/halpand; (br) Andrew R. Wright. **135** cultura Photography/Veer. **138** (t) The Crosiers/Gene Plaisted, OSC; (cr) Mary Paula Wiggins. **140** (t) Image licensed by Depositphotos.com/mandygodbehear. **144** (t) Giraudon/ The Bridgeman Art Library International. **146** (t) Gabriela Medina/Media Bakery. **147** (c) The Crosiers/Gene Plaisted, OSC. **148** (t) Laurence Mouton/Media Bakery. **151** (t) Media Bakery. **152** Brukenthal National Museum, Sibiu, Romania/The Bridgeman Art Library International. **153** (c) The Crosiers/Gene Plaisted, OSC. **155** (c) Media Bakery. **159** (t) Warling Studios. **161** (br) "Oscar Romero" © 2007 N. Oliphant • Reproductions at www.BridgeBuilding.com. **162** (t) Somos Photography/Veer. **163** (t) The Crosiers/Gene Plaisted, OSC; (b) Carolina Arentsen. **167** (br) Darren Greenwood/Media Bakery. **168** (t) The Crosiers/Gene Plaisted, OSC. **169** (br) Musee de l'Assistance Publique, Hopitaux de Paris, France/The Bridgeman Art Library International. **170** (t) SeDmi/Veer. **172** (t) The Crosiers/Gene Plaisted, OSC. **175** (t) Big Cheese Photo LLC/Alamy; (b) Jim West/Alamy. **176** (t) ZUMA Wire Service/Alamy; (bl) Evan Robinson/Alamy; (br) David Grossman/Alamy.

Unit 5: 177 Andrew R. Wright. **178** (bl) Andrew R. Wright. **179** (t) Ocean Photography/Veer. **180** (t) Mary Evans Picture Library/Alamy. **181** (br) The Crosiers/Gene Plaisted, OSC. **182** (tr) The Crosiers/Gene Plaisted, OSC; (bc) Wikipedia. **187** (t) Warling Studios. **188** (t) Mary Evans Picture Library/Alamy; (bl) Fine Art Photographic Library/Corbis. **190** Jeff Greenberg/Alamy. **191** (c) Peter Reali/Media Bakery. **192** (t) Jim West/Alamy. **196** (br) Franklin McMahon/Corbis. **198** W.P. Wittman Limited. **200** (t) Fancy/Media Bakery. **203** (t) Image Source Photography/Veer. **204** Tim Graham/Alamy. **205** (br) Hulton Archive/Getty Images. **206** (t) Frances Roberts/Alamy; (c) Jim West/Alamy; (b) Jeff Greenberg/Alamy. **207** (cl) Jim West/Alamy. **208** (t) Warling Studios. **209** www.audia.net. **212** (t) Tim Graham/Alamy. **214** (t) Alloy Photography/Veer; (br) Soichi Watanabe. **215** (cr) The Crosiers/Gene Plaisted, OSC. **219** (b) Media Bakery.

The Year in Our Church: 221 (cl) Jupiterimages; (cl) Plush Studios/Digital Vision/Getty Images; (cr, clockwise) Andrew R. Wright; (br) SeDmi/Veer. **222** (t) The Crosiers/Gene Plaisted, OSC; (ct) The Crosiers/Gene Plaisted, OSC; (cb) The Crosiers/Gene Plaisted, OSC; (br) The Crosiers/Gene Plaisted, OSC. **223** Warling Studios. (tr) © York Museums Trust (York Art Gallery), UK / The Bridgeman Art Library; (c) The Crosiers/Gene Plaisted, OSC. **225** (cr) The Art Gallery Collection/Alamy. **226** (cr) Media Bakery. **227** altrendo images/ Media Bakery. **228** Private Collection/The Bridgeman Art Library; (b) Private Collection/The Bridgeman Art Library; (c) © Radiant Light/The Bridgeman Art Library. **231** Warling Studios. **232** (t, b) SeDmi/Veer; (c) Private Collection/The Bridgeman Art Library; (br) W.P. Wittman Limited. **234** © Look and Learn/The Bridgeman Art Library. **235** (l) Friedrich Stark/Alamy; **236** Private Collection/ The Bridgeman Art Library; (br) Media Bakery. **238** Giraudon/The Bridgeman Art Library. **239** Craig Aurness/Media Bakery. **240** The Crosiers/Gene Plaisted, OSC. **241** (c) W.P. Wittman Limited; (b) W.P. Wittman Limited. **242** (tr) The Crosiers/Gene Plaisted, OSC. **243** © Glasgow University Library, Scotland/ The Bridgeman Art Library. **244** (c) © York Museums Trust (York Art Gallery), UK/The Bridgeman Art Library. **245** (cr) The Crosiers/Gene Plaisted, OSC; (br) The Crosiers/Gene Plaisted, OSC. **246** (c) He Qi, www.heqiarts.com. **247** John Block/Media Bakery; (b) Private Collection/The Bridgeman Art Library. **249** (bc) Helene Cyr/Media Bakery; **250** (c) Photo © Boltin Picture Library/The Bridgeman Art Library.

Prayers and Practices of Our Faith: 251–300 (bd) Greg Becker. **251** (ct) Design Pics CEF/Media Bakery. **251** (cb) © Hermitage Art, Inc./ Reproductions at www.Bridgebuilding.com. **251** (b) © Hermitage Art, Inc./ Reproductions at www.Bridgebuilding.com. **252** (cb) The Crosiers/Gene Plaisted, OSC. **253** Design Pics CEF/Media Bakery. **254** (br) Private Collection/ The Bridgeman Art Library. **255** (c) © Hermitage Art, Inc./Reproductions at www.Bridgebuilding.com. **256** (c) © Hermitage Art, Inc./Reproductions at www.Bridgebuilding.com. **256** (b) © Hermitage Art, Inc./Reproductions at www.Bridgebuilding.com. **257** (c) Michael Runkel Ethiopia/Alamy. **258** (c) © Hermitage Art, Inc./Reproductions at www.Bridgebuilding.com. **258** (br) Orsanmichele, Florence, Italy/The Bridgeman Art Library. **259** Araldo de Luca/Corbis. **260–261** (c, b) Penelope Dullaghan. **260** Penelope Dullaghan. **261** Penelope Dullaghan. **262** Corbis Photography/Veer **263** (b) Private Collection/The Bridgeman Art Library. **264** Christina Balit. **265** (bc) Giraudon/ The Bridgeman Art Library. **266** (cr) Cerezo Barredo. **266** (b) Jim Craigmyle/ Media Bakery. **267** (cl) Warling Studios. **267** (cr) Warling Studios. **268** (c) Rick Becker-Leckrone/Shutterstock.com. **272** (bl) The Crosiers/Gene Plaisted, OSC. **273** Warling Studios. **275** (bl) © Fondation Alberto & Annette Giacometti, ACS, London—Succession Alberto Giacometti ADAGP, Paris and DACS, London, 2012/The Bridgeman Art Library © 2014 Succession Alberto Giacometti (Fondation Alberto et Annette Giacometti, Paris)/ADAGP, Paris/VAGA and ARS, New York, NY. Art © Alberto Giacometti Estate/Licensed by VAGA and ARS, New York, NY. **276** (cl) The Crosiers/Gene Plaisted, OSC. **276** (br) The Crosiers/ Gene Plaisted, OSC. **277** (c) Kunsthistorisches Museum, Vienna, Austria/The Bridgeman Art Library. **278** (c) The Crosiers/Gene Plaisted, OSC. **279** Greg Kuepfer. **280** (cr) The Crosiers/Gene Plaisted, OSC. **280** (br) The Crosiers/Gene Plaisted, OSC. **281** (cr) The Crosiers/Gene Plaisted, OSC. **281** (br) The Crosiers/ Gene Plaisted, OSC. **282** (l) James, Laura/Private Collection/The Bridgeman Art Library. **282** (cl) James, Laura/Private Collection/The Bridgeman Art Library; (cr) James, Laura/Private Collection/The Bridgeman Art Library; (r) James, Laura/Private Collection/The Bridgeman Art Library. **283** James, Laura/Private Collection/The Bridgeman Art Library. **284** (t) Alessandra Cimatoribus; (c) Alessandra Cimatoribus. **284** (b) Alessandra Cimatoribus. **285** (t) Alessandra Cimatoribus; (ct) Alessandra Cimatoribus; (cb) Alessandra Cimatoribus; (b) Alessandra Cimatoribus. **286** (b) The Crosiers/Gene Plaisted, OSC. **287** (l) Warling Studios; (r) W.P. Wittman Limited. **288** (t) Warling Studios; (c) Warling Studios. **289** (cl) The Crosiers/Gene Plaisted, OSC; (c) Private Collection/The Bridgeman Art Library; (cr) Louvre, Paris, France/Giraudon/The Bridgeman Art Library; (bl) © Radiant Light/The Bridgeman Art Library; (bc) The Crosiers/Gene Plaisted, OSC; (br) Photo © Boltin Picture Library/The Bridgeman Art Library. **290** (c) cultura Photography/Veer. **291** Warling Studios. **292** (br) Anthony Lee/ Media Bakery. **293** Ocean Photography/Veer. **294** (b) Jupiterimages. **295** (cr) Warling Studios; (cr) Warling Studios; (cr) Warling Studios; (b) Warling Studios. **296** (br) Godong/Media Bakery. **297** (bl) The Crosiers/Gene Plaisted, OSC. **299** (cr) Alex Mares-Manton/Asia Images/Getty Images. **300** (cl) Jim West/ Alamy; (cr) Jim West/Alamy.